The Complexi

New Cultural Studies

SERIES EDITORS
Joan DeJean
Carroll Smith-Rosenberg
Peter Stallybrass
Gary A. Tomlinson

A complete list of books in the series
is available from the publisher.

The
Complexion of Race

*Categories of Difference in
Eighteenth–Century British Culture*

Roxann Wheeler

PENN

*University of Pennsylvania Press
Philadelphia*

10 9 8 7 6 5 4 3 2 1

Published by
University of Pennsylvania Press
Philadelphia, Pennsylvania 19104-4011

Library of Congress Cataloging-in-Publication Data

Wheeler, Roxann.
The complexion of race : categories of difference in eighteenth-century British culture / Roxann Wheeler.
    p.   cm. — (New cultural studies)
Includes bibliographical references and index.
ISBN 0-8122-3541-X (acid-free paper)—
ISBN 0-8122-1722-5 (pbk. : acid-free paper)
    1. Great Britain—Race relations—History—18th century.   2. Race awareness—Great Britain—History—18th century.   3. English fiction—18th century—History and criticism.   4. Difference (Psychology)—History—18th century.   5. Great Britain—Social conditions—18th century.   6. Great Britain—Civilization—18th century.   7. Race in literature.   I. Title.   II. Series.
DA125.A1 W448   2000
305.8'00941'09033—dc21

                                                    00-025539

To My Parents

*Whose lives first modeled how to work
joyfully toward important goals*

Contents

List of Illustrations   ix

Introduction. The Empire of Climate: Categories of Race in
Eighteenth-Century Britain   1

1. Christians, Savages, and Slaves: From the Mediterranean
to the Atlantic   49

2. Racializing Civility: Violence and Trade in Africa   90

3. Romanticizing Racial Difference: Benevolent Subordination
and the Midcentury Novel   137

4. Consuming Englishness: On the Margins of Civil Society   176

5. The Politicization of Race: The Specter of the Colonies
in Britain   234

Epilogue. Theorizing Race and Racism in the
Eighteenth Century   288

Notes   303

Index   363

Acknowledgments   369

Illustrations

1. Commerce and Character　8

2. The Complexion of Man　10

3. "A Description of the Habits of most Countries in the World"　18

4. The New Golden Age　34

5. Four Continents, Four Kinds of People　36

6. Robinson Crusoe and European Xury on the West Coast of Africa　63

7. Robinson Crusoe and Negro Xury on the West Coast of Africa　64

8. Negroized Caribbean Islanders　82

9. Man and Woman of St. John's, Cape Verde Islands　118

10. Uzbek Tartars　120

11. The Baptism of Zoa　165

12. Chart of Racial Casts　212

13. The Chain of Being　218

14. The Laplander　243

15. The Chinese　244

16. The African　245

17. The American　246

18. Five Varieties of the Human Race　247

19. Humanized Apes and Comparative Racial Profiles　292

20. Chart of Facial Angles　294

Introduction

The Empire of Climate

Categories of Race in Eighteenth-Century Britain

Nor is blackness inconsistent with beauty, which even to our European eyes consists not so much in colour, as an advantageous stature, a comely symmetry of the parts of the body, and good features in the face.

—ROBERT BOYLE
"Of the Nature of Whiteness and Blackness" (1664)

[C]olour, whatever be its cause, be it bile, or the influence of the sun, the air, or the climate, is, at all events an adventitious and easily changeable thing, and can never constitute a diversity of species.

—JOHANN FRIEDRICH BLUMENBACH
On the Natural Variety of Mankind (1775)[1]

WHEN present-day North Americans and Britons think about race, we are likely to default automatically to skin color. Preconceptions about skin color and about other differences between what we now call races are so ingrained in our contemporary culture that many of us hardly think twice about the complexity of the terms *black* and *white*. This association between color and race first became commonplace during the eighteenth century and obtained particular currency in the new discipline of natural history. Even today, however, *black* and *white* are simplifying, though powerful, cover stories for a dense matrix of ideas as closely associated with cultural differences as with the body's surface.

As the epigraphs indicate, skin color and race as we know them today have not always been powerful tools to convey difference. At various times in European history, they have fostered meanings incongruent with the current ubiquitous conviction about their significance to identity.[2] Colors, especially embodied in black and white skin tones, functioned on several registers during the eighteenth century: Climate, humors, anatomy, Christianity, and neutral description were all available paradigms.[3] The ancient Greeks and Romans believed that climate was responsible for the complexion of a nation's inhabitants, particularly air temperature and exposure to the sun. *Complexion* referred to inhabitants' temperament or disposition; it arose from the interaction of climate and the bodily humors (blood, bile, phlegm, and choler). Skin color, then, was only one component of complexion. Eighteenth-century Europeans maintained great faith in the strong effects of climate on the body. Their other traditional frame of reference for skin color derived from Christian semiotics, which combined moral and aesthetic meanings, primarily in the binary pair pure white and sinful black. This powerful color construction referred to internal turmoil, actions, spiritual states, and external coloring.

Two contemporary fields of inquiry, medicine and travel, contributed to the reification of skin color as a discrete item of analysis. The "new" anatomical body of the seventeenth century was a model that eventually helped detach skin color from the larger matrix of temperament in humoral theory. Under this rubric, skin color resided in a thin layer of the skin rather than in a changeable balance of the internal bodily fluids and the temperature of the environment. A 1677 injunction from the Royal Society of London to travelers in foreign countries noted skin color as one of many characteristics of foreign people that travelers were supposed to record. The several articulations of skin color I have outlined could work singly or in conjunction, but as I explore throughout this book, they carried assumptions that were not always compatible with each other. Moreover, the context of individual usage did not always clarify that author's adherence to a single meaning. Writers referred to complexion and skin color synonymously as well as using them as discrete concepts.

This array of possibilities for thinking about complexion and skin color may seem complicated to us today, and even eighteenth-century Britons found the shifting meanings of complexion confusing.[4] An example from the *Spectator* 262 (1711) illustrates the multiple definitions of complexion that coexisted. In a chatty meditation on his attempt to instruct yet delight his readers, Joseph Addison mentions the mental process he goes through to protect the individuals who are the models for his sketches of contemporary manners. "If I write any thing on a black Man," he explains, "I run over in my Mind all the eminent Persons in the Nation who are of that Complection . . . that it may not bear any Resemblance to one that is real."[5] When he mentions "black" and "Complection" in the same sentence, Addison does not refer to men of African descent, as we might think today, nor does he refer to an Englishman with a dark complexion whom he is going to lampoon, as some of his contemporaries might have thought. The only way to discover the meaning of "black Man" and "Complection" is to consider the context.

Addison writes that he is careful to protect private persons and disguise references to contemporary public figures in his delineation of faulty characters. The full quotation reads: "For this Reason when I draw any faulty Character, I consider all those Persons to whom the Malice of the World may possibly apply it, and take care to dash it with such particular Circumstances as may prevent all such ill-natured Applications. If I write any thing on a black Man, I run over in my Mind all the eminent Persons in the Nation who are of that Complection. . . . I examine every Syllable and Letter of it, that it may not bear any Resemblance to one that is real" (517–18). Addison thus refers to a wicked man.

Clearly, *black* had a range of meanings unavailable to us today, and the several possible meanings *black* presented to contemporaries are underscored by a misreading of this anecdote. Addison's use of "black Man" in the example above is a secular adaptation of Christian semiotics crosshatched by humoral theory. Samuel Johnson, some decades later in *A Dictionary of the English Language* (1755), misunderstood the reference as a neutrally descriptive one, because he uses Addison's quotation to illustrate the definition of "complexion" that means the "colour of the external parts of any body." The twentieth-century editor of the *Spectator* follows Johnson in his misreading by glossing "a black Man" to signify a man with a dark complexion (518), a meaning that was indeed part of contemporary vocabulary, just not applicable in this case.

Of course, there were black people, that is, people of African ancestry, who appeared in eighteenth-century texts. Britons' references to their skin color in travel narratives and in contemporary newspapers ranged from value-laden to neutrally descriptive. When it came to skin color, however, people around the world in the eighteenth century had perceptions of others and self-perceptions that were sometimes surprising. People with black skin did not necessarily regard that attribute in the same way we do today. In *Journal of a Voyage up the Gambia* (1723), for example, the English narrator describes the skin color of the native translators vital to the success of their expedition as "Black as Coal." Noticing the particular hue of dark skin was not unusual for eighteenth-century Britons, nor was the apparently paradoxical statement that followed concerning these same African translators: "Here, thro' Custom, (being Christians) they account themselves White Men."[6] Remarkably, the Englishman accepts the translators' construction of color identity, which is evident in a tally of the people embarking on the inland expedition to chart the settlements along the Gambia River. The narrator includes the African "linguisters" among the white men because of their religious affiliation (243). The neutrally descriptive fact of the translators' skin color is not their primary form of identity among Englishmen on the slave coasts of Africa. The linguisters claim the status associated with Christian belief, which meant that a black man could, in some contexts, be a white man. This anecdote speaks volumes about the elastic way that skin color could operate in the eighteenth century and about the status Britons accorded to Christian profession.

Other stories in contemporary documents testify to a superficial notion of human variety. The susceptibility of noses, heads, and skin color to environmental changes and to human manipulation were among the most popular. One type of commonly told tale involved mismatches between parental color and their newborn's color. Many physicians observed that children of American Indians and Africans were born with reddish but light-colored skin, like Europeans, and that they became darker gradually—over a period of days, weeks, or even months. Other evidence offered of color's mutability included white-skinned babies born to two black parents (albinism was not well understood at the time); children of one black-complected and one white-complected parent who were partially white and black, or sometimes spotted; and Europeans who became dark-skinned after living in the torrid zones. It was commonly reckoned that it would take at least ten generations for Englishmen in the torrid zones to turn into Negroes or for Negroes in England to turn into northern Europeans. Civil society could also enhance color's mutability. For example, in his enormously influential *Natural History: General and Particular* (1749), Buffon repeats an incident from Tavernier's seventeenth-century travels in South Africa about a Hottentot baby whom the Dutch removed from her home a few days after birth. Brought up among the Dutch, she "soon became as white as any European."[7] From this story, Tavernier and, by extension, Buffon conclude that all Hottentots would be equally fair if they "did not perpetually dawb themselves with dirt and black paints" (3:400). In fact, Buffon remarks on the largely artificial differences distinguishing black Africans from Europeans: "In a succession of generations, a white people transported from the north to the Equator, would undergo this change, especially if they adopted the manners, and used the food, of the new country" (406). Other writers who sought to account for the naturalness of dark skin likened black complexion to "an universal freckle."

Skin color was not the only—or even primary—register of human difference for much of the eighteenth century, and climate was not the only factor believed to shape appearance and influence behavior. Commerce, for example, was reckoned a powerful force in its own right. Henry Fielding was not alone in his observation about the profound effects of Britain's commercialization on the inhabitants: " 'Nothing has wrought such an Alteration in this Order of People, as the Introduction of Trade. This hath indeed given a new Face to the whole Nation, hath in great measure subverted the former State of Affairs, and hath almost totally changed the Manners, Customs and Habits of the People.' "[8] Fielding notes the way that commerce triggered social change, and he represents the effects of increased trade in the language of natural history. Other contemporaries believed that Britain's peculiar form of government, which fostered several ranks of people and many professions, shaped the character of the inhabitants by making them more industrious and liberal. An example of the profound effect Britons believed institutions had on character appears in a typical distinction between the English in England and the English who move to Ireland. One commentator on various national characters observes that the Irish are known for the "gaiety and levity of their dispositions," and that when the English are transplanted to Ireland they in turn "become gay and thoughtless, more fond of pleasure, and less addicted to reasoning. This difference of disposition cannot properly be said to arise from climate or soil . . . but merely from the nature of their government."[9] Still others regarded the literary achievements, the proliferation of manufactured goods, the advanced maritime technology, and the luxury of the upper orders as signs of Britain's special eminence. Most Britons attributed their flourishing civil and political institutions to the felicitous English climate. The several examples of the ease with which visible change occurred to individual bodies and to the body politic suggest that Britons' understanding of complexion, the body, and identity was far more fluid than ours is today.

I have purposely featured examples of the elasticity accorded black and white skin color and of the mutability of identity because they belie our current sense of color's intractability. Eighteenth-century Europeans were just beginning to analyze human variety according to Nature rather than relying primarily on received knowledge from writers such as Aristotle and Hippocrates. The textual authority of the Ancients was still a powerful force despite the testing of their theories through empirical experiments and comparative observations (and tentative rejection of them, in some cases). A study of contemporary racial ideology confirms that Britons' beliefs were slow to change, even when "objective" evidence refuted customary views of the effects of climate on skin color or on national character. In the ensuing chapters, this book demonstrates more fully that there was not yet consensus among Europeans about the extent to which humans were different from each other, what caused these variations, or about how to value the visible differences. Was a black man in England different from a black man elsewhere? Were English colonists in the West Indies constitutionally changed by exposure to the new climate? These questions worried eighteenth-century pundits, philosophers, and scientific investigators.

As Clarence Glacken's magisterial *Traces on the Rhodian Shore* (1967) shows, seventeenth- and eighteenth-century Europeans were preoccupied with assessing whether, and to what extent, culture or the arts and sciences could offset the influence of climate. No systematic answers resulted from the myriad speculations, experiments, or experiences. A view of the Enlightenment that has stressed the empirical orientation of philosophy and science, privileged rationality or the impulse to control nature over received knowledge from classical texts, belief in astrology, practice of folk knowledge, Christian teaching, and the fairly quirky speculations that pepper eighteenth-century texts, has told only part of the story. This view of the Enlightenment expunges the persistence of alternative knowledge in the haste to identify the emergence of the new and the breaks with the old. The historical record, in fact, militates against such a monologic interpretation of the Enlightenment in general and racial ideology in particular.

* * *

This book analyzes the significance of race to eighteenth-century Britons by examining what constituted human difference and how it was narrated. Most generally, I am interested in the fluid articulation of human variety, as it was called, during the period 1680–1800 in Britain, a time and location not usually distinguished for its own notion of race. I argue that throughout the eighteenth century older conceptions of Christianity, civility, and rank were *more explicitly* important to Britons' assessment of themselves and other people than physical attributes such as skin color, shape of the nose, or texture of the hair. Embodied in dress, manners, and language, the concepts of Christianity, civility, and rank were not simply abstract categories of difference; they constituted visible distinctions that are difficult for us to recover today. A distinguishing feature of my book is integrating the writings of the Scottish Enlightenment philosophers on civil and savage societies into our sense of Enlightenment racial ideology. With its emphasis on economic organization and social manners, covering everything from the protection of private property to men's treatment of women, four-stages theory arguably offered a more significant form of racialization of the body politic than the categories concerning the physical body found in natural history.

The surface of the body, however, raised other problems of categorization, and compared with the more traditional categories associated with Christianity and civil society, complexion and facial features elicited the most uncertain responses from British writers and proved the most difficult to narrate coherently. The assurance that skin color was the primary signifier of human difference was not a dominant conception until the last quarter of the eighteenth century, and even then individuals responded variously to nonwhite skin color. To be sure, Renaissance scholarship has demonstrated that complexion had mattered greatly to Britons at least since the early modern period and that it was a magnet for reflections on European superiority.[10] However, the eighteenth century is notable, I contend, for the reassessment of complexion's meanings.

Overall, this book traces how English religious and commercial categories designated the manifold excellence of British civil society and how a white and rosy complexion was, on occasion, called on to bolster the picture of British commercial eminence. The new prominence accorded skin color was not uniform within the newly forming human sciences nor throughout other cultural, political, and economic realms, as my investigation of the novel, travel narratives, and commercial discourse demonstrates. The larger issue at stake in analyzing relevant continuities in racial ideology in light of changes in emphasis and shifts in epistemology is how to theorize race in a way that accounts for its emergent character.

The elastic conception of race I have sketched above is largely absent from most critical interpretations of race in the Enlightenment.[11] One omis-

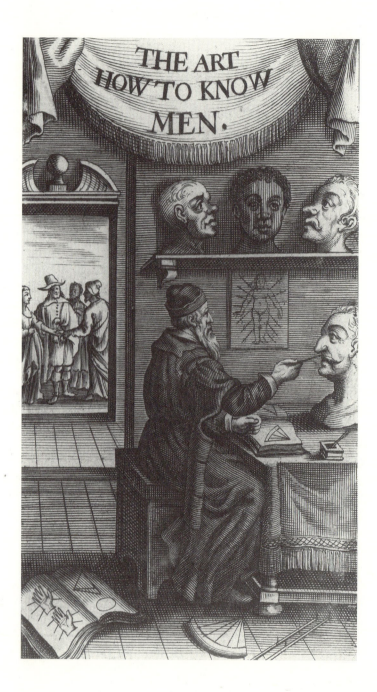

sion I seek to redress is that most histories of race have not adequately acknowledged the power of residual proto-racial ideologies, or older conceptions of national and religious difference that persisted despite the fact that the socioeconomic conditions which gave birth to them changed. What it meant to be a Christian in a Christian nation, for example, was integral to Britons' everyday lives, and this notion appears in travel accounts and novels, not in contemporary scientific or philosophical discourse, which is often the only body of texts studied in the history of race during the Enlightenment. An issue related to accounting for residual proto-racial ideologies of difference is acknowledging the sedimentation of racial ideology. Twentieth-century critics too often interpret the new scientific practices as dominant ones, which has skewed our sense of the extent and immediacy of changes. Many old and new beliefs and practices coexisted and cross-fertilized each other. Rarely was there a complete break with older ways of thinking.[12] A similar failure to account for historical variation arises when racial ideology in Britain is erroneously conflated with contemporary American or West Indian notions of race during the eighteenth century. Ideas about human differences developed at a different pace in England than in the colonies, and they had different histories in the West Indies, North America, Australia, New Zealand, and the East Indies.

I give a history to complexion and skin color largely absent from historical treatments of literature by showing their peculiarly eighteenth-century resonances, some of which no longer obtain today. My contention that skin color emerges as the most important component of racial identity in Britain during the third quarter of the eighteenth century, particularly noticeable in natural history and other scientific texts, distinguishes this study from others, especially literary interpretations, which have generally assumed that complexion is already the most significant factor.[13]

In emphasizing the elasticity of race in the Enlightenment, I also demonstrate that the deployment of racial discourse mattered in relation to popu-

Figure 1. Commerce and Character. Marin Cureau de la Chambre, *The Art How to Know Men* (London, 1665). Physiognomy, or divining the character of people by the shape and proportion of their facial features, had long been part of European folk knowledge, as numerous seventeenth-century almanacs attest. This frontispiece depicts the scholar's mathematical examination of European and African facial features in the foreground. The left background shows a European man buying gloves for his wife, possibly from an Armenian merchant. The information gleaned from judging character at a glance could be used to gauge exchanges with strangers in a commercial society. William Andrews Clark Memorial Library, University of California, Los Angeles.

Figure 2. The Complexion of Man. Johann Caspar Lavater, *Essays on Physiognomy* (London, 1789–98). The Swiss Lavater was aware of the little credibility given his approach. He estimated about 90 percent of the people who spoke about physiognomy were against it, often because they rightly feared the way it would be used "to the disadvantage of their fellow-creatures." Many natural historians, including Buffon, tried to divorce their work from the amateur pursuit of physiognomy, even as they drew on its commonplaces applied on a global scale. For instance, knowledge about what a flat forehead, "frizzled" hair, or a long nose signified shows an intimate connection to humoral theory. Department of Printing and Graphic Arts, Houghton Library, Harvard University.

lations other than Africans, and I show it at work in regard to North Africans, East Indians, and Native Americans. Too often, race has been treated only as a subset of slavery and colonialism, an emphasis that has reinforced the fallacious belief that race is primarily about blackness or African origins.[14] On the contrary, Europeans believed that all groups of people shared equally in a set of defining physical and cultural features—some of which were perceived to be distinctly more favorable than others. Although there has been a welcome recent shift in attention to the other side of the color binary, another problem has been brought into relief by the new emphasis on whiteness. Namely, some historians and literary critics have treated whiteness the same way blackness has been treated—in an essentialist way, a definition anachronistic to the time period. Similarly, they often conflate whiteness and Englishness, and one result is that neither term is fully explored for its historical pertinence. Understandably, some critics have thought it important for political reasons to analyze social formations and literature in black and white terms, and this emphasis has raised key issues about the connection between English aesthetic and economic realms. Nevertheless, this line of inquiry has also resulted in an impasse in our understanding of racial

ideology. By not pursuing the nuances of eighteenth-century racial thinking, our current preoccupation with chromatism is reproduced rather than
challenged by historical difference. My work encourages a more precise periodization of when race and colonialism, as well as race and slavery, became
intimately codependent and when other factors, such as political and economic issues, predominated.

In literary studies of the British eighteenth century, there has been,
to date, little treatment of race and color. With a few notable exceptions,
eighteenth-century literary historians have not generally perceived racial
ideology to be central to their research.[15] Because most literary critics have
treated Britain as a nation and not also as a colonial power, race has not
seemed significant to their inquiries.[16] Although Laura Brown, Markman
Ellis, Moira Ferguson, and Felicity Nussbaum have tried to redress this
omission, much work remains in studying the intersections of race and colonialism during the eighteenth century.

*   *   *

My study of British attempts to reckon with human variety is situated in a specific view of eighteenth-century Europe. There was a historically unprecedented establishment of exploitative power relations with
non-European people on a global scale. Among other effects in Britain,
this contact with other people triggered a boom in the acquisition of consumer goods, helped provide the monetary base for the Industrial Revolution
and more jobs in manufacturing and domestic service, and generated enormous profits and a higher standard of living.[17] These benefits, however, were
neither evenly distributed throughout the British populace nor continuous in
their effect (Brewer, 191). The various sorts of commercial and colonial contact also provided the data for scientific speculation. Although the data were
decidedly not uniform, they paved the way for mid-nineteenth-century scientific racism, a cultural and economic heritage we are still grappling with
today in the Atlantic region.

As the historian John Brewer shows, structural changes in Great Britain facilitated overseas expansion, and one fruit of the colonial growth was
a new accession to European dominance. By the 1760s, "Britain was able to
shoulder an ever-more ponderous burden of military commitments thanks
to a radical increase in taxation, the development of public deficit finance (a
national debt) on an unprecedented scale, and the growth of a sizable public administration devoted to organizing the fiscal and military activities of
the state. As a result, the state cut a substantial figure, becoming the largest

single actor in the economy."[18] A concomitant issue that historian Nancy Koehn raises is that conceptions of the empire shifted during this concentration of state resources and acquisition of new territory: "During the first half of the century, primarily militaristic conceptions of empire gradually gave way to commercial ones," a transition enacted by Daniel Defoe's fictional characters in the Caribbean, Africa, and the Americas.[19] At this time, according to Kathleen Wilson, British political culture disseminated competing images of the empire, nation, Englishness, and Otherness.[20] Thus, prevailing theories of human variety must be assessed in regard to an increasingly aggressive fiscal-military state and divergent visions of empire.

Some of the most striking differences in colonial practice from the nineteenth century include the stated aim, follow-through, and policies of empire building. During the eighteenth century, the British constituted an uneven presence in many landscapes, and their policies focused on trade more than on the transformation of other societies. As Koehn notes about the eighteenth century, "The central objectives of imperial management were increased sales of British manufactures and prudent fiscal administration," which is not to say that Britons did not resort to individual acts of violence, collective force, coercion, and chicanery to secure these ends.[21] Despite the fact that Britain maintained an official noninterventionary stance in relation to American Indian, East Indian, and Aborigine societies through the early nineteenth century, these same policies indirectly altered indigenous societies through the introduction of disease, clearing of land, and cruel labor practices.

Trade itself, while it fostered exploitative practices in some cases, was, in its discursive manifestation, based on mutual needs and a broad concept of utility in global exchange. In fact, it was a significant factor mitigating the perception of difference at this time. Take, for instance, Addison's unabashed celebration of London as "a kind of *Emporium* for the whole Earth." The narrator revels in mingling with the world's merchants in London's Royal Exchange and in the delights of "Traffick," which redistributes the world's products.[22] Over five decades later, the former slave Ignatius Sancho, in what Markman Ellis calls "a broadly sentimental account of the power of commerce in establishing sociable relations of virtue," observes that " 'Commerce was meant by the goodness of the Deity to diffuse the various goods of the earth into every part—to unite mankind in the blessed chains of brotherly love, society, and mutual dependence.' "[23] Given this intellectual constellation and its related practices, it is imperative to theorize race, its connections to the concept of empire, as well as its discontinuities from it, with the historical and economic conditions of the eighteenth century in mind. Otherwise, theory creates a transhistorical approach to race and colonial power.

There was not unalloyed celebration of intensified commercialism. Many writers of the day detailed the loss in traditional ways of living and in national character wrought by the more pervasive cash nexus. The underbelly of improvement included Parliament-supported land enclosures and the associated practices of rack-renting and short-leasing, policies that forced people to leave their parishes for the cities or colonies and resulted in a greater polarization between the wealthy few and the rest.[24] One indication of the enormous internal changes in Britain is that during the long reign of George III, the wealthier landowners appropriated more than six million acres of land (96). At the same time, there was, through Parliament and the courts, increased criminalization and control of poor people.[25] As Raymond Williams demonstrates in *The Country and the City* (1973), these changes appeared in contemporary domestic literature—transmogrified and obfuscated through what he calls "a dialectic of change" (71)—as celebration of rural innocence and melancholy for an irretrievable past.

Nevertheless, there was a certain seduction connected to the profound changes that contemporary Britons registered, particularly in regard to the proliferation of merchandise. The British economy itself was more integrated nationally and internationally than ever before, an effect particularly noticeable after midcentury.[26] Many Britons believed that their development of technology and pursuit of commerce made them a great society, an impression that was substantiated by the generally booming economy and by the outcomes of many of their encounters with peoples around the globe in which their ships, guns, and goods paved the way for favorable terms of trade and colonization. The economic transformation of Great Britain involved significant developments in industrialization and manufacturing concerns, such as the upsurge in textiles, metal works, and ship building; all of these changes took place in relation to the continuation of agricultural production, although it declined in overall economic importance by century's end.

The increased involvement in trade did not simply alter other societies with whom the British had contact but changed Britain's own landscape and inhabitants' manners. The transformation within Britain's infrastructure of trading arteries was visible, including the midcentury surge in the building of canals, roads, and turnpikes.[27] These changes in the countryside were accompanied by an explosion in the volume of goods that circulated within Great Britain and passed through its ports. "Between 1700 and 1800, imports into Great Britain expanded by more than 500 percent. Exports grew more than 560 percent and reexports by over 900 percent."[28] In fact, Britain's commerce "was increasingly dependent on foreign consumption of British manufactures and external provision of the raw materials used in manufacturing production and agricultural processing" (49). It was also increasingly dependent on the slave trade and commercial control in East India and North America.

Over the century, Europe itself became a less significant market for British goods than the colonies in America, which were the fastest growing sector: "By 1770, Europeans purchased only 30 percent of Britain's exports. In place of Dutch, French, and German consumers, a growing number of American customers—both in the mainland colonies and in the West Indies—bought 44 percent of Britain's exportable goods. India took almost 10 percent and Ireland 5 percent" (50). Most pundits and politicians believed that the African slave trade was largely responsible for this wealth. All of these changes meant that Britons were more connected to each other, albeit more stratified than ever before, and their fortunes more intimately tied to others'. Given the extension of British power through numerous voyages of discovery and the related national economic transformation, it is unsurprising that human differences became an object of study in the newly forming human sciences and in literary, travel, and historical narratives. Empire, Europe, and Britain were reimagined in the eighteenth century; skin color and civil society, the two main coordinates of this book, emerged as critical categories that helped define these related constructions. Before detailing the secular racial ideologies promulgated in natural history and four-stages theory and the way that climate theory was central to both, I will briefly examine older ways Europeans had for reflecting on their culture and their bodies.

*   *   *

Two of the most important ways that Europeans conveyed differences between themselves and others were with reference to religion and clothing. To be sure, there were other residual ideologies that eighteenth-century Britons could and did marshal as racial categories of difference, but religion and clothing consistently occupy the foreground of contemporary interest. Classical Greek and Roman texts, geographies of the four known continents, travel narratives, and the Bible were the main resources for Europeans' knowledge about other parts of the world. These texts offered rubrics for seeing as well as "raw" data for interpretation. Each genre, whether secular or religious, featured selective information, and there was little attempt to reconcile the various representations. Nevertheless, these resources provided the categories of difference that Europeans drew on and refined. Initially, they were mainly religious and political concepts, such as Christianity and civility; later, they were concepts related to physical appearance. The authority of Greek and Roman texts should not be underestimated in providing ruling-class men, in particular, with the distinction between themselves and barbarians, an essentially political concept based on differences in language and government.[29] The Bible, of course, offered the most general of all pictures about humankind and could be a guide to minimizing or exaggerating perceptions of others' differences. As early modern scholars have noted, Christian lore traditions were often at a far remove from the Bible, a situation enhanced by low levels of literacy. These biblical stories circulated along with more "official" knowledge, sometimes offering fanciful secular adaptations of biblical passages that Britons used to think about other people.[30]

Most Britons, if pressed, likely would have explained the variety of human appearances and behaviors as divinely ordained, based on the biblical account of the Creation and the common descent from Eve and Adam. This theory of shared human origins is now called monogenesis. Britons believed that the subsequent changes in complexion and manners, called "degeneration," sprang from natural occurrences to people as they dispersed over the earth. Variations in temperature and lifestyle, compounded by long amounts of time in the places where they settled, made the differences even more pronounced. The ethnocentric assumption that all people were born with white skin or the more startling claim that Africans, among others, had white souls stemmed from the conviction of a shared descent from Adam and Eve, whom Europeans often envisioned in their own image.[31] In this understanding, diversity among humankind was technically insignificant. Even though traditional Christian belief about similarity of bodies, minds, and souls was largely unchanged during the Enlightenment, it was increasingly questioned after midcentury, especially by slave owners, philosophers, and a few men of science.

Religion, in fact, was arguably the most important category of difference for Britons' understanding of themselves at various times during the century.[32] Notably, it was not always the most important rubric for seeing others, however. In eighteenth-century texts, Christianity often functions like a proto-racial ideology that flourished on its own and worked in conjunction with other categories. All in all, Christianity was a political, religious, and cultural concept on its own that was also a dense transfer point— a repository of qualities available for diversion into British national character and whiteness.

Before Europe, there was Latin Christendom, which rooted cultural resemblance among diverse nations in shared religious doctrine. To be a Christian was to be fully human, an association that reverberates throughout the seventeenth and eighteenth centuries in global confrontations. "Religion," Denys Hay reminds us, "rather than race or government or geography formed the common basis of all groups in western society."[33] Well into the seventeenth century, Hay contends, Christendom existed side-by-side with a conception of Europe (96, 115). Religious difference had structured the political and economic landscape of the Middle Ages and early modern era. In this vein, Winthrop Jordan maintains, "Until the emergence of nation-states in Europe, by far the most important category of stranger was the non-Christian." The contemporary term *heathenism* was an umbrella concept for the negation of all that was Christian.[34]

Before European involvement in the slave trade and settlement in the Americas, the most important Other was the Muslim. Through the contrast between Christian Europe and the Islamic Turkish Empire, the concept of freedom first arose when Europeans contrasted their lot to the despotic fate of Ottoman subjects. Indeed, according to Jordan, the spread of Christianity was often held responsible for the decline in bond slavery within European borders (50). Religion continued to be a significant category in the new colonies to distinguish Europeans from the indigenous people and the slaves. For the early English settlers in America, Jordan contends that "the heathen condition of the Negroes seemed of considerable importance" (91)—so much so that it was initially more important than their skin color, a situation that changed, in his view, only by the end of the seventeenth century in North America, when chattel racial slavery emerges (98).

The Church of England provided the main sense of British Christian identity after the sixteenth century, but the nuances of doctrine were noticeably less important for political alignment with Protestant nations —the Dutch and Germans—against Catholic powers. For the Anglican Britons of the eighteenth century, however, Protestant Dissenters, Catholics, Jews, Muslims, and heathens were all subject to prejudice and politico-economic punishment in varying degrees within their borders and outside them. In Britain, for instance, Catholics were excluded from civil and university positions; heathens and Muslims were candidates for enslavement. One indication of religion's central role in identity formation is Linda Colley's beginning *Britons: Forging the Nation, 1707–1837* (1992) with a chapter entitled "Protestants." Anglicanism was a unifying bond as Britons confronted other European and non-European peoples in the reaches of the new empire, in as much as it also helped unify the populace internally against Catholics. In the abstract attacks from pulpits and the particular instances of

mob violence, religious animosity toward Catholics was overdetermined because it was usually tied to local political and economic issues.[35] Anglicanism
was a coordinate of identity that synthesized English patriotism and ven-
eration of the Parliament-limited monarchy in the post–Civil War period;
Britons' peculiarly liberal government was believed to be part of the Protestant inheritance. Demonstrating the ideological connection between Protestantism, freedom, and prosperity, Colley argues that it was "on this strong
substratum of Protestant bias from below that the British state after 1707
was unapologetically founded" (43).

Other than Christianity, clothing was another category of difference
that Europeans saw as crucial to their own and others' identity. Important
as residual ideology and refashioned as part of the consumer revolution in
the eighteenth century, clothing draws on the vectors of Christian tradition
and secular subordination. It was key to the constitution of religious, class,
national, and personal identity during the eighteenth century. Dress fulfills
several functions, including protecting the body (a sort of artificial climate),
showing modesty, differentiating groups of people from one another, and
ornamenting the body. Like Christianity, dress also serves as a proto-racial
ideology and is a multiply determined concept. From at least the seventeenth
century, notes Daniel Roche, clothing was at the center of debates about
wealth, luxury, and necessity, and in this oblique way, a concern with apparel was a commentary on the empire: "In the Christian moral vision, both
Catholicism and Protestantism, it served as a means to measure how manners adapted to ethical requirements." In the Christian tradition, clothes
were an aspect of social and moral conduct. Conventionally, clothing functioned as an index of character: it was supposed to reflect a person's quality
of mind, which was enforced by sumptuary laws until the early seventeenth
century.[36] Clothing revealed so much about a person—or an entire group
of people—and Britons had an acute eye in regard to the social symbolics
of dress. As Marjorie Garber insists, one anxiety seventeenth-century ser-
mons and sumptuary laws conjured up was distinguishing properly between
the sexes. Clothing often functioned as if it were a reliable cultural norm.
Commercial society, however, made dress—to some extent—a less reliable
sign of status and character because it became a commodity in the public
domain and key to social mobility. Vital to social regulation, dress distinguished among the ranks, regions, and the sexes long after sumptuary laws
were abandoned.[37]

Although eighteenth-century fashion was less easy for Britons and visitors to interpret than before, especially in cities, apparel assumed a new general importance based on colonial and imperial experiences. If commercial

A Description of the Habits of most COUNTRIES in the WORLD.

The Habit of a Chinese
The Habit of a Mogul
The Habit of a Persian
The Habit of a Turk
The Habit of a Tartar
The Habit of a Polander
The Habit of a Muscovite
The Habit of a Laplander
The Habit of a Hungarian
The Habit of a Dutchman
The Habit of a Spaniard
The Habit of a Hottentot
The Habit of a Negroe
The Habit of a Moor
The Habit of a Mexican
The Habit of a Virginia Indian
The Habit of a Florida Indian
The Habit of a Scots Highlander

society tended to destabilize clothing as a legible sign of status, then European encounters with native people tended to establish anew the comparatively stable significance of specifically European clothing norms. Nakedness signified "a negation of civilization" on several counts.[38] Clothing assumed a new value in the repeated confrontations between fully garbed Europeans and lightly clothed "savages." Some Africans, Malaysians, Pacific Islanders, and Americans often substituted ointments and other external preparations for textile protection. It is little surprise, then, that the British Christianizing process, albeit weakly pursued in North America and the Caribbean, involved clothing. The degree to which native assimilation to religious instruction was gauged successful was perceptible in the dress that native converts adopted—or failed to adopt (146). Using clothing to measure the success of Christian instruction and Europeanizing others is evident throughout this book.

As the ensuing chapters explore, adoption of European clothing also signaled proper gender and political subordination in novels. In nonfiction accounts, writers and travelers regarded British ready-made clothing as vital to good trade relations with sovereign native people (and with colonial subjects, for that matter) in Africa and the Caribbean.[39] Reports of the consternation aroused by European clothing in the four corners of the earth are some of the funniest in an all too grim series of global encounters, not least because they often invert British ethnocentrism and show mutual systems of othering in operation. European clothing seemed to obscure vital information other people wished to access about the visitors/intruders. There are several incidents of British men stripping off their clothing and displaying their penises to satisfy other people that they themselves were human. For instance, in the first exchanges between Australian Aborigines and Europeans in 1788, it soon became clear that "there was some early confusion on the issue of gender because the [British] visitors were clean-shaven. Even their voices, overlaid with peculiar intonations, did not prove that they were

Figure 3. "A Description of the Habits of most Countries in the World." *A Collection of Voyages and Travels . . . Compiled from the Library of the Late Earl of Oxford* (London, 1745). This frontispiece shows the most typical expression of British interest in other people of the time period—in the variety of dress and its indication of local manners. Eschewing a straightforward scheme of four lines of people representing the variety on each continent, the ethnographic plate groups the Spaniards, Moors, and Highlanders with the countries Britons considered the least polished in the world. Partial nudity links Americans and Africans, but the Hottentots and Negroes are singled out as the only nonwhite people. Courtesy of the John Carter Brown Library at Brown University.

men, and the Aborigines considered the possibility that they were misshapen females." The suspense comes to a head when a party of Aborigines signaled to the Britons "that they wanted to know 'of what Sex we were,' and some of the humbler European men, no doubt under orders, 'satisfied them in that particular.'"[40] The discovery that the Europeans were, in fact, men like themselves prompted the Aborigines to extend a more cordial welcome than the previously guarded exchanges.

In other situations, clothing is key to religious identity, and British men peeling off their clothing to confirm their possession of uncircumcised "Christian" penises—or refusing to—is not unusual. The Scot Mungo Park undergoes untold hardships in his commission to find the source of the Niger River on behalf of the African Association at the century's end, and he is prey to the whim of his hosts and captors. Park finds himself subject to numerous indignities among Muslim Moors because he is a Christian; they regard his tight-fitting European clothes and white skin with contempt, not unlike the Brobdingnags' treatment of Gulliver. One group of Moorish women wish to discover whether Christians are circumcised like Muslim men, and they ask Park to remove his clothing. In a delicate social negotiation, he dissuades them from this inspection. In fiction, however, there was no such coyness about European men stripping down. An early episode in Defoe's *Captain Singleton* (1720) concerns whether the boy Bob Singleton is a circumcised Muslim or an uncircumcised Christian—an important piece of information obscured by his clothing. The European pirates force him to drop his breeches. This action saves his life and establishes his kinship with other Christian Europeans.

European clothes, it seems, were often viewed as odd extensions of the body; the copious clothing obscured where the European body began and ended. For example, a Briton who was shipwrecked among the Pelew islanders found himself the object of much curiosity. When he took off his hat for the first time, he reported that the people were amazed. Apparently to gratify them, he then unbuttoned his waistcoat and took off his shoes, in order that they might see that they were not attached to his body, "'being of opinion, that at first sight of me, they entertained a notion that my clothes constituted a part of my person; for, when undeceived in this, they came nearer to me, stroked me, and put their hands into my bosom to feel my skin.'"[41] Considering the importance Europeans themselves attributed to their clothing as a sign of their identity, the Pelew islanders guessed correctly.

European clothing was a spectacle to other people—both for the improbable amount of it in hot climates and for its intricacy. Early in the century, Lady Mary Wortley Montagu reported the astonishment of the naked

Turkish women in the baths who viewed her layers of clothing and under-garments with dismay. Montagu declined to remove her garments in order to bathe, and she reported that the women considered her elaborate apparel, especially her undergarments, as a form of imprisonment devised by a jeal-ous husband. At century's end, Anna Maria Falconbridge recorded how her dress, rather than her white complexion, was a spectacle to the people in Sierra Leone: "The people on the island crowded to see me; they gazed with apparent astonishment—I suppose at my dress, for white women could not be a novelty to them." [42] Her response to their native attire was not astonish-ment as much as injured "delicacy." Her diligent efforts to interact with Prin-cess Clara, daughter of King Naimbana and wife of the local British agent, centered around the drama of clothing. Falconbridge spent several days with Clara, during which time she tried to persuade her to dress in the Euro-pean manner. Falconbridge's efforts notwithstanding, Clara "would tear the clothes off her back immediately after I put them on" (62). Whether these apocryphal stories are true is hardly the point: one of their functions is to remind readers how integral dress is to Christian European identity, even in hot climates.

*   *   *

If Christianity and clothing helped Europeans articulate a shared hu-manity on the one hand and important distinctions on the other, climate theory was the secular rationale for various skin colors, behaviors, and abili-ties. The linchpin to understanding most eighteenth-century pronounce-ments about the body's appearance is climate. Positing that all bodies (minds, emotions, and the like) responded similarly to the environment, cli-mate theory also suggested that some environments were better than others for enabling humans to fulfill their potential. In the following sections I treat climate in its association with the body, complexion, and what eighteenth-century Britons called "understanding." Then, I examine climate's role in natural history, the main venue for establishing norms of human appearance, and, finally, I assess its role in four-stages theory, the chief way of discussing norms of cultural and economic activity. Comprehending the profound re-spect Europeans granted climate accounts for their superficial and malleable beliefs about skin color and race during the eighteenth century.

Despite ubiquitous claims to examine Nature during the Enlighten-ment, Europeans remained indebted to classical truisms about climate. Climate and humoral theory, in one form or another, provided the most im-portant rubric for thinking about human differences in the eighteenth century, in regard to both complexion and civil society.[43] The primary rubric for understanding temperament since its origination in the East Indies and development in classical Greece and Rome, climate and humoral theory were both the primary alternative to religious explanation and a companion to it. Although most British natural historians subscribed to Christian beliefs, they propounded a secular rationale of differences among people in their writings. These natural differences, they believed, arose from geographic variation, climatic conditions, and a people's related cultural habits; the most influential factors were exposure to the sun, the absence of winds, elevation of land above sea level, proximity to large bodies of water, fertility of the soil, and diet of the inhabitants. In this model, human characteristics, they believed, were formed over time by external forces working on the body.[44] These insights were adapted from the most reputable ancient authorities, including Hippocrates, Plato, and Galen, who had written extensively about how weather, waters, and places conditioned human bodies and understanding.

The ancient Greeks regarded complexion as a holistic concept. It encompassed people's disposition and cast of mind, as well as their general health and skin color. Humor theory linked the environment to the mind and body in a symbiotic relationship.[45] Conventionally, each region of the earth produced nations with a particular cast of humors that dominated the behavior and appearance of the inhabitants. Greeks and Romans believed that people in the northern and torrid regions possessed a mixture of positive and negative qualities, and regarded them as opposites. From the temperate regions, Greeks and Romans ascribed the best qualities the two extreme zones offered to themselves (70). Formulated at a time when people were not very mobile, this theory assumed each person was born with a complexion that was established at the moment of conception and "in some way persisting throughout life."[46] In this way, complexion was connected to familial inheritance and climate but not reducible to them. Complexion changed over the course of one's life, through age, conditions of living, geographic region, and even according to whether one was a man or a woman. Subject to fluctuation, the humoral body was porous and thus easily affected by what went in it and on around it, and it was especially sensitive to heat and cold, the major forces understood to alter bodies externally and internally.[47] In the Middle Ages and Renaissance understanding, complexion "was never an absolute but always a relative quality" (Siraisi, 103), a characteristic that continues to inflect it throughout the eighteenth century, even as complexion undergoes certain changes in usage. Complexion, or humoral theory, was often called on to explain psychological, social, and physiological characteristics as well as to formulate stereotypes (103). A vast majority of eighteenth-century Europeans still believed that cultural, educational, or environmental change altered the humoral mix and thus affected both appearance and behavior.[48]

Ancient writers from the Mediterranean region had originally designated Britain a northern climate and its people of a cold and moist constitution—hence people with strong bodies and a fierce spirit who were prone to excessive drinking and were dull-witted. Conventionally, the barbaric people from the northern regions, such as Britain, were believed to be phlegmatic, or sluggish in disposition; they were perceived as good for producing hardy laborers as well as fine mechanical and manual arts. Their chalky white complexion signified this mix of characteristics. Ancient writers imagined that the southern zones, including Africa, yielded a somewhat more feeble-bodied but intellectual and creative people. Their black complexions signified this array of qualities. The higher levels of civilization were, of course, reserved for the Greeks and, later, the Romans. In ancient texts, these middle, or temperate, climatic zones gave rise to a people with the best balance of humors and hence the most beautiful complexion midway between white and black, which characterized the two extremes, and a balance of bodily strength, intellect, and creativity. This picture changed, however, over time.

According to Mary Floyd-Wilson, climate theory was transmogrified through centuries of incipient nationalist and Christian tinkering. Climate theory was reworked to suit the needs of a shift in power to the northern parts of Europe, especially in the seventeenth and eighteenth centuries. Two changes occurred in traditional climate/humoral theory. In some versions, Britain became part of the temperate zone; in other versions, Britain remained in the northern regions but shed its negative traits. At the hands of several writers, Britain was imaginatively reconceptualized as part of the temperate region, particularly in the seventeenth and eighteenth centuries.[49] Former temperate regions, such as Greece and Italy, then became the outposts of the temperate zones or, occasionally, part of the less attractive southern regions. The new northern regions were somewhat more nebulously defined—sometimes including parts of Scotland, sometimes outside of Europe altogether. Now Britain and Scandinavia—the former northern zones—became the center of eighteenth-century civilization, at least to many British minds, and white skin color no longer had the pejorative associations associated with classical climate/humoral theory.

In the eighteenth century, proximity to Europe and to temperate climates generated a theoretical hierarchy—not a scale of horizontal differences—that placed Europeans, and a few groups from the Middle East and

North Africa, at the top and Africans and Laplanders at the bottom. Because of the excessive heat that was believed to enervate the body, mind, and morals, commonplaces about the torrid zone being the home of dark-skinned people who were indolent, lascivious, and subject to tyranny often seemed confirmed when Englishmen confronted social and political life as well as labor arrangements that were alien to them. In the same vein, excessive cold was believed to produce effects similar to hot climates, and the contemptuous descriptions of the physical features and cultural life of the populations from the torrid and arctic zones were largely interchangeable. For instance, in *The Philosophy of Natural History* (1790), William Smellie reproduces the typical contemporary contempt for populations outside the temperate regions. He claims that the skin of Greenlanders is very tawny and, in fact, his entire description of the inhabitants of the north is almost verbatim what some of his contemporaries wrote about black Africans: "All those races [of the arctic area] resemble each other not only in deformity, in lowness of stature, and in the colour of their hair and eyes, but likewise in their dispositions and manners. All of them are equally gross, stupid, and superstitious."[50] Smellie's insights into color and cultural traits derived from humoral/climate theory.

In other revisions of the humoral/climate paradigm, Britain remained a northern nation, but only in the positive sense of being the seat of industry and expansion (this last construction was far more popular in the nineteenth century). Writers of the seventeenth and eighteenth centuries abandoned some aspects of humor and climate theory and reorganized others. They kept many of the positive traits traditionally associated with northern nations and altered them slightly; they also co-opted the positive traits associated with the old temperate zones to themselves. Climate/humoral theory was, in the Gramscian sense, the common sense of the day and a magnet for contradictory beliefs. To be sure, it was probed and prodded, partially refuted by a few, but it was also easily adapted to new conditions.

Humoral and climatic theory persisted in one form or another despite attempts to revise it or abandon it well into the nineteenth century. This effort to question traditional assumptions began in the mid-seventeenth century. Humoral theory informed conceptions of human variety but did not fully explain the way all Europeans were thinking about it. For example, Sir Thomas Browne's mid-seventeenth-century inquiry into the origin and transmission of blackness encapsulates concerns about traditional humor and climate theory that were unresolved or ignored in the eighteenth century because of a greater adherence to external climatic factors and a failure to design acceptable alternative explanations. Following the ancients, Browne gives great weight to the heat of the sun in the determination of black complexion, but he finds it inadequate to explain completely the occurrence and transmission of dark skin color in various parts of the world. This inadequacy prompts him to consider the possible effects of other natural factors that might generate black skin, including a pregnant woman's ingestion of certain waters that darkened the fetus or the interaction between a mother's imagination and her environment during pregnancy, which might impress itself on the baby's body or in its constitution. As a physician, Browne is especially drawn to chemical explanations, which are also much indebted to the humoral tradition. Likening the damage that fire and water can cause to things, or the way that cutting an apple soon darkens it by exposing it to the air, Browne speculates about skin color by analogy: "And so may the Æthiopians or Negroes become coal-blacke from fuliginous efflorescences and complexionall tinctures."[51] Indeed, he wonders if an excess of black humor, black dye, such as in fruit, or an "Atramentous condition" in the blood might possibly turn Moors into Negroes (528). Like most seventeenth- and eighteenth-century thinkers, he reaches no firm conclusions. Browne believed that color, however first established, was transmitted subsequently by sperm, a conclusion his contemporary Robert Boyle shared.[52]

Humors, climate, and skin color continued to evince a fraught relationship, as is evident in *The Primitive Origination of Mankind* (1677). Some thirty years after Browne's speculations, Matthew Hale conceived of human groups each possessing several categories of features, which he divides into figure, stature, color, complexion, and humor—all arising from the effects of climate.[53] To us, his somewhat confusing separation of color, complexion, and humor suggests a tentative siphoning off of physical factors (skin color) from psychological (humor) and physiological factors (complexion), a process that intensifies in the eighteenth century and later periods.

Eighteenth-century scientific attempts to uncover the mysterious origins of color differences or to place humans in taxonomies were not fully disentangled from a complexional understanding either. Although some physicians claimed that humors were not responsible for skin color, they continued to connect humors to temperament and behavior. Nevertheless, many influential natural historians, including Blumenbach, speculated that black complexion arose from the excessive secretion of black bile, one of the four humors.[54] The black secretion, they believed, was communicated to the skin's surface from the liver where it accumulated. A stellar example of humoral theory's lingering influence is nowhere more apparent than in Linnaeus's *System of Nature*. In 1735, Linnaeus first characterized *Homo sapiens* as varying by skin color, but his more complete rendering of humans as part of natural history in 1758 entailed adding the predominant humor associated with Europeans, Asiatics, Africans, and Americans. By the time James Cowles Prichard refers to them in his *Researches into the Physical History of Man* (1813), the humors appear in an extensive footnote after he exhaustively examines cultural and physical aspects of the various human groups; oddly, the humors seem to apply only to the variations among European nations.[55] The impact of humoral/climate theory on the history of race is considerable. What many of us may have been led to consider physical "racial" traits that Europeans assigned themselves and others are, to a considerable extent, filtered through the humoral and climatic sensibility. The antinomies from humor and climate theory were, it appears, adapted to a color paradigm and were fully unmoored from their original context by the mid to the late nineteenth century.

Part of the explanation for the confusion in contemporary usage of complexion or skin color was that color was shifting out of an elastic climate/humoral sensibility and onto a more rigid anatomical model; however, this transition was not completed during the eighteenth century, nor was it even clearly articulated by contemporary writers. The reduction of complexion to skin color is particularly remarkable after the 1770s, at which time humoral assumptions are absorbed more completely into anatomical and strictly geographical models of human variety. The first edition of the *Encyclopaedia Britannica* (1771), for instance, signals that the transition from the humoral understanding of complexion to the anatomical one was under way. The definition of *complexion* reads: "Among physicians, the temperament, habitude, and natural disposition of the body, but more often the colour of the face and skin."[56]

If Europeans did not explain complexion by humoral and climatic theory, they refered to skin color through the relatively new discipline of anatomy. When skin color was articulated through an anatomical understanding, the differences between whites and blacks were, it was argued, quite slight. In 1664, Robert Boyle, a founder of the Royal Society of London, reckoned that skin color was present only in the very thin top layer of the outward skin; all other layers were exactly the same in blacks and whites (37). Eighty years later, John Mitchell's widely read "Essay upon the Causes of the Different Colours of People in Different Climates" (1744) dismissed the relation between skin color and humors, even though the title of his essay clings to the notion of climate's relation to color that originated with the humors.[57] He found that the actual difference in the seat of color was insignificant, too, although somewhat differently located than Boyle. There was a thin layer underneath the epidermis, or outward skin, that transmits color: "*All other Parts are of the same Colour in Them* [black people] *with those of white People, except the Fibres which pass between those Two Parts*" (109). He concludes, "However different, and opposite to one another, these two Colours of Black and White may appear to be to the Unskilful [sic], yet they will be found to differ from one another only in Degree" (130). Skin color was not a "deep" concept yet, and it continued to reflect its traditional association with humoral theory even when articulated through anatomical terminology.

The anatomical body derived from William Harvey's theory of blood circulation and Vesalius's experiments in dissection. Physician to King Charles I, Harvey offered the main challenge to humoral theory. As John Harris put it somewhat confusedly his *Lexicon Technicum* (1704), the theory of the four humors "is cashiered, since the Invention of the Circulation of the Blood. Yet they are found when the Blood preternaturally departs from its due Temperature."[58] Composed of layers of skin, nerves, muscles, and arteries, the anatomical body was more solid than its porous counterpart, the humoral body. A particularly important element of the anatomical body was the nervous system, which connected the body to the mind. Sensational psychology was the basis of sensibility, a theory elaborated by Newton and Locke in the seventeenth century and honed by the Scottish moral philosophers in the eighteenth century. It borrowed the assumption from humoral theory about the effect of the body on the mind. The brain, or soul, is the termination point for the nerves, or instruments of sensation. Physical exertion could strengthen the nerves as too much intellectual study could weaken them.[59] Similar to humors, one could be born with a certain degree of sensibility that could be affected by early upbringing, education, and life pursuits. One explanation for the ease with which humoral sensibility was engrafted onto the theory of blood circulation is that the interior of the body was still seen as containing flowing liquid, now reduced from the four humors to the blood.

Anatomy and humors were rival theories of the body and its mechanics but tended to be combined syncretically rather than treated as mutually exclusive. Although other theories of the body slowly took hold beginning in the mid-seventeenth century and had gathered momentum by the early nineteenth century, the humoral body was still the dominant personal and medical heuristic. For example, contemporary practices of blood-letting, dietary restrictions for gout, bathing in mineral springs, and purging were all attempts to restore humoral balance or, in the new parlance, brace the nerves. As historian Jonathan Barry demonstrates, the eighteenth-century medical world was characterized by a mix and match approach that reflected the uncertain assimilation of the new science: "Galenic, Hippocratic, chemical and iatro-mechanical systems all jostled for acceptance and were combined eclectically by each physician."[60] It is a sluggish process, then, in which theories of human variety register the implications of the hardening body.

I have devoted a great deal of space to the humoral body and its association with climate because they have both been strangely omitted in recent eighteenth-century studies. When it is mentioned, humoral theory is discussed primarily in relation to theories of sexual difference or relegated to the realm of medical science of the day. This fact is particularly curious given what Clarence Glacken claims about the way humoral assumptions permeated many other aspects of eighteenth-century life: They "had a long and exciting life lasting well into the eighteenth century." The humors were "the theoretical basis of the older theories of climatic influence. The doctrine of the four elements strongly influenced the history of soil theory, chemistry, and agriculture—hence ideas of the nature of the physical environment as a whole—and the doctrine of the humors influenced theories of psychology and physiology, making prominent the supposed changes brought about in both the mind and the body by climate as a whole, sudden temperature change, and the seasons."[61] Humoral theory has profound implications for the study of early modern and eighteenth-century notions of racialism. It accounts not only for the surface and malleable notions of complexion current at the time, but it also reveals the ways in which old modes of thinking were not abandoned in the face of the new science associated with the Enlightenment but coexisted with it and were partially reworked.

*   *   *

Possibly because many writers of natural histories were also physicians, they were steeped in the humoral tradition and overwhelmingly committed to accounting for various physical traits through the workings of climate. The method of eighteenth-century natural history adapted humoral/climate theory to geographic models of human difference. The eighteenth century is now known as the great age of natural history because of the first systematic efforts of luminaries such as Linnaeus, Buffon, and Blumenbach to tame the overwhelming variety of the natural world and to find principles of categorizing it. The new discipline of natural history provides considerable insight into the ideology of human variety during the eighteenth century. Michel Foucault's *Order of Things* (1970) contends that natural history emerged as a new way of narrating history in the eighteenth century; that is, there was a new cultural imperative to arrange and label living phenomena.[62]

Although focused on plant life, Foucault's observations apply to taxonomies of humans, which, it should be noted, were never as compelling as exotic plants and animals to contemporary audiences. In broad terms, the methodology of natural historians involved reducing the complexity of similarities and differences to a description of visible features (137). A science of surfaces was thereby instituted by the late eighteenth century, and classification was based on "the principle of the smallest possible difference between things" (159).

In terms of humans, this way of seeing raised a problem not pertinent to the plant and animal kingdoms because most thinkers believed that all humans possessed the same nature and capabilities. Between 1650 and 1800, it is possible to detect the new scientific impulse to track increasingly minute distinctions among humans. In 1677, Sir William Petty devised two scales of animate creatures. Man was the linchpin in the two systems—at the bottom of one scale with God at the top, and at the top of the other scale with the smallest visible animal at the bottom. Petty worried over which creature approximated man in the scale. His own preference was for an elephant or possibly the bee. The elephant's "Memory & understanding," he reasoned, qualified it for this position as did the bee's spirituality and art of government, which "seems to bee [*sic*] the most considerable faculty of a Man."[63] If he were to follow his inclination and privilege the senses other than sight, either of these two candidates would work, as would the parrot, which sounds like a human. But when he bowed to "the Opinion of most men" of his day and considered sight as the most important faculty, he selected bodily shape as the best heuristic and thereby chose the ape to place next to man in his scale of creatures (2:2). Petty momentarily digresses from his larger enterprise of creating scales of animate and heavenly creatures to note that the greatest combination of differences among humans exists between Middle Europeans and Guinea Negroes on the one hand, Guinea Negroes and Negroes living near the Cape of Good Hope on the other hand, and all of these groups and Laplanders. In this scheme, Petty adheres fairly closely to ancient Greek divisions of the earth into cold, temperate, and hot regions with populations reflecting the traits associated with their climate.

The majority of taxonomies appeared in natural histories; like geographies, their basis was information selectively culled from travel narratives. From the 1670s through the 1720s, the taxonomic impulse is fairly quirky: some writers followed ancient convention by grouping humans according to the three or four continents; some chose form of government, others degree of literacy. For instance, Thomas Sprat's *History of the Royal Society* (1667) divides humans into two categories: one of learned and civil people and the other of the unlearned and barbarian. The first group is familiar with the arts and sciences, and the second group are people who do not appreciate the arts or pursue the advancement of the sciences; they do not have written texts or architectural monuments. Among the ancient barbarians, Sprat mentions the Gauls, Britons, Germans, Scythians. The barbarians of the present include Turks, Moors, East Indians, and Americans. The civilized and barbaric binary is extremely elastic throughout the seventeenth and eighteenth centuries; it can be invoked in great detail or generically.

The relatively new interest in describing and ordering human variety according to strictly visible physical variations (as opposed to cultural criteria) was not equivalent to a sudden settling of disagreement. If anything, debate intensified over where to draw the line between human groups. In the 1790s, for example, the eminent German natural historian Blumenbach recorded at least seven other ways his contemporaries divided humans, ranging from two to six groups. Nevertheless, Sir William Petty's hesitations and quirky preferences had been largely expunged from taxonomies a century later. With the publication of Buffon's *Natural History* (1749–88), slight variations in human skin color became a new norm of scientific inquiry.[64] Before Buffon, most taxonomers were content with limited color schemes in ways suggested by Aristotle's division of the earth into the northern, southern, and temperate zones, which loosely corresponded to people with white, black, and light brown skin. Buffon declares complexion to be one of the three most important features separating human groups. The colors he features include several intermediate distinctions within a black-and-white spectrum: copper, purple, tawny, olive, yellow, and brown. This range of color reflected the previous eighty years of empirical evidence garnered from travelers who had been enjoined to observe people in foreign lands for specific data.[65]

The third quarter of the eighteenth century is especially crucial to consolidating complexion as a significant visible human difference, partly because of the impact of Buffon's *Natural History* and because of Linnaeus's several revised editions of his *General System of Nature* (1735), including the expanded categorization of *Homo sapiens* in the tenth edition of 1758. Both of these landmarks in natural history feature complexion as a key factor in grouping humans; indeed, joined with the emergence of "homegrown" British systems of natural history in the 1770s, most notably Oliver Goldsmith's, they all signpost a burgeoning conviction that there were myriad differences, physical and cultural, among humans. To be sure, there were several other important factors influencing the selection of complexion as the primary feature of difference, which Chapter 4 details.

Even though reference to skin color in natural histories increasingly specified shades of difference over the century, the way that individual colors signified for eighteenth-century writers varied considerably. For example, "tawny" could mean black, brown, reddish brown, or even olive green, and it could be a descriptive term or an insult, depending on the context and user. In 1795, Blumenbach complains, "The indefinite and arbitrary sense in which most authors use the names of colours has caused vast difficulty in all the study of natural history."[66] One group that highlights the rather imprecise way in which color was perceived is Native Americans; they were alternately described as copper, tawny, white, and black. The main check to this imprecision regarding skin color was the increasing insistence on identifying Europeans as white as opposed to Christian, and the designation of Africans as black. Because of these competing tendencies within the color paradigm—the formation of a black-and-white polarity laden with value and the recognition of multiple color differences with comparatively unfixed meanings—complexion requires closer study in individual texts and in broader cultural trends.

The terminology associated with natural histories also provides a sense of the emergent character of race at this time. Notably, the appearance of new terms in the eighteenth century marks changes in ideas about human variation. In fact, race accrued new definitions and shed others over the century. Until the very end of the century, *variety*, not *race*, was the scientific term of choice to designate different groups of people. There was one human race divided into several varieties of "men."[67] I have retained this sensibility by referring to "human variety" and "human difference" when possible instead of the more familiar "race." In its most common usage, *race* simply meant a group. In this construction, one group could be identified by its particular combination of differences from some other. Conventionally, *race* meant family lineage, and it could apply generally to "the race of man" (as distinct from animals); to a subgroup of people, such as the Irish race; or even to nonhuman objects, such as the vegetable race.[68] Unlike today in Britain or the United States, race was not primarily a characteristic of minority populations. During the late eighteenth century, the word *race* was used by some writers in a recognizably incipient form of its modern sense—denoting a fairly rigid separation among groups. At this time, skin color was the most typical way to differentiate "races."

By the century's end, most natural historians and comparative anatomists concurred that each variety of human possessed a distinctive complexion and set of defining characteristics. These racial identities were more precise than the older nomenclature of *European* or *Christian*, and they marked identity on the surface of the body by skin color. In the final decades of the century, many Britons appeared to believe that human differences were less superficial, less changeable, and more a reflection of interiority than before. Race seemed more fixed and, some suspected, unalterable by changing climate, intensified commerce, or by education than at the beginning of the century.

The changes that I have sketched must be considered in light of Britons' particular pursuit of natural history. According to historian of race Nancy Stepan, religion "played a larger role" in British science and distinguished it from the Continent and America in the eighteenth and nineteenth centuries.[69] One of the main effects of their longer and stronger adherence to Christian tradition showed up in the initial reluctance to abandon climate as the source of change in humans. Another effect was less concern with detailing human variety than other European traditions. For example, James Cowles Prichard observed in the preface to *Researches into the Physical History of Man* (1813) that the British were slower than their Continental counterparts even to evince interest in the "physical diversities which characterize different races of men," an omission he seeks to rectify (1). His complaint may be read as more than self-promotion because the Germans, Swiss, and French were at the forefront of human natural history and comparative anatomy studies.

The eighteenth-century interest in surface, physical variation gave way, in part, to a new emphasis on structure. In the nineteenth century, Foucault argues, a science of surfaces is transformed into a science that promotes a relatively stable relationship between surface and depth. In new scientific practices, natural historians made the visible correspond to the invisible structure beneath and "then to rise upwards once more from that hidden architecture towards the more obvious signs displayed on the surfaces of bodies."[70] To be sure, this methodology can be traced in its incipient form to Bacon, Harvey, and a few other seventeenth-century representatives of the new science, but Foucault identifies its institutional dominance. In the first few decades of nineteenth century, scientists and philosophers renew inquiry into the mind/body symbiosis that had been part of Western culture for centuries, an emphasis which registers in the methods of natural historians. This paradigm shift rehearses a new way Europeans conceived of human differences and helps account for the emerging conviction that a person's exterior appearance spoke volumes about their mental capacity or, conversely, that skeletons or cranial measurement, now tools of scientific study, revealed civilizational proclivities for entire groups of people. During the last decade of the eighteenth century, research by French and German scientists in the

new discipline of comparative anatomy focused attention on the shape of
the skull as a mark of beauty and intellect. Eventually, comparative anatomy
became more important to scientists than skin color in delineating human
difference.

By the mid-nineteenth century, many Britons believed that race was
destiny—that one's skin color, skull shape, place of birth, or even hair type
largely determined one's potential, a dramatic change from previous thinking. Nancy Stepan aptly characterizes the difference before and after the
mid-nineteenth century in Britain as involving "a change from an emphasis
on the fundamental physical and moral homogeneity of man, despite superficial differences, to an emphasis on the essential heterogeneity of mankind,
despite superficial similarities. . . . By the middle of the nineteenth century,
everyone [in Britain] was agreed, it seemed, that in essential ways the white
race was superior to non-white races" (4). Even though many Britons ultimately subscribed to a deterministic notion of race, this conception was not
historically inevitable, as this book demonstrates.

*   *   *

As I have suggested, Britons put great faith in the arts and sciences,
clothing, and religion as ways to distinguish themselves from others. The
Scottish Enlightenment secularized and elaborated many of the symbolics arising from these proto-racial ideologies. A sizable body of literature
and offhand remarks about the advanced state of English arts and sciences,
as well as England's excellent government and active commerce, saturated
British writing at least from Samuel Purchas's influential collection of travel
narratives, *Hakluytus Posthumus; or, Purchas His Pilgrimes* (1625), but the development of a coherent theory about their origin, flourishing, and decline
did not occur until the 1770s with the publication of Adam Ferguson's *Essay
on the History of Civil Society* (1767), John Millar's *Origin of the Distinction
of Ranks* (1771), and Adam Smith's *Wealth of Nations* (1776). Notions of
polished, barbaric, and savage societies were elaborated and honed through
this school of thought. The assumptions about civil society informing four-
stages theory were indebted to publications such as the *Spectator*, which
popularized reforming the manners of a newly commercial and urban people;
to notions of climate and terrain's effect on people's manners, theorized cogently in Montesquieu's *Spirit of the Laws* (1748); and to the effects of the
circulation of money and of trade, formulated in David Hume's essays.

The "new" people whom Britons had been meeting in the trade networks and colonial outposts organized their societies quite differently from

Figure 4. The New Golden Age. *Atlas Geographus* (London, 1711). The human embodiment of the four continents typically appears on decorative maps and frontispieces to collections of travel narratives as well as books of geography and commerce. Here, the Greek goddess Astrea, now resident in England, holds the scales of justice. She is flanked by the civil societies of Asia and Europe on the left and the savage societies of Africa and America on the right. The cathedral in the left background reinforces the significance of altering nature to the determination of refinement. America and Africa are figured against the background of a natural setting on the right, unchanged by human labor and art. Courtesy of the John Carter Brown Library at Brown University.

Europeans. In trying to account for what contributed to these vast differences, some contemporary academics assessed why societies had developed at various paces by comparing socioeconomic arrangements around the globe and throughout history to analyze the causes and effects that seemed to operate. Although not hierarchical in all of its formulations, four-stages theory tended to establish superiority based on the organization of what John Millar calls "the common arts of life."[71] Most contributors to this theory emphasized how the division of labor shaped manners.[72] Particularly useful for explaining the former barbarity of an advanced civilization like Britain, four-stages theory also accounted for the contemporary existence of "savage" societies in parts of Africa, America, Asia, and the Pacific islands. This way of thinking used mythical, historical, and present-day "savages," "barbarians," and polite people to make its points. The stages of civilization model described the attributes of the most "primitive" societies, which comprised isolated families engaged in hunting, fishing, and foraging activities typical of nomads. Shepherd-based societies were also considered rudimentary in comparison with the settlement and institutions characteristic of the third stage, or agriculturally based societies. The fourth stage of society was commercial civilization. For instance, American Indians were the archetypal example of people who hunted or fished for sustenance. Typical shepherd societies were the Scottish Highlanders and Arabs. Both of these "savage" societies were nomadic or seminomadic. The civil societies were restricted to those people who had settled on the land permanently and cultivated it. To regulate agricultural and commercial societies and bolster the power of the landowners, legal and economic institutions instilled social order in civil societies. These institutions were integral to the perception of a developed society. The ancient Greeks and Romans were usually associated with the agricultural stage of society, and modern Europeans monopolized the commercial stage of civilization. Just when it seemed like natural history, with its emphasis on physical characteristics, might displace cultural conceptions of pagans and savages, four-stages theory kept them alive and well.

Most moral philosophers assumed that human nature was uniform throughout time and responsive to environmental and institutional forces.[73] Undergirding four-stages theory is a belief in the progress and the perfectibility of society. This belief should not be mistaken for a teleological theory. Progress was usually perceived as part of a cycle in which eminence characteristically preceded decline. For instance, when Malachy Postlethwayt celebrated Britain's great achievements and attributed them all to commerce and trade in his *Universal Dictionary of Trade and Commerce* (1774), he also summed up the vulnerability of a polite society to degeneration. The bounty

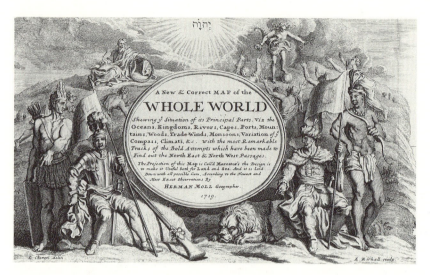

Figure 5. Four Continents, Four Kinds of People. Herman Moll, *A New and Correct Map of the Whole World* (London, 1719). The unusual cartouche shows the continents represented by men instead of women. Through the various accessories and details, the cartouche conveys the main difference between societies similarly to figure 4. Here, a polished country is paired with a rude one: the clothed European and the barefoot American appear on the left, and Asia and Africa are similarly juxtaposed on the right. This arrangement demonstrates the change from poverty to plenty and from savagery to refinement. Typically, complexion is not attended to as closely as cultural accessories. Courtesy of the John Carter Brown Library at Brown University.

afforded by trade, if indulged in too much, results in idleness and effeminacy among polite people. People who indulge excessively in the enjoyment of luxury and do not counteract it by industry usually decline into savagery. Such a decline had, of course, befallen the Roman Empire, which many educated Britons looked to for comparison. More recently, the Spanish and Portuguese empires had overextended themselves and had ceded their position to France and Britain.[74] British eminence, then, seemed a precarious condition at different moments in the eighteenth century rather than a permanent one. Some Britons worried that their own emergence from barbarism to civility was temporary, if not regulated closely. Although working from a non-color-based paradigm, Scottish Enlightenment thinkers reached a similar conclusion to other Europeans who were interested in complexion: Differences between human groups could be identified, and they revealed a hierarchy of excellence. Socioeconomic factors, in addition to skin color, were visible testimony of contemporary identity.

The 1770s was a key decade for registering the combined implications of natural and civil histories. In general the same differences contemporaries had noted over the century were seen as greater and more significant, and traditional explanations based on climatic degeneration from a common original seemed inadequate to some Europeans to account for the extent of variation. Because of a dynamic internal to early scientific inquiry, the mounting public pressure to discuss the economic and moral viability of the slave trade, and an expanding empire, among other factors, ubiquitous commitment to human similarity was beginning to show a few weak spots by the 1770s, a sentiment that had gained momentum by the 1790s. Thus, there was a newly receptive audience for alternative theories that accounted for human variety. Polygenesis, or multiple divine creations, was a radical departure from centuries of assumptions about the shared nature and capabilities of humans. A minority theory, tentatively conjectured by a few Europeans, including Lord Kames and Edward Long, polygenesis did not have its heyday until the mid-nineteenth century, and even then it was still a minority theory in Britain, though with more widespread intellectual backing than in the previous century.[75] In its eighteenth-century version, polygenesis relied on biblical authority, especially the passages about the Flood or the Tower of Babel, to account for the striking differences among people. The separate origins of some people explained these great differences.[76] At different times over the century, a few writers speculated that either American Indians, Africans, or Pacific islanders originated in a different manner than the rest of the world's peoples, either because they were believed to look and act so differently from Europeans or because their social development did not seem subject to the same laws as Europeans and Asians. In his studied response to Lord Kames's assumptions in *Six Sketches on the History of Man* (1774), David Doig fingers Hottentots, Negroes, and Native Americans as proof that there was no automatic progression from universal savagery to universal civilization because these three groups showed signs of regression and a preference for freedom over refinement. He concludes, "There appears in savages a natural and rooted aversion to a civilized state . . . by the efforts of their natural genius alone, they never would have raised themselves above their original character."[77] Despite their extremely different conclusions, monogenecists and polygenecists, as well as natural historians and proponents of the secular four-stages theory, shared the ethnocentric belief that England—and much of Europe—was the best place on earth.

By the late eighteenth century, then, there were several paradigms to account for human differences, paradigms that could be mutually reinforcing or at odds. The origins, causes, and interpretation of human variety had become a preoccupation of intellectual inquiry, not just a passing interest. Despite their sometimes divergent political implications, all systems relied on the same assumption: Visible differences mattered, possibly more than ever before, and difference often meant inferiority to Europeans. These theories of human variety were fully articulated when racial and gender rights became pressing issues in the political economy of Europe during the late 1780s and 1790s. Lessons drawn from comparative anatomy, natural history, and moral philosophy helped contain the force of their challenge.[78] This is one of the most important implications of the nineteenth-century epistemic shift Foucault accounts for in *The Order of Things*. The focus on visible qualities was buttressed by speculations about the social meaning of skin colors and skeletal variations; some scientists and other powerful men translated their "findings" into statements about mental capacity and suitability for certain occupations—childbearing for women and civilization through Christian conversion, increased labor and commerce for black Africans.

*   *   *

Because of the several old, revised, and emergent articulations of human variety characteristic of the eighteenth century that I have detailed above, *multiplicity* is the key theoretical concept that I call on to analyze stories of colonial encounters and human dissimilitude.[79] Although multiplicity is often interpreted as signifying an absence of hierarchy, I use it to signify imbrication and overdetermination. A concept of multiplicity allows discussion of racial ideology in its nascent stages and intimates its embeddedness in related economic and political concepts. In fact, my use of multiplicity resembles the first definition for complexion that Samuel Johnson notes in his *Dictionary of the English Language* (1755), which is the "inclosure or involution of one thing in another." In the ensuing chapters, I emphasize several historical manifestations of multiplicity, including the way that discourses of civility, Christianity, and commercial society constituted racial ideology; the way that skin color was the most volatile component of racial ideology; and when and why gender was important to understanding human variety. For instance, when William Smellie commented on the short stature and clothing of the inhabitants of Greenland, he used European gendered conventions in a racialized manner. Smellie writes about the Arctic inhabitants: "The women, among all these nations, are as ugly as the men, and resemble them so much, that the distinction is not easily to be perceived."[80] That is, finding a lack of adequate distinction between the sexes in the shape, dress, and manners of the Lapps, Samoyeds, or Tartars reveals the importance of pronounced gender distinction to the concept of Britishness.

An awareness of multiplicity is based on the premise that in historical terms, ideologies and practices do not disappear; rather, they coexist with new ways of thinking and living, are revised partially to fit new conditions, or "go underground" for a while and resurface later. This understanding holds true for notions of race in the seventeenth through nineteenth centuries.[81] As I use it, a theory of multiplicity also acknowledges the various components of racial ideology and attends to differences within a single binary term as much as between binary pairs. Multiplicity seems particularly apt to study theories of human difference since Britons amalgamated beliefs about the body we generally associate with medical discourse, notions of beauty from classical texts on aesthetics, truisms about clothing from archaic sumptuary laws, class hierarchy, and Christian belief. These meanings were shaped by a growing empire, the height of the slave trade, and *contestations to both* during the eighteenth century. A focus on the elasticity of race at this moment is not to say that it was unconstrained, but its articulation was far more heterogeneous than is usually conceded today. Hence, a theory of racial multiplicity is best understood as situated within structures of domination, such as capitalism, patriarchy, colonialism, which were themselves not monolithic in their effects.

When I began investigating the meanings eighteenth-century Britons attached to complexion in the early 1990s, the black-white binary dominated studies of race, and white feminists were first enjoined to study whiteness. At the same time, the study of race was being taken up in postcolonial theory and thus detached somewhat from the context of slavery and its heritage. Moreover, the academic engagement with the Rodney King beating highlighted the shortcoming of the black-white dynamic to address the contemporary racial conflict in Los Angeles. These formative influences led me to examine anew the black-white binary as well as those articulations of race that did not immediately fit into that rubric; hence I have tried to incorporate both historical manifestations of difference and multiplicity.

The intense theoretical and historical focus on difference has yielded important insights about multiply constituted and constrained subjects as well as about power relations. The past twenty years of African-American, materialist, and Third World feminisms have complicated received notions of race, class, and gender by rendering them historically specific and treating them as mutually determinate categories rather than homologous ones, which is a significant advance over other feminist approaches, not to mention Marxist ones. The works of Hazel Carby, bell hooks, Valerie Smith, and Michele Wallace are key to my present reading of power and race relations through the critical concept of difference because they engage issues of erasure and marginality in light of larger historical, social, and economic factors. African-American feminisms also helped initiate the study of whiteness.[82] For instance, the idea that "woman" is a designation primarily reserved for the dominant heterosexual white culture and not equally available to various minorities has revolutionized the study of gender and race as well as their articulation across class and sexuality.

The emphasis on whiteness as part of the racial matrix finds one of its most provocative articulations in Peggy McIntosh's trenchant essay entitled "The Invisibility of Privilege," which focuses attention on the many institutional cachets white skin color obtains in present-day America. This essay prompted my investigation of the "invisible" ways of racializing Britons and Others and led me to consider that religion as well as consumer and trade activity functioned this way in the eighteenth century. In a similar vein, Third World feminism has been especially attentive to the manifold inequities of the international division of labor and flows of capital (present and historical). This global focus distinguishes its political analyses and is a necessary context for any understanding of the post-fifteenth-century Atlantic world in its interdependence. Overall, these feminisms have modeled highly nuanced analyses based on attention to multiple factors of oppression and alternative conceptions of power.

My focus on binary difference and multiplicity as it pertains to race has been further informed by poststructuralist theory, which has greatly enabled the denaturing of race. The work of Derrida, Irigaray, and a host of others has unveiled the powerful hold binary sensibility has on the Western intellectual tradition. Several insights from deconstruction inform my choice of situated multiplicity as a mode of analysis to put into tension with eighteenth-century documents. Binary pairs, such as white and black, male and female, are not equivalent terms. As we well know, in practice, the first term is the more socially and politically powerful. Nevertheless, the terms mutually define each other in their plenitude or lack and, in that sense, are intimately linked.[83] The other point, which is the main departure for this book, is that a binary understanding simplifies complex situations and phenomena. In fact, eighteenth-century European scientists were self-conscious about their own use of a binary sensibility. Oliver Goldsmith made a typical comment when he noted that changes were so slight among neighboring nations that one had to compare people from distant climates in order to identify remarkable difference. This is one of several explanations for the eighteenth-century focus on Europeans in their myriad differences from Africans. My attention to multiplicity is a way to reinvest binaries with some of the intermediate and structuring terms that routinely are occluded and to show that binary thinking, while a powerful shorthand, simplifies more than it elucidates. Laying bare the historical underpinnings of our current assumptions about race and racism, as well as the language in which they are articulated, is a significant part of this book's goal.

One of the most important revisions of binary thinking that inflects multiplicity is indebted to poststructuralist engagement with postcolonial theory. Terms such as *ambivalence* and *hybridity*, popularized by Homi Bhabha's theory of colonial states, have connected the study of national and colonial contexts because those terms imply that there are no pure terms of authority, identity, or culture for either colonizers or the colonized.[84] Similarly, Trinh Minh-ha's *Woman, Native, Other* (1989) works against the rigidity of binary understanding. Her text is exemplary in theorizing gendered subjects in terms of multiplicity, a much needed corrective to Bhabha's genderless colonial subjects (but who are, nonetheless, implicitly masculine).[85] A particularly insightful strategy that Trinh presents is to attend to differences within seemingly monolithic entities such as the ethnic female subject and the First World (and thereby shift the gaze of difference back to its customary point of origin). Trinh's concept of difference disengages the Manichean binary grip by studying variations within a single binary term as well as between binary pairs. To accomplish this task, she contends that pairs should be treated as different from each other, not as rigid opposites, thereby focusing on untraditional juxtapositions and offering a useful counterpoint to the analysis of difference only as oppression. This method offers a fruitful approach to issues typically raised by eighteenth-century colonial texts, but it, like Bhabha's, must be integrated with a specific view of historical and economic factors that constitute power relations at this time. Two examples of historically specific and theoretically sophisticated studies of binaries and multiplicity are Nicholas Thomas's *Colonialism's Cultures* (1994) and Ann Laura Stoler's "Rethinking Colonial Categories" (1989), which have successfully shown the variety and conflicting interests among colonizers and among colonized.[86]

The Marxist theories of Althusser, Gramsci, Volosinov, and Raymond Williams help situate binaries in a larger matrix of factors; their work has enabled my study of eighteenth-century social formations, ideology, and texts. Stuart Hall has provided the most fruitful dialogue with these theorists in regard to the study of race, colonialism, and their legacies by regarding them as variable historical formations. Even though Althusser et al. privilege twentieth-century models of state power, the reproduction of capitalist relations of domination, the dynamics of class fractions and relations, as well as the class struggle over cultural signs, their methods are useful, with adaptation, to the analysis of other power relations.[87] As Williams so elegantly shows in *The Country and the City* (1973), capitalism itself and remnants of other modes of production were, of course, at different stages two centuries ago. Nevertheless, the concepts of ideology, hegemony, and social formation, most closely associated with these twentieth-century Marxists, can offer certain insights into eighteenth-century conditions and the analysis of texts. A concept of ideology helps analyze race because it addresses its sedimentation—the complexity and simultaneity of its historical components. It is also particularly geared to account for continuity in belief systems. Ideology, in my usage, refers to a historical organization of signifying practices which help turn human beings into social subjects; this constellation of representational systems structures everyday lives. Ideology works on our conscious and unconscious and manifests itself in actions as well as in language use and in this sense has a materiality; its effects are uneven and variable.

As my study of racial ideology makes clear, occasionally economic conditions give rise to representational practices, but not always, and not always in predictable ways.[88] For this reason, I subscribe to Hall's position that a social formation predicates "complexly structured societies composed of economic, political and ideological relations, where the different levels of articulation do not by any means simply correspond or 'mirror' one another, but which are—in Althusser's felicitous metaphor—'over-determining' on and for one another."[89] This formulation allows the following supposition about the eighteenth century: ideological categories often arise, flourish, or transform themselves according to their own laws of development, although they may have been generated out of given material conditions.[90] Williams puts this understanding somewhat differently: a social formation is a complex, interactive amalgam of dominant, residual, and emergent ideologies. The historical convergence, coexistence, and sometimes competition among racial and proto-racial ideologies account for the simultaneity of old and new ways of thinking, which characterizes the eighteenth century. This distillation of ideology has fallen out of fashion somewhat with the more recent poststructuralist emphasis on discontinuity and rupture. While my indebtedness to poststructuralist theory, its challenge to traditional methods of interpreting texts and "objective" renditions of history should be clear, I am unwilling to abandon the explanatory force of Williams's terminology, which is apt for a historical period not as quickly affected by new knowledge or modern communication technologies, which disseminate trends and transform subjectivity more quickly than eighteenth-century print culture and its life in oral transmission. This way of thinking about the past suggests that the present is constituted by historical forces which continue to function as constraints on discursive articulation (148). Indeed, the understanding that ideologies change by articulating and disarticulating ideas (discursive recycling), rather than by one concept replacing another, is a more generative notion of the way theories of human variety and racisms have, in fact, flourished, waned, and been challenged (434).

Racisms, Hall contends, have different historical specificities in which they become active, and their forms may be various, as are their relations to other structures and their effects on people (435). Quite simply, this insight, combined with the argument that "racism and racist practices and structures frequently occur in some but not all sectors of the social formation; their impact is penetrative but uneven" (435), suggest the urgency of developing historical analyses that attend to the various realms in which racialism and racism flourish and realms in which they do not. As this book argues in detail, writers of imaginative literature, among others, promulgated superficial and changeable notions of human difference long after scientists and philosophers "discovered" profound distinctions among human groups. Another example of the uneven penetration of racism in eighteenth-century Britain is apparent in the economic and religious realms. Slave labor was vital to the enormous profits investors made and to the consumer boom in Britain, yet the numerous treatises on commerce constructed Africans as consumers and trading partners. Similarly, the Anglican Church continually reassured planters that baptizing slaves would not affect their temporal condition as property, yet Christian belief underwrote the insistence that Africans and Englishmen were descendants of Adam and Eve, and it posed the most significant ideological challenge to slavery. These contradictions substantiate Hall's argument that "we need to understand better the tensions and contradictions generated by the uneven tempos and directions of historical development" (435).

Within this historical and dynamic weave, a concept of ideology is often more useful than a theory of discourse for analyzing social formations and texts, even though this is not a book about subjectivity, or the multifarious ways that Europeans and others lived their lives in light of racial categories, as much as a book about how Britons wrote about the categories themselves. The Foucault of *The History of Sexuality*, in particular, is an absent presence in many of the questions that I ask and the conclusions that I reach; discourse analysis is generally less successful than ideological analysis, however, in examining the continuity that seems so important to theorizing race at this historical moment. It may well be that Foucault's theory of discourse, with its incitements to speak, spirals of power and pleasure, and emphasis on new methods of power, such as surveillance, normalization, and administration, is more suited to the nineteenth and twentieth centuries than to previous periods.[91] This conceptualization of power, as Foucault recognizes, relies on the increasingly rigid disciplines of medicine and science typical of the latter nineteenth century, not to mention quicker and cheaper forms of print that were more widely available.

Accounting for the disjunction between ways of thinking, representational practices, and the ways people lived—or were forced to live their lives—is possibly beyond the reaches of any theory, but it is more likely to be broached through ideological analysis than a theory of discourse on its own. The explanatory capability of ideology includes elucidating the sometimes contradictory beliefs people acted on about race. The insight that ideology, like discourse, is articulated in and through language but is not equivalent to it, is particularly important to understanding one of the odder aspects of contemporary discussions in England.[92] In regard to eighteenth-century slavery, for example, the daily brutality and violence intrinsic to many slaves' lives was not, in fact, explained in Britain by arguments that they were less than human. Given that ideology presumes subjects who act with partial knowledge, it is not reducible either to subjectivity or to political and economic relations at any given historical moment.[93] This theory of ideology assumes that it has material effects as well as linguistic manifestations (166).

My use of ideology registers its multiple functions, especially in regard to its manifestation in texts. Too frequently, a dogmatic notion of discourse or ideology's single function results in partial or clumsy analyses based on a very few selected texts. The variety of eighteenth-century documents I have consulted are best served by a view of ideology that recognizes its several possible manifestations in texts and social formations. Occasionally, for instance, I take eighteenth-century ideologies of human variety and colonialism at face value in order to assess their manifest content seriously. At other points, I refuse this surface construction in order to probe the investments of this ideology more closely. To wit, sometimes the best analytical tool generated by ideology critique is to examine the assumptions that ground ideology or probe what the text does not "say" but should, and thus to uncover the operative silences. At other times, the tradition of symptomatic interpretation is more helpful. This theory of interpretation attends to moments when the text "stumbles" because it offers conflicting rationales or presents unresolved (and unresolvable) contradictions; these moments, made evident through a text's structure or language, hint at suppressed stories and connections vital to comprehending a particular historical articulation of race. Some texts, especially literary ones, reveal eighteenth-century Britons' attempts to address pressing but unspoken issues, especially those arising from a newly felt urgency about interpreting human difference. It is also the case that literary texts often provide imaginary resolutions to real problems. For example, many midcentury novels make a point of mentioning European characters' negative response to dark skin, yet they all promptly deny that nonwhite complexion matters. The imaginary solutions these novels offer dark-skinned characters include Christian conversion and marriage to Europeans; in exchange for transferring their wealth to England, they obtain a new life in civil society. In this way, some texts seem to manage anxieties generated by social problems by establishing fictional precedents at quite a remove from a less palatable reality. At any rate, the stories that Britons told themselves about complexion and race demand scrutiny so that we may understand the past in its difference from the present and the ways it continues to inflect our present.

As a historical and theoretical concept, then, *situated multiplicity* may also help revise much postcolonial and race theory that has focused on the period most commonly associated with European colonization and racism—the nineteenth and early twentieth centuries. Indeed, the eighteenth century has been absent from the most influential theories of colonialism and race.[94] Most colonial and critical theorists silently base their assumptions about race on the mid-nineteenth-century heritage of biological racism. This formulation assumes an anxiety about cultural and racial purity, pervasive white supremacism, the white man's burden of civilizing native populations, and an interventionary political rule largely absent from the eighteenth century.[95] The real differences in intensity of racial ideology and the dynamics of colonialism require any theory to be sensitive to historical change.

*   *   *

In terms of subject matter, the texts that I analyze in the ensuing chapters reflect the main direction of contemporary British political and commercial interests in the periphery of Great Britain's own borders, its most lucrative overseas colonies, and its trading partners in Africa and East India. The range in genre, though by no means comprehensive, suggests that the analysis of race and colonialism is not exhausted by the study of literary, scientific, or economic discourse alone.[96] One of the connecting threads among the selection of texts is the actions of the historical and fictional characters who inhabit the colonial landscapes and imperial trade networks. They stage highly selective versions of the confrontation between various stages of civilization, different "races," and conflicting interests. The other similarity in the various cultural documents I consult is that their authors all believe that racial ideology is not self-evident; I have focused on the constructed-ness of human difference precisely because the authors treat it as something that must be explained.

The chapters are arranged chronologically in order to examine more carefully shifts in racial ideology and to track the germane continuity. Each chapter investigates an important eighteenth-century issue distilled by the new attention to human variety: namely, the persistence of older proto-racial ideology based in Christianity and savagery; the various uses to which complexion was put in colonial narratives; the relationship between slavery and race in Britain; and the role of consumer desire, certain kinds of labor, and trading activity in retarding the force of racist conceptions. Each chapter is framed by a twentieth-century impasse in historicizing race. In one way or another, each impasse I analyze stems from treating race and racism as more rigid and less historically nuanced than is warranted.

The first two chapters introduce the geographies of colonization and the slave trade most significant to Britain's economic situation in the early eighteenth century: the West Indies and Africa, respectively. Through readings of Daniel Defoe's *Robinson Crusoe* (1719) and *Captain Singleton* (1720), these chapters contend that the religious and political categories *Christian* and *savage* develop primarily in relation to British masculine identity in a colonial context during the early eighteenth century and that they rely strongly on the play of absence and presence of clothing, hospitality to strangers, agricultural cultivation, and manufactures. In fact, *Christian* and *savage* participate in a visible economy of race outside of a color paradigm. Although *slave* was already overdetermined as a category in regard to Africans, I demonstrate that to Britons, slavery was not inextricably connected to skin color at this time; it was primarily a political and economic condition rather than a racial one—a phenomenon arising from trade and necessary to the livelihood of the colonies, the center without which the empire would evanesce.

Featuring romantic attachment between Britons and non-Europeans, rather than the commercial and colonial relations between men featured in the first two chapters, Chapter 3 examines constructions of human variety in intermarriage novels. This little known literary phenomenon of the mid-century shows racial ideology in transition from an older conception of difference based on religion to a newer one based on complexion. Intermarriage novels depict dark skin color as unsettling to Europeans initially but surmountable through the greater power of love and through Christian conversion. Even at midcentury, it was still possible for Britons to subordinate a discomfort with dark skin to the profession of Christianity and high rank in relation to some populations.

Chapters 4 and 5 illustrate how deficient consumer activity helped designate segments of the British and colonial populace as subordinate subjects of empire. An examination of Edward Long's *History of Jamaica* (1774) and Samuel Johnson's *Journey to the Western Islands of Scotland* (1775) in Chapter 4 reveals that, like most of their contemporaries, they believed in the power of civil society, ownership of property, and involvement in trade to improve people. Despite their different convictions about colonization and slavery, both Long and Johnson assumed that social, sexual, and economic contact with the English improved Africans and Scots. In marshaling these discourses, Johnson and Long assess the place of Scotland and Jamaica in the empire based on judgments about their inhabitants. By bringing this unusual pairing of texts together, I show the tension between ideologies of skin color and civil society in the 1770s.

A more color-conscious concept of human difference is analyzed in Chapter 5. This chapter situates Equiano's slave narrative in the context of other abolitionist writings in order to examine the difficulties that arose for an antiracist agenda when theories of human difference are invoked to argue against slavery. The limits of climate theory are revealed in the contradictions it gave rise to. These logical limitations tend to undermine the abolitionist mantra that skin color, though literally remarkable, was not significant. Despite these problems, I show that Equiano's narrative avoids collapsing whiteness with Englishness because they are not yet essentialized terms nor has one sublated the other.

Since this book purports to fill a gap in literary analysis, it remains firmly rooted in distinctly eighteenth-century trends, although it occasionally glances back to the seventeenth century and forward to the nineteenth century when necessary. This book begins in the 1720s when there is a nuanced difference in racial ideology from earlier periods; for example, the insistent linking of human difference to black and white aesthetics in poetry and drama, ably analyzed by Renaissance scholars, has subsided somewhat, albeit temporarily, and the pervasive iconography of sexual difference and territorial discovery that so many early modern critics have examined has largely disappeared. Notably, the paradigm of colonial relations associated with Crusoe and Friday is more apt to characterize eighteenth-century British conceptions of themselves and others than the tragedy enacted in *Oroonoko* (1688). As the chapters all demonstrate, Britons maintained an optimistic sense of the efficacy of Christianity, education, and commerce in redressing unpolished manners or in erasing the importance of dark skin color, which is evident in their embracing select Others as various subordinate, but fellow, subjects of the British empire: as servants, trading partners, soldiers, and wives in literature and in historical fact. By beginning with Friday and ending with Equiano, I am able to examine a broad change in the general character of racialism. Over the century, Europeans' self-perception broadly shifted from defining themselves in relation to each other, Muslims, and the naked, pagan savage to distinguishing themselves from black Africans.

Ultimately, this book traces Britons' uncertainty about the signifiers of human difference, especially skin color. This study unravels the intertwined hierarchies structuring racial ideology, colonial oppression, and imperial authority during the eighteenth century. In the chapters that follow, I lay the groundwork not only for making certain Britons more visible as racial subjects but also for questioning the contexts that we choose in the present for analyzing eighteenth-century literary production. In this way, I hope to initiate a different conversation about the place of race in eighteenth-century studies.

Chapter 1

Christians, Savages, and S[

From the Mediterranean to the Atlantic

Christianity has so long prevailed in these Parts of the World [Caribbean and American colonies], that there are no Advantages or Privileges now peculiar to it, to distinguish it from any other Sect or Party; and therefore whatever Liberties the Laws indulge to us, they do it to us as *English-Men*, and not as *Christians*.

—LORD BISHOP OF ST. ASAPH
Society for the Propagation of the Gospel
in Foreign Parts (1711)[1]

AN analysis of Daniel Defoe's *Life and Adventures of Robinson Crusoe* (1719) and its critical tradition exemplifies the way that a theory of multiplicity helps to recover the emergent character of race in the early eighteenth century. Because skin color became a more important racial category to the British only later in the eighteenth century, a color binary of black and white does not help to elucidate British reactions to other Europeans, Moors, West Africans, or native Caribbeans or, indeed, their representation of them. Of course, *Robinson Crusoe* does not perfectly reflect English culture or economic investment in the first two decades of the century, but it does present some fascinating ideological dilemmas conjured up by eighteenth-century articulations of human difference and colonial power relations.

Because *Robinson Crusoe* marshals categories of difference, such as savagery, slavery, and Christianity, it appears to define precisely the boundaries between people in various racial terms and thereby elicits a picture of European superiority. Despite this apparent precision, the novel has fostered readerly confusion about the status of the Caribbean islander Friday, the Spanish Moor Xury, and even the English Crusoe in its many subsequent interpretations. Indeed, the novel's difficulty in situating Friday in a stable category of cannibal, slave, or servant reflects a cultural uncertainty about the signifiers of racial difference in the early eighteenth century and their significance, an idea seldom explored in critical assessments of Defoe's novel or other early eighteenth-century literature. Beginning with a recent interpretation of *Robinson Crusoe* emphasizes the problems that arise when an analysis seeks to confine an eighteenth-century colonial text to a color binary informed by current notions of race.

*   *   *

In 1992, when Toni Morrison introduced *Race-ing Justice, En-gendering Power: Essays on Anita Hill, Clarence Thomas, and the Construction of Social Reality* and sought to make sense of Supreme Court Justice Clarence Thomas's position in relation to racial politics in the United States, she chose a comparison to *Robinson Crusoe*. Morrison identifies Friday's subservience to Crusoe as a particularly appropriate analogy for Thomas's relationship to the Bush administration.[2] Overall, because her attention is focused on Thomas, the effect of Morrison's comments is to homogenize race to a rigid binary that divorces the literary text from its cultural context. The result is a narrative about racial relations in *Robinson Crusoe* that seems remarkably contemporary.

Morrison's "Introduction: Friday on the Potomac" juxtaposes Clarence

Thomas's Senate confirmation hearings with scenes from *Robinson Crusoe*. Her critique of Thomas and the Bush administration is first introduced in the epigraphs, which include comments by Thomas and Anita Hill as well as the scene in which Friday bends his head to Crusoe's foot. Arguing that the significance of the hearings is, in part, the interpretation of "history" and suggesting that the Hill/Thomas investigation was "the site of the exorcism of critical national issues" by being "situated in the miasma of black life and inscribed on the bodies of black people," Morrison's essay deftly unveils the way that U.S. racial politics played out in 1992, exposing the structure of racial discrimination in which both Thomas and Hill were placed by the media and other Americans.[3] Morrison contends that the Senate Judiciary Committee and the media coverage of the hearings positioned the two main players within a discourse derived from slavery that featured two stereotyped responses of slaves to their masters—codependency and rebellion—or the "tom" (Clarence Thomas) and the "savage" (Anita Hill). In her interpretation of the hearings and the aftermath, Morrison shows the ease with which this binary was adopted and claims that the hearings were a process "to re-order these signifying fictions ['natural servant' and 'savage demon']" (xvi). Not surprisingly, perhaps, these terms are the very terms in which *Robinson Crusoe* works out Friday's position, but in a way that is obscured by Morrison's invocation of them.

A comparison of Morrison's recollection of *Robinson Crusoe* with the novel itself reveals how she overlaid a late nineteenth-century racial sensibility on it. This change enables the racial dynamic between the English Crusoe and the Caribbean islander Friday to characterize Clarence Thomas's position in relation to the Bush administration. Beginning the comparison between the present and the past, Morrison spotlights Friday: "On a Friday, Anita Hill graphically articulated points in her accusation of sexual misconduct. On the same Friday Clarence Thomas answered . . . those charges. And it was on a Friday in 1709 when Alexander Selkirk found an 'almost drowned Indian' on the shore of an island upon which he had been shipwrecked. Ten years later Selkirk's story would be immortalized by Daniel Defoe in *Robinson Crusoe*" (xxiii).[4] Morrison's version of the novel's origin is mistaken, but such a confusion, especially about Friday, has been part of the novel's critical history since its initial publication. First, it is arguable whether narratives of shipwrecks on Juan Fernandez Island in the South Seas are the basis for Crusoe's Caribbean island. There were two instances of solitary individuals on Juan Fernandez Island that Morrison's version conflates. One involved a Guyanese man, the Mosquito Indian Will, who was not shipwrecked but left behind accidentally by his shipmates in 1681; the other was the Scotsman

Alexander Selkirk, who was not shipwrecked either but abandoned by his captain in 1704. Thus, Selkirk did not find an Indian, drowned or otherwise. Will had been rescued by another buccaneer ship in 1684.

Transferring an Indian from *Robinson Crusoe* to Selkirk's narrative creates space for a character Morrison refers to as a black, savage cannibal to replace the Caribbean native Friday in her recollection of *Robinson Crusoe*. Morrison has recalled a fiction of the fiction: "There [in Defoe's novel] the Indian becomes a 'savage cannibal'—black, barbarous, stupid, servile, adoring. . . . Crusoe's narrative is a success story, one in which a socially, culturally, and biologically handicapped black man is civilized and Christianized—taught, in other words, to be like a white one" (xxiii). Notably, in this passage, Morrison superimposes a more recent conception of race on *Robinson Crusoe*.[5] In the novel, Friday is not "black," "stupid," or considered "biologically handicapped" (xxiii), though I agree with Morrison that Friday is taught to behave like a white man, and a certain kind of white man—a servant. The stereotypical features that she lists are the products of mid-nineteenth-century racism and a North American, post–civil rights critique of the construction of race. They are also a measure of black power to act as proxy for all other oppressed groups. In the novel, the "savage" is not an African but a Caribbean islander, who is attached to a sociopolitical group with specific customs, religious and social beliefs, and rules of governance.[6] The novel carefully depicts Friday in a way that it refuses to depict the other "savages."

Morrison observes that the interaction between Crusoe and Friday takes place on Crusoe's terms, not Friday's, because of the way that power differences are structured by language use: "The problem of internalizing the master's tongue is the problem of the rescued" (xxv). Commenting on Friday's assimilation to Crusoe's version of British culture, particularly the loss of his "mother tongue," and the associated consequences of internalizing the norms of the master's language, Morrison concludes that Thomas and Friday "are condemned . . . never to utter one single sentence understood to be beneficial to their original culture" (xxix). Of Clarence Thomas and his political allegiances, Morrison writes: "If the language of one's culture is lost or surrendered, one may be forced to describe that culture in the language of the rescuing one. . . . It becomes easy to confuse the metaphors embedded in the blood language of one's own culture with the objects they stand for. . . . One is obliged to cooperate in the misuse of figurative language, in the reinforcement of cliché, the erasure of difference, . . . the denial of history, . . . [and] the inscription of hegemony" (xxviii).[7] Morrison's critique of Thomas's reinforcement of cliché and the resulting denial of history

is applicable, in a different sense, to Morrison's own erasure of the Caribbean Friday and to the association of blackness with servility. Substituting a
black man for Friday in her recollection of *Robinson Crusoe* inadvertently repeats the material eradication of native Indian cultures (through disease and
population manipulation as well as slaughter, despite their resistance, and,
of course, through rewriting history) on a figurative level. This replacement
also fails to articulate the historical connection between native Caribbean
populations and African slaves, especially the forced introduction of African people to the Caribbean and mainland Americas as slaves to supplement
a native labor force that Europeans could not adequately command or had
destroyed. By making internalized racism seem eternal, Morrison's greater
truth about Clarence Thomas's unthinking assimilation to hegemonic norms
misses the historical difference I wish to untangle in this chapter.

Morrison emphasizes similarities between the past and the present. Her
logic is reminiscent of the current political hegemony in the United States
that encourages the construction of only one Other at a time. (Hence the
confusion and general failure to find a way to discuss the ideological similarities between Thomas and Hill or the differences between a Caribbean
Friday and an African one.) A corollary to acknowledging only one Other
at a time is that if the black/white color binary breaks down, it tends to be
in racist ways, such as in the construction of a "model minority."[8] An important implication is that, in general, only one group at a time is positioned
as Other, marginalized, or disenfranchised from a white norm in the contemporary moment. Nevertheless, Morrison's trenchant critique of dominant U.S. racial politics allows us to discern a troublesome aspect of the
black/white binary: the way that race is made equivalent to blackness in the
United States. Of course, the black/white opposition is never borne out in
social reality, but it does constitute the metaphysics of present-day racism in
the United States.

Despite my critique of Morrison's substitutions and embellishments,
that they appeared in 1992 is symptomatic of a relatively recent binary understanding of race. As I show below, a binary sensibility has largely informed
critical attention to *Robinson Crusoe* and fostered cogent analyses of it. By
also bringing a theory of multiplicity to bear on this material, I offer a more
dynamic conception of early eighteenth-century ideas about human variety.
Significant reasons for textual ambiguities about racial differences at this
time include vast economic changes in the intensity of colonialism and a
massive change in the population mixture of the Atlantic colonies. *Robinson Crusoe* harks back to the cataclysmic shift from a diversified subsistence-
based or moderate profit economy to a single crop, profit-oriented economy

dependent on African slaves that occurred first in the British West Indies. In fact, between about 1645 and 1665, the proportion of Europeans, Caribbean islanders, and African slaves changed dramatically, especially on Barbados, from one of European dominance in numbers on the settled islands to one of African majority in numbers.[9] *Robinson Crusoe* conjures up older New World Others, however, and manifests a desire for European difference to be constructed in relation to Caribbean peoples.[10]

*   *   *

Peter Hulme's *Colonial Encounters: Europe and the Native Caribbean, 1492–1797* (1986) has been instrumental in framing *Robinson Crusoe* as a study of colonial discourse and in making visible the significance of cannibalism to constructions of European identity.[11] Hulme and other critics have tended to regard the novel primarily in its construction of European superiority, and certainly such an emphasis is warranted given that, overall, power relations in the Atlantic benefited Europeans. Most of this scholarship, however, has focused only on the island segment. My analysis links the Caribbean to other geographies of imperialism in the early eighteenth century and attends to the way that a theory of multiplicity, not simply difference, helps interpret the representation of the relations between the English Crusoe and the Spanish Moor Xury and between Crusoe and the Carib Friday.

In examining eighteenth-century discourses about savages, Christians, slaves, and servants, it appears that race as we understand it today did not fully anchor European perceptions of difference at this time and cannot analyze colonial relations adequately. *Robinson Crusoe* corresponds to a particular episode of the colonial process when practices were not justified by relatively seamless ideology. In this early stage of colonialism, the representation of racial differences was not as systematized as it became later in the century. Indeed, the novel reflects the fact that only some differences were belatedly cobbled together to justify European domination. To eighteenth-century Britons, *savage* and *Christian* were crucial concepts of difference, while only to a lesser extent were slavery and skin color relevant. In practice, of course, both skin color and slavery effectively distinguished others from Europeans in the colonies, but a coherent ideology had not yet emerged to match the de facto situation. As scholars are just beginning to explore, British slavery and colonial life were structured as much, if not more, by custom than by law, the latter of which worked on a need-to-have basis rather than on a strictly ideological one, especially until the slave trade and conditions of enslavement came under parliamentary scrutiny in the late 1780s.

By emphasizing an interpretive practice based on the analysis of difference and multiplicity, it is possible to read *Robinson Crusoe* as a vindication of the European, specifically the British, colonial spirit *and* an exploration of its fissures.

Several colonial factors give impetus to the plot and align Crusoe indisputably on the colonizer's side. For example, *Robinson Crusoe* rehearses the early stages of European colonial contact in the Atlantic twice, once in Brazil and then on the Caribbean island. Before Crusoe has even left Britain, the novel betrays its colonial underpinnings in Crusoe's desire to improve his middling station in Britain through speculative trading schemes and sea voyages as well as in his ability to travel voluntarily to diverse parts of the world. On the island, his fear of bodily harm from the Caribbean islanders, the eventual necessity of eradicating the cannibals, and his desire to domesticate Friday all bespeak the imbrication of fear, violence, and optimism in forging an empire. All in all, the differences between Crusoe and the Others with whom he comes in contact establishes the superiority of enslaver to enslaved: the Africans he trades in, the Spanish Moor Xury whom he sells as a slave, and the Carib Friday whom he relegates to perpetual servitude.

In the first part of *Robinson Crusoe*, the hero travels between Britain, Africa, and Brazil. He encounters Moors, West Africans, the Morisco Xury, and other Europeans.[12] Initially, Crusoe's desire for advancement beyond the station allotted to him propels the plot forward and takes him well beyond England's borders. Crusoe's wish for advancement materializes when he joins a trading expedition to Guinea: "That evil influence which carried me first away from my father's house, that hurried me into the wild and indigested notion of raising my fortune . . . whatever it was, presented the most unfortunate of all enterprises to my view; and I went on board a vessel bound to the coast of Africa."[13] Although Crusoe reiterates that his desire to travel and to amass wealth is inexplicable, a modern-day reader might explain these goals as a result of the unprecedented capital accumulation in Europe made possible through global trade and colonization from the sixteenth century onward. Expanded trade routes and new colonies stripped parts of what was called the "uncivilized" world of their natural and human resources and permanently altered those economies and ways of life to satisfy spiraling British consumer desire—including a desire for adventure and travel.

The novel establishes Crusoe's method of rising in the world as possible because of a developed colonial labor force and because of the demands of trade. African trade, particularly in slaves, provides Crusoe's capital and labor base for his profitable production of sugar in Brazil. Crusoe notes that by joining a slaving expedition, "This voyage made me both a sailor and a merchant." The gold dust he brought back yielded him £300 in London, and "this filled me with those aspiring thoughts which have since so compleated my ruin" (40). The even greater desire to increase this wealth leads to another African voyage, but Moorish pirates take him prisoner, and he is enslaved in Morocco. In North Africa, piracy fills the narrative function that the hurricane does in the Caribbean, "accidentally" situating Crusoe in a historic power struggle for European hegemony. The Moors function similarly to the later shipwreck because they both impede Crusoe's success as a slave trader.

The Mediterranean was, of course, the first place of European imperialism; it was significant to Christian identity and fodder for exotic tales long before the Caribbean was. The representation of the Moors in *Robinson Crusoe* is more favorable than one might imagine given the way that the Moors had traditionally symbolized the Antichrist and had frustrated European aspirations in the Holy Land during the Crusades. By the early eighteenth century, Moors were not as Other as they once had been. For centuries, their appearance on the theatrical stage and in popular literature had been one of the main ways that the British signified religious and cultural difference.[14] The Moors who enslave Crusoe are represented as frightening rather than inferior or savage. This depiction derives from the centuries of maritime and financial power wielded by the Moors and Turks, which was historically more threatening and much better known to eighteenth-century Europeans than either the history or civilization of the Caribbean islanders or West Africans. In this instance, neither the nature nor the customs of the Moors defines their status in relation to Europeans; their power does. Not surprisingly, perhaps, one of the first attempts to group the world's known people according to physical appearance in the late seventeenth century decisively included the Moors with Europeans.[15] Religious difference was not coterminous with physical difference.

The depiction of Crusoe's enslavement in Morocco by a Turkish pirate underscores that difference and multiplicity cannot be separated conceptually in the analysis of racial ideology. What might seem the most significant alteration in Crusoe's status receives little narrative attention; consequently, critics have not commented much on this part of the novel. At the level of plot, it is in Moroccan slavery, strangely enough, that Crusoe's status as a free Englishman is most compromised and his body suspended from its self-mastery. The juxtaposition of Crusoe, his Moorish owner, and Xury, another slave who is a Morisco or Spanish Moor, represents a collection of national identities thrown together by the fortunes of international power differences. At the height of Corsair activity in the mid-seventeenth century, thousands of Europeans were enslaved by the Moors. Some were periodically released for ransom money or became wealthy renegades by converting to Islam.[16] Many European captives were ransomed by Catholic religious orders or by European secular authorities. Petitions were regularly presented to European monarchs asking for ransom monies and negotiation.[17] Crusoe's enslavement is one of many signs that Defoe relied on older concepts of difference. During the sixteenth century and before, international warfare occurred frequently between the Turks and Christians, and the enslavement of Christians and Muslims resulted from these engagements. In fact, historian Winthrop Jordan reminds us how numerous and popular accounts of European captives and slaves were.[18] Thus, the association between slavery and religious difference was customary by the eighteenth century but not necessarily related to skin color. In historical terms, then, it is no surprise that Crusoe becomes a prisoner to a pirate and his household slave; Crusoe's change of fortune results in a temporary decline in status from a planter/merchant to a slave, a change that has nothing to do with his nature or national affiliation per se. The novel offers Crusoe's ingenuity in escaping as a significant difference between Crusoe and other slaves.

Indeed, the predilection to regard enslaved Europeans differently from other slaves was not unremarked by Englishmen. One of Defoe's contemporaries condemned the ubiquitous double standard that regarded a European slave in Barbary as less debased than an African slave in the West Indies: "Doth he [the European] thereupon become a Brute? If not, why should an *African*, (suppose of that, or any other remote part) suffer a greater alteration than one of us?"[19] Morgan Godwyn's treatise questions common practice and assumptions about African slaves in the late seventeenth century, and he records the reasons West Indian planters gave for their low regard of Africans, which included color, national origin, and slave status itself.

A theory of multiplicity is especially important in relation to the analysis of slavery because Crusoe is an Englishman; the enslavement of European Christians is a little remembered historical phenomenon, particularly for men. As Godwyn notes, there are some powerful binaries newly pertinent to Englishmen in the colonies by 1680: "*Negro* and *Slave*, being by custom grown Homogeneous and Convertible; even as *Negro* and *Christian*, *Englishman* and *Heathen*, are by the like corrupt Custom and Partiality made *Opposites*; thereby as it were implying, that the one could not be *Christians*, nor the other *Infidels*" (36). The semantics of colonial power relations prepare us for the binaries of racism. Even though *slave* signified "African" or "Negro" in common colonial usage, slavery was not a condition reserved only for Africans. In the novel, the section on Crusoe in Morocco follows European convention by depicting slavery in Asia and Africa as more benign than in European colonies. This part of the novel suggests that Crusoe was treated more as a household servant than as a slave and certainly not subject to re-culturation like Xury or Friday. In such a context, slavery does not appear to be a particularly clear boundary of permanent difference between people, since it can happen to anyone in spite of religion, national origin, or skin color. In *Robinson Crusoe*, slaves are Moriscos, European Christians, black Africans, and Caribbean islanders. Nevertheless, the novel seems quite clear about the difference between Moors and West Africans: Moors are not savage, naked, or unfamiliar. In this part of *Robinson Crusoe*, savagery rather than slavery or the Islamic religion appears to draw the greatest distinctions between Europeans and Others.

Savagery constitutes the dominant contrast between Europeans and Others in the first part of the novel. After their escape from slavery, Crusoe and Xury sail southward from Morocco "to the truly Barbarian coast." Crusoe speculates about their reception there, "where whole nations of negroes were sure to surround us with their canoes, and destroy us; where we could ne'er once go on shoar but we should be devoured by savage beasts, or more merciless savages of humane kind" (45). Even though Crusoe fears human savages in Africa, the novel offers only savage animals. Crusoe is terrified by the disturbing cacophony that the beasts create: they hear from their boat "the horrible noises, and hideous cryes and howlings" on the African shore (47). It is aural, not visual, difference that is so remarkable and a much under-explored sensation in eighteenth-century texts. Finally, Crusoe and Xury sail far enough south to spot people. The narrative calls attention to the West Africans' skin color and nakedness, the features that most clearly separate them from the English Crusoe and the Morisco Xury. Crusoe's first obser-vation of the inhabitants notes these outstanding attributes: "We saw people stand upon the shoar to look at us; we could also perceive they were quite black and stark-naked. I was once inclined to ha' gone on shoar to them; but Xury was my better councellor, and said to me, 'No go'" (50). Clothing was one of the most important visible signs of Christian profession and Euro-pean class hierarchy; in secular custom, apparel separated the higher from the lower ranks at a glance. To Europeans, naked people were hard to read; in fact, most "naked" people were simply scantily clad rather than without any clothing. Nakedness was a metaphorical sign of strangeness and indicated a lack of hierarchical society. Although blackness and nakedness seem to con-stitute visible signs of the Africans' alleged savagery, they are not sufficient to account for Crusoe's conviction that these people are cannibals.

It must be said that Crusoe's fear of African cannibals is completely unfounded in terms of the novel, which suggests it was an easy assumption to make about "savages." The narrative exposes Crusoe's fear of African canni- balism as a faulty perception of difference based on misinformation. As op- posed to his violent and anonymous encounter with the Caribs later, Crusoe meets and communicates with a group of people on the west coast of Africa who offer to aid him, not to eat him. For instance, the people bring him food and water, a gesture that transforms their representation. Crusoe observes: "I was now furnished with roots and corn, such as it was, and water, and leaving my friendly negroes, I made forward" (52). The novel quickly reveals that these "savages" eat wild game (like Europeans), not men. The scene in which Crusoe gratifies the Africans by shooting "a most curious leopard" for their culinary delight confirms this crucial difference and exposes the precon- ception versus the "reality" of the encounter (52). Crusoe departs with provi- sions and a changed perspective. The phrase that Crusoe invokes to describe the Africans who have succored him and whom he has repaid is "my friendly negroes." Using this phrase links Crusoe to a well-known English slaving voyage of the sixteenth century, the text of which used a similar phrase to de- note the helpful middlemen vital for successful trade.[20] At any rate, many of Defoe's contemporaries had noted that cannibalism in Africa was limited to the unknown interior peoples and was suspected, even then, to be fictional. Cannibalism in Africa, Defoe confirms, is a strategy of keeping Europeans from penetrating their trading networks. Since the novel does not strictly maintain the savagery of the Africans as it does the Caribs,' the only real can- nibals, then, are the Caribbean Indians, whose several flesh feasts punctuate the latter part of Crusoe's island sojourn.

The depiction of the Morisco Xury also demonstrates the efficacy of joining theories of racial difference and multiplicity. Xury's and Crusoe's interaction foreshadows Crusoe's subsequent relationship to Friday; in both cases, the novel depicts Crusoe's association with a younger, non-Christian man who does not fall easily into categories of difference. Aspects of colo- nialism structure the two relationships in which the English Crusoe acquires a young male servant. In the context of Moroccan slavery, Xury and Crusoe resemble each other more than they differ. At first, Crusoe's greater age seems to be the only distinction between the two slaves. The similarity be- tween Xury and Crusoe is further emphasized by their common difference from the Moors; their shared European origin counts most in this respect. Once out of the context of slavery, a different configuration is formed — first in relation to black Africans and then in relation to Europeans. When they escape, Xury and Crusoe are allied in their fear of the Moors who enslaved them and then in their initial fear of the people on the coast of West Africa.

The potential danger of the "wild mans" and the resulting fear of being eaten lead Crusoe to notice that which most clearly separates Xury and himself from the West Africans: their light skin color and clothed bodies.

While Xury is neither as powerful as Crusoe nor as abject as the Africans on the west coast, his status in the novel is not stable, reflecting British uncertainties about difference in the early eighteenth century. Xury is a household slave like Crusoe; the Moors emphasized Moriscos' European descent, and the Spanish denigrated Moriscos because they maintained Muslim cultural practices, even those who had converted to Christianity.[21] Thus, Spanish Moors were one of the most vulnerable populations in the Mediterranean, likely to be enslaved by Turks or Christians. They occupied a liminal position, considered neither fully European nor fully Muslim; in fact, their name, meaning "little Moors," was conferred on those who chose to convert to Christianity, and those who were forced to, in 1501.[22] The Moriscos were part of the blending of Arab and Spanish populations that arose from the Arab conquest of the Iberian peninsula in the eighth century. Following the Christian reconquest in the fifteenth century, the condition of Moriscos worsened in Spain: some were forced to emigrate, and those who remained in Spain were forced to convert. The Moriscos who left Spain dispersed around the Mediterranean basin, and there was a considerable community in Salé, where Xury and Crusoe were enslaved (14). Because of their profession of Islam, they often worked on behalf of the African Moors, especially the pirates.

Upon escape from slavery, Xury is not free like Crusoe is; his value is compromised from the beginning because the narrative construes him only in terms of his usefulness to Crusoe. For example, Crusoe remarks about his master's kinsman: "I could ha' been content to ha' taken this Moor with me, and ha' drowned the boy [Xury], but there was no venturing to trust him. . . . I turned to the boy, who they called Xury, and said to him, 'Xury, if you will be faithful to me I'll make you a great man'" (45). Crusoe's age and initiative position Xury as a particular kind of subordinate—a servant. Crusoe orders him to kill wild beasts and to perform menial tasks, yet Xury also advises Crusoe and they hunt together (47). Theirs is not a relationship of equals but of roles that can be assumed by a trusty servant in relation to a master. Friday and Crusoe repeat such a pattern later.

The arrival of the Portuguese slave ship alters Xury's status vis-à-vis Crusoe even further. If the least difference between Xury and Crusoe is discernible when they are slaves to the Moor, the greatest difference occurs when they are in the presence of other Europeans. In this context, Crusoe assumes the position of the owner of the goods, which he had stolen from his owner. The Catholic Portuguese captain treats Crusoe as an equal, even though he possesses only the stolen boat—and Xury. Crusoe explains his actions among strange Europeans: "I immediately offered all I had to the captain of the ship, . . . but he generously told me he would take nothing from me" (53–54). Indeed, the captain identifies with Crusoe's plight: "'I have saved your life on no other terms than I would be glad to be saved my self'" (54). The captain offers to purchase Crusoe's goods, and it is at this point that Xury's status slips from servant and occasional partner in adventure to a slave because he is considered a legitimate object of exchange by both the older European men. Xury's position as an object of exchange between the two Europeans becomes a sign of their friendship and newly established equality. Crusoe's reluctance to part with Xury prompts the captain to mitigate Xury's permanent servitude to a temporary term. Although the eventual conditions of Xury's sale are more akin to indentured servitude than to permanent enslavement (ten years' labor with freedom contingent on conversion to Christianity), Xury is a slave, not a servant, precisely because he is understood to belong to Crusoe, who has no contractual rights to his labor or person. Typically critics interpret Crusoe's treatment of Xury as a relationship of master to slave, and certainly Crusoe's selling Xury to the Portuguese captain confirms this idea. Yet Xury's status is even more complicated by his religious affiliation.

Xury's ability to be a "free" subject is silenced by the Europeans' ostensible concern for his spiritual welfare. The importance of Christianity as a significant bond between Europeans overrides even historical differences between the Church of England and Catholics by representing the greater difference as that between Christianity and Islam. It is clearly not Xury's Spanish national origin that casts him as a slave but his Islamic religion.[23] In this novel, Christianity represents the most significant category of difference that excuses European domination and establishes the conditions for enslavement. Xury, however, is not a permanent slave; he is linked to Europeans by his shared fear of being eaten by the "wild mans" on the west coast of Africa (47). In comparison to naked, black Africans, Xury is reassuringly similar to Crusoe. It is important, then, to distinguish between Xury's national origins, which separate him from West Africans (and from Friday), and Xury's Islamic profession, a religious category that compromises his similarity to Crusoe.

Xury, like Friday, has given rise to conflicting interpretations. His non-Christian religious status and his being sold by Crusoe have meant that he has easily slipped into categories of difference not licensed by the novel. Despite the fact that the first illustration of Xury in *Robinson Crusoe* depicts

him as a boyish replica of Crusoe, including the same clothing and coloring as well as the possession of a gun, there has been a persistent Negroization of Xury.[24] For instance, in an eighteenth-century abridged edition of
Robinson Crusoe, the editor Negroizes Xury by intensifying his pidgin English to approximate stereotypes of slave speech common on the stage. Similarly, in the Dublin edition of 1774, Xury alerts Crusoe to the savage animals
in the following terms: " 'Look yonder, Meyter,' says he in his broken tone,
'and see dat huge Monster dat lies asleep on de side of de Rock!' "[25] The
Negroization of Xury occurs in the illustrations as well. In a 1781 illustration, Xury appears with dark skin and short black hair; in this version, he
is no longer a young version of Crusoe. One of the least powerful groups
of people, neither fully European nor Islamic, Morisco is synonymous with
slave in this context. In *A Collection of the Dresses of Different Nations, An-
tient and Modern* (1757), there are several pictures of people from Egypt and
other North African states, including an African woman, a noble lady of
Alexandria, a woman of Fez, an Ethiopian, and a Morisco slave (illustrations
were commonly copied from seventeenth-century travel narratives). Of all
these people, the Morisco slave's features are the most stereotypically Negro.
This is surprising in many ways, not least because *Morisco* was decidedly not
equivalent to *Negro* for the Spanish and Portuguese; if anything, *Morisco* designated an Islamic man of Arab descent who wore a long, close-fitting robe.
As Morgan Godwyn notes about the equivalency between slave and Negro
in the colonies, the signification of slave as black African seems fairly stable,
at least in some eighteenth-century British illustrations.

Just as Crusoe made his first fortune in England by trading "trifles" on
the African coast for slaves and gold, so the sale of Xury and other goods
stolen from the Moor establishes him in Brazil as a land-rich plantation
owner. After staying with a man who has a sugar plantation, Crusoe perceives sugar as the best path to improving his fortune: "Seeing how well
the planters lived, and how they grew rich suddenly, I resolved, if I could
get licence to settle there, I would turn planter among them" (55). He follows the pattern of European settlement in the Americas first by buying
land, working it with his own labor, and eking out a living. Noting that
his neighbor is in the same circumstance, Crusoe comments about the difficulty of producing profit: "We rather planted for food than any thing else,
for about two years. . . . [In] the third year we planted some tobacco, and
made each of us a large piece of ground ready for planting canes in the year
to come; but we both wanted help" (55). In the narrative time of the mid-
seventeenth century, this choice places Crusoe in Spanish-controlled Brazil
when it was the world's leading exporter of sugar. Crusoe complains that all

R.Crusoe & his boy Xury on the Coast of Guinny shooting a Lyon. *Vol.I.P.28.*

Figure 6. Robinson Crusoe and European Xury on the West Coast of Africa. Daniel Defoe, *The Life, and Strange Surprizing Adventures of Robinson Crusoe* (London, 1726). The illustration is set on the west coast of Africa and shows the Morisco Xury as a young replica of Crusoe. *Morisco* did not signify "Negro" to the Spanish and Portuguese, but it sometimes did to the British. The naked black bodies above the two escaped slaves offer the main contrast to Crusoe and Xury's shared color and clothing style. Brown University Library.

Figure 7. Robinson Crusoe and Negro Xury on the West Coast of Africa. Daniel Defoe, *The Life, and Strange Surprizing Adventures of Robinson Crusoe*, in *The Novelist's Magazine* (London, 1791). In this illustration, Xury appears as a black African. This same elasticity of complexion and national origin characterizes the illustrations of the Caribbean islander Friday. Reproduced by permission of the Huntington Library, San Marino, California.

the work is by the labor of his own hands and that his standard of living is lower than it was in England. Twice in the novel, Crusoe regrets parting with Xury, not out of loneliness or ethical regret but because he wishes to benefit from his unpaid labor. When Crusoe's plantation begins to produce a profit, he desires Xury's presence to enhance his income. To augment his profits, Crusoe purchases European and African labor. The ownership of property—land and especially slaves—permits the apparent equality of different nationals of European descent on the Portuguese ship and in Brazil. Thus, the status of European men in a colonial economy depends on the labor supply they command, which was overwhelmingly either Indian or African in South America.[26] An important explanation for the absence of strife in the colonies, especially between countrymen, involves shared economic benefits in the Atlantic empires. From the mid-seventeenth century onward, successive travelers noted the undiluted friendliness among Caribbean planters. Important political and religious differences between Englishmen, particularly in the seventeenth-century British colonies (and to a lesser extent between European nationals), were often suppressed to pursue common economic goals.[27]

In the first section of the novel, then, Defoe marshals categories of difference, including the Christian, savage, and slave to distinguish Crusoe favorably. *Christian* is the only category that is not undermined by its liminality. Europeans of various national origins are connected by their common Christian heritage and desire for economic advancement in exploiting African labor power and natural resources in the colonies. Neither ideologies of savagery nor slavery adequately maintain differences between Europeans and Others in Morocco or West Africa. In the novel, the hospitality of the black Africans replaces their savagery, though their color and lack of clothing still distinguish them from Europeans and Xury. Given the significance of West African slaves to European colonialism in the late seventeenth century and beyond, they strangely do not appear in the novel en masse in the role of embodied plantation slaves. Moreover, slavery is not represented as a permanent condition for Xury or Crusoe. While the novel fosters certain European differences from Moors and West Africans, the differences have little to do with complexion. Crusoe's distinction from the Caribs is far greater and far more important to the plot.

The performance of labor is a more reliable index of status than other activities or physical attributes. Crusoe's final action that lands him on the Caribbean island is his scheme to buy slaves in Africa and then sell them illegally in Brazil on behalf of himself and other planters who were inadequately supplied by the Spanish government (58–59). Crusoe periodically bemoans the manual work he must perform. His own labor arrangements depend on profits from his sugar crop, and he augments his small labor force when possible: the more workers, the more land planted, and the greater the profits. The relations that Crusoe enters into as owner of others' labor are much more perfunctory than his relationship to Xury or Friday. In Brazil, Crusoe purchases one European servant under six years' bond, one permanent European servant, and one African slave. When Crusoe sets out on a third voyage to Africa, he characterizes his plan to buy slaves as a fulfillment of passion rather than a rational decision (60). A shipwreck arrests his trip to the slave coast, and he arrives on the uninhabited Caribbean island. The narrative initially validates Crusoe's prosperity in the colonies; on the other hand, it reveals the manipulations, expropriations, and betrayals his newfound status requires to attain power.

*   *   *

The same racial categories that were relevant in an African context apply to the Caribbean: savage, Christian, slave, and indentured servant. The narrative emphasis on the absence of clothing is more fully developed in relation to the Caribs than to West Africans. There are three related issues that I explain by focusing on difference and multiplicity in the Caribbean: the discursive construction of Friday as neither a savage nor an African in the novel; the depiction of Friday and the Caribs as Negroes in the 1720 frontispiece to *Serious Reflections on the Life and Surprizing Adventures of Robinson Crusoe*; and the changeability of Friday's status as a servant and a slave. Even though Friday displays a lingering penchant for human flesh and is reluctant to give up his belief in Benamuckee, his god, the novel distinguishes Friday from other "savages" in remarkable ways.

The remainder of *Robinson Crusoe* locates the main character in the Caribbean on an uninhabited island and then briefly in Europe. Unlike the frequent encounters with other populations in Africa and Brazil, Crusoe spends much of this part of the novel alone. His significant relations are with the mostly absent Caribs, Friday, and other Europeans, especially the Spaniard and the English captain who appear at the end of the novel. A colonial pattern similar to the one on the mainland repeats itself on the island: Crusoe acquires land, improves it with his own labor, and then acquires Friday as additional labor power. Before this point, when Crusoe is convinced he will remain on the island alone, he notes that his desire for advancement had dissipated because there are no competitors. By his fourth year, Crusoe is self-sufficient: "I had nothing to covet; for I had all that I was now capable of enjoying; I was lord of the whole manor; or if I pleased, I might call my self king or emperor over the whole country which I had possession of. There were no rivals; I had no competitor" (139). There is neither surplus nor a circuit of exchange. This fulfillment should end a novel driven by Crusoe's desire for economic gain, but another motivating factor takes over the colonial plot: distinguishing Europeans from savages. At the point of apparent stasis in the plot, when his pecuniary desire has subsided, Crusoe sees a footprint, and the fear of cannibals takes over as the driving force of the plot (162–67, 171). Fear renews his plans to escape the island, but when he rescues Friday, the desire to domesticate his newfound servant soon replaces his desire to leave.

Savage had a long history of signifying European Christian superiority. A religious, cultural, and political category, it came into use in regard to people in the sixteenth century, according to the *OED*. As several studies of the early modern era suggest, the savage was linked to ideologies of European empire and human difference at this time.[28] In general, the diverse tribes lumped under the generic term *Americans* or *cannibals* constituted the most significant population of savages during the eighteenth century, and the Caribbean islanders were distinguished among their peers for their resistant behavior to European conquest and enslavement: "Few groups were deemed more savage than island Caribs."[29] Savagery embraces many attributes, particularly cannibalism, paganism, social disorder and nakedness; dark complexion is not ideologically necessary, though it does bolster the negative image when it is present. The most casual assumption in Defoe's novels is just what a "savage" might be; the word litters the text and is the primary label of difference.

The outstanding characteristic of the savage was cannibalism, and in the European imagination, this practice stood in for religious belief. Until the eighteenth century, Caribbean islanders conjured up "the most extreme form of savagery. Truculent by nature and eating human flesh by inclination, they stood opposed to all the tenets of Christian and civilized behaviour."[30] Frank Lestringant contends that Defoe's influential characterization of monstrous cannibals represented the mainstream English attitude.[31] Not surprisingly, then, cannibalism is the motivating fear most constitutive of Crusoe's (fictional) subjectivity and of his ideas about the inhabitants. Crusoe's fear is subsequently justified in narrative terms by his repeated witnessing of cannibal festivities. Initially, however, the unsubstantiated fear of cannibals results in Crusoe's altering his mode of production from a subsistence-based to a surplus economy (164). Later the first visual verification of cannibalism leads Crusoe to vomit at the scene of frenzied ingestion.

Immediately he thanks God "that had cast my first lot in a part of the world where I was distinguished from such dreadful creatures as these" (172). Eventually, of course, cannibalism justifies Crusoe's colonization project, which is instituted when he murders scores of island Caribees. Crusoe's security in his difference from cannibals participates in a larger cultural phenomenon; in *The Man-Eating Myth* (1979), W. Arens demonstrates that "anthropology has a clear-cut vested interest in maintaining some crucial cultural boundaries—of which the cannibalistic boundary is one—and [in] constantly reinforcing subjective conclusions about the opposition between the civilized and savage."[32] This same desire to maintain the boundary between the civilized and the savage may be found in most European travel literature and fiction located in the Atlantic, of which *Robinson Crusoe* is a well-known example.

Since the early sixteenth century, Spaniards had used cannibalism as a justification to enslave Caribbean people who refused their overtures to trade and colonize their land; indeed, Europeans had long distinguished between friendly Indians and cannibals—at least in theory. Europeans believed that compliant native people were members of sovereign nations. Cannibals had foreclosed the question of rights by virtue of their threatening behavior and resistance to European plans, and they thereby became legitimate candidates for slavery.[33] This combination of cannibalism and enslavement constitutes a major racial boundary exploited in *Robinson Crusoe*. Friday is an enslavable cannibal (at least initially) who turns out to be a friendly Caribbean islander. In volume 2, *The Farther Adventures of Robinson Crusoe* (1719), Defoe revises the identification of Friday and his people as Caribees—long synonymous with cannibals—and thereby erodes a "valid" reason for their massacre in volume 1. Modern anthropologists and historians are still divided over the historical existence of cannibal practices in the Caribbean.[34] Nevertheless, it is appropriate to conclude, as historian Philip Boucher does, that *cannibal* should be viewed as the nomenclature signaling a dynamic political contest.[35]

Historically, one way that Europeans had made Caribs and cannibals equivalent was to connect their threatening behavior to their allegedly monstrous appearance. From Columbus's third voyage onward, there was a close association between cannibals and hideous appearance. Europeans did not have to witness acts of cannibalism to confirm that a certain group of people were, in fact, cannibals and hence eligible for guilt-free forced servitude or eradication: they could tell by looking at the Caribs (Arens, 48). Furthermore, Columbus's text introduces cannibalism as a theme once the possibility and profitability of a slave trade seemed likely to materialize. This increasingly naturalized cluster of terms should alert us that where Europeans find cannibals, their enslavement often ensues.[36] Europeans developed the concept *cannibal* complete with an imaginary visual referent for the failure to comply with their terms, a pattern that *Robinson Crusoe* repeats. Despite this powerful mode of representation, there was another history of representation that can help elucidate the depiction of Friday, who looks and acts so differently from the other Caribs.

The novel's difficulty in defining the precise nature of Friday may be explained by the minority European tradition of representing Indians positively, which was fostered predominantly by French writers and is now called the noble savage tradition.[37] In this view, traceable to classical conceits about the golden age, Indians were gentle and intelligent; they lived simply without the corruption of civilization. In the eighteenth century, significantly, writers who found Indians physically similar to Europeans often adopted this approach. The category of Carib was not fixed, then, especially not in terms of representation. Although Caribbean Indians were occasionally considered black, they were more likely to be considered visually akin to Europeans, much more so than Africans. In 1667, Jean Baptiste du Tertre's observation provides a typical example of perceiving essential kinship between Indians and Europeans: "Only skin color distinguishes them from us, for they have bronzed skin, the colour of olives."[38] Similarly, in *A Philosophical Account of the Works of Nature* (1721), Richard Bradley conveys a positive perception of Indians in his taxonomy of human variety when he characterizes them as "a sort of *White Men* in *America* (as I am told) that only differ from us in having no *Beards*."[39] In the seventeenth and eighteenth centuries, Indians were often illustrated as naked, beardless versions of Europeans; frequently, they were considered white because *artificially* colored (by roucou). Even writers who ascribed to the permanent effects of climate on skin color reported that Caribbees were quite similar in coloring to the Portuguese, Spaniards, and Italians, being only a slightly more tanned version.[40] Despite an occasionally more favorable representational history than Negroes, Indians did not escape murder or enslavement either. These two representational histories help explain not only how the character Friday appears to be so different from other cannibals but also how Toni Morrison envisions Friday as the native image of the English Crusoe.

One of the main reasons for the negative representation of Indians was their failure to be Christians. The paganism of savages is threatening in a different way than their cannibalism even though the two are often sublated, and the Caribbean Indians are the ideological center of this concern in the novel rather than the Moors or West Africans. In *Robinson Crusoe*, Crusoe's most thoughtful and extended musings about differences between people concern religion. Crusoe couches religious difference in the language of light and dark—those to whom God reveals the light and those from whom God hides the light—referring not to skin color but to knowledge of divine revelation. Crusoe can account for this difference only in terms of a rough geographic injustice, which permits some nations to be Christian and "forces" others to be sinners and punishes them in their absence from God (172). The ideological work of Crusoe's religious speculations makes unequal access to God's will seem divinely ordained instead of man-made and temporally convenient to excuse European domination. As Hayden White suggests in his analysis of the Wild Man, the Christian tradition promoted the equation of Christianity with humanity and savagery with sinfulness: "Christianity had provided the basis of belief in the possibility of a humanity gone wild by suggesting that men might degenerate into an animal state in *this* world through sin. Even though it held out the prospect of redemption to any such degenerate humanity, through the operation of divine grace upon a species-specific 'soul,' supposedly present even in the most depraved of human beings, Christianity nonetheless did little to encourage the idea that a true humanity was realizable outside the confines either of the Church or of a 'civilization' generally defined as Christian."[41] As a result of his colonial experiences, Crusoe undergoes a conversion of sorts, to an active Christian, a shrewd narrative decision that undisputedly positions the solitary Englishman outside the savage realm.

Yet Crusoe's musings on religion also underscore that there is no human difference that explains the lot of savages. For example, Crusoe's delight in Friday prompts him to question what he had previously believed: that God had taken "from so great a part of the world of His creatures, the best uses to which their faculties and the powers of their souls are adapted; yet that He has bestowed upon them the same powers, the same reason, the same affections, the same sentiments of kindness and obligation, the same passions and resentments of wrongs, the same sense of gratitude, sincerity, fidelity, and all the capacities of doing good and receiving good, that He has given to us; . . . this made me very melancholly sometimes, . . . why it has pleased God to hide the like saving knowledge from so many millions of souls" (212). It is worth emphasizing that this meditation on savages, with Friday uppermost in his thoughts, leads Crusoe to enumerate all of the similarities between the Carib savages and European Christians. The single greatest difference is not located in appearance, mental prowess, or technological sophistication but in God's inexplicable will. Crusoe finds "so arbitrary a disposition of things" worrisome, and it makes him momentarily disbelieve (212). He notes, however, "But I shut it up," and he concludes in a stunning non sequitur that "if these creatures were all sentenced to absence from Himself, it was on account of sinning against that light" (212). Note the shift here from an arbitrary to a just God; these disruptive questions lead not to permanent doubt but to a comforting reinsertion of polarization, such as Hayden White investigates.

Crusoe offers a purely religious explanation for the Indians' plight rather than the climatic one common to early science. For instance, in his poetic taxonomy of human variety, "The Nature of Man" (1711), Richard Blackmore attributes all variations in intellectual faculties, disposition, and passions to a country's exposure to the heat of the sun. Although his understanding derives closely from humoral theory, Blackmore discovers much greater distinctions between Europeans and Indians than Defoe, and he insinuates that natives of Africa, the arctic, as well as East and West Indians seem "a middle Species."[42] According to Blackmore and others who subscribed to the effects of humors and climate, the torrid zones did not foster human potential: "Their Spirits suffer by too hot a Ray, / And their dry Brain grows dark with too much Day. / . . . Their Spirits burning with too fierce a Fire / Unqualify'd by proper Flegme, acquire / A Disposition so inept for Thought / Few just Perceptions in their Minds are wrought" (180).

The section of the novel featuring religious difference uses extremely vague language to assign actual difference. At the points when Crusoe seems most convinced of the savages' difference, the text often fails to account for it satisfactorily. Working on political and religious registers, the several terms referring to the Caribs are a symptom of such a failure. Crusoe alternately calls the Caribs "criminals," "prisoners," "sinners," and "sovereign nation," and it is never clear which terms will suffice to represent their relationship either to God or to Crusoe—except through ad hoc practice. Finally, it seems, Crusoe's deliberations lead him to conclude that the national character of the Carib crimes means he cannot intervene or kill them because they have not harmed him by their rituals of cannibalism (179, 233). The Caribs' status as a sovereign people triumphs momentarily over religious difference—until the sight of a European victim completely reverses Crusoe's intentions toward the Caribs. Thus, significant issues of human difference are raised only to be falsely resolved into the previously available paradigm of European and Christian superiority. Similarly, as a convert, Friday crosses the most significant boundary of European identity, and this event is awkwardly resolved. As *The Farther Adventures of Robinson Crusoe* suggests, Crusoe persisted in referring to Friday as "my trusty savage" despite his servitude, European clothing, English-language acquisition, and conversion and adherence to Christianity (18). Volume 3, *Serious Reflections* (1720), offers a more redemptive and interventionary view of Christianity because Crusoe sees it as legitimating conquest.[43] Nevertheless, this logic leads him to the conclusion that the practice, not the profession, of Christianity is the key point; on this account, he condemns the nominal Christians of Barbados and Jamaica for not instructing their slaves or baptizing them (143). In this way, the three volumes of *Robinson Crusoe* are typical of many other eighteenth-century documents that are not uniform in their approbation of British colonists or slavery.

If paganism and cannibalism are crucial factors separating Europeans and Others, the absence of clothing helps maintain important visible differences between savages and Christians. The significance of clothing to identifying European difference from savages should not be underestimated; its absence or scantiness signified a negation or paucity of civilization.[44] As Gordon Sayre demonstrates, contemporary European documents offered conflicting accounts about whether various groups of Indians were clothed and whether they manifested any signs of civilization (145). In both Africa and the Caribbean, Crusoe repeatedly notes the nakedness of the people; on the island, neither the gender nor the skin color of the Caribbean islanders warrant mention. Conventionally, a state of savagery is a state in which there is little distinction between the sexes in physical appearance, labor, or dress.

The several scenes focusing on clothing emphasize European superiority at crucial junctures in the novel. For example, when Crusoe is determined to attack the cannibals, he indicates their inferiority in this way: "I do not mean that I entertained any fear of their number; for as they were naked, unarmed wretches, 'tis certain I was superior to them" (232). The symbolic value of clothing distinguishes Crusoe from savages in two other scenes. First, Crusoe accounts for why he cannot bear nakedness despite the weather: "It is true that the weather was so violent hot that there was no need of cloaths, yet I could not go quite naked; no, tho' I had been inclined to it, which I was not, nor could not abide the thoughts of it, tho' I was all alone" (144). The blistering sun does not fully account for his lack of inclination, but it may be more understandable given that clothing helps maintain his difference from savages. Crusoe reveals uneasiness about the issue of clothing, indicating that it is impractical in the tropical climate though necessary as a sign of his distinction from naked savages. At different times, Crusoe is nearly naked or burdensomely overdressed.[45] Another crucial scene involving the presence of clothing concerns securing Friday in his new status as "not cannibal." Notably, it is only after Crusoe discourages Friday's lingering desire for human flesh that he is clothed European style (210).

In spite of the importance of clothing and technology to notions of European superiority, there is a recognition that these are, in fact, cultural artifacts, not innate differences. On these occasions, European difference from savages seems entirely accidental; nevertheless, they also serve as moments to conjure up disgust at the animal-like behavior of savages. For example, realizing that tools and clothing obtained from the ship separate him from savages, Crusoe worries: "How I must have acted if I had got nothing out of the ship; . . . that I should have lived, if I had not perished, like a meer savage; that if I had killed a goat or a fowl, . . . [I] must gnaw it with my teeth and pull it with my claws like a beast" (141). As Lestringant notes, Friday's religious conversion is accompanied by an "alimentary conversion" in one of the more improbable scenes of the novel when Crusoe interests Friday in goat's flesh to wean him off humans (141). Even the sensitive issue of cannibalism is both abhorred (for savages) and understood as a potential survival tactic for Europeans (192). Indeed, Crusoe's distrust of the Englishmen who arrive at the end of the novel is dramatized by Friday's comment that Englishmen will eat prisoners as well as savage men (250). The double standard for clothing and cannibalism is, then, another way that *Robinson Crusoe* offers contradictions and qualifications of its seemingly rigid divisions.

Unlike cannibalism and nakedness, complexion is not fully exploited for its potential to carry ideological difference. Instead, skin color plays a significant secondary role in distinguishing Europeans from Others. In terms of the Caribs, Crusoe connects the ugliness of their color to a general sense of their disagreeableness, not unlike the traditional association between cannibals and hideous appearance discussed earlier. The Caribs' skin color is not represented directly in the novel, even when Crusoe describes the cannibal scenes; instead, he refers to their color obliquely as "ugly yellow nauseous tawny" in the description of Friday, whose attractive color is "very tawny" (208).[46] Crusoe uses white skin color as an identifying distinction of Europeans (as opposed to Friday, who uses the presence of beards as an alternative system of difference). This is one of many instances in which the novel opens up the possibility for alternatives to Crusoe's interpretation. Hence, it is important not to mistake the ideology associated with Crusoe with Defoe's point of view. Because Crusoe's culturally produced criteria associate Christians, Europeans, and white, bearded men, his seeing a European fall victim to the cannibals is a major turning point in the colonial plot. When Friday alerts Crusoe that the next victim of the cannibals "was not one of their [Friday's people's] nation, but one of the bearded men, who he had told me of, that came to their country in the boat," Crusoe responds to this revelation with righteous indignation: "I was filled with horror at the very naming the white bearded man. . . . I saw plainly by my glass a white man who lay upon the beach . . . and that he was an European, and had cloaths on" (233).

This emotional and visible kinship leads to the destruction of those who are clearly Other (234).

Crusoe's first contact with the Spaniard on the island reveals the array of terms to refer to nonsavages and their interchangeability. Crusoe "asked him in the Portuguese tongue what he was. He answered in Latin, 'Christianus.' . . . I asked him what countryman he was, and he said, 'Espagniole'" (235). Obviously, in terms of representing Europeans to each other, "white" was not an appropriate response, but it is notable that religious markers carry more meaning than national ones at this point. *White* is not a term of subjective identification but an attribute. As Theodore Allen aptly notes, when the terms were used to write colonial laws, there was a world of difference between laws in favor of whites and laws in favor of Christians.[47] In regard to Europeans, the novel vacillates between using the designation *Christian* and *white* (the Spaniard identifies himself as a Christian, and Crusoe sees him as a white European), and *free* remains a crucial, if repressed, subtext always distinguishing Europeans in the Atlantic.[48] Thus, complexion is most frequently part of a larger cluster of differences and not able, on its own, to signify racial difference. Nevertheless, it is the visible differences between Europeans and savages that trigger Crusoe's anger and result in the massacre of the cannibals. This scene of a potential European victim marks the change in the island from an individual to a corporate colonial relation in which the Europeans command a domestic labor population composed of Friday and his father and in which they all fight the native enemies of Friday's village.

Changes in terms of European colonial identity after the first century of English colonization were linked to the use of slave labor. In the seventeenth and eighteenth centuries, religion lost its edge as the most important difference in the colonies. In addition to Christianity, national origin, slavery, and skin color all served as competing divisions between Europeans and people of both Native American and African descent. The epigraph reflects this transition. In finessing the use of *Christian* by replacing it with *Englishmen* to reassure planters that converting their slaves would not alter their temporal status, the Lord Bishop of St. Asaph unwittingly revealed why the term *Christian* declined over the course of the century: it no longer denoted only Europeans and was not as reliable in its signification as *free* or *white*. *Free*, of course, had long referred to landowning men in Britain. Only men who were not dependent on others could truly be said to think and act for themselves: only a minuscule proportion of the English were truly free. Nonetheless, Britons in general could, at times, laud their freedom in comparison with Catholic, Islamic, or pagan countries. Parliament, a limited monarchy, and the constitution were widely believed to make Britons peculiarly free, even in comparison with fellow Europeans. Since landownership devolved on many European servants after the expiration of their service in the colonies (Barbados is a notable exception), they too were newly "free" people, both in contrast to slaves and in the sense of land ownership.

Complexion was also a relatively new category at this time, replacing *heathen* or religious denomination by continental origin in many cases. Its predominance was not yet guaranteed in Britain, although some contemporary authors used it more than Defoe did—the novelist William Chetwood, for example. Historian of race Winthrop Jordan argues that in the mid-seventeenth century, there was more than one shift in the terminology that colonists used to describe themselves in relation to other colonial populations: "From the initially most common term *Christian*, at mid-century there was a marked drift toward *English* and *free*. After about 1680, taking the colonies as a whole, a new term appeared—*white*."[49] In addition, between 1660 and 1690, slavery became a more permanent state by becoming lifelong and hereditary in most cases; it is at this time that the term *white* emerged *in the colonies*, especially in reference to European indentured servants.[50] That *white*, in its inception, was a term saturated with laboring-class associations suggests that it was not easily conflated with Englishness, which, at its heart, was a concept born of aristocratic inflections.[51] In 1680, Godwyn had to explain to English readers that *white* and *European* were used interchangeably in the colonies; almost one hundred years later, Edward Long still felt compelled to inform his British readers that Europeans in Jamaica were called whites.[52] Even though the terms differ—*free, white, Christian*—they all singularized Europeans in relationship to other people whom they encountered in the Atlantic. Indeed, in *Robinson Crusoe*, the differences among Europeans are not as important ideologically as their similarities. The novel situates Europeans in a kinship by virtue of a common Christian heritage, the wearing of clothes, use of firearms, light skin color, and linked national economies, especially between the Portuguese and English in Africa, Europe, and the Atlantic empire.

Although *Robinson Crusoe* tends to downplay differences among Europeans, the Spanish occupy a hybrid position worth noting: the Spanish are positioned between the civilized and the savage. While the novel never satisfactorily resolves this dichotomy at the level of explanation, it suggests that Catholicism and the ease with which Spaniards murdered native American peoples accounted for their reputation of savagery. The Spaniards' hybrid position is best shown in the scenes involving Crusoe, Friday, his father, and the Spaniard whom Crusoe also rescues from the cannibals. The British colonial architecture of power relations is most pronounced as these four prepare to increase food stores for the arrival of the other Spaniards and Portuguese residing with Friday's people. Crusoe chooses trees for use, Friday and his father cut them down, and the Spaniard is the trusty middle manager of their labor. Crusoe refers to the Spaniard as someone "to whom I imparted my thought on that affair [escape from the island], to oversee and direct their work" (246). This passage naturalizes British supremacy and highlights the way that supervising manual labor separates the men from the "boys." As with Xury and the Portuguese captain, other Europeans negatively impact the relationship between Crusoe and his servant/companion.

Based on English prejudice and on sixteenth-century policy, the Spaniards' ruthless behavior as colonizers helps account, in part, for their liminal position. Musing on Spanish colonial relations as evidence of their tendency to participate in barbarity, Crusoe decides not to attack the Caribs because "this would justify the conduct of the Spaniards in all their barbarities practised in America, where they destroyed millions of these people, who, however they were idolaters and barbarians, and had several bloody and barbarious rites in their customs, . . . were yet, as to the Spaniards, very innocent people" (178). Because of this "unnatural piece of cruelty," "the very name of a Spaniard is reckoned to be frightful and terrible to all people of humanity, or of Christian compassion; as if the kingdom of Spain were particularly eminent for the product of a race of men who were without principles of tenderness" (178). Rejecting the Spanish model for conduct in the Americas, Crusoe temporarily finds more comfort in being "not Spanish" than in eradicating cannibals. Later, Crusoe claims that his fear of the Spaniards exceeds his fear of dismemberment by the cannibals. Imagining being made a prisoner in New Spain, where an Englishman was certain to be made a sacrifice, Crusoe observes: "I had rather be delivered up to the savages, and be devoured alive, than fall into the merciless claws of the priests, and be carry'd into the Inquisition" (243). In volume 2, Crusoe continues his diatribe against Spanish savagery, conceding at one point that the Spanish Inquisition was preferable to being at the mercy of the northern Chinese (249). In the more philosophical mode of volume 3, Crusoe explains Spanish cruelties as the will of God and thereby dismisses them (224). These far-fetched claims use the most extreme form of difference from Europeans to denigrate Catholicism. Crusoe's inadequate solution to the Spaniards' potential savagery and treachery is a contract with them. Even though contracts did not necessitate equivalence between the parties, as marriage and labor both suggest, its ideological manifestation encouraged this view. Certainly a contract is out of the question in terms of Crusoe's relations with Caribbean islanders (notably, a contract defines Xury's terms of servitude). The novel uses savagery as the linchpin not only to separate Europeans from those with whom they came into violent conflict in the Atlantic but also to create hierarchies among Europeans.

In this depiction of Spaniards, the novel reveals profound anxiety about the price of European control of the Caribbean islands—the potential of domination tipping over into savage behavior and the likelihood of slave owners being corrupted by their own power. Both of these anxieties attest to a vulnerable conception of identity, not a monolithic one. At the same time, however, the novel helps obscure the role other European powers had in making colonial conditions dangerous for each other. Many historians have documented the almost equal danger from the Caribs and other Europeans to the British in the West Indies especially during wartime when the Caribbean was a major theater of intra-European aggression.[53] In the novel, however, the similarities among Europeans far outrank national differences and sectarian Christianity in the colonial context, implicitly indicating the overriding importance of European unity against the indigenous peoples. Such a desire for unity, however, rarely transpired in the Atlantic empire. The major European nations capitalized on national and tribal rivalries among Indians to their advantage against each other, as did the Caribs and other native Americans, in their turn. *Robinson Crusoe* assumes that because the Spanish are European and Christian, they are within nonsavage boundaries, even though they acted like savages toward the native populations whom they murdered and colonized. This rough sense of European similarity is, of course, dramatized by the contrast to savages in the same way that taxonomies of human difference collapsed stereotypical national characteristics to produce a homogeneous European at this time. An interest in national characters had produced well-known stereotypes of various European nations for centuries. While these ideas persisted, largely undisturbed, the composite European emerged in racial taxonomies, which was a powerful parallel construction.

* * *

Two pivotal scenes in the novel illustrate the way that *Robinson Crusoe* simultaneously establishes and undermines racial differences. These scenes seem to promote rigid distinctions between the English and Caribs, yet they are ultimately more interesting for the way that they question the stability of racial boundaries. In each case, the passage describes the appearance of Friday and Crusoe through Crusoe's "eyes." The most significant feature in comparing the two is the lack of symmetry in the narrative object: Crusoe defines Friday by his body and himself by his clothing.[54] Both feminist and postcolonial scholars have noted that one of the persistent forms of producing and maintaining a sense of inferiority in Western, patriarchal culture involves focusing on the body of the Other. Despite this telling difference, the effect of these scenes makes imprecise the boundary between savage and European Christian. At first glance, the description of Friday appears to attend only to how he differs from Crusoe. Ultimately, however, the representation of Friday furthers the case for multiple rather than singular difference between Europeans and Caribs. The careful description intersperses taxonomic detail with approbation of what Crusoe sees:

He was a comely handsome fellow, perfectly well made; with straight strong limbs, not too large; tall and well shaped, . . . twenty six years of age. He had a very good countenance, not a fierce and surly aspect; but seemed to have something very manly in his face, and yet he had all the sweetness and softness of an European in his countenance too, especially when he smiled. His hair was long and black, not curled like wool; his forehead very high and large, and a great vivacity and sparkling sharpness in his eyes. The colour of his skin was not quite black, but very tawny; and yet not of an ugly yellow nauseous tawny, as the Brasilians, and Virginians, and other natives of America are; but of a bright kind of a dun olive colour, that had in it something very agreeable, tho' not very easy to describe. His face was round and plump; his nose small, not flat like the negroes, a very good mouth, thin lips, and his fine teeth well set, and white as ivory. (208–9)

This passage is key in preparing us to read Friday not primarily in his difference from Crusoe but in his difference from other Amerindians and black Africans.[55] Most critics who mention this passage reiterate that Friday is not of African descent but not that he is similar to Europeans. Defoe's idealized portrait of Friday is even more remarkable when one considers Philip Boucher's argument that an eighteenth-century male Carib would likely have had ear and lip plugs, scarification, and probably a flattened forehead and nose.[56]

To eighteenth-century Britons, Crusoe's first observations about Friday carry positive connotations, including his seeing a European countenance as somehow present in Friday's visage. Mostly the physical description distinguishes Friday from a stereotypical African slave. Notably, Crusoe also distinguishes Friday from stereotypes about cannibals in terms of attitude and skin color. This hybrid physical description mirrors Crusoe's treatment of Friday, who is alternately a laboring slave, trusted servant, affectionate companion, and fellow Christian. Clearly we are meant to share in Friday's *je ne sais quoi*, which is neither fully Carib nor European but a pleasing mixture of the two. Among the first attributes that Crusoe notes are Friday's "strength and swiftness" (205); it is not until four pages later that he mentions Friday's nakedness and preference for eating men's flesh—the two overriding and, in fact, sole characteristics of the group from which Friday comes that are acknowledged in the novel. Such an important contradiction stems from the narrative desire for Friday to be simultaneously a savage and a Christian. Although the novel introduces Crusoe's initial intention to treat Friday as a slave or servant (it is not clear which status will prevail), his subsequent desire to convert Friday to Christianity raises the issue of whether Friday's status then may be "upgraded." An ideological compromise constructs Friday as an exceptional savage and silences this issue.

Not surprisingly, Crusoe's self-representation implicitly establishes his difference from Africans and Caribs, but the description also singularizes him in regard to other Europeans. In the representation of Friday cited above, Crusoe tries but fails to establish a sharp picture of Friday's distinction; here, Crusoe represents himself in his difference from contemporary readers and from himself as he was in England. As part of the system signifying *European*, Crusoe describes what is on his body rather than the body itself, as with Friday. For instance, he imagines "had any one in England been to meet such a man as I was, it must either have frighted them, or raised a great deal of laughter; and as I frequently stood still to look at my self, I could not but smile at the notion of my travelling through Yorkshire with such an equipage, and in such a dress. Be pleased to take a sketch of my figure, as follows" (158). The description centers on Crusoe's clothing: goat skin hat with a flap hanging down behind, a short jacket of goat skin falling to his mid-thigh, open-kneed breeches with goat hair hanging down to the middle of his legs, and buskins to cover his legs. Carrying a saw and hatchet on his belt, a powder pouch and shot on his body, Crusoe also totes a basket on his back, a gun on his shoulder, and the goat-skin umbrella. In terms of his complexion, Crusoe is relatively unchanged despite his exposure to the elements: "As for my face, the colour of it was really not so moletta-like as one might expect from a man not at all careful of it, and living within nine or ten degrees of the equinox" (158). Crusoe's one concession to fashion rather than functionality is his whiskers, which, because of their style and length, visibly distinguish him from other Europeans who wear beards and from Moors and Amerindians who do not: "I had trimmed [my mustache] into a large pair of Mahometan whiskers, such as I had seen worn by some Turks who I saw at Sallee; for the Moors did not wear such, tho' the Turks did, . . . they were of a length and shape monstrous enough, and such as in England would have passed for frightful" (159). Indeed, while a beard was traditionally a mark of virility, whiskers were considered slightly inferior and worn mainly to frighten enemies in war.[57]

Here, Crusoe represents his body as laden with Western artifacts and tools, although his European fashion is fabricated with native materials. Moreover, Crusoe's body is a fortified body, not unlike the structures he builds to protect himself from the savages. His facial hair, clothing, and accouterments, however, are every bit as foreign as the Caribs' nakedness. Yet the presence of the whiskers connects him to the Spaniards, who, among Europeans, were most attached to whiskers and beards (76). Overall, there is very little in his self-representation to distinguish him as a European, even though his own color, "not so moletta-like" from the intensity of the sun as he imagined, changes the least of all. Even so, in terms of skin color, Crusoe fails to correspond to other Europeans who are called "white." His color is closer to Friday's: tawny and mulatto were often associated in the seventeenth and eighteenth centuries.[58] In these examples, complexion bears no relation to subjectivity and provides no key to character.

In the description of Crusoe and Friday, it is possible to detect a pattern of partially collapsed boundaries of difference. On first reading, the representation of Friday seems to suggest an unadulterated colonial desire for the Other only as different; in the case of Crusoe, his self-description at first seems to confirm the way he re-creates himself in the image of a typical European. Yet, as I have indicated, neither passage maintains a stable boundary between savage and European: in the one, there is a Europeanized savage; in the other, a barbaric-looking European. The collapse of absolute difference between savage and European helps support the idea that the *savage*, and *Carib* in particular, is a complicated representational category, especially in terms of Friday.

Friday compromises the effort to maintain traditional distinctions between Europeans and savages in terms of clothing and physical features. Curiously, although *Robinson Crusoe* describes black Africans for us, the novel does not provide a single physical description of the cannibals, despite Crusoe's intensive gazing and habitual monitoring of their feasts. Their difference is embodied in acts of cannibalism; the description of Friday, on the contrary, is one of the most sustained in the novel. In fact, Friday is *Robinson Crusoe*'s solution to the often undetectable boundary between friendly natives, or unenslavable inhabitants, and cannibals. The text retains the "hideous" cannibals (many of whom are massacred by the Europeans) but puts one of them (who does not resemble the others) in servitude, thereby providing a relationship in which power clearly remains in European hands but allows an individual Caribbee's spiritual welfare to be attended to. Friday's treatment after his religious conversion parallels the terms of Xury's exchange between Crusoe and the Portuguese captain, but this time Crusoe does not require liquid capital and keeps possession of Friday's labor. The economic nature of their relationship disappears almost from the beginning as the spiritual and affectionate aspects are emphasized. Historically, Caribs successfully resisted religious and political "hegemonization" but not trade relations.[59] The pairing of spiritual welfare and religious conversion with "free" labor allows Crusoe to fill the role of a benefactor rather than an exploiter in terms of colonial plot and theme. Such a role, however, carries a great deal of historical irony. As sixteenth- and seventeenth-century documents reveal, many Caribbean and Native American groups had befriended colonists, making their survival possible. Historically, the benefactor was not the European but the native, a reverse Robinson Crusoe and Friday situation. Thus, there is a splitting within the representation of Caribbean islanders—of an individual from the whole. Everything other than Friday's savagery is foregrounded. Such an embrace of another on an individual basis is perfectly compatible with the exercise of European colonial power because it is nonthreatening, piecemeal assimilation. Acceptance of these Others reflects the ubiquitous conviction about the changeability wrought by influences of climate or education—that exposure to English climate or ways of living would rehabilitate savages.

The analysis that I have offered above works satisfactorily only if one ignores the illustrations of the novel and the several changes in the narrative language to describe the cannibals and Friday. Since the novel defines Friday's features and color so precisely, the first illustration of Friday as a black African comes as a surprise. Beginning his illustrated life as a black man, Friday is physically undifferentiated from the other savages. In the frontispiece to *The Serious Reflections During the Life and Surprising Adventures of Robinson Crusoe* (1720), Friday appears with short, black curly hair and a black body, as do the rest of the Caribbean islanders featured at a cannibal feast.[60] By the 1780s, however, the illustrated Friday is an idealized Caribbean Indian, which follows the text closely. In the nineteenth century, Friday is a black African in some of the illustrations and in pantomime versions of the novel. In general, Defoe's novel emphasizes Friday's resemblance to Europeans, but the illustrations emphasize his affiliation with Negroes and Indians.

Despite the novel's precision about the Caribs' yellow color and savage attributes, and that the island is not off of the African continent but in the Caribbean, an aspect duly noted by the title page, the idea of *savage* signified Negro rather than Carib, as the 1720 illustration reveals: those who were

Figure 8. Negroized Caribbean Islanders. Daniel Defoe, *Serious Reflections During the Life and Surprising Adventures of Robinson Crusoe* (London, 1720). A seldom analyzed phenomenon, the Negroization of Friday, occurs early on and sporadically throughout the novel's illustrated and written history. In the foreground is a black Friday with short curly hair who is dressed identically to Crusoe. Their goatskin fashions distinguish them from both the naked cannibals and the conventionally clothed Europeans. In illustrated editions of the 1780s and 1790s, Friday usually appears as a brown noble savage or occasionally as a white one. Reproduced by permission of the Huntington Library, San Marino, California.

most clearly different from the Englishman Crusoe were blackened. There are several ways to account for the slippage between Indian and African. A brief consideration of colonial labor conditions, ideological pressures, and clues from the novel may help elucidate the periodic Negroization of Friday. Possibly the most important reason for the interchangeability of Africans and Caribbean islanders is due to the practices of labor-hungry planters who enslaved both groups on a temporary basis as well as for life; for instance, in the Caribbean plantations, there were quarters known as "Indian houses." Additionally, by the late seventeenth century, hundreds of Native American men had been taken into slavery in New England alone, and by the first decade of the eighteenth century, about one-quarter of all slaves in South Carolina were Indians.[61] Routinely, colonists transported them to the West Indies in exchange for African slaves to forestall rebellion and lesser forms of resistance. So there was literally an exchange of Indian bodies for African ones to meet labor requirements and to ensure the dominance of planters. For Europeans, the exchangeability between different subordinate groups may be explained by a desire for a numerous, inexpensive, and docile labor force.

Changes in the laboring population were not the only factor resulting in confusion between Carib and African. Friday's Negroization in eighteenth-century illustrations is also connected to the makeup of the colonial population. The movement of bodies from Europe and Africa to the Americas and between the Americas and the Caribbean gave rise to many blended identities. This hybridity is nowhere more evident than in the people who were known as the Black Caribs. Several slave shipwrecks over the sixteenth to eighteenth centuries resulted in the Islanders assimilating the survivors.[62] Because of intermarriage and concubinage between Africans and Caribbean islanders, there was a literal blending, giving rise to a population the British called *Black Caribs*, who were considered particularly dangerous to Europeans and to indigenous people alike.[63] Moreover, on St. Vincent in 1674, there were reports of Africans as well as Englishmen (who had been carried off when young) living with Caribees. Of the African population, many women married the Caribees, and many men were enslaved; others, who were Maroons, inhabited a separate part of the island. All in all, there were about 4,000 Black Caribs on St. Vincent alone at the end of the seventeenth century and possibly twice that number a century later.[64] Some of the confusion about the difference between Caribs and Africans did not result solely from European policy of substituting an imported labor force for the indigenous one, but from maroonage and other instances of oppressed populations resisting European assimilation.

A rarely noted factor contributing to the Negroization of Friday is the discrepancy between the narrative time and the publication date. Published in 1719, *Robinson Crusoe* takes place between the 1640s and 1690s. The events of the book correspond roughly to the political and economic situation of the mid-seventeenth century as opposed to the time of publication, although *Robinson Crusoe* does not reflect either historical period accurately.[65] Between the narrative time and 1719, the changes in territory, trade, and labor conditions in the British colonies alone were sufficient to introduce several possibilities for confusion between Caribbean and African people. Written during the year when the duke of Chandos was reinvigorating the Royal African Company, and British involvement in the slave trade was skyrocketing, the novel harks back to Spanish- and Portuguese-dominated sugar production. By the 1660s, the British West Indies had shifted broadly from a labor system of indentured servants with some slaves in a diversified economy to a slave economy with a few European servants for the production of sugar. After the mid-seventeenth century, people of African descent outnumbered the European population for the first time on many islands; the black population in the West Indies increased over sevenfold in the second half of the seventeenth century.[66] Indigenous people still occupied some of the Caribbean islands and were considered formidable enemies. In narrative time, Crusoe's confrontation with the cannibals takes place at a crucial moment in England's empire formation. Between 1665 and 1688, the island Caribs were in constant conflict with the English colonists and sought French aid in their endeavors (never an affiliation endearing to the English). After 1688, their numbers decreased dramatically through the kind of violence depicted in the novel and through demographic attrition. By 1719, native inhabitants were scarcely a threat to Europeans. In this way, England gained security in the leeward island region, which was a major factor that intensified the sugar boom and slave trade of the eighteenth century.[67]

Conditions of slavery and servitude changed for Europeans, Africans, and Native Americans throughout colonial contact; in general they improved only for Europeans. Similarly, the ability to be defined as *free* rather than as a slave or servant changed continually for all populations. The category of *slave* signified abject difference from free Britons and was a real as well as an ideological force. In the Caribbean, *slave* primarily referred to Africans but also to Amerindians who were enslaved. Because *slave* signified both African and Indian difference from Europeans, on the one hand, and difference between Africans and Caribbean islanders, on the other hand, it was an unstable category in theory. As many historians have contended, Europeans treated Caribs and Africans differently sometimes and similarly at other times. The Caribs' relation to Africans and to Europeans was not firmly established in the realm of representation either. The transition to a monocrop economy with intensive labor requirements meant that *slave* became a much more rigid category, especially for people of African descent. In the mid-seventeenth century, the status of Africans as slaves in British colonies was less rigid than in 1719 because not always permanent or hereditary: "It was only in the period from 1680 to 1710 that hereditary lifetime African slavery was first regularly instituted."[68] Even though colonists enslaved both Indians and Africans, by the time *Robinson Crusoe* was published in 1719, *slave* was a condition most particularly associated with Negroes, partly because most Caribbean Indians were still considered to be members of sovereign tribes and partly because their enslavement was never as visible to Britons who were familiar with the Guinea trade. In Jamaica, Indians were legally removed from the slave category in the 1740s. These tremendous changes in labor and colonial power relations help explain why Crusoe refers interchangeably to Friday as a savage, slave, servant, and Christian.

Servant designated any population, though most commonly it signified people of Irish, Scottish, and English descent who initially dominated the category of indentured servants. There were other less exalted categories of servants. European redemptioners arranged with a ship's captain to exchange the passage for payment of the fare upon arrival in the colonies or at a specified time thereafter. Failure to pay resulted in sale of the European, usually at an auction. Convicts were sent by the English government to serve for a specified period. Between 1654 and 1685—crucial years during which Crusoe is on the island—about ten thousand servants of various kinds sailed to the West Indies and Virginia.[69]

Indeed, in the mid-seventeenth century, the distinctions between a slave and an indentured servant were not always as significant as the similarities in terms of their value and treatment as individual labor units and as an overall workforce. As a slave in Morocco, Crusoe exemplifies such a blurring of status as do both Xury and Friday in relation to Crusoe. Hilary Beckles's *White Servitude and Black Slavery in Barbados, 1627–1715* (1989) focuses on the connections between slave and servant status in the British West In and on the way that African slavery systematically replaced other forms of servitude in the mid-seventeenth century.[70] Noting that British planters were committed to a white indentured labor force before the midcentury shift to a sugar-driven economy, Beckles provides convincing evidence for the negligible planter distinction between indentured servants and slaves *in terms of the market use of their labor* until after the 1660s (77).[71] Both indentured servants and slaves, no matter what their national origin, worked in the fields and at other unskilled manual labor jobs. Other similarities extended to the conditions of their labor. Both populations were subject to kidnapping from their country of origin, to restraining in the ship's holds during the middle passage, and to general conditions of trade, such as medical inspection and auction (65).[72] In the colonies, both groups were corporally punished and used to repay debts (33), and they were valued in terms of other commodities such as cotton bales or livestock for trade or sale (72).

Eric Williams attributes these deplorable conditions for all laborers to the general welter of the age (13). Of course, one crucial difference was that planters regarded indentured servants, even Irish political prisoners, as "temporary chattels" (171). In fact, until the African slave economy dominated the West Indies in the mid-seventeenth century, indentured servants were considered a better short-term investment because they did not require training and were a preferred form of debt repayment. The supply of indentured servants never met the demand, and it was not until the end of the seventeenth century that planter demands for indentured servants abated. By then, the price of slaves had decreased dramatically and the price of servants had doubled (Beckles, 168, 170).

In as much as there was a certain blurring of distinction between slave and servant in terminology and treatment, the novel also encourages a sliding between Friday's status as a servant and his status as a slave. In *Colonial Encounters*, Peter Hulme accounts for the persistent connection of Friday and slavery: Crusoe's relationship to Friday, he argues, functions as "a veiled and disavowed reference to the more pressing issue of black slavery."[73] A confusion between Caribs and Africans arises possibly because Caribs are the focus of the novel precisely at the time when Africans had become the most significant laboring population in the Atlantic world. Indeed, the connection between Friday and slavery is inconsistent at best in the novel, but one of the most frequently illustrated scenes from the 1780s onward was Friday's moment of submission to Crusoe after Crusoe saves him from being devoured by other cannibals.[74] Crusoe uses the word *slave* only this one time when interpreting Friday's putting his head beneath Crusoe's foot. The reinvention of Friday as an African was under way from the first illustration in 1720, and it depends on an intersection of European labor needs with the discourse of savagery and slavery that was first solidified during the eighteenth century, earlier in the colonies and later in Britain. Friday is most often remembered as Crusoe's slave, and *slave* has come to be connected almost exclusively to black Africans.

Nevertheless, at other times, Crusoe refers to Friday as his servant. Indeed, Crusoe's efforts to convert Friday to Christianity suggest his servant status, since slaves were routinely denied baptism and conversion at this time in the British colonies. Initially, when Crusoe sees Friday, before he meets him, he automatically connects Friday to servitude. This unthinking association is saturated with the colonial assumptions already in place: "It came now very warmly upon my thoughts, and indeed irresistibly, that now was my time to get me a servant, and perhaps a companion or assistant; and that I was called plainly by Providence to save this poor creature's life" (206). The uncertainty about Friday's future relationship to Crusoe is dramatized in the slippage among servant, companion, and assistant, which persists until the novel ends. Before Christianity is introduced as the determining difference in the interpretation of Friday, Crusoe perceives him as a political prisoner (207). *Prisoner*, as Chapter 2 details, translates as "enslavable." In terms of the law of nations and of a militaristic conception of empire, the taking of slaves was legitimated by conditions of warfare, much like the conflict between Muslims and Christians in the Mediterranean and Atlantic regions. Even more strangely, it is not mainly through the lens of Crusoe's desire as much as Friday's actions that lead Crusoe to think of him as a slave. Crusoe explains Friday's slavish reaction as stemming from fear of him: "I cou'd then perceive that he stood trembling, as if he had been taken prisoner, and had just been to be killed, as his two enemies were. I beckoned him again to come to me, and gave him all the signs of encouragement[;] . . . he came nearer . . . kneeling down every ten or twelve steps in token of acknowledgment for my saving his life[;] . . . he kneeled down again, kissed the ground, and laid his head upon the ground, and taking me by the foot, set my foot upon his head; this it seems was in token of swearing to be my slave for ever" (206–7). Later, Crusoe also refers to Friday as a companion (213), but as the adventures with Xury demonstrate, *companion* is entirely compatible with a subordinate.

During the narrative time of *Robinson Crusoe*, the category of servant was not reliably different from slave in many instances; slaves could become servants and indentured servants could become free servants. Winthrop Jordan has argued for a similar elasticity among the laboring categories in the seventeenth and early eighteenth centuries.[75] Although there were legal and cultural distinctions between servants and slaves, particularly from the late seventeenth century onward, including diet, clothing, and punishments, terminology and custom often lagged behind legal distinctions until well into the eighteenth century in some cases. For instance, it was not uncommon for masters to refer to slave laborers as servants even though the legal and social standing of the two groups was different.

While the text wavers between defining Friday as either a slave or a servant in the Caribbean, Friday's status as Crusoe's servant seems more secure when they travel in Europe, where it was not uncommon for Britons to have

African or East Indian servants (often unpaid).[76] In fact, Friday seems to be the model servant that Defoe had in mind when he wrote *The Great Law of Subordination Consider'd* (1724). Two of his main complaints are that British servants were increasingly difficult to distinguish in dress from their masters and that they lacked a due sense of their subordination. Masters were partially responsible for fostering this "insolence" by giving servants high wages, a problem resulting from the colonies' depleting Britain of working bodies, especially women.[77] Of course, Friday's skin color, gratitude, and unpaid status solve all the problems Defoe diagnosed in British master-servant relations.

There is a homogenizing tendency detectable in British culture itself that encourages a sense of exchangeability between Indians and Africans. Britons believed that Caribees and Africans lived lives far less polished than their own: both groups were scantily clad non-Christians. There was also a crucial difference between the way Britons viewed slaves and Indians and the way settlers in the colonies viewed them, a difference frequently noticed at the time. (Britons were considered much more hostile to slavery and less prejudiced in regard to dark skin color.) Thus, the distinctions between Indians and Africans commonly made in the colonies were not as important or discernible to Britons who had never been to the Caribbean. The overall effect of the difference between the novel and its illustrations was to promote divergent colonial stories. Combined with selective cultural memory, *Robinson Crusoe* encourages confusion about cannibals, Indians, and slaves that periodically surfaces in critical commentary. The portrayal of Friday as a black man in some illustrations and abridged editions, combined with his changeable designation as savage, slave, servant, and companion to Crusoe, reflects and participates in the ideological confusion generated by the far-reaching changes in colonial relations and in the makeup of the labor force.

To return briefly to Toni Morrison's claim that the Senate confirmation hearings reordered the signifying fictions of "natural servant" and "savage demon" through the bodies of Clarence Thomas and Anita Hill (xvi): my analysis of savagery, servitude, and slavery suggests that their sole application to people of African descent was not inevitable historically. Like Thomas and Hill, Friday and the Caribs represent the splitting of these two signifying fictions in *Robinson Crusoe*. That they later became a crucial legacy of North American slavery is another, though related, story.

A focus on Xury, Friday, and Crusoe demonstrates that emergent racial categories of difference are indeed produced but are not stable in either the novel or the social formation that gave rise to their representation. On the one hand, *Robinson Crusoe* revises colonial relations by featuring a more palatable version of power differences than existed in practice; for instance, the depiction of Friday, Crusoe, and Xury focuses on slavery as an individual and even temporary phenomenon and not as the systemic oppression necessary to a successful colonial empire based on the large-scale production of sugar in the West Indies, cotton and tobacco in North America. On the other hand, the novel can hardly be read as a simple vindication of the colonial enterprise. The hesitations Crusoe shows in his treatment of Africans and Caribs, the disconcerting questions Friday asks about Christian doctrine, and the lack of coherent logic in many of Crusoe's musings undermine a monolithic notion of empire or race.

In fact, Defoe's contemporaries did not wholly endorse the depiction of Xury, Friday, or Crusoe. In a wonderfully satiric commentary on the improbability of *Robinson Crusoe*, Charles Gildon stages a dialogue between the author and his two main characters. Crusoe complains to Defoe about the disconcerting religious toleration he is made to espouse, especially in regard to "Papists." Friday's grievance is that Defoe makes him a blockhead through his pidgin English, which never improves.[78] In a later section when Gildon has abandoned the fictional confrontation, he makes Xury's broken English a point of criticism by suggesting its ethnocentric bias. Gildon argues, "It had been more natural to have bade Robinson speak broken Arabick" (13). Finally, Gildon objects to the consideration Crusoe affords savages over slaves: Crusoe's acting as supercargo on a slave ship does not offer "any check of Conscience in that infamous Trade of buying and selling of Men for Slaves" compared with his scruples about killing the cannibals (14).

Analyses that have relied primarily on a binary sensibility to elucidate the novel or eighteenth-century racial ideology, for example, by opposing Crusoe to Xury and Friday, have erased a significant aspect of European colonialism—its contradictory history of contact and oppression. Thus, a reading practice emphasizing the multiple components of racial ideology makes a difference to the way in which modern readers interpret the novel. By selecting connections between Xury and Friday rather than simply focusing on their difference from Crusoe, I have argued that despite British participation in the African slave trade and domination of the Caribbean islands, *Robinson Crusoe* reflects some of the confusion that changing colonial practices elicited. *Robinson Crusoe* makes obvious the fact that colonialism was not simply staged between white and black men—nor even between Europeans and Caribbean Islanders—and brings to the foreground the way that the desire for clear boundaries of difference has always informed both the writing and subsequent readings of *Robinson Crusoe*.

Chapter 2

Racializing Civility

Violence and Trade in Africa

[Negroes are] a Race of People who appear to be different from the rest of Mankind; their Hair being woolly, and their Colour black; their Noses flat, and their Lips large; but whether these are an original Race, or whether the Difference arises from the Climate, the Vapours of that particular Soil, the Manner of breeding their Children, and from the mothers forming of their Features, is not here determined.

—FRANCIS MOORE
Travels into the Inland Parts of Africa (1738)[1]

[A Negro is] an individual (esp. a male) belonging to the African race of mankind, which is distinguished by a black skin, black woolly hair, flat nose and thick protruding lips.

— *Oxford English Dictionary* (1933)[2]

Savage = oposite of civil

UNTIL the mid-1990s, critics and theorists alike tended to equate the analysis of race with the study of the European representation of Africans and black skin color; accordingly, most previous studies of race during the seventeenth and eighteenth centuries investigated European writing about black Africans or privileged this material. Certainly, a focus on color difference seems warranted given that England escalated its participation in the slave trade between 1660 and 1720 and given that the current study of race was initially a by-product of the civil rights movement in the United States. Two of the most influential historians of black Africans outside of Africa, Winthrop Jordan and Peter Fryer, date racial slavery in the English colonies—as opposed to religious or economic slavery—to about 1700 and find evidence of black color prejudice even earlier. It is not surprising, then, that few scholars have wondered if the link between race and Africans is suspect or if skin color ranked among the most important embodiments of English claims to superiority at this time. Indeed, perhaps because there has been so much fine analysis of the way blackness functions in the early modern period, the tendency among literary critics has been to assume that racism intensifies or blackness carries the same meaning from one historical period to another. This chapter seeks to unsettle teleological and presentist conceptualizations of race and racism by untangling the customary equation of slavery and race and by considering the significance of complexion anew. A theory of multiplicity is historically and theoretically useful when the focus is on Africans and Europeans.

One way to sort through the several theories of human variety and complexion in the early modern period and their bearing on eighteenth-century social formations and literary texts is to establish what was culturally available versus what was dominant ideology. Moreover, it is helpful to inquire whether divergent ideas about complexion and civility were coexisting or competing. The English narratives about Africa of the 1720s and 1730s that I focus on in this chapter reveal a range of coexisting responses to Africans and Europeans in Africa, and they indicate the ideological limits of English writing about Africans during the first three decades of the eighteenth century. In these accounts, concepts of the *European* and *African* are still in formation and not overdetermined by racist ideology.[3] Moreover, as both eyewitness accounts and Daniel Defoe's *Captain Singleton* (1720) illustrate, the dominant preoccupation at this time was with masculine identity and the enterprising male figure. European and African men engaged in trade emerge more fully than their female counterparts in early representations of imperial contact and in conceptions of human difference.[4]

This chapter examines eyewitness accounts of Africa, particularly Wil-

liam Snelgrave's *New Account of Some Parts of Guinea, and the Slave-Trade*
(1734), and Daniel Defoe's *Captain Singleton*, an early novel that depicts
twenty-seven European pirates who find themselves stranded in Madagascar and their journey from Mozambique, across central Africa, to Angola
with sixty African men whom they enslave to carry their baggage. The issues
raised by this conjunction of texts primarily concern the relationship between trade and racial ideology. Thus, I depart from the assurance of a negative or fixed African difference to study the inconsistencies of racial ideology, which are also important to understanding British culture and the
history of race. While some negative conceptions of Africans carried over
from previous centuries, they did not simply intensify during the eighteenth
century, nor were they unchallenged. There was an uneven, not a cumula-
tive, development of racial ideology. Moreover, skin color, even in the case
of black Africans, was not the primary issue when the British considered
human differences in the first half of the eighteenth century.[5] Racial ideology
forms mainly around English responses to certain customs, dress, religion,
and especially trading—in short, around a concept of civility. It was through
these means that early eighteenth-century ideology encouraged a keen sense
of the visibility of differences, both of the British themselves and of others.
Early eighteenth-century British narratives about Africa did not tend to link
slavery to skin color.

In discussions of slavery during the first half of the eighteenth century,
issues of population overflow and European profits are the primary justifications of the trade with Africa, not the phenotyping of Africans. In narratives
of voyages to Africa, novels, and debates on trade, writers claim that commercial contact and slavery are motivated and justified by a legitimate desire
for economic gain. There was a widespread sense that the slave trade was an
economic boon and integral to England's glory.[6] Although there was consensus about the benefits to England of trade to Africa, support for slavery
was not universal, and glimpses of some moral uneasiness are detectable in
the literature. An anonymous writer supporting the slave trade in 1746 acknowledges the primary form that dissent over the slave trade took before
abolition: "Many are prepossessed against this Trade, thinking it *a barbarous,
inhuman, and unlawful Traffic for a Christian Country to trade in Blacks.*"[7] All
of these factors suggest that more careful attention to the precise meaning
of race in the earlier periods is warranted and that black skin color should
not be the main point of analysis.

*   *   *

Literary critics of the Renaissance have made a significant contribution to the analysis of race, especially the largely negative ways in which blackness signified in English culture during the early modern period. Published soon after *Women, "Race," and Writing in the Early Modern Period* (1994), Kim Hall's *Things of Darkness: Economies of Race and Gender in Early Modern England* (1995) offers a black feminist approach to reading Renaissance texts. Similar to the claims that Margo Hendricks and Patricia Parker offer, Hall argues for understanding race as unstable and as not forming a coherent ideology at this time.[8] The motivating concern of her study is to integrate an analysis of racism with the study of racial imagery, even though a terminology of race does not exist at this time (255, 261). Predominantly a study of literary convention and the way blackness is embedded in early modern language, Hall's book contends that dark and light, rather than simply conjuring up beauty or moral categories, are conduits through which English people articulated their own and others' identity (2). Black and white, she demonstrates, is a central binary for expressing fears about the conflict between cultures in imperial interaction. In the vast amount of textual evidence that she amasses, Hall provides a nuanced sense of the mutability of blackness. Despite this nuanced approach, Hall supports the sense that blackness and Englishness are mutually exclusive categories (12). Hall contends that the seventeenth century, especially after 1650, is a time when "dark skin color and certain physical features" posed a problem "for a culture that believed that God made man in his own image" (13). Similarly, the Vaughans' "Before *Othello*: Elizabethan Representations of Sub-Saharan Africans" (1997) sees this as a time when "with few exceptions, the emerging composite picture portrayed African skin as unattractive and, in some texts, as the stigma of divine punishment."[9] Both the Vaughans and Hall focus on skin color and thereby give it undue emphasis.

Hall's analysis of whiteness is somewhat more problematic, however, than her investigation of blackness given its general absence in early modern texts (171). Nevertheless, she rightly observes that whiteness was not a reliable register of value at this time (51). Mapping the black/white binary onto a present/absent axis in her discussion of *The English Moore* by Richard Brome (1631), Hall argues periodically throughout her book that whiteness works by its invisibility in ways comparable to those outlined by Peggy McIntosh. McIntosh's "On the Invisibility of Privilege" highlights the myriad benefits daily accruing to people who have white skin that are completely taken for granted—a sort of invisible and silent affirmative action on behalf of white Americans.[10] The main result, according to McIntosh, is general institutional empowerment for white people, including a range of material advancements, such as opened doors in education and employment, as well as ease of access to basic social and economic services. In fact, whiteness does not function this way in the early modern period and eighteenth century. Its invisibility is moot in a political and social space in which it need not be either hypervisible or invisible. Whiteness was visible, but it was not as important as other constituents of Englishness. It may appear "invisible" to some critics because, in fact, it was not central to identity at this time.

Emily Bartels has undertaken a critique of the way that difference has been theorized in Renaissance literary criticism and critical theory. She points out that many critics assume that identity is formed only through the concept of difference and that European cultural dominance is both the beginning and the end of many analyses.[11] Bartels expresses dismay over the general tendency in theorizing identity "to start with struggle and work backward—to read identity through conflict, cross-cultural encounters through conquest, race through racism" (47). Her timely critique may be furthered by noting that notions of struggle and domination associated with this theoretical model of identity and difference are relatively new racial concepts popularized through Darwin's work on natural selection and adopted in Marx and Engels's writings to shape their conceptions of class and capitalism in the 1840s and beyond. These assumptions have informed cultural studies and often have been the silent basis of theoretical models. To assume the efficacy of this view of race and identity in the seventeenth and eighteenth centuries, rather than testing it, is misleading. Furthermore, drawing conclusions primarily from literary sources gives, at best, a partial picture of culture in any time period.

*   *   *

Between 1700 and 1750, about four times as many books were published on Africa as were published during the seventeenth century.[12] Not all of this information was new or significantly different from previous texts, but the increase in the number of books reflects Africa's new prominence in British culture. In the early eighteenth century, there were several sources of ideas about Africa. Even though very little was known about most of the continent, Africa was not considered homogeneous; on the contrary, many writers throughout the eighteenth and nineteenth centuries believed it contained the most diversity of any quarter of the world. Inquiries treating the entire continent commonly divided it into several regions. The countries in northern Africa, or the Barbary region, were the most familiar. In geographies, the many principalities in western Africa could be represented as completely Other to Europe. Summaries such as the one found in *The Compleat Geographer* (1723) provide an appraisal of Africans typically available to English readers and to students of geography. The value-laden description works on the binary polite/unpolished. Behavior, not appearance, is the important focus of the analysis: "Those People [Africans] in general are the most unpolish'd of the three ancient Parts of the World. Along the Coasts of the *Mediterranean*, where the *Arabs* formerly extended their Conquests, they are most civiliz'd; that Nation, renown'd in those Days, having still retain'd something of their former Government, and more human Way of Living. The inner Regions, less known to us, as scarce ever frequented by other Nations, continue in greater Ignorance, and entire Deprivation of all politeness; and the most Southern are altogether brutal and savage."[13] The contrast between Europe and Africa was comprehensive. The description of Europe in the same volume is typical of the way Europe appears throughout the century: The mild climate is complemented by "the Beauty, Strength, Courage, Ingenuity and Wisdom of its Inhabitants; the Excellency of their Governments, . . . and which Surpasses all, the Sanctity of their Religion" (n.p.). The fact that Europe had "discovered" half of the earth and founded colonies in the New World numbered among its most stellar achievements. The excerpt is useful for revealing the way that Africa might appear in contemporary educational books as Europe's opposite and the way that racial thinking worked generally in regard to people in southern climates.

This negative view of Africans in *The Compleat Geographer*, based on the organization of their government, civil institutions, and manners is confirmed by a factor for the Royal African Company, who offered perhaps the most favorable depiction of West Africans in the early eighteenth century. Indicating dominant English assumptions in his *Travels into the Inland Parts of Africa* (1738), Francis Moore reports, "The Natives, really, are not so disagreeable in their Behaviour as we are apt to imagine."[14] His statement attests both to the influence of received epistemology encouraged by publications such as *The Compleat Geographer* and to new appraisals characteristic of many other eighteenth-century writers. The problem of cultural interpretation was compounded by the language barrier, which few Englishmen sought to transcend.

In many of the accounts by men associated with the slave trade, like Francis Moore, Africa appeared as a complex society but inferior in some ways to Europe. To the extent that various versions of Africa and Africans were available at this time, we may conclude that the physical body had an uncertain place in this matrix of representation. The earliest taxonomies of physical features were based on visible differences at the level of an increas-

ingly stylized and stereotypical body. Many Europeans who tried to make
sense of the heterogeneity among people viewed the world through a black-
and-white polarity in which the physical typology of northern Europeans
was the model of humanity. These early efforts to make sense of humans
as part of the natural world reveal a search for the most extreme differences
in appearance. The French traveler François Bernier separates black Africans from other populations in "A New Division of the Earth" (1684) because of their "thick lips and squab noses," the texture of their hair and skin,
their slight beards, and their blackness.[15] His work is particularly notable because he is conscious of characterizing the global population in a new way.
His extensive travels had given him the idea of dividing the world according to differences in physical appearances among people rather than adopting
the north to south, east to west axes that other geographers had customarily followed. By identifying four or five species of men, Bernier offers the
most modern taxonomy until Linnaeus's. According to Bernier, the largest
group consists of people in Europe, Malaysia, north India, north Africa, and
North America who resemble each other; the second group contains the rest
of Africa; the third division encompasses Malaysia, Thailand, Japan, and
China; and the last division includes people from Lapland. Tellingly, when
Bernier discusses attractive women he encountered, he includes some black
African women whose features most resemble Europeans': "I have also seen
some very handsome ones among the blacks of Africa, who had not those
thick lips and that squab nose" (363). European facial features and the proportion of parts matter more to his sexual aesthetics than skin color.

Bernier's decision to employ physical resemblance as an organizing
principle did not immediately establish a trend, and some thirty-five years
later, it is possible to see how at least one writer accommodates old and new
ways of thinking. In *A Philosophical Account of the Works of Nature* (1721),
Richard Bradley's depiction of the world is indebted to the ancients' division of the earth into northern, temperate, and southern zones. He up-
dates it by abandoning place for face; that is, he emphasizes complexion
and variety within the three main climatic zones by identifying two kinds
of white men, two kinds of black men, and one group of intermediate-
complected mulattos. Bradley continues the precedent set by Bernier and Sir
William Petty, his seventeenth-century predecessors, by reckoning that skin
color and hair texture separated various populations. Typical of his contemporaries, Bradley was unwilling to associate physical distinctions with mental differences, although he uses white men with straight hair as the standard by which to measure others. Bradley's idiosyncratic division begins with
white, bearded Europeans and progressively separates populations as they

vary from this model. The second remove from Europeans is white men in America with no beards; copper-colored mulattos with straight black hair is the third; blacks with straight black hair is the fourth; and last, the blacks of Guinea with curly black hair, who represent the most differences from Europeans.[16] After describing their physical features, Bradley adds, "As to their Knowledge, I suppose there would not be any great Difference, if it was possible they could all be born of the same Parents, and have the same Education, they would vary no more in Understanding than Children of the same House" (169). In sum, while many late seventeenth- and early eighteenth-century writers concurred that black Africans were different from Europeans in appearance, dark color was not yet the primary signifier of their identity or status even in proto-scientific speculation, which tended to focus on visible differences more than other realms of discourse.

This is not to say that some Englishmen did not find black skin un-attractive—some did. Dark skin had long been remarkable to the lighter-complected English, but its status as a sign of inferiority, in and of itself, was not well established in the 1720s and 1730s when several narratives about Africa were published. Many twentieth-century scholars have understandably emphasized the pejorative European comments about Africans' physical appearance and organization of their societies that began to appear more frequently in the seventeenth and eighteenth centuries. These scholars have linked negative European responses to Africans to the eighteenth-century writers' investment in slavery or to their anxiety about it; however, these negative views were not the only responses. There was also a tendency to acknowledge what we now call cultural relativity in the eighteenth century—or at least an ethnocentric form of it. Indeed, many writers mentioned that Africans, Pacific islanders, and Australian Aborigines often found whiteness disagreeable or frightening. Mungo Park, for one, records that Moorish women "shudder" at his white complexion.[17] Similarly, English customs seemed as outlandish to Africans as some African manners did to the British who traded with them. Britons who came in contact with others frequently had the experience of seeing themselves through others' eyes—as unhygienic, bizarre, and as gendered differently, especially in regard to the clothes that they wore. Many Britons who experienced or who read about other people understood the artificiality of their own preferences.

While there was usually a mixed response to Africans, the negative commentary was more likely to concern their religion or polygamy than their complexion, and observations about dark skin color were not predictably negative. Indeed, many Britons found depth of color (in both whites and blacks) more attractive than intermediate colors and complexion less significant than shape of features and texture of hair. For instance, the tendency to notice other features more distracting than color surfaces when an author remarks that the African Jalofs are "blacker and handsomer" than Mandingos, partly because of their "not having the broad Noses and thick Lips peculiar to those Nations."[18] Similarly, John Ogilby's extremely popular *Africa* (1670) offers a mixed commentary in his observation that the natives of "Negro-land, or the Countrey of Blacks" are "very black; but the Features of their Faces, and their excellent Teeth, being white as ivory, make up together a handsom Ayre, and taking comeliness of a new Beauty: they are well Limm'd, and much addicted to *Venus*."[19] In these observations, it is possible to detect a tension between older conceptions of beauty that featured proportion and shape of features and newer ideas that singled out complexion, a phenomenon also remarkable in taxonomies of human variety. As many of the comments of seventeenth- and eighteenth-century writers suggest, perceptions of physical beauty could easily be combined with negative views of cultural organization, as in Ogilby's throwaway comment, derived from humoral/climate theory, about people in hot climates being disposed to passion.

Not coincidentally, in some usages, *black* had shifted from an adjective to a noun by the 1720s, but *Negro* and *black man* were commonly preferred. *Black* is not always equivalent to *Negro*; for example, some British commonly referred to East Indians as blacks.[20] An important indication that complexion and even facial features were not indelible components of identity is the fact that more writers than not believed that features such as flat noses or full lips resulted from infants being carried on their mother's back and rubbing against it.[21] Combined with a belief in the darkening effects of sunlight, or sometimes separate from it, dark complexion was believed by some to be manipulated through the application of ointments. In these cases, darkening occurred gradually, sometimes over a period of years.[22] Similar to the emergence of *black*, *white* first appears as a noun in the 1670s, also in colonial contexts. These nouns will prove to have lasting importance, but at this time they mark the intensification of color-based identity (in some locations and under certain circumstances), not the achievement of it. Indeed, Linnaeus's influential 1735 taxonomy of four types of men from four continents helps dissolve the conception of the world in black-and-white terms, a trend even more characteristic of the second half of the eighteenth century.

In early eighteenth-century Britain, short essays about the causes of black complexion or brief speculations about the origin of skin color were more common than taxonomies of human variety. Even though complexion was not yet as important to racial ideology as it became later in the century, it was a source of great interest to some travelers and essayists. Attempts to account for the origins and causes of different skin colors eluded Enlightenment scholars. They singled out blackness in many cases as an especially puzzling phenomenon, and it was around this mystery that the most speculation occurred. Uncertainty about how to explain various skin colors was accompanied by ambivalence about how to judge them. One of the earliest and most complete inquiries into human complexion was Sir Thomas Browne's "Of the Blacknesse of Negroes" in *Pseudodoxia Epidemica* (1646), which went into six editions by 1672. Browne's three chapters on skin color comprise an extended meditation on the multiple causes of skin color and visible variations in inhabitants even within a given country. Browne rules out some popular misconceptions about the cause of color variations. (As Chapter 5 shows, little progress was made in terms of explaining the causes of skin color by the late 1780s.) By presenting exceptions that called standard explanations into question, Browne eliminates the most commonly cited single factors believed to cause dark skin color, such as the heat of the sun or God's curse. Rejecting the most prevalent rationale of the sun's heat as a single cause of the variety of complexions, Browne does not leave it far behind when he speculates that the air temperature and the proximity of people to rivers also influence skin color but are ultimately insufficient, in and of themselves, to explain the kinds of variations reported by travelers. Unable to solve the riddle of the origins of blackness, Browne finally concedes, "However therefore this complexion was first acquired, it is evidently maintained by generation, and by the tincture of the skin as a spermaticall part traduced from father unto son."[23] In a related point about the significance of skin color, Browne consults conflicting ideas about beauty in mid-seventeenth-century Britain: Some people believe beauty "to consist in a comely commensurability of the whole unto the parts, and the parts betweene themselves" (520–21). Others, however, "and those most in number, . . . place it [beauty] not onely in proportion of parts, but also in grace of colour" (521). Similar to his contemporaries Robert Boyle and Matthew Hale, Browne's meditations acknowledge an important change in English ways of seeing from a primary emphasis on stature to skin color. This transition occurs during a time of major colonial expansion in the Caribbean and North America. Nevertheless, Browne's essay also suggests that aesthetic value, which often equated beauty with fairness or whiteness in literary convention, was not identical to moral value or to practices of scientific observation at this time.

Other sources of speculation about human complexion that commanded a large readership were periodicals, which perhaps best indicate the range of popular beliefs about complexion. The *Athenian Oracle*, in its third edition by 1728, collected the significant issues of the *Athenian Mercury*, a periodical which first appeared in the 1690s; its readership was drawn from "the middle ranks of life—tradesmen, literate artisans, and small professional people" and from "'the politer sort of mankind.'"[24] Its format featured answers to questions in divinity, law, philosophy, trade, and the like. To the (erroneously conceptualized) question of why, in the same climate, such as India, some people are black, some white, and some tawny, the editors offer the most popular explanations, including that dark-skinned inhabitants are the descendants of Cain (they are dark because the God-given mark of disobedience was black skin, which was an explanation not given any credence by the editors); dark- or light-skinned babies result from the power of a woman's imagination or a whimsical desire during pregnancy; and color is variously produced by proximity to the sun, to mountains, and to bodies of water.[25] The editors believe that the most convincing explanation for variously colored inhabitants of India was the last option—exposure to the sun. To the more risky question, *"Whether Negroes shall rise so at the last Day?"* the editors symptomatically reframe the religious issue into an aesthetic one: Was white or black the better color? (1:435). They repeat commonplaces that in European culture black is associated with night and terror and that white connotes light and beauty, yet they consider blackness "an accidental imperfection," and so when Negroes rise to heaven, they will be white (436). Assuming an original whiteness from which all populations degenerated neatly reconciles English chauvinism with the sense of common human origins.

Although early taxonomies of human variety, such as Bradley's, highlight physical features of populations, visible bodily characteristics were not yet the primary way that all Britons singled out others as inferior. Instead, Christianity still dominated English concepts of self versus Other in the culture at large, as did convictions stemming from humoral theory about people in north, south, and temperate regions; generic ideas of savagery also continued to influence English concepts of Africans. In the wake of Winthrop Jordan's influential *White over Black: American Attitudes Toward the Negro, 1555–1812* (1968), it has been difficult to discuss eighteenth-century human variety without privileging skin color. I am in agreement with Michael Adas, who remarks on the current critical overemphasis on physical features to the exclusion of religion and social organization when discussing Africans.[26] Contemplation of human variety occurred in a larger matrix than much twentieth-century research acknowledges, although I agree with the implicit assumptions of such work: British conceptions about human differences are more significant in relation to populations enslaved by the British because this epistemology later approximated, in some arguments, a cause-and-effect relationship between visible characteristics of African bodies, invisible qualities of their intelligence, and the appropriateness of their enslavement.[27] Taken together, taxonomies, geographies, and travel narratives reveal a sense of otherness traditionally lodged in social organization, and hence subject to change, colliding with a newer interest in the generic body in which complexion was an important feature, though uncertainly configured.

* * *

An examination of British narratives of West Africa, rather than accounts of the colonies, explores the formation of racial ideology in a landscape where European men were still tenuously placed and where they were engaged in commercial and political relations with local power bases.[28] The context of contact in Africa differed dramatically from the colonies; most often contact was for trade. The Africans and mulattos with whom Englishmen had dealings were wealthy merchants working on behalf of their states, regional middlemen, or local potentates, and the power dynamic with Europeans was the opposite of that in the British colonies.[29] It is clear from accounts that many African business people preferred not to allow Europeans on shore, so trade took place on the ships at anchor. Africans wished to safeguard inland slaving and trading routes and to conceal the location of gold mines.[30] In cases when they were permitted on shore, Europeans were carefully contained, and their experiences of the land and people were usually highly ritualized by the local people in charge. Limited by terrain and by the availability of guides, Europeans were generally restricted to areas designated for trading. As Anthony Barker reminds us about the differences between the African in Africa and in the colonies, "The Negro had been known by Englishmen as an African even longer than he had been known as a chattel slave."[31] More important, many Africans of both sexes distinguished themselves in a crucial fashion from slaves by their position as brokers in trade and by their wearing of elaborate dress and adornment. (Slaves designated for the Atlantic trade often arrived at the coast with negligible clothing and accessories.)

The early eighteenth-century accounts of the slave trade and the African coast written by William Snelgrave, John Atkins, and Francis Moore occur, like *Captain Singleton*, during a period of phenomenal increase in the slave trade. As Snelgrave notes, in 1712, twenty-three ships left England for Africa; in 1726, two hundred did. By this time, about 20,000 slaves were transported yearly to the European Caribbean and about 1,000 to the North American ports.[32] Reasons for the tenfold increase in Guinea-bound ships had to do with Britain winning the Asiento (the potentially lucrative privilege of supplying slaves to Spanish colonies in the Atlantic), with the duke of Chandos's efforts to revive the monopoly trade of the Royal African Company after 1719, and with the expansion of sugar plantations in the Caribbean. Snelgrave, Atkins, and Moore represent the range of early eighteenth-century British responses to Africans in their eyewitness accounts. These texts detail trade, agriculture, ways of living, and conversations that belie sweeping generalizations about Africans, such as *The Compleat Geographer* features, and individual accounts often contain claims both about African barbarity and about polite trading exchanges. Ideas about dark skin color, other human differences, and slavery are not at all coherently connected at this point, nor do they necessarily correspond to an individual's economic stake in the slave trade in any direct way. To illustrate, Snelgrave, a slaving captain for many years, was an enthusiastic supporter of the slave trade, but he believed in a single creation and showed grudging admiration for local power brokers. On the other hand, the physician John Atkins was the writer most vociferously opposed to the slave trade, and he vehemently refuted rumors of cannibalism fostered by Snelgrave; yet he suspected that the great physical dissimilarity he perceived between Africans and Europeans suggested their separate origins. Of all the narrators, Moore, a factor for the Royal African Company in Africa, is the most evenhanded author in tone and approach to Europeans' shared humanity with Africans, despite his devising a system to ensure a constant supply of slaves to English ships.

The early eighteenth-century narratives evince a tension between perceptions of cultural difference and the experience of commercial exchange. Revealing the contradictions generated by frames of reference Englishmen brought with them to Africa versus their experience, the writers' representation of African trade permits an analysis of typical modes of othering and the simultaneous fracture of them through the pressure of trading situations. A significant aspect of British identity other than Christianity was commercial behavior. Over the eighteenth century, trade and the resulting civility were increasingly key to the formation of English identity. As J. G. A. Pocock, G. J. Barker-Benfield, David Solkin, and David Shields demonstrate, a change in national manners resulted from the new demands of commercial capitalism. At its most abstract, civility was a centuries-old concept concerned with mitigating conflict between powerful strangers or in a competitive social space, such as a court.[33] Civility was an individual attribute but could apply to entire societies. It signified freedom from barbarity and elegance of behavior.[34] As the narratives to Africa reveal, trading encounters also infuse the concept of civility. In England and abroad,

the large number of encounters between the British and strangers, including other businessmen, required a new form of politeness in which, theoretically, a code of fairness, piety, and agreeableness predominated. In this
way, regular arrangements were facilitated, which suited most merchants because stability and goodwill gleaned more profits over the long term. Notions
of civility appear in eighteenth-century domestic fiction through terms such
as *courteous, complaisant,* or *genteel* and are most frequently associated with
men of the middling and upper ranks. In a colonial context, civility takes on
the added qualities of a good trader and of bravery, attributes which were
often underwritten by aggression and seemingly at odds with the domestic
ideal of civility. Many comments about trade in Africa, however, suggest that
English slave traders were slower to emulate this model than their domestic counterparts. The large number of private traders inevitably resulted in
maverick behavior that shut down coastal regions for trade.

Snelgrave's text is especially interesting when analyzing the clash between civility and racial ideology, since he had traded in Africa for decades,
was staunchly committed to the slave trade, and freely circulated rumors
of African cannibalism; clearly, he does not appear as a good candidate for
a sympathetic depiction of Africans. His narrative begins with the political history of the rise of Dahomey power in the region of Whydah and its
effect on trade. Snelgrave minutely reports his conversations with the victor
and the vanquished. Notwithstanding that these conversations take place
through a translator and that the reportage is based on Snelgrave's memory
(i.e., it is a highly mediated text), an intriguing phenomenon is still discernible. The extensive amount of conversation conveys not a uniform sense of
English superiority but a sense of the mutual jockeying for position and, in
some cases, for understanding. Thus, as Snelgrave's text reveals, there is an
odd mixture of mutual suspicion, cultural arrogance, and occasional admiration in British accounts of Africans at this time.

Snelgrave does not reveal a uniform investment in depicting Africans'
inferiority to Britons, although confrontations between Snelgrave and African potentates occasionally show the superiority of Christian morals, the
"barbarity" of natives, and the triumph of English terms of trade as the
resolution to all difficulties. In the following scenario, a social visit is soon
transformed into an opportunity for trade in which Snelgrave brings into
play the most typical sense of difference between the English and Africans:
Christianity. On an invitation from a chief man, Snelgrave goes to his village, where he sees a boy tied to a stake. Snelgrave inquires why he must
die, and the king replies the boy must be sacrificed to his god Egbo for continued prosperity. At this point a breach in hospitality occurs when Snel-

grave orders one of his own armed men to release the child, an action that demonstrates Snelgrave's failure to accommodate himself to his hosts. In response, the king's man advances, also armed. Snelgrave pulls out a pistol; at this point, the king remonstrates, and there is a heated exchange of words through an interpreter. The king accuses Snelgrave of violating the laws of hospitality, and Snelgrave grudgingly concedes the breach in a way that illuminates his investment in his own greater humanity. Justifying himself, Snelgrave explains his intervention in local ritual " 'on account of my religion, which, tho' it does not allow forcibly taking away what belongs to another, yet expressly forbids so horrid a Thing, as the putting a poor innocent Child to death.' " Simultaneously confirming the cross-cultural sanctity of private property, which includes slaves, and notions of fair exchange (money for people), Snelgrave's account of his actions promote an image of the benevolent slave trader, which is an oxymoron to us today. The king finally accepts Snelgrave's payment in return for sparing the child's life, and Snelgrave reassures readers that he sells the boy to a good master in the West Indies. A successful transaction solves not only the tension of religious difference but also the trespass on hospitality. This fascinating trading encounter legitimates the English participation in the slave trade through the interference of Christianity: Christians' greater humanity preserves the life that Africans would sacrifice. Contradictorily, it casts African religion dismissively as pandering to a desire for gain that Christianity evidently does not foster.

Other episodes, especially those concerned with more conventional trading situations, are more ambiguous, and the English assurance of superior difference is often deflated because, in reality, they occupied a less empowered position than the Africans in trade negotiations. One of the most interesting encounters in Snelgrave's text is the settlement of future trading rights with the king of Dahomey. Snelgrave records the signs of a civil society as he travels inland to meet the leader: well-paved roads, populous villages, and pleasant, cultivated countryside leading to the capital. There, the king is richly dressed in his court, and he receives gifts from Snelgrave. To be sure, this is neither a naked savage nor the leader of what elsewhere Snelgrave refers to as a "barbarous, brutish" nation.[35] The king sits cross-legged on the ground, and Snelgrave must, out of courtesy and protocol, do the same, even though he finds it uncomfortable (60). The negotiating that ensues appears to give Snelgrave the upper hand, but it is suitably uncertain, not least because it depends on Snelgrave being feminized in relation to the king—an almost unprecedented phenomenon in early English travel literature. Apparently, the king wants to encourage European trade now that the wars are over to help replenish his finances and secure hegemony in the region; he is a powerful conqueror and initiates the bargaining by expecting what the defeated king of Whidaw formerly received. Snelgrave counters with flattery: since the king of Dahomey is so much greater than the vanquished king, he will not require as much from the Europeans. The king finally says to Snelgrave that " 'he would treat me as a young Wife or Bride, who must be denied nothing at first' " (62). Snelgrave is disconcerted by this wording but is led by the interpreter and the king to be encouraged by the allusion to marital bliss. So he offers the king half of what Whidaw received, and the trading "marriage" is cemented. Finding the land, leader, army, and inhabitants well organized, prosperous, and brave, Snelgrave's sense of religious difference, so obvious in the previous example, is diminished by the myriad signs of power and civilization as well as by the realities of trade.

Even when the text highlights African difference from a European norm, Snelgrave's narrative often does not maintain it. In his account, meetings with chief men typically elicit an uneasy combination of similarity and difference. As part of cultivating ongoing trade relations, Snelgrave invites one of the great men from the Dahomey court to visit him at the factory where the British based their trading operations. Just as Robinson Crusoe is grateful to Providence for the shipwreck that afforded him a knife with which to prepare his food and eat, thus saving him from feeding "like a beast," Snelgrave highlights silverware in his meeting with a local potentate.[36] On his own turf, Snelgrave serves the visiting dignitary ham and minced meat pie on plates with silverware to use. Observing how awkwardly the African man uses the fork, Snelgrave finds it amusing. Readers, Snelgrave assumes, will find humor in the clumsy manners of the African and share this evidence of European superiority. This "superiority" was of fairly recent date and not ubiquitous, even among the nobility. As Fernand Braudel demonstrates in *The Structures of Everyday Life* (1979), the use of spoons and knives was not widespread until the sixteenth century; the fork appeared on the scene somewhat later.[37] In fact, the Italians, but not the French or English, were known as fork users in the early seventeenth century; for instance, it was still a novelty worth mentioning by an English traveler in Italy. In Britain, table forks did not appear in individual household inventories before 1660: "Their use only became general in about 1750." Louis XIV, for instance, was noted for the skill with which he ate chicken stew with his fingers (206).

The fork incident in Snelgrave's narrative initiates the theme of superior European polish that punctuates his account of the meal. When the visitor asks Snelgrave how the pie is made and admires it extremely, the

Englishman retorts that his wife made it and put it in earthenware pans to keep six months, even in the great heat. The guest then asks how many wives Snelgrave has, and he laughs when Snelgrave replies that he has only one. He owns he has five hundred wives and wishes fifty could prepare the meat as Snelgrave's wife had done (79). On the one hand, this encounter is remarkable for what is rarely shown—a shared taste and a joke.[38] The joke reveals a common ground for English and African men: a belief in women's subordination to men, but the joke is more at the expense of African women whose domestic skills do not compare with their English counterparts. On the other hand, undercutting this sense of similarity between the men is the polygamous Other who manipulates the protocols of politeness and *dashees*, or bribes, customary to maintaining trading privileges. This is nowhere more evident than the final scene of their exchange when the duke, as Snelgrave calls him, admires the plates and silverware as well as the food, and Snelgrave, ever sensitive to the necessity of maintaining good relations, feels the pressure of polite behavior. In the end, he offers the duke the single place setting as a civil gesture, but the duke "misunderstands" the offer and takes them all, much to Snelgrave's irritation.

Snelgrave concludes his narrative with the happy ending of successful trade relations established in the region. He ends up with six hundred slaves and gets a good market for them in Antigua, where he loads sugar and returns to London. Yet Snelgrave mentions a litany of complaints about the ill usage he receives in Africa from the chief man of Jaqueen, who refuses to pay a balance owed to Snelgrave, and about his storehouses being plundered; this situation gives rise to his accusations of their barbarity. As all of these examples show, successful trade relations turn "brutish" people into esteemed trading partners, but a sour deal can reconfirm ideas about African barbarity. There is thus an intimate relationship between the significance of difference and successful trade, and this symbiosis carries over to Defoe's *Captain Singleton*.

Early narratives of voyages to Africa, such as Snelgrave's, reveal it as a place of power politics between European and African men and among Africans themselves, as a coast controlled by middlemen, and as a site of ritualized business dealings and trade constantly renegotiated because of European breaches of protocol, individual whim on both sides, and changes in local power structures. In most of these narratives, there is a remarkable separation between the discussions of African people and of slaves destined for overseas transportation. For instance, Snelgrave's text has two parts, one about the power politics of the Dahomey region and the other about the slave trade; in fact, included in the subtitle of his book is "The manner how the Negroes become Slaves." Similarly, Atkins physically separates observations

about the life of the inhabitants from his account of slaves. These discursive patterns reflect a larger ideological separation of Africans into two kinds
of inhabitants: people and slaves. The relatively positive perception of Africans noticeable here will be inverted by advocates of slavery in the 1770s and
1780s, as Chapters 4 and 5 explore; they emphasize the savage condition of
Africa in order to relieve British anxiety about the conduct of the slave trade
and the revulsion at planter treatment of West Indian slaves.

At this time, the benefits of the African trade overshadow interest in
confirming rumors of savagery circulated in educational geographies and
in some eyewitness accounts, but the experience of trade does not prompt
a large-scale revision of European convictions about Africans' differences
from themselves; characteristically, the two modes of expression coexist. In
turning to *Captain Singleton*, I examine the differences as well as similarities
in the depiction of Africans when real contact and profits are not at stake.
On the one hand, Defoe transforms Africans and trade quite dramatically
from the available reports; on the other hand, he treats the land similarly to
other contemporary writers, leading a recent literary historian to speculate
whether *Captain Singleton* was "deliberately designed to stimulate interest in
the potential value of the interior of Africa."[39]

*   *   *

In 1720, no European was known to have traveled more than a few hundred miles up major coastal rivers and certainly not across Africa. *Captain
Singleton* has long been interesting to critics because of the overland African
journey that occurs in the first half of the novel, and that portion of the novel
has garnered the preponderance of attention over the years. Not surprisingly,
several scholars have insisted on the travel book quality of the novel, and
many have devoted their essays to source studies and to ascertaining what
kind of geographical knowledge about Africa was available to Defoe.[40] Since
Secord's study of Defoe's narrative method over seventy years ago, most concur with his conclusion that Defoe shows an astute use of commonly available speculation about the interior regions.[41] In what follows, I am not as
interested in the accuracy of Defoe's depiction per se as in the function of the
overlaps and differences from contemporary accounts and in developing the
arguments laid out in previous sections about various English responses to
Africans. *Captain Singleton* is an especially important text because it shows
the opposing pressures on the formation of *European* and *African*, which include both a glorification of European technology and a critique of European behavior in Africa.

On the whole, the novel significantly alters the conditions of contact characteristic of contemporary eyewitness accounts. For instance, in the novel, European access to the coast and to the interior is largely unhampered by local challenges, and the bulk of the African interlude takes place in the interior—far from the main African-European trading centers; consequently, there is more scope for departure from contemporary reports of the west coast.[42] Given free access to the interior, what is discovered? Other than some generic changes in the terrain (a series of fertile river beds, deserts, vast lakes, and mountains), punctuated by running herds of elephants, fierce leopards, the de rigueur crocodile attack, and regular trading encounters, there is ivory—miles and miles of it—and gold. Defoe thus fuses the two main perceptions of the unknown interior common at the time: it is uninhabited, barren in parts (during a 1,000-mile stretch of desert, there are no inhabitants and the Europeans and their slaves nearly starve [105]), and it is a treasure chest. In the thousands of miles covered, there are no extensive trading towns, no mines, and no Africans in charge of the routes over which they travel. On Madagascar and the mainland, European authority is easily asserted over the land, climate, and people and is regularly achieved through the use of guns and through technological feats such as building ships, keeping meat from rotting, removing salt from seawater to provide drinkable water, and coercing natives to work either as slaves or for a pittance. The novel envisions an Africa emptied of a commercial infrastructure, including trading and communication networks. People are no longer serious obstacles either: in the novel, the challenge is European survival in a dangerous environment.

Apparently not in contact with their neighbors, the African inhabitants in *Captain Singleton* all live in primitive, isolated bunches with little discernible government. There are no challenging trade negotiations, and there is no question that the Europeans are in charge. Remarkably, wherever the Europeans discover ivory or gold, there are no inhabitants to contest their taking it. Several contemporary writers noted the unrealized potential of the African landscape. They attributed it to the alleged disregard Africans had for labor or for turning a profit because, they believed, the torrid zones enervated a people's industry; the climate also seemed to generate fruitful crops and trees more easily than in northern Europe. Whether it was hundreds of miles of untouched ivory tusks, rivers full of unmined gold ore, or fertile land aching to be tilled and sowed, many British men expressed more than a passing interest in realizing Africa's promise that the inhabitants had apparently neglected.[43] These speculations reflect contemporary interest in exploring the interior of Africa and what it could mean for increasing commerce, a desire finally realized in Mungo Park's 1795 journey to ascertain the direction in which the Niger flowed, under the auspices of the African Association formed in 1788. Willem Bosman, a Dutch agent in Africa, perhaps the most widely acknowledged European expert on Africa in the early eighteenth century, believed that the potential of the mainland interior to yield riches was unrealized by the inhabitants, and he arrived at a conclusion frequently repeated in other texts: "I doubt not but if this country belonged to the *Europeans*, they would soon find it to produce much richer Treasures than the *Negroes* obtain from it."[44] The novel proves over and over again the "truth" of Bosman's belief: Singleton and the Portuguese pirates repeatedly discover gold and ivory that the natives either do not know about or have no use for, scenarios that completely belie the extensive African trade in ore and the reputation of certain Africans for their artisan skills in jewelry and mask making. Ironically, Bosman and others who had long-term dealings with Africans frequently noted the agricultural abilities of certain groups, whom the British colonists particularly sought as prized slaves.

If Defoe's novel rehearses certain cultural fantasies of expanding the empire through plundering Africa and describing a continent ripe for English commercial development, the novel underestimates African people proportionately. Strangely, the many fictional trading encounters in *Captain Singleton* function as opportunities for emphasizing the primitive state of African society. Instead of a continent characterized by agriculturally based societies with extensive trading networks and frequent warfare (like contemporary Europe), Defoe offers a more primitive Africa composed of scantily clad cowherds, which places Africa among the barbaric stages of civilization and to which Europe's superior commercial aspirations are contrasted. Unlike the eyewitness accounts of Snelgrave, Atkins, and Moore, *Captain Singleton* creates the greatest sense of human difference around situations of trade and labor.

Many twentieth-century critics have emphasized the oddity of the novel's almost exclusive focus on trade, especially the Europeans' repeated acquisition of gold in the transcontinental journey. Historians have argued that the early eighteenth-century image of Africa and Africans was heavily influenced by the first European traders and colonizers, the Portuguese, and their fifteenth- and sixteenth-century accounts, which were still being reprinted in Britain.[45] These narratives focus less on the nature and description of the people than on (potential) trade relations. Before the Americas and the Caribbean had been partially settled and commercially exploited, Europeans "had seen African potential largely in terms of trade. Profits were made not by seizing the mineral resources of Africa but by invigorating existing African commercial systems" (4). The novel, it seems, is written in the spirit of sixteenth-century English commercial interests when "the English-men's principal interest lay not in obtaining servants for use back home but in training guides and interpreters for forthcoming expeditions."[46] In *Captain Singleton*, the appearance of this older understanding of trade with Africa underscores the desire to expand the nonslave trade even more.

Increasing commercial interest in the African interior is not the only function of the many trading encounters. Indeed, in *Ends of Empire* (1993), Laura Brown comments on Defoe's anachronistic glorification of the gold trade in the novel as obfuscating the trade in human beings dominant at this time.[47] *Captain Singleton* is placed in the 1690s; even by then, gold had become incidental to the slave trade, except in Sierra Leone.[48] Historically, the shift from the 1640s onward to sugar plantations in Barbados (and later in the century elsewhere in the Caribbean) led to England's greater participation in the slave trade and to more widespread interest in it. The Dutch West India Company dominated the transatlantic slave trade in the mid-seventeenth century; in 1660, Charles II granted a charter to the Company of Royal Adventurers, the predecessor of the Royal African Company. Its principal objective was to search for gold in Africa.[49] It was not until 1663 that the slave trade was first mentioned as an objective of the Company of Royal Adventurers.[50] Both entities were monopoly joint stock companies responsible for overseeing trade on the western coast of Africa. Laura Brown's argument that the novel's focus on gold obfuscates the actual trade in slaves possesses a good deal of explanatory power, yet Defoe, among others, was interested in increasing trade of all kinds with Africa. In fact, the discovery of gold was a desire present in contemporary French accounts, which speculated that enormous amounts of gold could be easily extracted by people with proper instruments and knowledge.[51] Knowledge, practice, and ideology were not well coordinated following the scramble to keep up with the colonists' demand for slaves, which resulted from the sugar boom in the West Indies.

Laura Brown also contends that Defoe's focus on trade helps define a peculiarly English notion of civility and superiority, a point which I develop below. Her related statement that "trade and money are the catalysts here, producing in the context of an assertion of racial superiority the text's *only* acknowledgment of racial difference" is, however, questionable (163–64, emphasis added). In the novel, one of the main ways of indicating the state of civilization of other people and conveying positive responses to them is through their willingness to trade with Europeans. Essentially, there is a geography of civility: all European writers about Africa concurred that coastal people who were engaged in trade were more civilized than the (un-

known) inland tribes. According to this standard, *Captain Singleton* represents inhabitants as "Barbarians" if they "will not allow any Trade or Commerce with any *European* Nation" (238). Indigenous people who refuse to
trade with the Europeans or fail to welcome their presence meet with similar treatment—casualties by the score (213). Through creating a periodic
sense of conflict in the pirates' encounters with unknown regions and people,
Defoe not only adds interest to the plot but also encodes resistance to European encroachments. The issue dramatized in *Captain Singleton* by Africans'
refusal to trade is native inhabitants who want the Europeans to leave and
the negative—often violent—European response to thwarted trade. Eyewitness accounts of Africa, in contrast, emphasize a healthy desire for exchange on both sides. In *Captain Singleton*, refusal to trade and underesti-
mating the value of goods underscore the savagery of unknown Africans in
the interior regions.

   The narrative treatment of different villages that Singleton and the Portuguese encounter in Madagascar and between modern-day Mozambique
and Angola may be gauged by their alacrity to trade and their ingenuity for
it. The northern people of Madagascar are considered "courteous" (37, 39);
Singleton's perception of Malagasy civility rests on their recognition that the
Europeans "were in Distress for want of Provisions" (37). In fact, civility
in Madagascar seems equivalent to cost-free supplies, not to trade, because
these people give the Europeans goats and steers and refuse to accept anything in return—a situation unparalleled in any other contemporary account.
Moreover, the northern people of Madagascar freely offer other food as well
as their labor to the Europeans: one scene describes a captain of the natives
"seeing some of our Men making up their Hutts, and that they did it but
bunglingly, he becken'd to some of his Men to go and help us. . . . They were
better Workmen than we were, for they run up three or four Hutts for us
in a Moment, and much handsomer done than ours" (38). At the other end
of the courtesy scale are the natives of southern Madagascar, who are perceived as civil only out of fear of the armed Europeans (14). They are worse
than the natives from other places: "scarce human, or capable of being made
sociable on any Account whatsoever" because initially they do not engage
in trade with the Europeans on European terms (21). Nevertheless, the narrative transforms these very same unsociable natives into "very civil" people
when later they bring food to Europeans and try to barter (22, 27). In these
examples, civility is determined through willing interaction and trade with
Europeans, yet civility also connotes shrewd trading, even boldness in a colonial context. For instance, in the novel, the Africans accustomed to European trade "were a more fierce and politick People than those we had met

with before; not so easily terrified with our Arms as those, and not so ignorant, as to give their Provisions and Corn for our little Toys. . . . But as they
had frequently traded and conversed with the *Europeans* on the Coast, or
with other Negro Nations that had traded and been concerned with them,
they were the less ignorant, and the less fearful, and consequently nothing
was to be had from them but by Exchange for such things as they liked"
(122). Europeans reaped less benefit from "Europeanized" Africans, even if
they admired them more for reflecting aspects of themselves that they prized
most.

   Although the common sense of Defoe's day was that Africans who
traded with Europeans were more civil because of that contact and the very
action of trading, the novel also offers an alternative interpretation of the
effect of European contact on Africans. Singleton observes that some Africans who have traded with Europeans have been cozened by them so that
they are hostile and corrupt, not civilized: "Those who had seen and traf-
ficked with the *Europeans,* such as *Dutch, English, Portuguese, Spaniards,* &c.
. . . had most of them been so ill used at some time or other, that they would
certainly put all the Spight they could upon us in meer Revenge" (108). There
are, in fact, three competing versions of African politeness represented in
the novel: contact with Europeans has rendered Africans more civil, but it
may exist at the cost of European economic domination; Africans' civility
signifies their lack of knowledge about trading and technology—the most
courteous and good-natured inhabitants are also the most ignorant of European exchange value; and European contact is pernicious, not beneficial to
either Africans or Britons.[52] Taken together, these examples suggest that as
much as Britons glorified the civilizing aspects of trade, trade was not always
beneficial to others in quite the way it was believed to be. These conflicting
versions of civility may result as much from real contradictions as from the
characterization of Singleton and the Portuguese as pirates. They were not
particularly educated nor were they devout Christians. Civility was understood to arise from Christian gentleman merchants interacting with each
other in designated trading areas, not from chance frontier encounters. Even
so, at moments like these in the novel, critique of dominant ideology is available though the presence of inconsistent statements.

   As I have intimated, it is not only trade per se that defines one people as
civil and others as barbarous; the trade must acknowledge a European concept of value. *Captain Singleton* emphasizes the great gains Europeans can
obtain for "Trifles"—that is, natives do not seem to share the same sense of
exchange value as Europeans. For example, the pirates, stranded in Madagascar, are embarrassed when the natives bring them food: "We were in the

utmost Confusion on our Side; for we had nothing to buy with, or exchange for; and as to giving us things for nothing, they had no Notion of that again. As to our Money, it was meer Trash to them, they had no Value for it. . . . Had we but some Toys and Trinckets, Brass Chains, Baubles, Glass Beads, or in a Word, the veriest Trifles . . . we might have bought Cattel and Provisions enough for an Army" (27). The cutler in their group spends a fortnight converting European coins into bracelets and necklaces of metal birds and beasts.[53] Singleton patronizingly observes that they "were surprized to see the Folly of the poor People. For a little Bit of Silver cut out in the Shape of a Bird, we had two Cows" (28). Similarly, he comments on the Madagascar natives who exchange fresh beef for dried beef, an exchange which, he believes, reveals their stupidity: "They were so pleased with it, and it was such a Dainty to them, that at any time after they would Trade with us for it, not knowing, or so much as imagining, what it was; so that for Ten or Twelve Pound Weight of smoked dry'd Beef, they would give us a whole Bullock" (38–39). The higher the stakes, the more gleeful Singleton is about the natives' alleged ignorance: "Our Artificer found a Way to make other People find us in Gold without our own Labour"; he "sold his Goods at a monstrous Rate; for he would get an Ounce of Gold, sometimes two, for a Bit of Silver, perhaps of the Value of a Groat, nay if it were Iron; and if it was of Gold, they would not give the more for it; and it was incredible almost to think what a Quantity of Gold he got that Way" (136).

Defoe's fictional rendition of trade belies the historical record. Iron "was a rare instance of a European import that could be put to productive use by Africans" because "it went into weapons and agricultural implements."[54] Since the 1680s, England had exported a large amount of iron to enhance trade in Upper Guinea (185). In addition, the novel offers only a one-way flow of gold—from Africans to Europeans. In fact, Europeans routinely traded in gold with local businessmen. John Atkins, for one, reported that to appease a lapse in payment for the ability to obtain water for English slave ships, the captain offered local potentate John Conny six ounces of gold and about eight imperial gallons of brandy.[55] In the examples from the novel that feature issues of value, two aspects of trade with Africa are erased routinely: the European labor that provides adornment or dried beef and African cultural dynamics that value local status display. The natives trade cattle for bracelets of carved animals or for dried beef, because they are already fulfilling basic needs that the Europeans are not. They trade foodstuffs for luxury items, especially ones with value-added European labor.[56]

As the scenarios cited above suggest, Defoe's picture of European trade with the Africans in the novel was not commensurate with knowledge about the Guinea trade. Africans are made to appear more childlike and ignorant than in most eyewitness accounts of trade with which Defoe was familiar. In fact, Europeans frequently complained of native hard bargaining and savvy business sense on the west coast.[57] Moreover, modern historians of the African trade have noted that the items of barter Defoe features were among the least desirable to Africans: "For both Europeans and Africans, the numerous items of trumpery were placed at the bottom of the scale of values. It was said in 1607 [in a travel account included in *Purchas his Pilgrimes*] that bells, garlic, and other 'trifles' and 'toyes' were by themselves incapable of purchasing anything but foodstuff."[58] All kinds of weapons were popular, and guns were among the most coveted items of trade in Africa. "Weapons stood at the other extreme from trinkets" (173): Africans demanded them, and some Europeans feared their passing into African hands. It was the Dutch, English, and French who introduced firearms in any quantity in the later seventeenth century.[59] Private traders and pirates were mainly responsible for selling heavy weapons to African rulers in the late seventeenth century; at that time, a trade in swords was more acceptable to other Europeans (174). Defoe, however, uses weapon technology as a major distinction between civil Britons and savage Africans. Such a large discrepancy in the novel's representation and the actual relations of trade also appears in Defoe's nonfiction about the African trade. While Defoe notes the putative ignorance of Africans who trade gold bullion for trinkets in his novel, he reveals the terms of trade by which many Europeans secured profits in his nonfiction. Because the Portuguese who first settled in Africa "found the Natives, Wild, Barbarous, Treacherous, and perfectly untractable as to Commerce, and therefore to maintain the Trade, which they found profitable, they made little Settlements there. . . . They found it at last necessary to fortify themselves, and maintain their Possession by force. . . . [This lesson has] taught us, *if we please to learn* this Maxim in the *African* Trade, that it is no way to be carried on but by Force; for a mere Correspondence with the Natives as Merchants, is as impracticable, as it would be if they were a Nation of Horses."[60] An intimate part of trade, violence secures profits and underwrites British civility. In *Captain Singleton*, the violence that energizes European masculine presence abroad fractures the distinction that civility is meant to confer.

*   *   *

Although the alacrity and ingenuity to trade was a significant economic and cultural phenomenon on which to base concepts of human difference, the novel establishes a sense of difference in other ways that hark back to knowledge commonly available in geographies and travel narratives. Nevertheless, Defoe scholars frequently have noted the difficulty of recovering much useful information in the novel about early eighteenth-century British views of Africans. For instance, one critic complains about the inscrutability of the text and paucity of real information about Africans in the novel: "They are, in fact, almost identical with the South American cannibals of *Robinson Crusoe* and the islanders of *A New Voyage*, and there is nothing here but the most superficial and elementary of pictures."[61] Laura Brown also subscribes to Defoe's generic depiction of Africans, but she places it in a racial context rather than an aesthetic one: "Because they are not seen as human, their difference, racial or otherwise, from the European adventurers is at first barely recognized" (162). Ironically, this superficiality produces apparent legibility: "Their characteristics are so repetitive that they are easily catalogued" (Scrimgeour, 26). While these observations correctly characterize the paucity of physical descriptions, they ignore other forms of racialization, including the many trading scenarios that offer a positive distinction from the cannibals in *Robinson Crusoe* who were so monstrous that Crusoe never envisioned any kind of commerce with them. It seems to me that the novel defeats the ease of decipherability other critics have maintained in regard to black Africans precisely because of the contradictions noticeable in the trading encounters enumerated above and in Defoe's use of the terms *savage*, *naked*, and *slave*.

Despite the frequent trading encounters in the novel, which offer an uneven sense of African civility, Africans' savagery and nakedness are their most frequently cited qualities. Unlike the Caribbean Indians in *Robinson Crusoe*, savagery does not signify cannibalism nor does it conjure up polygamy or fetish worship, as in other contemporary narratives of Africa. In the novel, *savage* refers less to real fierceness or hostility toward Europeans than to those who simply are not European. For example, *savage* applies equally to native people who are known and friendly as well as to those who are unknown and threatening. Compare the following statements about savages: "The second Journey he went, some more of our Men desired to go with him, and they made a Troop of ten white Men, and ten Savages" (134); and "At one of the Towns of these Savage Nations we were very friendly received by their King" (130). As the examples dramatize, there were two unequal categories of men: white ones and savage ones.[62]

Even for those early eighteenth-century writers who judged Africans most harshly, unqualified savagery was an ideological stretch to characterize their experiences of the inhabitants; however, the Englishmen who went to Africa at this time tended to work with two unequal categories of identity: white men, or Christians, and black men. These labels function similarly to Defoe's scheme of savage and nonsavage and with similar homogenizing effects. For instance, Snelgrave's *New Account of Guinea* illustrates the tendency to group people in white-and-black terms by his constant qualification of admiration for local leaders. The king of Dahomey's brother, he observes, is a "Person endowed with the most amiable qualities I ever met with amongst Persons of his Colour."[63] This reference to two unequal categories of men also appears in Bulfinch Lamb's comment about King Trudo Audati of Dahomey, with whom Snelgrave transacted business: " 'And though he seems to be a Man of great natural Parts and Sense as any of his Colour, yet he takes great Delight in trifling Toys and Whims.' "[64] For Britons on the colonial and imperial littorals, visual categories of identity often superseded religious and cultural ones in comparison with those who never left Britain.

That savagery had assumed a generic quality and that it was relatively free of color specificity is reflected in the characters' references in *Captain Singleton* to the inhabitants in Africa and Australia as "Indians," by which a savage is meant. Because *Indian* became a synonym for savage in the post-Columbus era of Caribbean and American colonization, the term was used in the eighteenth century to refer to any group of native peoples considered unpolished by European standards. Despite repeated narrative encounters that demonstrate the civility of Africans, they are persistently called "savages." Strangely, the Africans' reputation never matches the European characters' encounters with them. For example, upon first arriving on Madagascar, Singleton concedes the power of European hearsay about the torrid zones in constructing negative expectations of Africans: "At our first coming into the Island, we were terrified exceedingly with the Sight of the barbarous People; whose Figure was made more terrible to us than really it was, by the Report we had of them from the Seamen" (13–14).[65] Yet, on the continent of Africa, Singleton notes, "We had Nations of Savages to encounter with, barbarous and brutish to the last Degree" (48). None of these encounters proves this initial claim. In fact, the same disjunction is noticeable in the novel as it is in the eyewitness accounts. Smith, Snelgrave, and Atkins include references to African barbarity *and* numerous encounters and conversations that belie this received knowledge. Although the novel conjures up savagery to signify Africans, it does so neither with as many resources as it might have nor with much textual evidence. In fact, Scrimgeour remarks dryly that Defoe "does not exert himself to use what information was available."[66] While this fact may indeed reveal something about Defoe's imaginative process, it also points to the sense that a "realistic" narrative technique did not require a very detailed knowledge of Africans or much proof of their savagery. Despite repeated encounters that demonstrate the civility of Africans in *Captain Singleton*, conventions associated with trade did not triumph over previous frames of reference in the novel. Africans are civil when they trade with the Europeans, yet they remain savages because of their poor sense of value and their underclothed bodies.

Lack of clothing, rather than skin color or particular customs, tends to signify most strongly Africans' alleged savagery in the novel. Less clothing than Europeans and lack of an urban setting seem key factors in negative judgments. Tzvetan Todorov traces the generic quality created by lack of clothing to Columbus, who found the Caribbean Indians similar to each other because they wore few clothes and were thus bereft of class and cultural distinctions at the level of the body *that he recognized*.[67] When Europeans referred to other people's nudity, however, they usually meant partial covering, which signified at once a non-Christian (Adam and Eve had learned to hide "their shame" by clothing), a less civilized and more impoverished society, and occasionally a people who had a freer sexuality than Europeans, although this last construction usually relates to the hot climate. Contemporary narratives explain nakedness in a particular fashion. Most writers first claim that Africans are naked, then they qualify that statement by pointing out that only male and female torsos are bare. Finally, they all note when men and women are fully clothed—a sign of their high rank. The conventions of African society equated rank with the quantity and unusual colors/patterns of cloth, though on a rather different scale from the English. In fact, since the early seventeenth century, many African regions had imported cloth from Europe and exported textiles to Europe. On the Gold Coast, the average cloth consumption per year for a man was about three or four meters and for each female a bit more, a quantity that could hardly sustain the allegation of nakedness.[68]

Given this historical evidence of widespread conspicuous consumption in Africa, it comes as some surprise, then, that in the many encounters with interior people in *Captain Singleton*, the phrase "These People were all stark naked" appears over and over again (118).[69] Strangely, Defoe suggests by his use of the word *stark* that there is not even scanty covering. Despite this ubiquitous inaccuracy, the novel does not elaborate on nakedness as many contemporary travel narratives did, although it is frequently cited. The effect of African nakedness is to emphasize European superiority, especially their technological superiority over physical strength. Singleton's comment about confronting strange Africans dramatizes the gulf between nakedness and technological savvy:

Man & Woman of St. John's in their best Habits   *Man and Woman of the Island of St. John*

T. Kitchin sculp.

Figure 9. Man and Woman of St. John's, Cape Verde Islands. *A New General Collection of Voyages and Travels* (London, 1745). This double portrait of a couple in their best dress and in everyday wear supports the European belief that clothing should distinguish between men and women at a glance. In loin cloths, the distinction between the two is minimal because they both have muscled bodies and similar hair styles. Women's involvement in manual labor and their partially clothed bodies contributed to the maxim that there were slight differences between the genders in the ruder stages of society. When fully clothed, the woman's covered head and body distinguish her easily from her male counterpart. Courtesy of the John Carter Brown Library at Brown University.

We found them a fierce, barbarous, treacherous People, and who at first look'd upon us as Robbers, and gathered themselves in Numbers to attack us.

Our Men were terrified at them at first . . . and even our black Prince seemed in a great deal of Confusion: But I smiled at him, and shewing him some of our Guns I asked him, if he thought that which killed the spotted Cat . . . could not make a Thousand of those naked Creatures die at one Blow? (73)

As the narrative reveals, nakedness is not just a sign of cultural inferiority to Europeans; it has an important material aspect, too. Nakedness reduces Europeans' potential gain, especially for pirates in search of booty: "There was no great Spoil to be got, for they were all stark naked as they came into the World, Men and Women together; some of them having Feathers stuck in their Hair, and others a kind of Bracelets about their Necks, but nothing else" (77). The example suggests that little was to be gained from conquest in which land was not the objective and where the people possess little in the way of weaponry or personal adornment of value to Europeans. Rather than signifying a potential market for British woolens or India cloth (as, in fact, was the case), their nakedness represents a lack.[70] Such an absence from the depiction of Africans in *Captain Singleton* encourages an even greater sense of their distance from Europeans, since they seem to possess no other distinguishing cultural traits, religion, or history.

If nakedness most defines Africans, then clothing and a fortified body are most significant to demarcating Europeans. Like *Robinson Crusoe, Captain Singleton* intimates on several occasions that European appearance is frightful to Africans (46, 68). It is their association with violence, as much as their light skin color or beards, that usually frightens people: "They [Portuguese pirates] brought Word, that they had seen some of the Natives, who appeared very civil to them, but very shy and afraid, seeing their Guns; for it was easy to perceive, that the Natives knew what their Guns were, and what Use they were of" (22). There is also the sense in which this awful spectacle of Europeans laden with guns handily subdues resistance. Other people admire Europeans because of their guns and power to kill. After shooting at resistant natives, Singleton remarks about the significance of European technology to Africans' behavior: "Several of them [Africans], as they recovered themselves, came and worshipped us (taking us for Gods or Devils, I know not which, nor did it much matter to us)" (53). European masculine identity signifies most strongly through lethal weapons, an acknowledgment of the visible economy of violence that produces the European man in Africa.

Both Captain Singleton and Robinson Crusoe underestimate the technological capacity and scientific knowledge of Africans. This plot element corresponds to Michael Adas's conclusions in *Machines as the Measure of Man: Science, Technology, and Ideologies of Western Dominance* (1989). Adas contends that mastery of the natural world was increasingly important to European definitions of themselves during the eighteenth century. Nevertheless, most European travelers actually failed to grasp the extent of European technology or to weigh it more than differences in religion, dress, or facial features, particularly before the eighteenth century.[71]

Figure 10. Uzbek Tartars. *A New General Collection of Voyages and Travels* (London, 1745). Treated similarly to the Cape Verdean couple in figure 9, the Uzbek Tartars are both garbed in three-quarter-length robes. The distinction between the man and woman is in the greater amount of material in the woman's dress and in their head dresses; the mustache and weapon visibly masculinize the man. While their clothing suggests that they are from a civil society, the text claims that they live an idle life supported by robbery and plunder and that they have no arts and sciences. Courtesy of the John Carter Brown Library at Brown University.

Defoe's disregard for religion, dark color, and sexuality as ways to signify African savagery suggests a greater interest in the European adventure
story than in detailing Africans' otherness. Indeed, the virtual absence of
Christian references is noticeable, possibly because the main character is a
pirate. Christian religion is far less important in defining Europeans positively or other populations negatively than in other geographies or in other
narratives about Africa. Unlike most travelers to Africa who did remark
at length on the incomprehensibility of African religious practices, *Captain Singleton* refers to African religion only once (58). Significantly, Singleton's onetime meditation on his absolute difference from Africans converges
with his first religious sentiment. These two feelings occur at a moment of
supreme power over the Africans he has helped enslave. He promises the
African men that he will not kill them; on the contrary, he will feed them
and protect them from wild animals. The leader of the enslaved men, the
Black Prince, urges Singleton to clap his hands toward the sun to assure the
men of his benign intentions. The obedient response of the Africans to his
signal of fidelity leads him to reflect: "I think it was the first time in my Life
that ever any religious Thought affected me; but I could not refrain some
Reflections, and almost Tears, in considering how happy it was, that I was
not born among such Creatures as these, and was not so stupidly ignorant
and barbarous: But this soon went off again, and I was not troubled again
with any Qualms of that Sort for a long time after" (61). Singleton employs
religious feeling to distinguish himself from the Africans even as he imitates
their religious ceremony by clapping his hands toward the sun. Reflecting
the inseparability of Christianity and subordination, Singleton's most profound religious insight occurs at the moment when the Africans submit to
him. The only other moments in the novel when the category of *Christian*
obtains currency is when Singleton and his gang discover Europeans living
with non-Europeans; in these instances, the narrative evokes sympathy for
Europeans who are forced by circumstances into "going native" (158, 226).

From the beginning to the end of the African journey, the novel highlights European control and exploitation of African labor. The novel need
not depict plantation slavery or the slave trade to evoke an important definition of European men in an imperial landscape. One of the defining features
of European men in Africa or in the colonies, of course, is that they do not
perform manual labor despite their being pirates and of low rank. Instead,
they amass wealth through extracting surplus labor from Africans, and they
trade in attractively manufactured commodities, not raw materials. Niceties
about performing manual labor indicate a deeply ingrained prejudice most
closely associated with distinctions of rank in Great Britain; in Africa, Euro-

pean preconceptions about manual labor are easily adapted to racial distinctions, especially in regard to slaves.

Unlike *Robinson Crusoe*'s obsessive focus on the Caribs' cannibalism and paganism, *Captain Singleton*'s preoccupation is Africans' labor. Financial gain accrues because Europeans force Africans to work. For instance, a rescued Englishman, a few Portuguese pirates, and some helpful slaves take a side trip from the camp and bring back gold dust and "fifteen Ton of Elephants Teeth, which he [the Englishman] had, partly by good Usage, and partly by bad, obliged the Savages of the Country to fetch, and bring down to him from the Mountains, and which he made others bring with him quite down to our Camp" (133). In addition to deriving profits from forced African labor, Europeans discover that commanding subordinates' labor proves crucial to enhancing equality among themselves. Singleton encourages the other pirates to exploit the labor potential of slaves: "I offered it to them to consider whether it would not be the best Way for us, and to preserve the good Harmony and Friendship that had been always kept among us, and which was so absolutely necessary to our Safety, that what we found should be brought together to one common Stock, and be equally divided at last. . . . I told them, that if we were all upon one Bottom, we should all apply our selves heartily to the Work, and besides that, we might then set our Negroes all to Work for us, and receive equally the Fruit of their Labour" (94–95). Hoarding, chicanery, or any other antisocial behavior becomes unnecessary when slaves augment European wealth so significantly and eliminate their own menial labor. In the many instances of shared material benefits from coercing Africans to work, *Captain Singleton* shows the way that slave labor enhances European male sociability (in the colonies and imperial outposts especially).

The narrative emphasis on external markers of identity, such as wearing clothing, carrying guns, or performing certain kinds of labor, is as significant to a sense of colonial identities in formation as are the contradictions in the uses of *savage* and *naked*. A notion of identity expressed through one's accessories is at odds with another assumption fostered in the novel—that European masculine identity possesses a core that remains untouched by intensive commercial and colonial contact. The anxiety that Englishmen were tainted by contact with others was much more prevalent in descriptions of the English landowners in Ireland, the planters in the West Indies, and the behavior of settlers in the North American colonies than in narratives about the temporary contact with people in Africa, East India, and China. In Africa and other torrid zones, the debilitating effects of a warm climate—lack of industry and increased sexual desire—were also greatly feared as much as the influence of barbaric customs. Nevertheless, the popularity of captivity narratives suggests a widespread interest in gauging the resiliency of European identity. The obverse assumption, that Africans and other foreigners became more civil because they traded with Europeans, suggests a more malleable sense of the Other's identity than of Europeans'.

The double standard in notions of identity comes together in the character of an Englishman discovered deep in the African interior in *Captain Singleton*.[72] Although the narrative space that he occupies is relatively small, this Englishman commands a great deal of marketability. In fact, the title page features his story by highlighting Singleton's "meeting with an *Englishman*, a citizen of *London*, among the *Indians*." Paramount to this interlude is the contrast between civility and savagery. At the heart of the African overland journey, the Europeans rejoice at signs of a civil people: "We perceiv'd some Hutts of Negroes not many, and in a little low Spot of Ground some *Maise* or *Indian Corn* growing, which intimated presently to us, that there were some Inhabitants on that Side, less barbarous than what we had met with in other Places where we had been" (119). Agriculture distinguishes these people from other Africans, but the real reason for their superiority is soon revealed: An Englishman lives with them. In return for their receiving him cordially, he inserts them properly into the global economy. He teaches them "how to value the Product of their Labour, and on what Terms to trade with those Negroes who came up to them for Teeth [ivory]" (124).

Initially, however, Singleton is unsure about this European man's status because, although he is "a White Man," he is "stark naked" (120). Once Singleton discovers the white man is English, the doubt about his ambiguous status lessens, and he responds well to the naked Englishman. The description of his multicolored skin reflects the hybrid position he occupies at first: "He was a middle-aged Man . . . tho' his Beard was grown exceeding long, and the Hair of his Head and face strangely covered him to the Middle of his Back and Breast, he was white, and his Skin very fine, tho' discoloured and in some Places blistered and covered with a brown blackish Substance, scurfy, scaly, and hard which was the Effect of the scorching Heat of the Sun; he was stark naked, and had been so, as he told us, upwards of two Years" (121). Because he is an English gentleman, "naked" suggests vulnerability, not savagery, and despite the man's nude torso covered by the long hair on his head, Singleton observes, "He appeared to be a Gentleman, not an ordinary bred Fellow, Seaman, or labouring Man; this shewed it self in his Behaviour, in the first Moment of our conversing with him, and in spight of all the Disadvantages of his miserable Circumstance" (121). The mannered Englishman is absolved of responsibility for his "savage" appearance. Civil behavior is a code legible to and valued by Europeans, especially among themselves. The continued narrative emphasis on this man's behavior erodes the problem of his nudity and his "savage" physical appearance; the description of the naked Englishman demands the cover story of his manners. In fact, Singleton effuses, "We found his Behaviour the most courteous and endearing I ever saw in any Man whatever, and most evident Tokens of a mannerly well-bred Person, appeared in all things he did or said" (121–22). Defoe's other writings also feature this aspect of gentlemanly comportment; to Defoe, manners were the essence of a gentleman, not his birth or even his physical body.[73]

Reassuringly, the Englishman's identity is intact: no hybridity of behavior or appearance lingers. Singleton and the other Europeans transform the Englishman outwardly to match his behavior. They cut his hair, shave him, and clothe him; they also arm him to complete his transformation. In the quotations cited above, the rapid change from savage to civil relies on a notion of an unchanging core, which tends to belie a sense of change arising from climatic susceptibility or from exposure to savage ways. When the English merchant is clothed and armed, he leads the rest of the expedition and gains them all even greater riches by his "native" knowledge of gold and ivory—and by his ability to coerce Africans' labor. The gentleman is a citizen of London who had been a factor for the Royal African Company, but who had been ousted from his position by French rivalry for coastal hegemony in the slave trade. Unaided by his monopoly employers, the former factor turned separate trader and then finally traded only for himself, thus exhausting the gamut of British trading options in Africa—none of which prove safe or profitable. Eventually he ends up cohabiting with an inland tribe. The gentleman slave trader has no long-term success through legitimate commercial transactions. It is only through illegitimate, ad hoc exploitation of African land and labor that he reaps a profit, which is the same pattern that the pirate Singleton fulfills. Given Defoe's commitment to defending the Royal African Company in pamphlets, this picture of illegal success may very well be a veiled reproach to the English government for failing to back the Royal African Company as the legitimate vehicle of British imperialism.

*   *   *

Although references to savagery, nakedness, and manual labor are the central discursive indications of Africans' difference as the Europeans cross Africa and engage in trade, the focal point is not so much the unknown Africans encountered as much as the sixty men whom the pirates enslave. There are some significant narrative avoidances noticeable in the treatment of these slaves that suggest a discomfort with the dehumanizing aspects of bondage typical of slavery in the European colonies. One of the most noticeable narrative singularities is that neither *slave* nor *servant* is used in relation to the Africans who are forced to accompany the Europeans across the interior of Africa. The preferred reference to the Africans whom the pirates enslave is the political term of warfare, *prisoners*. Appearing insistently in the beginning of the journey across Africa, this denomination functions to legitimate the Europeans' enslaving Africans and suggests a temporary status rather than the permanent bondage customary in the colonies.[74]

Avoiding terms that signified forced labor for others and subordination to Europeans is strangely reinforced by the narrative refusal to connect English agency with the taking of slaves—an interesting effect since elsewhere in his writings Defoe shows no such reluctance.[75] In the novel, the first instance of disassociating agency from the slave trade translates European aggression immediately into native perfidy, which then justifies European armed defense—and the "happy" result of taking slaves legitimately. After Singleton's design to provoke a quarrel to take slaves as prisoners of war, a proposal rejected by the Portuguese, "the Natives soon gave them Reason to approve it" because they cheat in trade (51). There are two significant features of this scene of armed conflict between Africans and Europeans: Singleton's initial design for acquiring slaves is not approved by the Portuguese because there is no just cause for picking a fight with natives; second, the desire for getting "free" help with their baggage is rapidly fulfilled by rechanneling it and cathecting it to a legitimate cause: native treachery, not European aggression. After initial resistance, the African men willingly, even though handcuffed, aid the European enterprise (54). This scene simultaneously avows and disavows the deliberate warfare by which most slaves were obtained, which was sometimes fomented indirectly by European trade. In terms of British commercial desires, Defoe replaces Africans who procure slaves for trade on the coasts with Singleton and the Portuguese; the narrative envisions Europeans in charge of transporting slaves from inland regions and selling them at the coast. In the novel, then, Europeans gain limited control over the supply of slaves. The novel presents both the originary scenario of violent European desires for procuring African labor by any means available and its cover story: the methods of obtaining slaves are sanctioned by the law of nations, and the slaves' attitude toward labor is not resistant.

In another case of disassociating European agency from the slave trade, the novel depicts Singleton and the other pirates literally running into a ship full of slaves with no European masters. The question raised by this freak accident is not whether to free them but which nation to sell them to (164). Enormous profits from illegal sales of slaves to the Portuguese in Brazil accrue in the same way profits from gold accrue in Africa: the land and sea simply offer up bounty for the taking. There is no little irony in Singleton finding a ship of slaves, because Defoe proved absolutely committed in his *Review* to arguing on behalf of the Royal African Company as the most reliable provider of slaves to the European plantations. Despite Defoe's belief in the benefits of a slave-trade monopoly to the nation, interlopers or private traders (sometimes equated with pirates in the early eighteenth century) were the means by which Britain "developed and eventually dominated the slave trade."[76] As all of these examples reveal, there are considerable narrative acrobatics that make exploitation appear more legitimate than convenient to the Europeans; they demonstrate a certain cultural anxiety about equating humans with commodities.

In this vein, the chief African character is a particularly interesting illustration of this uneasiness. The leader of the sixty African men whom the Europeans temporarily enslave to carry their provisions and booty is a character called the Black Prince. Laura Brown notes the resemblance between the Black Prince and Aphra Behn's Oroonoko.[77] Although they are both Europeanized to signal their exceptional status, they are not Europeanized in the same way: they both are assigned illustrious lineages, but the Black Prince is not given European facial features, as Oroonoko is to emphasize his heroic stature.

When the Black Prince is first introduced, the narrative positions him midway between the Europeans and other Africans. Because of his high status with his countrymen, Singleton makes use of him as an overseer and mediator: "There was among the Prisoners one tall, well-shap'd handsom Fellow, to whom the rest seem'd to pay great Respect, and who, as we understood afterwards, was the Son of one of their Kings. . . . As I found the Man had some Respect shew'd him, it presently occured [*sic*] to my Thoughts, that we might bring him to be useful to us, and perhaps make him a kind of Commander over them." (57) The Prince's difference from the other Africans, which is based on his distinguished birth, is marked by the Europeans' different labor expectations for him. The Prince relays his men's needs to the Europeans and vice versa: he is the conduit for maintaining stable power relations, which translates in narrative terms as their willing subordination to the Europeans (60, 65). Singleton's willingness to upgrade the Prince's status from a common laborer is based on the prospect of gain and the same *je ne sais quoi* that Crusoe detected in Friday, or what Singleton perceives as "evident signs of an honourable just Principle in him" (62). Distinguishing the Prince, however, follows a pattern typical of plantation management, not of European brotherhood. The Prince's position is similar to the slave driver in the colonies. A slave's status improved through rewards of better and more clothes, food, and lodging for being an overseer.[78] It is this position of overseer, rather than any kind of "whitening" or European facial features, that marks the Prince's difference from his fellow Africans. Although it is tempting to attribute the Prince's narrative position to European recognition of individual merit or of honoring local hierarchies of rank, the novel emphasizes the expediency of exploiting local power relations to ensure cooperation in gaining profit.

Despite the noticeable cross-fertilization between slaves and Africans embodied in the depiction of the Prince, he is both obedient and manly and comparable to a Christian in his behavior: "Never was [a] Christian more punctual to an Oath, than he was to this, for he was a sworn Servant to us for many a weary Month after. . . . I took a great deal of Pains to acquaint this Negroe what we intended to do, and what Use we intended to make of his Men; and particularly, to teach him the Meaning of what we said . . . and he was very willing and apt to learn any thing I taught him" (58–59). Similar to Friday's position in *Robinson Crusoe*, the Prince's masculinity is not threatening because it is underwritten by his ready subordination: "He made great Signs of Fidelity, and with his own Hands tied a Rope about his Neck, offering me one End of it" (61). The fictional Prince and Friday are, however, quite unlike the men with whom Snelgrave, Atkins, and Moore interact—whose empowerment posed danger to Englishmen.

Although there are many signs of the Prince's similarity to Europeans, occasionally the narrative reminds us of his kinship to the other slaves. Unlike Oroonoko, who is forced to embody his rebelliousness through castration and dismemberment at the end of Behn's novella, the Prince in *Captain Singleton* is linked to his men in ways that conjure up European technological and intellectual superiority. Weaponry provides the occasion for demonstrating the way that the Prince is similar to the other slaves, yet also different. For instance, before Singleton shoots a gun, he informs the Prince: "Tell your Men not to be afraid. . . . The poor Negroes looked as if they had been all going to be killed, notwithstanding what their Prince said to them. . . . Four or five of them fell down as if they had been shot. . . . We made Signs to their Prince to encourage them, which he did, but it was with much ado that he brought them to their Sense; nay, the Prince, notwithstanding all that was said to prepare him for it, yet when the Piece went off, he gave a Start as if he would have leap'd into the River" (65–66). The narrative emphasis on technology, especially weaponry, secures European supremacy over African men and reminds readers of the violence underwriting European masculinity in imperial and colonial landscapes.

One of the most striking ways that the Europeans distinguish the Prince is their consideration of him as an agent worthy of autonomy. At the end of the African journey, the Prince's fate differs from many of the others: "The *Negro Prince* we made perfectly free, clothed him out of our common Stock, and gave him a Pound and a half of Gold for himself, which he knew very well how to manage" (137). He is literally valued at a little less than half a European, all of whom receive four pounds of gold! (Previously, when the Europeans had been rewarded with three and a half pounds of gold, the Prince received one pound [97].) European clothing, understanding the value of gold, and freedom of movement define both Europeans and, to a lesser extent, the Prince. The nameless other African men do not fare as well as the Prince. Singleton mentions in passing that at the end of the journey, some "of our Negroes as we thought fit to keep with us" continued with them as subordinates; in fact, Singleton takes two African men with him—whether to Cape Coast Castle or to England is not made clear (137).[79]

At first glance, Singleton's callous disregard for the laboring Negroes seems at odds with the pains taken to reward the Prince. This split in the Europeans' behavior, however, arises from common distinctions fostered by trade and explains the representation of two "types" of Africans, also evident in *Oroonoko* and in narratives by Atkins and Snelgrave; the enslavement of a vast majority and the dealings with middlemen and local powers as near equals. This second group was assimilated into European consciousness chiefly by means of domestic paradigms of station, masculinity, and manners. As the representation of the Prince dramatizes by contrast, the novel relies on treating a majority of Africans as faceless masses who labor—not because they are pagans, black-complected, or lacking in the advantages derived from developing the arts and letters, but because doing so benefits Europeans.

The ideology of race as we are familiar with it today does not excuse European aggression in the novel or indeed in most publications of the 1720s and 1730s; on the contrary, aggression is a manly part of consolidating imperial power, even though it seems at odds with the concept of civility that was so important to English identity. At this time, there was little need to justify slavery by reference to African cultural inferiority or to their physical appearance because advantageous trade was a sufficient rationale; there was also no systematic way to justify slavery through specifically racial ideology because it was still in formation. None of this means, however, that European exploitation of Africa was not mediated and palliated through narratives such as *Captain Singleton*, through its characterization of legitimate slavery and of beneficial commercial contact, or through the representation of Africans' failure to maximize their land's potential. In early eighteenth-century accounts, the preferred British justifications for enslaving Africans centered not on ideas about physical inferiority but on African overpopulation of their continent, their historic practice of enslaving prisoners of war, and the usefulness of slaves to British sugar plantations.[80] Indeed, in *A Voyage to Guinea*, John Atkins mentions typical justifications of the slave trade: Some people claimed that British slavery ameliorated Africans' living conditions and attended to their spiritual welfare (the last point he dismisses as ludicrous). Atkins concedes that by European standards, it is easy to deduce that Africans live a "very poor and mean" existence, but they do not starve and, he contends, they should not be taken from their homes (177–78). Thus, other than enumerating the economic benefits to themselves, Britons primarily justify slavery in cultural terms during the first half of the century.

Reading British narratives to Africa in conjunction with *Captain Singleton* allows present-day readers to fathom the particular shape of colonial and racial ideology at this time. The representation of European and African contact is asymmetrical: if the "prisoners" cheerfully work for the Europeans, they have been subdued by guns, slaughter of their countrymen, and then tied together to prevent escape. Even though in *Captain Singleton*, slavery was not justified through physical typology, it is justified through narrative acrobatics to make exploitation appear more legitimate than convenient to the Europeans. *Captain Singleton* thereby reveals, even as it disavows, the structures of power that promote selective representations of European-African contact.

*   *   *

While previous sections of this chapter have demonstrated that the representation of African men is intimately connected to the validation of European masculinity, this final section examines how this masculinity secures itself through the desire for non-European, but chiefly African, women. In an imperial context, a European masculinity is also constructed through sexual contact with Other women and the inscription of power relations on their bodies as they become commodified, usually in exchanges between men. Emergent racial ideologies discernible in *Captain Singleton* do not veil European violence and power; on the contrary, European men are always represented as the aggressor in the novel, and constructions of Europeans and Africans rely on such distinctions.

The representation of native women symptomatically appears in scenes of trading and accumulating wealth. While *Captain Singleton* and *Robinson Crusoe* leave readers with the notion that the acquisition of wealth is a man's business, the early travel narratives to Africa offer a different picture. Women appear there as willing sexual partners for white men and as signs of African men's status when they are one of numerous wives or concubines. Chiefly, however, contemporary writers mention women as the primary laborers in Africa. One of the few visions that Atkins and Snelgrave agree on is the excessive luxury debilitating the king of Whidaw, the loser to the king of Dahomey in local warfare. The numerous women always mentioned in conjunction with him function as a sign of his corruption and weakness, not as a marker of his power: Whidaw is "indolent and lascivious, having in his Court several thousands of Women, by whom he was served in all capacities. . . . Being thus soften'd by his Pleasures, he grew intirely negligent of his Affairs."[81] From William Snelgrave's narrative to Mungo Park's at the end of the century, African women play momentarily significant parts in their accounts. Sometimes the encounter between Englishmen and African women positions the narrator as the African woman's savior. For example, Snelgrave reunites a child destined to be sacrificed by a chief man with its enslaved mother. Other times, African women are used to satirize European women. William Smith's *New Voyage to Guinea* (1744) includes a lengthy scene in which he is given a woman to enjoy temporarily by a local potentate, and he becomes her lover despite his distaste for her color.[82] In the suspiciously stylized encounter reported by William Smith, the function of the African woman is to smooth relations between himself and the local leader — to facilitate an interracial male bond. Smith's account of his experience of being given a woman as a temporary gift wavers between concern about the woman's color and a desire to use the situation, especially her "natural" manners, to critique European mores. He writes about the physical appearance of the woman: "She made methought no despicable Figure, and though she was black, that was amply recompenc'd by the Softness of her Skin, the beautiful Proportion and exact Symmetry of each Part of her Body, and the natural, pleasant and inartificial Method of her Behaviour" (253). Although the end of the interlude is tinged with regret because her dark color mitigates her considerable accomplishments and Smith's desire, the goodwill she has produced between the men is infinite: "She seem'd to be a Woman of a good natural Judgment, and I took great Delight in her Conversation, and had she been White, I should have begg'd her of the King" (257). Smith's response to the African woman reinforces the dynamic detectable in the two unequal categories of men mentioned in the travel narratives—white ones and black ones.

Just as critics have long written about *Robinson Crusoe* without commenting on the Indian women who figure belatedly in the novel as the means by which Crusoe's colony flourishes in his absence, the African women who appear in *Captain Singleton* have received scant mention.[83] And little surprise: They are as incidental to the masculine adventure story of crossing Africa as they are to the piracy segment of the novel. The novel depicts cooperative inter-European and interracial relations among men, which in turn produce the basis of successful imperial relations. This fantasy of an all-male world—or at least one where white men return to Europe—reveals the traces of desire for clear-cut boundaries, boundaries impossible to maintain with the common practice in the African trading zones of interracial sexual and marital relations. Moreover, British men negotiated sexual relations with native women variously: Some married sisters or daughters of local potentates, and some lived with slaves and later freed their partners, educated their mulatto children, or gave them personal fortunes; others did not.

In the following incidents of interracial sexual contact in *Captain Singleton*, native women either facilitate relations between European men or rupture a peaceful coexistence between white and black men (a powerful European myth belying their intervention in Africa). In each case, the relations between men are emphasized rather than those between European men and African women. In the first instance, the novel is coyly silent about what happens—whether it is rape or consensual sex, although the resolution is mediated through the English gentleman with a hefty compensation to a local man, which indicates European use of force: "Here we stay'd thirteen Days more, in which time we had many pleasant Adventures with the Savages, too long to mention here, and some of them too homely to tell off;[84] for some of our Men had made something free with their Women, which, had not our new Guide [the Englishman] made Peace for us with one of their Men, at the Price of seven fine Bits of Silver, which our Artificer had cut out into the Shapes of Lions, and Fishes, and Birds, and had punch'd Holes to hang them up by (an inestimable Treasure!) we must have gone to War with them and all their People" (130). This crucial transaction prevents slaughter and preserves the pirates' stockpile of gold, which provided the original occasion for the sexual encounters.

A similar encounter occurs in Sri Lanka, and the narrative tone is tolerant, even indulgent, toward the violations (i.e., it exemplifies a "boys will be boys" attitude). In this instance, the interracial conflict between men is not resolved through the provision of compensatory commodities but through violence: "We had a little Skirmish on Shore here with some of the People of the Island, some of our Men having been a little too familiar with the *Homely Ladies* of the Country; for Homely indeed they were, to such a Degree, that if our Men had not had good Stomachs that Way, they would scarce have touch'd any of them" (218). European men's sexual violation is mitigated by the women's putative appearance and is immediately recuperated into interracial male violence: the pirates' unnamed, transgressive actions provoke warfare. When Singleton narrates his own innocence, he offers a more restrained version of colonial masculinity that sets him apart from the Portuguese pirates: "I could never fully get it out of our Men what they did, they were so true to one another in their Wickedness; but I understood in the main, that it was some barbarous thing they had done, and that they had like to have paid dear for it; for the Men resented it to the last Degree, and gathered in such Numbers about them" (218). The argument that deters the pirates from slaughtering more than the seventy men they already had is that murder diverts from their quest for wealth (219). But there is another compelling argument: the Sri Lankan men were acting as they ought because they resented European aggression against their women. Singleton's cohort, the English Quaker William, pacifies the pirates by reminding them that it was natural for men to vindicate the abused women: "He convinc'd them that . . . the Men had a Right to their own, and that they had no Right to take them away: That it was destroying innocent Men, who acted no otherwise than as the Laws of Nature dictated" (219). Notably, Singleton, like Crusoe before him, refrains from sex with native women. Unlike most of his fictional and actual counterparts, Singleton finds native women in Ceylon and Africa too unattractive to pursue. Another way to account for his and Crusoe's prolonged celibacy is the leadership position that the two men occupy; sexual restraint distinguishes the upwardly mobile, self-fashioning Protestant leader from his Catholic cohorts. A final possibility is, of course, suggested by critics such as Hans Turley and B. R. Burg, who contend that the homoeroticism of pirates offers an alternative to heteronormative characters and plot trajectories.[85]

Another example of interracial sex from the novel demonstrates the way that controlling slave women's bodies encourages friendly trading relations among European men. An African woman is used to cement a friendship between European men of different nations in their commercial transaction. When William the Quaker seeks to sell slaves to the Portuguese in Brazil, he initially contacts only one planter with whom he becomes so cordial that, in return for provisions and a night's dining, William wishes to match the civility, "and he invited the Planter on board his Ship, and in Return for his Kindness, gave him a Negroe Girl for his Wife" (166). Here, the African woman facilitates cordial relations between European men; she is a "gift" that establishes goodwill for the trading of other slaves. The narrative notes, "This [gift] so obliged the Planter" that he sends generous amounts of fresh provisions in return (166). With so much goodwill flowing between them, William soon sells him thirty slaves. The feminist philosopher Luce Irigaray proves helpful to elucidating the way that women's treatment as commodities facilitates relations between men: "She has functioned as merchandise, a commodity passing from one owner to another, from one consumer to another, a possible currency of exchange between one and the other."[86] This observation assumes an even more trenchant critique of women's position in patriarchy when the subject is a slave woman. In the first example of interracial sexual contact that I cited from *Captain Singleton*, neither the woman nor her sexual services initially function as a commodity exchanged between African and European men, but they become commodified as the price of peace is negotiated. In the last example, the African woman is a commodity from the beginning because of her slave status; she further becomes a sign of a European male bond and the embodiment of the promise to exchange the other goods. Thus, while the African woman's sexual services have a certain use value in the first example for Europeans, they become exchange value through the appeasing gift of silver animals; in the second case, because the woman is a "gift," she is already assigned a value based on her reproductive and sexual person as well as on her laboring potential as a slave woman.

The last instance of interracial sexual contact in the novel occurs on a slave ship and represents the most violent aspect of commerce: a seaman rapes two slave women. This encounter is most explicitly about European men's exploitative power, yet the novel dwells more on the Europeans' brave defense of the ship, when the Africans take over after the rapes, than on the scene of sexual violence itself. In this case, a white man's forcible sex with two African women defines at once their disempowerment through their status and gender and the husband/father's different kind of powerlessness. The novel reports the conversation between Singleton and an African on the slave ship:

Then he told us, that the white Men used them barbarously; that they beat them unmercifully; that one of the Negroe Men had a Wife, and two Negroe Children, one a Daughter about sixteen Years old; that a White Man abused the Negroe Man's Wife, and afterwards his Daughter, which as he said, made all the Negroe Men mad; and that the Woman's Husband was in a great Rage, at which the White Man was so provoked, that he threaten'd to kill him; but in the Night, the Negroe Man being loose, got a great Club, . . . and that when the same *Frenchman* (*if it was a* Frenchman) came among them again, he began to abuse the Negroe Man's Wife; at which the Negroe taking up the Handspike, knock'd his Brains out. (161–62)

This incident raises several issues about the split between Africans and slaves and the liminal space of ships. Unlike the Sri Lankan men who were naturally resentful of Europeans violating their women and who were entitled by the laws of nature to attack the Europeans for their transgressions, these men do not have that right by virtue of their slave status and because they are not on their home territory. In fact, an earlier scene in Africa in which the Europeans instruct the sixty slaves in the law of arms suggests that all Africans lack this basic European knowledge of rightful aggression (69).

All of these examples of interracial sexual contact center on the way that African women either foster violence between African and European men or prevent it between Europeans in a colonial landscape. Unlike Englishwomen who are largely absent from both novels and travel narratives about Africa (until they write their own at the end of the century), African women punctuate scenes of trade and are valued similarly to the trade for provisions: European men desire free access to such a market. African women did, in fact, often serve the function of cementing civil exchanges and keeping open certain trade regions. As the next chapter shows, Englishwomen may have been key to fostering Englishmen's polished manners by conversing with them in a domestic context, but Other women, who are outside the domestic space, underwrite the trade which was the cornerstone of civility and profits. Examining the novel's connection of interracial sexual relations to violence (its threat or realization) suggests a more critical way to interpret emergent racial ideology.

The representation of native women in *Captain Singleton* offers a critical view of European men, but both Singleton and Crusoe return from accumulating wealth abroad and marry an Englishwoman. It is significant that in both novels the Englishwomen appear only at the end of the novel, both as a reward for the hero and as a recipient of colonial or imperial profit, a phenomenon Jonathan Swift lampoons in the final pages of *Gulliver's Travels* (1729). The domestic Englishwoman is important as the primary beneficiary of the plunder. Singleton reports, "I pitch'd thus upon *William's* Sister . . . [as] the Object of my first Bounty" (276). The generosity of Singleton and his partner in piracy, William the Quaker, make it possible for William's sister to ascend into a higher rank: Their money allows her to close her business as a London shopkeeper and to become a property owner in a nearby village. Without her, Singleton would be unable to enjoy his wealth without guilt and would have no reason to feel allegiance to one country more than another: "I did not doubt but I should purchase something of a Refuge for my self, and a kind of a Centre, to which I should tend in my future Actions; for really a Man that has a Subsistence, and no Residence, no Place that has a Magnetick Influence upon his Affections, is in one of the most odd uneasy Conditions in the World" (276). The Englishwoman fixes Singleton's wanderlust and puts it to good use for the nation. Through her, the domestic economy reaps the profits plundered from abroad. Defoe and some of his contemporaries who wrote about the benefits of the slave trade in nonfictional paeans to commerce saw women's dietary and clothing fashions as intimately linked to the profits of forced labor and, in fact, used the one to legitimate the other: "Those who know how far our Plantation Trade is Blended and interwoven with the Trade to *Africa*, and that they can no more be parted than the Child and the Nurse, need have no time spent to convince them of this; The Case is as plain as Cause and Consequence: Mark the Climax. *No African* Trade, *no* Negroes *no* Negroes; *no* Sugars, Gingers, Indicos, &c. *no* Sugars, &c. *no* Islands; *no* Islands, *no* Continent; *no* Continent, *no* Trade; that is to say, farewel [*sic*] all your *American* Trade, your *West-India* Trade."[87]

Hazel Carby has analyzed the widespread domestic rewards of colonialism for Englishwomen in the historical past. In this way, she emphasizes that colonialism was not simply the all-male enterprise that prevails in Defoe's novels. Moreover, she links the benefits of slavery to the domestic scene in Britain: "The benefits of a white skin did not just apply to a handful of cotton, tea or sugar plantation mistresses; all women in Britain benefited—in varying degrees—from the economic exploitation of the colonies."[88] It is possible that Carby overestimates colonialism's payoff for most women of the laboring classes, especially the marginal position of female laborers in the expanding woolen (and later cotton) industries. Her analysis focuses more on women of the middling and upper ranks, whose domestic exploitation of laboring poor women tends to be eliminated. In this sense, Carby rewrites colonial ideology similarly to Defoe. Nonetheless, her attempt in the present to make visible European women's domestic participation in colonial oppression responds to narratives such as Defoe's which promote the ideological separation of European women from the benefits of empire. Although the Englishwoman as wife and consumer is neatly included into the colonial circuit on the receiving end in *Captain Singleton*, the return to England in the novel and in narratives of African voyages cleanly separates Englishwomen from all others geographically and narratively, seeming to erase any connection between them and the women who hunt for gold in Africa to trade for trinkets, the mother and daughter who are raped on a slave ship, or the female slave who is given as a present from one white man to another. In this way, the racialization of laboring and merchant British men and the people they encounter abroad occurs under different conditions and at a different pace than their female counterparts.

In analyzing how *Captain Singleton* and other narratives of the early eighteenth century create a visible economy of difference for European and African men that does not rely primarily on differences of color or bodily features, but on ideas about commercial behavior, clothing, and manual labor, I have argued that African slavery in the Americas did not elicit an ideology of race commensurate to Britain's involvement and profits in the slave trade at this time, although its nascent traces appear in some of the narratives examined here. In highlighting the role of violence (threatened or enacted) in securing European dominance and its palpable presence in underwriting imperial relations of trade and labor in *Captain Singleton*, I have suggested that the contemporary ideology of civility masked the global inequities that it relied on. I have also argued implicitly that the novel represents a picture of Africa that dovetails with contemporary British commercial desires, although it disregards the actual conditions of trade in Africa. Defoe's novel transforms Africa into a land that provides the raw materials (gold, ivory, and food) and labor power for European profits; its place in an increasingly global economy is not as a nation of consumers or of manufacturers, but as a nation that does not value consumption, an historical construction with important colonial ramifications, which are explored in Chapters 4 and 5. The repeated scenes of asymmetrical trading, the many references to Africans' lack of clothing, and the negligible spoils for Europeans from conflict all align Africa on a dangerous side of the imperial dynamic. Thus, in *Captain Singleton*, Africa and its peoples fit into the emerging empire as resources for European exploitation secured by superior technology and trading acumen.

Chapter 3

Romanticizing Racial Difference

Benevolent Subordination and the Midcentury Novel

[A] man ennobles the woman he takes, be she *who* she will; and adopts her into his own rank, be it *what* it will: but a woman, though ever so nobly born, debases herself by a mean marriage, and descends from her *own* rank, to that of him she stoops to marry.

—SAMUEL RICHARDSON, *Pamela* (1740)

Where there is no *Legal* Impediment, we find that differences of Nation—Religion, or even Color, cannot prevent People from marrying amongst each other.

—BENJAMIN RUSH, *A Vindication of the Address to the Inhabitants of the British Settlements, on the Slavery of the Negroes in America* (1773)

↳ most important Date

DEFOE's *Robinson Crusoe* and *Captain Singleton*, as well as many other early eighteenth-century narratives, punctuate their tales of colonial encounters and imperial adventure with interracial sex. The numerous sexual liaisons between European men and Other women allow us to see it as constitutive of European masculinity in forging an empire. To be sure, interracial sex is an unsurprising by-product of the colonial enterprise or vast networks of trade. Reproduction is absolutely necessary to the project of colonization. In the final pages of *Robinson Crusoe*, for example, Crusoe records the fate of his new colony. The Europeans, he tells us, invade the mainland to capture slaves and sexual partners in order to expand the settlement. In his own provisions for the island, he sends a variety of supplies from Brazil, including native women, and for the Englishmen he promises "to send them some women from England, with a good cargoe of necessaries."[2] The casual juxtaposition of sending goods and women, of kidnapping a subjugated workforce and securing women, all as necessary to the future of the colony, suggests the importance of reproduction (in both senses) to the continuation of the colonial settlement. This unsentimental treatment provides a startling contrast to the novels that I examine in this chapter, which focus on marriage between Englishmen and Other women rather than on casual or violent sexual relations.[3]

Popular assumptions about skin color and other distinctions commonly surface in tales of interracial sex and romance, not as a central preoccupation but as an indication of the ideological limits Britons accorded racial differences. Sexual relations between Englishmen and non-Europeans had long fascinated consumers of literary and travel narratives, but what distinguishes midcentury novels from earlier narratives like Henry Neville's *Isle of Pines* (1668) or "Inkle and Yarico" are the organizing tropes of Christian conversion and romantic love. Although Daniel Defoe's novels, for instance, point to the importance of Christianity as a defining feature of European men engaged in colonial exploitation, intermarriage novels suggest its significance in legitimating interracial desire for domestic British consumption. In midcentury, Europeans tend to find dark skin color initially unsettling but surmountable through the power of love and through Christian conversion, which proves necessary to happily resolving all intermarriage plots. Religious education is the main process of acculturation for the fictional Other, which marks the acceptance of these characters at once into the marital bond and English society. When dark color and religious dissimilarity are conjured up as temporary barriers rather than permanent impediments to marriage with non-Europeans, the ideology of race reveals its emergent rather than developed character.

By analyzing fictional representations of interracial desire that span the midcentury, I show that imaginative visions of human difference correspond to colonial practices or scientific inquiry only obliquely. Because midcentury intermarriage novels bear traces of older racial ideology, based chiefly on religious difference, and a newer concern with skin color, they capture ideology in transition by juxtaposing two distinct ideas about race. Midcentury novels demonstrate that even though racial ideology was based on a superficial conception of human variety, it worked in at least two registers that could be at odds with each other. The concern with dark complexion that momentarily surfaces in these narratives signals a notion of human variety that is visible on the body, a view that contrasts with a concept of difference that is defined by cultural practices, such as religion. Ideologically, then, it was still possible for the British to subordinate dark skin color to high rank and the profession of Christianity in relation to some populations. The way that midcentury novels resolve this sometimes awkward exceptionality was either not to assign characters from other climates darker complexions, to erase the significance of nonwhite color through Christian conversion, or to show that what was believed to be actual color difference was really racial masquerade. These narrative strategies reconcile a superficial perception of human variety with a discomfort about color difference.

*   *   *

The British avidly read intermarriage novels, including William Chetwood's *Voyages, Travels, and Adventures of William Owen Gwin Vaughan Esq., with the History of his Brother Jonathan Vaughan, Six Years a Slave in Tunis* (1736), James Annesley's *Memoirs of an Unfortunate Nobleman, Return'd from a Thirteen Years Slavery in America* (1743), *The Lady's Drawing Room* (1744), *The History of Cleanthes, An Englishman of the Highest Quality, and Celemene, the Amazonian Princess* (1757), *Memoirs of the Remarkable Life of Mr. Charles Brachy* (1767), Henry Brooke's *Fool of Quality* (1767–70), and *The Female American; or, the Extraordinary Adventures of Unca Eliza Winkfield* (1767). Little known today, these novels were a literary phenomenon of the midcentury. Attracting a considerable readership, they were all reprinted at least twice, many of them three or four times, a fact that made for a significant readership.[4] Part of their appeal derived from the favorable way that they presented Englishmen abroad and from the flattering picture of England as the seat of tolerance. Nonetheless, the narrative desire underwriting the intermarriage novels is to erase divisions, not to establish them. Unlike actual colonial and imperial relations, these narratives happily resolve religious conflict and dissimilar complexions through conversion and marriage. While these novels did not encourage readers to think of race as deterministic, they did promote highly selective versions of encounters with Others that "whitewashed" the imperial enterprise, especially in regard to Native Americans.

As Nancy Armstrong, Jane Spencer, James Thompson, and Janet Todd have observed, conflicts over the social and economic aspects of marriage and courtship are vital to understanding the midcentury novel. Intermarriage novels participate in the plot constructions and characterizations of their more famous counterparts and unite typical interests of the early novel: courtship; the vogue for Oriental romance and other exotic tales, which often feature female virtue in distress; and voyage and adventure tales, a trend "fostered by a growing English spirit of commercial and colonial imperialism."[5] There is an even older literary tradition, however, that also helps explain the proliferation of stories about Christian conversion. As Jennifer Goodman shows, two of the most popular plots in medieval literature involve religious intermarriage: the one depicts a Christian lady marrying a pagan king and persuading him to accept her faith (usually in response to a child's birth) and a Saracen (Muslim) princess or Amazon queen converting in order to win the love of a Christian knight. Eighteenth-century intermarriage novels are indebted to both plots, but they tend to favor the second story line. Both narrative structures, however, "celebrate intermarriage as a means toward religious assimilation," which works only in the direction of Christianity.[6] The constants in the characterization over time include the Other woman's explicit passion; her actions to save the hero from a peril versus the comparative passivity of Christian heroines; the acceptance of Christianity's superiority; and the ensuing happiness of the couple. The changes over time mainly concern complexion: by the eighteenth century, dark complexion routinely enters the plot as a factor that complicates the European characters' desire, and England, even more than Europe, exemplifies liberal governance, benign social subordination, and proper treatment of women as companions and not simply as sex objects or servants.

An analysis of the religious and racial politics informing *The History of Sir George Ellison* (1766), *The Voyages of William Vaughan, Memoirs of Mr. Brachy, The Fool of Quality, The Lady's Drawing Room,* and *The Female American* permits an examination of the fraught nexus of two distinct sensibilities about human difference. In scrutinizing the way that novels represent sexual and marital relations between Britons and black Africans, as well as exotic white Muslims, Hindus, and Native Americans, I show that complexion and religious difference matter differently in regard to four populations with varying degrees of commercial and political significance to Britain. The fictional manifestation of romantic desire for nonslave populations mainly predates but also overlaps with statements in Britain against amalgamation between Africans and Britons aired by proponents of slavery, which began appearing in print during the 1770s. The absence of black Africans in intermarriage plots suggests a narrative avoidance. In as much as enslaved Africans were crucial to bolstering the British economy, not to mention the other population with whom the British were most likely to have sex, they were banished from the pages of novels that depicted romantic love between Englishmen and non-European women. The more acceptable racial Others found in intermarriage novels embody and serve the narrative function of negotiating wider cultural anxieties invoked by a slave-based empire.

*   *   *

The epigraphs to this chapter hint at the complex legal and customary hierarchies that constrained desire. Contemporaries perceived that sexual desire—and the prerogatives of power—all too frequently resulted in the transgression of accepted boundaries of station, religion, and sometimes racial mixture. Almost all twentieth-century analyses of intermarriage focus on skin color or status (slave versus free), not on religion or rank. One eighteenth-century writer in particular has been routinely associated with anti-amalgamation discourse. Edward Long, an ardent anti-French, pro-slavery English patriot, lived in Jamaica and England. His negative view of interracial sex is best understood in the context of his other writings, one of which was the most detailed plan for the social ascent of mulattos in Jamaica. Selecting the Europeans with the swarthiest complexions (the Portuguese) and the Europeans who were most different from the British in terms of religious heritage, cultural organization, and physical features (the converted Spanish Moors) from the southernmost point of the continent, Long conjures up their degeneration to reflect on the contemporary scene in London: "The lower class of women in England, are remarkably fond of the blacks[;] . . . in the course of a few generations more, the English blood will become so contaminated with this mixture, . . . this alloy may spread so extensively, as even to reach the middle, and then the higher orders of the people, till the whole nation resembles the *Portuguese* and *Moriscos* in complexion of skin and baseness of mind."[7] Even though Edward Long's often-quoted opinion about the link between complexion and moral probity and the undesirable effects of racial mixture was an emerging minority position in Britain rather than an established concern, it is the primary view that historians and literary critics have transmitted of interracial sex in the eighteenth century. At this time, it is a peculiarly colonial construction.

A few social observers in Britain, mainly connected to the West India lobby, published their negative—and offhand—opinions about interracial sex in pamphlets following the 1772 Mansfield decision in the James Somerset case.[8] Their claims implied that sexual relations between English people and Africans threatened Great Britain's political interests and endangered the beauty of its population. Coming as they did, during the century of the greatest racial intermixture between blacks and whites in the colonies, these comments were at odds with the generally more tolerant attitude in Britain than in the colonies in regard to interracial liaisons, especially among the serving classes.[9] Unlike the world reflected in intermarriage novels, the most typical interracial couple in eighteenth-century Britain was a laboring man of African descent and a British serving woman; the transgression of boundaries of station were largely moot. In the colonies, however, the most common interracial sexual union was between British men (of various ranks) and women of African descent, or Euro-African descent, who were their slaves or other men's slaves. Widely practiced though frequently condemned in the colonies, interracial sexual relations were represented in public discussions most frequently in terms of convenience for men and as disgraceful for Englishwomen.[10] Laboring white women's unions with free blacks and slaves were represented as injurious, likely because they confounded white men's property rights and racially based patriarchal privilege in the colonies. Nevertheless, as Winthrop Jordan reminds us about North American colonies, "Community feeling was of course not monolithically arrayed against interracial union" (139). Antiamalgamation discourse was generally aimed not at landowners but at the lower classes and particularly at Englishwomen, who appear as agents rather than as objects of desire.

The negative view of interracial sex, while available to eighteenth-century Britons, became ubiquitous by the mid-nineteenth century. Abena Busia's analysis of expatriate novels about nineteenth-century Africa demonstrates that representing sexual relations between Africans and Britons at that time was fraught with tragic elements. She summarizes the ideology of miscegenation in these novels: "Sex between the races is never a good thing. Without exception, when it takes place, it is an unhealthy relationship with dire consequences. . . . Where there are children born of such a union who live, they are frequently the most morally degenerate of beings . . . who, contrary to genetic laws of breeding, manage to inherit both the repulsive physical and spiritual traits of their parents."[11] These nineteenth-century novels correspond to the quotation from Edward Long's *Candid Reflections*; they highlight the adverse social effects of interracial sex by invoking an ideology of race that assumes it is unchangeable and that it should be a natural barrier between people. This more familiar construction of interracial sexual relations differs greatly from mid-eighteenth-century novels: neither inter-racial sex nor the offspring of that contact are constructed negatively because they feature nonslave populations as marriage partners for Englishmen, and because the dominant ideology of human variety assumed the common origins of all people. Concepts of either contamination or degeneration did not yet inflect the way that most Britons perceived children of mixed parentage. Since novels did not, in general, depict relationships between Britons and free blacks or slaves, the most numerically significant interracial couple received the least representation. Representing black and white intermarriage would have raised confusing social consequences, especially about rank, that the midcentury intermarriage novels never confront, since the Other is always of exalted birth in his—or, most commonly, her—country of origin. As an explanation for enslaving other populations, religious difference was not entirely superseded by the practice of color-based slavery, especially in Britain.

Many of our current assumptions about interracial sex are based on the black/white model that Edward Long and many nineteenth-century Englishmen promoted and which has become closely associated with a peculiarly American history of slavery. Marriage does not frequently enter into most present-day analyses, possibly because it was banned in several North American colonies and later in many states until well into the twentieth century. The preferred eighteenth-century colonial reference to interracial sex and marriage was *amalgamation*, a term which highlights the bringing together of two people to produce a uniform whole; in contrast, *miscegenation* focuses negatively on the mixed-race progeny. The social taboo arising from interracial sex and marriage tends to be reinforced by interpretations offered by historians of slavery and of the Negro image. In the American context, Winthrop Jordan, for instance, is scrupulous in mentioning the multiple responses in North America to interracial sex and marriage as well as the variety of legislation that addressed the resulting blurring of power lines in the late seventeenth and early eighteenth centuries. Despite the nod to multiplicity, the upshot of his analysis is that North Americans largely disapproved of interracial sex and marriage and that amalgamation with Indians never bothered colonists as much as with Negroes.[12]

In the British context, Peter Fryer and Folarin Shyllon have tended to portray eighteenth-century Britons' intense animosity toward interracial sex and marriage. This claim is particularly strange in Fryer's case, since he carefully argues that English racism was largely attributable to the West India lobby and their efforts to circulate proslavery propaganda based on insinuations about racial difference, among other tactics. In fact, Fryer goes so far as to contend that hostility to miscegenation was at the base of racism *tout court*: "It is clear that by the 1770s racism had more than a foothold in Britain. In particular, the spectre of racial intermarriage and 'contamination,' incessantly invoked by the West Indians' propagandists, was haunting England."[13] Fryer's evidence for rampant hostility in the 1770s is five articles by or associated with the West Indian agents, which were published following the 1772 Somerset case.[14] Possibly, it is more appropriate to suggest that despite there not being much printed evidence for it, there are anecdotal and "reactive" statements, which suggest that offhand references in England to amalgamation escalated in response to the political and economic challenge to the slave trade in ways not unlike similar statements and actions against English intermarriage with the Catholics, Irish, Scots, and French. Thought of in this light, interracial sex and marriage are best treated in their multiple manifestations and not just in terms of single differences of skin color, status, or national origins.

Although there were laws in some of the North American colonies dating from the late seventeenth century that prohibited either fornication or marriage between people of African descent and Britons for economic and political reasons (which were not always enforced), there were no such laws in the West Indies prohibiting extramarital sex.[15] And, there were no such laws in Britain. Similarly, there was not a consensus among the British that interracial sex or the resulting children were more shameful than other forms of extramarital sex or children born out of wedlock. As George Fredrickson explains, most opposition to amalgamation in the late seventeenth and eighteenth centuries, even in the colonies, reflected a "traditional desire to prevent intermarriage between people of different social stations."[16]

While negative reactions to marriage between partners considered inappropriate for each other had a short but significant history in regard to the colonies, there was a much longer history of objection to certain transgressive unions in the domestic national space, a history that was invoked in a supportive response to the Marriage Act of 1753 in England. One contemporary author justified this act, the apparent purpose of which was to ban clandestine marriages, not only on the grounds that they produced many evils in society, but also because historically civil law "has appointed disabling Circumstances as to Marriage Contracts."[17] Included in the lengthy list of traditionally forbidden liaisons are marriages between people of different religious faiths, classes, and status. These restrictions originated with another imperial power, Rome, and all were punishable on the books, either as capital offenses or by slightly lesser penalties. The most pertinent example to contemporary Britain prohibited Christians and Jews from marrying (37).[18]

Henry Gally further reminds his readers that before there were religious interdictions, Romans were forbidden to marry Barbarians, although the Justinian Code later omitted this stricture (42). A difference in station between marriage partners within the same political state was also considered transgressive. For instance, the Law of Constantine forbid senators, or the governing elite, to marry a servant or the daughter of a maid servant, a freed woman, or the daughter of a freed woman; Gally complains that such a propensity to cross-class alliance "has too much prevail'd amongst our Nobility" (46). So, too, under Roman law, a free woman might not marry a bondman (49). In eighteenth-century Britain, rank was less determinant than religion in regard to marriage; legally, religious difference constituted the most significant barrier to marriage in Britain, not color, rank, or national difference per se. According to Gally, low class origins could be eradicated within two generations—a similar amount of time for upgrading "racial" status in many of the eighteenth-century colonies to full privileges of English subjects.

The 1753 Marriage Act was not the only lightning rod for laying bare assumptions about boundaries that should not be crossed. The English had banned interfaith marriages between members of the Church of England and Catholics as well as Jews, and the pope had banned Christian women from marrying Islamic Moors. In a colonial situation, Englishmen were legally restrained from marrying Irish women as far back as the fourteenth-century Statutes of Kilkenny. These strictures were not very effective in actually preventing intermarriage, although their primary purpose was to protect Englishmen from assimilating and confounding boundaries of political rule. The concerted written efforts in Ireland, North America, and other outposts to preserve the distinctiveness of English identity were less successful in practice.

Juxtaposing this history of forbidden marriages to the issue of racial intermarriage is instructive: marriage between individuals was an interest of the state, especially because of the effects on property and inheritance. Intermarriage also affected ideas about national identity, which was intimately associated with the Church of England and a limited monarchy. Anxieties about the various kinds of boundary crossing underwrote most of the arguments for and against the Marriage Act of 1753. Many of these same anxieties surface in the midcentury novels analyzed below only to be repressed. Comparing the sometimes hostile responses toward British and African amalgamation with the novels about Europeans marrying other non-European populations demonstrates the way that marriage imaginatively resolves concerns about some religious and color differences at this historical moment. In each novel, the narrative desire is to embrace, not reject, the mixed-race

heroine or non-European character. Below, I investigate the various conditions that contribute to this distinctive representation.

*   *   *

Even in the colonies, religious difference continued to be invoked in
public discussions of slavery well after it declined as the ostensible grounds
for enslavement. Christianity as well as complexion distinguished British
settlers from slaves in the colonies; for example, the Virginia Slave Code
defined slavery in terms of religious difference as late as 1753.[19] To understand the valence of Christian identity in the colonies, one need only consult Morgan Godwyn's 1680 treatise urging planters to Christianize Africans and Indians in the colonies. Planters objected strenuously because both
masters and slaves believed that baptism and Christian conversion rendered
slave status dubious despite the Church of England's assurances to the contrary. A customary planter response to the prospect of Christianizing slaves
employs a common term of abuse: "*What, those black Dogs be made Christians? What, shall they be like us?*"[20] Although "dogs" was a generic insult by
the seventeenth century, one of its older resonances points to religious difference. At least as far back as early medieval iconography, dog-headed men
commonly represented the uncoverted. The planter's retort underscores that
Christianity was still key to establishing a sense of fully shared humanity.
Until well into the late eighteenth century, many Britons believed that conversion or even setting foot in England constituted grounds for emancipation.[21] These issues inform the story line of Sarah Scott's *History of Sir George
Ellison* (1766); this novel best indicates the contradictory ways that Christianity, dark skin color, and colonial relations of slavery overdetermined the
contemplation of intermarriage at midcentury. Sir George Ellison, a reluctant slave owner, emphasizes several times that the present difference between Europeans and African slaves is "merely adventitious, not natural"
and that slaves are "fellow-creatures." Urging the rational appeal of his own
position, Ellison defends his remarks about the shared humanity of Europeans and slaves to a naysayer who had long been in the West Indies: "I
must call them so, till you can prove to me, that the distinguishing marks of
humanity be in the complexion or turn of features."[22] This comment reveals
the possibility in 1766 of still divorcing issues of skin color from determining degrees of humanity as well as the increasingly racist challenge to their
separation.

Ellison's belief in essential human similarity later proves a stumbling
block to a seamless narrative of racial commensurability when color differ-

ence is contextualized in regard to marriage. The narrator observes of Ellison's extended family: "Mr. Ellison's house contained also many children of
inferior rank; his servants had intermarried, the blacks with the blacks, the
white servants with those of their own colour: for though he promoted their
marrying, he did not wish an union between those of different complexions,
the connection appearing indelicate and almost unnatural."[23] Couched in
terms of a class issue—the many children are of "inferior rank"—the narrator's alarm seems to arise from racial intermixture, which, however, has
been avoided. Nonetheless, using the word *intermarried* in reference to the
color segregated married serving couples suggests an unintentional slippage
from separation to amalgamation. While the intraracial marriages eliminate
the possibility of interracial marriage, Ellison's approval of color-segregated
couples appears contradictory given his protestations about slaves being fellow creatures and about skin color being incidental, especially since his black
servants are recently converted Christians. The narrative contradictions of
Sir George Ellison permit us to glimpse the anomalous position of former
slaves in terms of racial ideology. This fictional rejection of interracial marriage between Ellison's servants matches Edward Long's concern about the
darkening of Britain if lower-class Englishwomen follow their inclinations.
Together these two texts suggest that, at times, the tolerant and even liberal
conception of human variety voiced by Ellison displays the same fear as an
overt racist such as Edward Long.

*   *   *

The midcentury literary focus on conjugal relations, rather than on a
master/slave dynamic, occurred when the nature of the British Empire was
shifting emphasis from territorial acquisition to issues of governance. According to Kathleen Wilson, the midcentury British Empire, as opposed
to other European ones, was ideologically and materially driven to civilize
the world via trade.[24] Through the representation of intermarriage, many
of these novels responded to British concerns about governing an empire.[25]
In fiction, a gendered power dynamic helped create a "natural," even benevolent, depiction of racial subordination through the conversion of the
non-Christian characters. Moreover, the novels feature the legitimate bond
of marriage rather than illicit or forced sex between genteel Europeans and
marriage partners of high rank from populations the British considered
white (Moors and Muslims), viewed as primitive Europeans (Native Americans), or believed were socially and commercially like Europeans (East Indians). The non-European and non-Christian characters all undergo a milder

version of the religious instruction and extensive acculturation that Friday experiences in *Robinson Crusoe*. Unlike the sexual and racial politics of *Sir George Ellison*, intermarriage novels feature either narratives in which religious difference constitutes the barrier between Christians marrying non-Europeans, or narratives in which religion and complexion both matter, but Christianity ultimately prevails as the more significant factor. Many intermarriage plots involve female cross-dressing and occasionally blackface in order to get the heroines safely to Europe. In each plot resolution, the non-European heroine of high rank embraces Christianity before her marriage, an event which signals proper social order and rational happiness. The consent of non-Europeans to this formative trope of British national identity enacts an unproblematic change of their religious and cultural affiliation: each time, their assimilation is successful.

Muslims from the reaches of the Ottoman Empire figure most successfully in the intermarriage novels. In regard to this diverse population, which the novel rendered in homogeneous terms, religious, not color, difference is most significant; in fact, many of these novels do not consider the Moors or Muslims to be dark complected (as many seventeenth-century texts did); rather, they are figured as exotic whites. One novel that features religious difference is *The Voyages of William Owen Gwin Vaughan* (1736). Reprinted three times, this novel was popular for twenty-five years after its initial publication.[26] A Christian slave narrative inset in the novel as a stand-alone story, Jonathan Vaughan's enslavement in Tunis conjures up the most common narrative tropes and devices developed more fully in later intermarriage novels. Conventional differences are established in the episode when Jonathan Vaughan becomes a slave to a Moor: Muslim/Christian, master/slave, illicit sexual desire/sanctioned romantic attachment, and activity/passivity. Because of the slave status of the Christian man and the religious and cultural otherness of the non-European woman, there is a certain fluidity in the depiction of gendered traits. In narratives with a European heroine and a non-Christian hero, gender configurations are more conventional. The resolution to all intermarriage novels restores benign patriarchal authority based on the superiority of a British model.

Jonathan Vaughan's slave narrative features the mutual desire of the Christian and Fatima, the daughter of his recently dead owner. Upon the master's death, the son of the Moor makes his desire for Jonathan known, an episode that contrasts with Fatima's more acceptable heterosexual desire.[27] Her attraction to the Christian slave is immediately linked to marriage and hence subordination. Jonathan receives a letter from Fatima, "the amiable Christian *Moor*," who pities his enslavement, and she confesses that when

she first saw him, she immediately loved him. Even though the novel emphasizes mutual visual attraction between the two, her marriage proposal privileges her religious status: *"I am a sincere Christian in my Heart, without Baptism."* A slave taught her to speak and read English; her favorite book is the
Bible. Claiming that she *"found so much sound truth* [in the Bible] . . . *that I
began to abhor the Absurdities of the Alcoran,"* Fatima rejects the Koran because
of the greater rational appeal of Christianity, which also heralds her rejection of patriarchal tyranny, polygamy, and other practices that the British
commonly associated with Islamic people.[28] Fatima's evolution from a Moor
into a suitable wife hinges on her private conversion to Christianity. Her
active desire for Jonathan and her proposal of marriage contradict the emerging norm of the British heroine in the novel; nonetheless, Fatima's desire
for Jonathan is sanctioned in the novel as understandable, even laudable.
Indeed, other legends of interracial couples, such as Pocohantas and John
Smith or Inkle and Yarico, agree with the premise that British men, especially their complexion and visage, are overwhelmingly desirable to Other
women. Of course, this inversion of the sexual desire British men regularly
acted on when abroad explains their unions with Other women in novels at
the same time that it erases their agency in forming them.

Religious and cultural differences of these Other women surface in their
masculine behavior. Fatima's gender ambiguity literally manifests itself in
the disguise that enables her to assume a new Christian identity. Despite the
fact that the Vaughan brothers mistakenly rescue another woman from her
brother's clutches, Fatima resourcefully boards their ship disguised as a male
youth. Fatima's gender disguise is a common device in English literature to
render women mobile yet unremarkable in public spaces; however, in most of
the midcentury romances, the heroine's momentary transgression of visible
gender boundaries always precedes her marriage. Restoring proper order on
many levels, the episode ends with all of the European and recently converted Christian characters embarking on a ship for Britain where Fatima
is formally baptized and takes the Christian name Maria before her wed-
ding. In *The Voyages of William Vaughan*, the designation of *Christian* denotes
exemplary morals and heterosexual object choice to distinguish the British
slave from his Muslim counterpart. Christianity also represents the criterion
for a perfect union—a marriage of proper subordination of one wife to one
man. The narrative insistence on conversion suggests that Christianity is the
umbrella term that encompasses a variety of other differences; this narrative
tic also reflects an external conception of human variety that was easy for the
British to maintain in regard to Moors and other Muslims.

The importance of shared Christianity to conjugal happiness is equally noticeable in *Memoirs of the Remarkable Life of Mr. Charles Brachy* (1767), but the narrative unfolding differs because the religious Other is a male character.[29] As in other intermarriage novels, Brachy's Muslim religion accounts for his "racial" difference. Similar to novels with non-Christian heroines, the corollary issue to Brachy's religious conversion is his learning to be a virtuous European. Chiefly, he must master an excessive desire for wealth. Reforming men's manners through the contrast to men of different religions and colors was one way the novel helped Englishmen prepare for their role in a newly commercial empire.

The protagonist introduces himself in Europe as Charles Brachy, but he is really Osmin Brachy—a Muslim, and not the Christian for whom he passes. Indeed, he passes so successfully (i.e., he neither *looks* nor *acts* non-European or non-Christian) that he wins the love of the French Henrietta and the consent of her parents to marry. Henrietta's distress upon discovering that he is an "infidel" does not overpower her love for Osmin, but she begs not to be forced to change her religion, and he grants her wish. His condescension notwithstanding, their religious difference drives the plot and introduces misgivings between the couple.

Osmin is the son of a renegade, born of European parents and raised as a Muslim in Algiers. His characterization reflects the fissures posed by this incongruity. The narrative makes him sympathetic and attractive in order to be the hero, yet treacherous because he is not a Christian. On the ship to Algiers, Osmin divulges his background to an incredulous Henrietta; his history strikes the reader as a solidly European account of accumulating colonial wealth. A younger son, Osmin has gained his personal fortune from prosperous commerce in the West Indies and six years' residence there. Wealth was not the only benefit that accrued to him in the West Indies: Osmin learned "that politeness which he had acquired by his commerce with civilized nations" (97). Like Englishmen, Osmin benefits from colonialism's spoils, and the accumulation of wealth and contact with European men polishes his manners. This approved method of amassing a personal fortune, through industry, slave labor, and exploitative commercial relations, contrasts with the putative Eastern mode: hoarding wealth and women. Osmin, poised between two religions and cultures, exemplifies aspects of both until his Christian conversion.

The narrative crisis occurs when Osmin's evil elder brother discovers that Henrietta and Osmin are married. Knowing he should flee and take Henrietta to Europe, Osmin is stymied by his conflicting desires between rescuing Henrietta and preserving his wealth. Several times, the novel focuses on Osmin's cupidity (presumably the trace of his Muslim education);

he is too attached to his treasures to escape (103). Osmin's inaction is offset by the resourcefulness of the sympathetic Muslim heroine Xamira, who is in love with a European man, who does not return her desire because she is not a Christian (83). The Algerian Xamira is depicted in sympathetic terms: she is lovely and virtuous; the only virtue lacking is "the light of Christianity" (111).

The narrative resolution of *Memoirs of Mr. Charles Brachy* involves gender and racial disguise. As a sign of her basic goodness, Xamira facilitates the reunion between a European couple by dressing the husband in woman's clothing; by disguising herself as a black male slave, she conducts Osmin and Henrietta to freedom. Her resourceful intervention is a conventionally masculine trait that signals her racial difference. Throughout the narrative, cordial relations between the sexes are all disrupted because of religious difference. Thwarted intimacy underscores the significance of shared religion to the development of trust. The discord produced by disparate religions is resolved at the end of the novel when Xamira and Osmin vow to become Christians (118). The return to Europe hinges on the reunion of husbands and wives, conversion of the rehabilitated Muslims to Christianity, disguise, and the renunciation of cupidity. The novel ends with the formal baptism of Xamira and Osmin and the marriage of Osmin and Henrietta newly legitimated.

How might the ease with which fictional Muslims are embraced as Christians be understood? And how might we account for the many romantic attachments between Europeans and people from the Ottoman Empire that occur in novels? Part of the answer involves the intersection of dominant racial and gender ideology; another part of the answer lies in the waning power of the Ottomans and the history of its representation. The half-century preceding these intermarriage novels produced a range of conflicting interpretations about Muslims and Moors; yet, of all other groups, Europeans consistently found these populations the most similar to themselves. In both travel narratives and protoscientific essays, writers assessed similarities between Europeans and Moors in terms of physical resemblance and difference in terms of cultural institutions.

By midcentury, new scientific interest in taxonomy had not settled on one interpretation of Muslims or Moors, nor had it divorced political judgments from scientific categorization in any obvious way. On the one hand, Linnaeus, the foremost taxonomer of the eighteenth century, included Moors in the category with Asiatics, whom he described as "fuscus," meaning sooty- or sallow-complected in the first edition of *The System of Nature* (1735). By the expanded tenth edition in 1758, Linnaeus delineates their other differences from Europeans in a static way in terms of disposition, clothing, and government. As a people, Asiatics were believed to be proud and covetous, to wear loose garments, and to be governed by opinions rather than a rational form of government.[30] Following conventional early modern literary representation of tawny Moors, Linnaeus's composite negative characterization reflects eighteenth-century Europeans' use of Asiatics to bolster their own sense of cultural superiority. On the other hand, Linnaeus's main rival, the natural historian Buffon, concedes that the Moors, Turks, and Persians have "acquired a degree of civilization" and he finds their complexion similar to Europeans'; for example, "the men are white, and only a little tawny" in Barbary.[31] Even more favorably, Laugier de Tassy, a contemporary who resided in North Africa, concedes that if persons prejudiced against natives of Barbary were "to converse unknowingly with *Mahometans* in a *Christian* Dress, they would look upon them to be just such Creatures as themselves, having the same Faculties and Dispositions."[32] De Tassy's observation dovetails nicely with the characterization of Fatima and Xamira by suggesting that only clothing divides the two populations. In a similar vein, almost all travelers regarded Muslim women as beautiful and emphasized their physical resemblance to Europeans. For example, Thomas Shaw's *Travels* (1738) contends that "the greatest part of the *Moorish* women would be reckoned beauties, even in *Great Britain*; as their Children certainly have the finest Complexions of any Nation whatsoever. In a note he corrects the common mistake that Europeans make in believing the Moors to be a swarthy people. Shaw captures the kind of revision that took place between the seventeenth and the eighteenth centuries when he adds that although the word *Moor* usually conveys "the *Idea* of a Person of a dark and swarthy Complexion," in his usage "it only denotes the situation of the Country he inhabits."[33]

Citing the older point of contention between them, de Tassy argues that the religious difference between Europeans and Islamic people is fundamental to the representation of them: "Prejudice against the *Turks, and all other Mahometans*, is so firmly rooted in the Breast of most *Christians*, that they seem to want Words to express the Bitterness of their Hearts." The prejudice to which de Tassy refers includes polygamy, men's bisexuality, and the putative tyrannical mode of government. In the setting for the Christian slave narrative, Tunis and Algiers, like Morocco, represent a mode of government antithetical to the British understanding of order. Positions of power were not necessarily hereditary and changed frequently; primogeniture was the least likely mode of succession in a state that valued individual qualifications or raw personal power.[34] Europeans believed Muslim and Ottoman institutions were highly flawed, and as Janet Todd contends, midcentury Englishmen "thought of themselves as peculiarly free of despotism ... and peculiarly just in their laws." [35]

The context of British representations of Moors and Muslims was not as overdetermined as that of the various populations in the colonies. Until the late seventeenth century, the Ottoman Empire was recognized as a formidable maritime and financial power. Between Europeans and Ottomans, there had been a rivalry for access to the Holy Land initially and later to Africa and the Atlantic, but by the mid-eighteenth century, the reaches of the Ottoman Empire had become a relatively innocuous space for Britons to work out a newly forming identity as a major European empire. Constructing a benign imperial identity posed more difficulties in relation to the Caribbean and the Americas than North Africa because, as some early abolitionists argued, the slave-based Atlantic empire was antithetical to Britain's identity as a Christian nation. In fact, as Linda Colley contends, by the end of the Seven Years' War in 1763, the territorial results of the victory "challenged longstanding British mythologies: Britain as a pre-eminently Protestant nation; Britain as a polity built on commerce; Britain as the land of liberty because founded on Protestantism and commerce." [36]

*   *   *

In turning to intermarriage novels in which dark skin color plays a more visible role, we can discern the simultaneous avowal and disavowal of complexion's significance that characterizes most other midcentury intermarriage novels. Combined with religious difference, dark skin color complicates marriage but does not prevent it in *The Fool of Quality*, *The Lady's Drawing Room*, and *The Female American*. These novels focus our attention on the way that some colonial practices obliquely infused British culture, particularly the spatial and discursive separation of the British from Others. Separating populations by custom or law, based on religion and/or skin color, was common in the colonies and commercial factories in Africa and India, where skin color was used as a point of identification earlier and more frequently than in Britain. Occasionally, segregation was mutually agreeable, such as European commercial enclaves like Madras, where the city was divided into a Black Town and a White Town. While some Englishmen found that black complexion inspired an inexplicable anxiety, there was also a sense that a negative response to something beyond human control was unworthy of rational Englishmen, especially around the midcentury. Intermarriage novels rehearse this cultural equivocation over complexion's significance in their repeated enactment of the Christian conversion of dark-skinned characters of gentle birth. This process erases the formerly felt significance of dark color.

The Fool of Quality, a beloved novel in its own time and reprinted throughout the nineteenth century, commanded wide respect for the noble sentiments exemplified by its heroes.[37] It charts the development and beneficence of two men of sentiment: Harry Clinton, the younger brother of the earl of Moreland, and the earl's second son, also named Harry. Significantly, both Harry Clintons are younger brothers to two generations of the earls of Moreland; both are benevolent men of feeling. Their actions exude sentiment—the increasingly favored (though still emerging) national masculine trait—and they embody the precepts of Adam Smith's *Theory of Moral Sentiments* (1759).[38] This novel develops a new eighteenth-century national hero based on financial generosity and proper sentiment, not only on the privilege of birth and inherited money, and this is the usual context critics cite for its analysis.

Less remarked on is the fact that these new men embrace women whose nationality, religion, or color differs from their own. In fact, *The Fool of Quality* features three generations of marriages, all of which cross "real" or figural religious and color lines. The first one involves the English Harry Clinton the elder, who marries the French Louisa, a Catholic of gentle birth. Their daughter marries a Moroccan emperor, and in turn the daughter of the Moor and European marries an Englishman, her cousin Harry. For both the Moor and his daughter, dark complexion is crucial to their narratives. The emperor's tawny color is brought up only to be underplayed, and his daughter's black color turns out to be a temporary fiction. In both cases, dark color is deemed important enough to address but ultimately dismissable because virtuous behavior matters more, a result of the Christian, sentimental, and racial ideology shaping the novel.

The first marriage in the novel is based on national and religious difference within Europe between the English Harry Clinton and the French Louisa. The racial tropes and plot devices in this segment foreshadow the ones in the two subsequent intermarriages and are made possible primarily by Louisa's Catholic faith and the way that it intersects with patriarchal authority. Twentieth-century scholars of religion in the eighteenth century have argued that Catholicism and Islam functioned similarly in securing Protestant British identity by negation.[39] *The Fool of Quality* uses them both to make such an imaginative connection. The Englishman meets his future wife when she is disguised as Lewis, son of a refined Frenchwoman. Her gender disguise involves physical deformity, including a dark complexion, although neither of these features seem to impede Harry Clinton's admiration: "Were it not that his complexion is sallow, and that he is something short of a leg, and blind of one eye, he would positively be the most lovely of all the human species" (5:118). The Englishman's heightened interest in Lewis is explained when the "blind, lame, and tawny Lewis" (5:126) metamorphoses into the beautiful Louisa, unwillingly betrothed to a French prince by her father. Her disguise allows her to escape a tyrannous father and a forced marriage. This example is the first of two in which the English heroes each find a tawny boy attractive, only to discover later that the boy is, in fact, a beautiful woman and his own destined wife.[40]

Initially, Louisa's disguise as a tawny boy eliminates the possibility of romantic attachment because of her apparent masculine gender, but the more significant barrier is a perceived difference of station, especially the Englishman's involvement in trade, which is reason enough for her father to forbid their marriage.[41] Louisa resumes her disguise as a tawny boy to flee Paris. Harry and Louisa marry and go to England with Louisa's mother and brother: the reconfigured international family is a midcentury British phenomenon. England, unlike France, protects women from the exercise of tyranny and encourages them to follow their romantic inclinations—within the appropriate range of rank, of course. Unlike France, England offers social order yet upward mobility for its younger sons of gentle birth: "the place where law was regent; where there was no apprehension of inquisitions or bastiles; and where the peasant was guarded, as with a bulwark of adamant, against every encroachment of arbitrary power" (162).[42] Of all the narratives, this one participates most obviously in the developing sense of Britain's singularity and excellence that was noticeable in various publications dating from the 1660s and gathering momentum in the 1760s. This felicity is linked to the climate, the land's plenty, commerce, and government. A contributor to the *Royal Magazine* includes the following address, a typical praisesong: "Hail Britain, happiest of countries! happy in thy climate, fertility, situation, and commerce; but still happier in the peculiar nature of thy laws and government."[43] As a nation, England stands for respect between the sexes (i.e., proper subordination) as well as a prudent exercise of power.

In contrast to England's moderation, contemporary travelers singled out the government of Morocco as "the most despotic of all *Barbary*, and the Subjects consequently the most wretched."[44] A reference to the governance of Morocco—or France—was enough to signify all that was inimical to the British love of liberty. These same sentiments about Britain's excellence are resurrected some decades later when Eloisa, the daughter of the English Harry and the French Louisa, and her husband, Abenamin, emperor of Morocco, adopt England as their permanent home because it is among Christians. In the story told of their courtship, both color and religious difference arise as initial barriers to their happy marriage, though not to their mutual desire. Depicting Muslim characters as exotic whites was not the only way to represent North Africans. *The Fool of Quality* puts forth a tawny Moor who is just as successful at assimilating to English norms as the lighter-colored characters, even though he formerly was a polygamous Muslim. Saved by the love of a European woman, the Moroccan emperor, who "exceeded all in his dominions for grace of person and beauty of aspect," gives up his other wives, allows his European wife freedom to practice her religion, and eventually converts himself and allows their daughter to be raised a Protestant (5:228). No coercion, no subterfuge, this non-European man truly deserves approbation even before he converts. A man of feeling rather than a tawny tyrant, he typifies a new ideal for Englishmen.

The emperor's religion is the one declared barrier inhibiting his European wife's perfect happiness. The emperor's conversion, both rational and emotional, signals a happy future and precedes his marriage to Eloisa. At this time, religious practice and complexion were both viewed as accidents of climate, geography, and custom. These novels repeatedly stage the changeability of both conditions. Yet it is the unwritten anxiety, raised by the effort to disavow the importance of the emperor's complexion, that is most noticeable. The disavowal is proclaimed several times, most notably by a spokeswoman for liberal sentiments, who calls on her travel experience to recommend the Moroccan emperor thusly in England: he "is the least of the tawny of any man I saw in Africa" (5:206).

The arrival in England of Abenaide, the daughter of the Moor and the European Eloisa, initiates the final intermarriage. Disguised as a black prince, Abenamin/Abenaide crosses the black/white boundary and the male/female one. Even though there is a sustained homoerotic attraction between the prince and Harry the younger, Abenaide's color and gender disguise are fictional barriers to the heterosexual plot resolution. In fact, their initial meeting does not bode well for a future union because Harry focuses on the prince's blackness.[45] Shortly after expressing his disgust at the prince's dark color, Harry responds to his own good impulses and recognizes the "inherent" nobility of the Christian prince, despite his color. Almost immediately, the black prince's affection for Harry converts his heart from irrational repugnance to respect. After his secular conversion, Harry tells the prince's European guardian: "I now perceive, madam, how ridiculous all sorts of prejudices are, and find that time and observation may change our opinions to the reverse of what they were. I once had an aversion to all sorts of blacks; but I avow that there is something so amiable in the face of this youth, and his eyes cast such a lustre over the darkness of his countenance, as is enough, as Shakespeare has it, to make us in love with night, and pay no more worship to the gaudy sun" (5:203). Harry's final lesson about generosity in a didactic novel about relieving needy and distressed Europeans of all ranks concerns "racial" generosity. Harry the younger makes the same discovery that Harry the elder made about the blind, lame, and tawny Lewis: Superficial traits are always less important than virtuous behavior. Nevertheless, the heroines are always exceptionally beautiful. In gender disguise and blackface, there is always a *je ne sais quoi* about their countenances that attracts the British. Thus, there is a contradiction between the ideological message and the textual example.

Although the intermarriage novels that feature European men in North Africa usually refer to illicit male Muslim desire for Christian men, in *The Fool of Quality*, homosexual desire operates, but in a way not threatening to dominant ideology because it is revealed to be heterosexual. The relationship between Harry and Abenamin quickly assumes homoerotic proportions (211). The prince is androgynous: on the one hand, he exemplifies the traits of an accomplished female by singing African songs and dancing African dances (214); on the other hand, the prince also participates in typically masculine activities by riding horses, running races, and wrestling with Harry—activities never associated with European heroines. At the height of the apparently mutual desire, the black prince reveals that he has a twin sister "as fair as I am black" and thereby recuperates the prolonged homoerotic fiction into sanctioned heterosexual desire (217). Love and affection between men are sanctioned because not explicitly sexually motivated. The moment that this attachment becomes more explicit, the masquerade is revealed. The sexual and racial "joke" is the amiable *je ne sais quoi* in the youth's face, which, we discover, is the fairness and femaleness underneath.

The Fool of Quality, like other intermarriage novels, demonstrates that complexion is a remarkable factor, but not a crucial one, in constitutional makeup. Even though dark complexion is repeatedly disclaimed as a problem (it functions as a "joke" in the final marriage), it must be safely banished before each union—along with any sexual ambiguity. If British men's identity was constituted by the crossing of many overdetermined dominant ideological boundaries (polygamy, interracial sex, gratuitous violence in the colonies), these were not appropriate thresholds for their wives (of any color) to transgress.

Once the deception is uncovered and the black prince and the white princess are shown to be the same, the story of her disguise is told. It is explained as the necessary subterfuge to counteract illicit male Muslim desire.

Abenaide's blackening helps her escape her native country and her father's heir, who "had long conceived an illicit passion for his young and lovely sister" (240). As in other narratives of interracial romance, desire of a Muslim man for a European (in this case, it manifests itself as incestuous instead of homosexual) is juxtaposed to "legitimate" heterosexual Christian desire. Abenaide permanently abandons her disguise when she marries Harry, the procession which ends the novel. Other intermarriage novels figuratively erase black skin color when it concerns women. In all of the examples of blackface examined so far, except the emperor's, dark skin is a temporary phenomenon that heroines undergo for their own safety. These novels eradicate the significance of black and brown complexions by avowing and then disavowing their importance before eliminating it. The male character is typically permitted to remain darker than his wife.

Unlike Defoe's novels that feature European men abroad amassing wealth and often having recourse to violence, these novels emphasize British men acquiring "racial" manners fit for national domestic happiness. In this way, the dominant eighteenth-century construction of upper and middling-class masculine identity, based on civility, was also conceived in response to Britain's growing empire. Both the elder and younger Harry Clinton are younger sons of titled men involved in international trade. These sons of gentle birth are exemplars of a new ideal. Strong in adversity, shrewd in business, these men are equally at ease in a drawing room as in foreign business negotiation. Intermarriage novels emplot the vital role of younger sons in the spread of empire. Their wealth is earned through industry and merit; their manners, acquired through their high birth, are honed through contact with foreign people. The discomfort characters in the novels all evince with these younger sons' pursuit of profit is undercut by their generosity to people in need and their rescue of women from foreign tyranny. As John Barrell shows, there is an increasing separation of the concept of a gentleman from the ownership of land under way in the eighteenth century, which is detectable in the *Spectator* and in Defoe's writings.[46] These novels are part of that process and part of the racialization of Englishness. The English male protagonists in the last two novels under consideration follow this model as well.

*   *   *

Under the auspices of the East India Company, Britain had a commercial relationship with various Mogul rulers when *The Lady's Drawing Room* (1744) was written. The East India Company was scattered in strategic locations, such as Madras, Bombay, and Bengal, and it maintained trading factories and small communities in the vast expanses of the East Indies. To the British, East India mainly signified desirable commodities, such as beautiful dress fabrics. Although most British fiction about East India was written after the 1770s, when its political and economic importance increased with the loss of the American colonies, an earlier novel concerns two generations of marriages: the marriage of the French Henrietta to an East Indian Banyan and the marriage of their daughter Zoa to the English Rodomond. These extremely popular stories first appeared as inset narratives in *The Lady's Drawing Room*; thereafter, they were printed separately in chapbooks and as single pamphlets until the 1820s. The novel's plot spans successive days when visitors to Ethelinda's London drawing room tell stories about men and women in complicated relationships and scrutinize their behavior. Zoa's and Henrietta's histories demonstrate how much religious difference endangers marital happiness.

The European woman's destiny is reflected in the title to her story, "The True History of Henrietta de Bellgrave. A Woman born only for Calamities: A distress'd Virgin, unhappy Wife, and most afflicted Mother." [47] Henrietta is stranded in East India without the protection of her parents because they died in a shipwreck. Cast ashore near Bombay, she is rescued by the Banyan's men. Henrietta's initial meeting with the nameless Banyan, who is a wealthy and powerful local merchant, creates a favorable impression, and she refers to him as if he were an eligible European suitor: "At last I saw a very graceful Indian enter" (129), who was "Master of a great deal of Politeness, and of all those arts so engaging to our Sex" (130). Of all the Hindu populations, the high caste Brahmins received the most praise for their intellect and business acumen, the same traits that often raised British suspicions. As the Banyan courts her, the novel features Henrietta's objections to his religious faith and, in this sense, promotes an older ideology of human difference. For instance, when the Banyan's desire for her becomes obvious, Henrietta urges the Banyan to fix his passion on "some Maid, whose Religion and Customs are more agreeable to your own" (142). His unspecified, though heathen, religion carries the burden of all other differences in her dialogue with him, but in her address to the readers, Henrietta alludes to the Banyan's dark complexion as a barrier to her romantic attachment.

Henrietta's concern about the Banyan's skin color escalates as the nature of their relationship intensifies to marriage plans. The Banyan accepts the naturalness of Henrietta's disgust at his complexion: "Our tawny Colour is irksome to your eyes." He reasons, "You cannot bear to look on what is so different from yourself" (139). Because of her vulnerable position, Henrietta finds it politic to insist that she was taught to esteem people by their actions and virtue, not by their complexion. This sentiment is the same that *The Fool of Quality* ultimately endorses, but it is suspicious in this novel as well given the main character's repeatedly calling attention to the Banyan's complexion. Henrietta's comments operate similarly to Sir George Ellison's vague sense that it is indelicate to mix complexions in a marriage.

Nevertheless, the Banyan's polite behavior leads her to contemplate him more favorably. Notably, the terms of her approbation are couched in the insignificance of his skin color to his identity: "How ridiculous is it, said I to myself, to confine our Liking to what is meerly owing to the Difference of Climates? Had I been born in *India*, I should have been of the same Colour with this *Banyan*. And what, except a Skin, is wanting, to render his Person as agreeable as any *European* I have ever seen?" (161). Visibly it is simply skin color—an accident of climate—that differentiates him from a European. Ultimately, such a slight difference can hardly constitute reasonable grounds for rejection, or so the apparent logic of the novel suggests. The obsessive return to complexion and the denial that it matters embody the narrative indecision about the significance of the Banyan's complexion.

Henrietta's concern about the Banyan's tawny color is compensated for by other resemblances he bears to Europeans, an ambiguity early taxonomies of human variety also reflected. Typically, contemporary racial taxonomies included East Indians from the Mogul Empire in a grouping with Europeans, although their darker complexion was usually noted. Based on his travels in the late seventeenth century, François Bernier conveyed the indefinable similarity between East Indians and Europeans: "It is true that most Indians have something very different from us in the shape of their face, and in their colour which often comes very near to yellow; but that does not seem enough to make them a species apart."[48] He included East Indians in a category with Europeans and Moors, despite their differences in color. Fifty years later, Linnaeus separated East Indians from Europeans by putting them in the Asiatic category. At midcentury, Buffon offered a far more nuanced approach by discriminating among the many populations of the East Indies based on color and approximation to European features. The olive-colored Moguls from the northern regions did particularly well in this scheme, since they were the whites of the East Indies (3:340–42). In *The Lady's Drawing Room*, Zoa's physical resemblance to Europeans was only slightly undercut by her brown skin color. Many British writers acknowledged that East Indians with whom they dealt were not black complected, even though they were often denominated *blacks*. Throughout the seventeenth and eighteenth centuries, the British frequently referred to East Indians as blacks in their letters and newspapers; racial taxonomies, however, generally distinguished between the lighter-complected inhabitants from the northwest and their darker-colored southern counterparts.[49]

The most significant change in the narrative treatment of complexion and religion occurs when the brown-skinned daughter Zoa is born, and this event highlights anew the importance of Christianity to European identity. Henrietta remarks to Zoa in her memoirs: "What Horrors did my poor Heart feel, when, regarding you with all a Mother's Tenderness, I reflected, that you must be train'd up in Infidelity" (168). To remedy such a defect, Henrietta secretly baptizes Zoa, but she is interrupted by the Banyan, who forces her to promise never to teach the Christian faith to their daughter. Some years later, Henrietta's dying bequest to Zoa is her memoirs, which includes all articles of the Christian faith. She gives them to her daughter, saying, "I cannot die, and leave you with no other Knowledge of yourself, than that you are the Daughter of an *Indian Banyan*, and an *Heathen*" (101).[50] In the end, the Hindu's failure to convert or to honor Henrietta's wish to practice Christianity ruins their marriage. Foregrounding the Banyan's tawny color intensifies his undesirability but does not delimit it. By contrast, the tawny Moroccan emperor of *The Fool of Quality* was amply rewarded by allowing his wife to practice Christianity.

Henrietta's story, like the other inset narratives, is framed by conversation in Ethelinda's drawing room. Each vignette of *The Lady's Drawing Room* is analyzed by the men and women who are Ethelinda's visitors. The social intercourse of the sexes, believed to be the primary means by which men acquired manners in civil society, is exemplified in London entertainment. As important as formulating appropriate commentary is to polishing manners is the model of politeness embodied in heterosocial conversation. It was a key factor in the change of manners suitable for a commercial nation. According to David Solkin, conversation was "the forum in which individuals learned to refine their sympathy and mutual understanding[;] conversation provided eighteenth-century commercial ideologies with the perfect vehicle for constructing an idealised representation of the social relations that existed at the heart of the marketplace."[51] Novelistic conversation often refers to people elsewhere in the empire and in the trade networks for positive and negative examples to discipline English people into a more polished state. In this way, *The Lady's Drawing Room* imitates in novel form the framing device of heterosocial exchange for Steele's famous rendition of "Inkle and Yarico" in *Spectator* 11.

To Ethelinda's visitors, the implicit message of Henrietta's history is not just an admonishment to men to permit women greater rational freedom in marriage; it is also a warning to women. Clearly, Henrietta's example demonstrates that European women had much to lose by putting themselves in the hands of a foreign system of patriarchy. As Chapter 4 explores at greater length, men's treatment of women was an index to an entire society's claim to sophistication. For example, the Scottish physician William Alexander concludes that "in the same proportion as we find the men emerging from ignorance and brutality, and approaching to knowledge and refinement; the rank, therefore, and condition, in which we find women in any country, mark out to us with the greatest precision, the exact point in the scale of civil society, to which the people of such country have arrived."[52] Readers may feel vindicated that they are more civilized than the Banyan and better off than Henrietta, who finishes her days as an isolated prisoner. Because of her tyrannical husband, Henrietta is denied a role increasingly recognized as a civilized woman's right—being a cultural agent who reforms her husband and who educates her daughter.

Upon hearing Henrietta's story, the drawing room company first reacts negatively toward Henrietta rather than the Banyan: "They cou'd no otherwise account for a *Christian* and an *European* being married to an *Indian Banyan*, than that she must have been one of those unhappy Persons, who, to avoide publick Shame in their own country, seek a Refuge in the Colonies abroad" (100).[53] The initial operative assumption is that Henrietta willingly allied herself to a "heathen" because she was sexually promiscuous, if not also of the lower class. In the 1740s, what other kind of European woman would go to the colonies or commercial outposts voluntarily unless she were transported as a convict or as an indentured servant? The full force of Edward Long's fears about interracial desire reassert themselves even in the most genteel society where a European woman's desire for a dark-skinned, non-European, and non-Christian man appears inexplicable. After the various members of Ethelinda's drawing room are assured that Henrietta was a woman of high birth who fell into unfortunate circumstances, they conclude that the Banyan displayed a want of delicacy in urging the marriage (178). One lady in the drawing room summarizes, "We wept, that her hard Fate condemn'd her to a Man, who . . . was every way unworthy of her[;] . . . she suffer'd not because she *lov'd*, but because she did *not* love" (176). In the frame narrative of *The Lady's Drawing Room*, Ethelinda's company interpret the story of Henrietta and the Banyan as an allegory of universal male/female troubles, not as a story about racial difference, although we can detect the way that nascent racial ideology attaches itself to domestic tales of conflict between the sexes to exaggerate, in this case, the tyranny of a loveless marriage.

If the story of Henrietta and the Banyan illustrates the problems that can arise from uniting different religions and complexions, their daughter Zoa and the English Rodomond's story signals the success of intermarriage when based in Christianity. Their courtship also raises the twin problems of religion and color differences but resolves them happily. Rodomond, a younger son of an ancient English family and junior merchant with the East India Company, becomes known to Zoa through his dealings with her father. The Banyan and Rodomond clash over commercial matters because Rodomond threatens the Banyan's local power base; the Banyan redresses the erosion of his authority by having Rodomond kidnapped and holding him hostage in a prison. Zoa, who falls in love with Rodomond at first sight, intervenes by disguising herself as a "*Negro* Slave" to rescue him and get them both out of Bombay (25). Marking her association with blackness, Rodomond sees Zoa for the first time as "the Shadow of something" (20–21). She then appears disguised as a black slave and Rodomond recognizes her only because of her voice.

Strangely, blackface and gender disguise mark the passage from mixed-race daughter to an English wife. As with other heroines, this plot device permits women unchaperoned access to the public domain, but in regard to the brown-complected Zoa, the blackening precedes the narrative purging of the significance of her color. By momentarily introducing the specter of a black male slave superimposed on the exemplary heroine, these novels betray a largely unspoken anxiety about European and African amalgamation. The frequent motif of cross-dressing and blackface heroines raises the question about their function beyond a conventional mechanism. Both are overdetermined acts, I submit, that are magnets for contemporary fears and desires.[54] Blackface and cross-dressing signify social and economic conflict and literally mark change at the level of the body; they are multiply resonant of displacements, slippages, and substitutions of gender, race, station, and religion.[55] If Marjorie Garber's analysis of cross-dressing reminds us how significant clothes are to distinguishing between sexes and discerning status, she also argues that clothing may be used to blur those boundaries. Clothing, then, is a malleable sign, and fictional transvestism signals what Garber calls a category crisis, a construction which is useful for understanding the momentary masquerade in intermarriage novels. Garber observes, "Category crises can and do mark displacements from the axis of *class* as well as from *race* onto the axis of gender" (17). A similar effect is associated with blackface. Both Michael Rogin and Eric Lott analyze the historical function of blackface in terms similar to Garber's examination of cross-dressing. Lott claims that the broadest conditions of possibility for nineteenth-century blackface were the European slave trade and miscegenation.[56] Even more

suggestively, Rogin contends that the history of miscegenation and assimilation both energize blackface in the twentieth-century cinema.[57] For Rogin,
racial masquerade is a symbolic substitute for the exchange of bodily fluids
between whites and blacks (421), a claim that furthers the analysis of blackface heroines in eighteenth-century intermarriage novels considerably. Assimilation into a dominant culture, then, has often occurred through the
medium of blackface since the slave trade reached its historic height in the
eighteenth century. Assimilation is achieved for some groups—in Rogin's
case for Jews—through the mask of the most segregated. In the context of
performance, according to Rogin, blackface offers upward mobility to the
wearer by keeping blacks in place (447).

After leaving Bombay, Zoa is symbolically whitened. She discards the
boy's clothes, washes off the dark color, and dons European clothes: Zoa
"put on an *English* Habit, which, tho' altogether new to her, she appear'd
perfectly easy and genteel in." Rodomond observes, "My Freind [*sic*], who
had never before seen her as a woman, was dazzled and transported when
he first came into the Room.—He confest he had never beheld any thing so
lovely" (31). This passage shows that the heroine's stunning beauty is partially constituted by English clothing and that the significance of her color
is being erased. At this moment, her gender and racial ambiguity subsides.

Zoa's physical beauty is very important, since it is emphasized several
times by the narrator and other characters. In all intermarriage novels, dark-
skinned characters whom narrators wish readers to accept are routinely described as tawny but beautiful. Readers know that Zoa is primed for acceptance in the drawing room when the narrator observes, "*Zoa* had every
Thing, except Complection, that cou'd form a perfect beauty, and even that
was less swarthy than I have seen in some that are born in Europe, and not
esteem'd unlovely" (97). Zoa's precise hue elicits the same "eyewitness" testimony that the Moroccan emperor's did—he who was the least tawny man
in Africa. If Zoa's brownness is inherited from her father, her loveliness reflects the noble lineage on her mother's side (31). Nonetheless, Zoa's cultural
and physical similarity to Europeans is insufficient, in and of itself, for acceptance into London society. She must be a Christian to be the heroine. By
demanding baptism and a profession of faith, novels depart from contemporary protoscientific discourse, which featured visible, external differences in
the demarcation of human variety. By having "The History of Rodomond.
And the Beautiful Indian" become part of the frame narrative, *The Lady's
Drawing Room* presents Rodomond and Zoa as subjects of a newly forming
empire welcomed into England's fold.

Many European travelers found Indian women attractive, despite their

Figure 11. The Baptism of Zoa. *The True History of Zoa, the Beautiful Indian* (Stourbridge, 1815). Unlike earlier frontispieces that accompanied Zoa's history, which commonly show her the same shade as Rodomond but in East Indian dress, here Zoa's particular shade of complexion is highlighted through the contrast to the lighter European men and to the darker Indians. The addition of the Indian figures is not supported by the text; indeed, it apparently relocates the East Indian and London narrative in the Americas. These introduced figures, however, help in the task of reassuring readers about Zoa's European features, dress, and lighter coloring. By permission of the British Library.

skin color, and Robert Orme's comments are typical: "Their skins are of a polish and softness beyond that of all their rivals on the globe. . . . [A]lthough in the men he [a statuary] would find nothing to furnish the ideas of the Farnesian Hercules, he would find in the women the finest hints of the Medicean Venus."[58] Other than the attraction some male European travelers evidently felt toward East Indian women and the physical similarities to themselves that some Britons perceived, is there any other explanation for the celebration of the marriage between an Englishman and a young woman of mixed parentage? At first glance, Zoa's heroine status seems questionable: her real-life counterparts were among the most unempowered groups in India. Many of them married British soldiers, became domestics in European households, or wound up as prostitutes in the British community.[59] The literary treatment of a mixed-race woman was thus much more benign than the reality. One explanation for their fictional success may be a function of the novel itself. As Nancy Armstrong cogently argues about the ideological effect of novels like *The Lady's Drawing Room*, "Domestic fiction represented sexual relationships according to an idea of the social contract that empowered certain qualities of an individual's mind over membership in a particular group."[60] Novels, then, were a primary vehicle for exemplifying the rewards of virtue and gentle manners; in this context, Zoa's brown complexion is ultimately inconsequential, since novels put a premium on gentle behavior.

Other than the generic conventions that allowed for the representability of Zoa's marriage to Rodomond, East India was one of the very few places where marriage with native women was encouraged to create a mixed community supportive of British commercial policies. This encouragement was based on the perceived resemblance between Britain and the East Indies, including a well ordered, caste-based society, an ancient civilization with visible artifacts, and the commercial savvy of the inhabitants. These factors led many Englishmen to perceive East Indians more favorably than some African societies, for instance: "In the seventeenth century the East India Company encouraged the growth of a Eurasian community as a support for English activities. In 1687 the Court of Directors wrote to their officials at Madras that 'the marriage of our soldiers to the Native women' was 'a matter of such consequence to posterity that we shall be content to encourage it with some expense and have been thinking for the future to appoint a Pagoda to be paid to the Mother of any child that shall hereafter be born, of any such future marriage, upon the day the child be christened, if you think this small encouragement will increase the number of such marriages.'"[61] The customary couple was a working-class Englishman and a low-caste Hindu or Muslim woman; letters reveal that as late as the 1770s, some officers in the Bombay army "did not feel it dishonourable to marry Indian women."[62]

Historically, the privileged status of male Eurasian children, in comparison with native males, was secure until the third quarter of the eighteenth century. As a group, these children functioned as economic allies to British interest in the region. It was not until British involvement in India intensified toward the end of the century that the Eurasians were treated as a threat rather than as a desirable buffer group. Eurasian youths usually became civil servants or officers in the Company's armies, but in 1791 the Court of Directors "resolved that Eurasians could no longer be appointed to the Company's civil, military or marine services." Despite exceptions in practice, the official policy marks a significant change in British perception, military involvement, and economic interests in East India. Not surprisingly, the reasons offered for such a change in policy parallel those that resulted in legislation against amalgamation with people of African descent in America and the West Indies: "At the turn of the [nineteenth] century there had been fears that a strong Eurasian community might be a political threat: there was talk of Eurasian leadership in the revolt in Haiti."[63] Political conflict ultimately encouraged derogatory and institutionalized racial ideology.

* * *

Possibly the most important region of European political conflict in the eighteenth century, the North American colonies, promoted a slightly different set of racial concerns than the East Indies. Set in seventeenth-century Virginia and the Caribbean, *The Female American* differs from other intermarriage novels because of the Indian heroine's death, an event that is typically generated by plots with Native American women.[64] Fictional tragedy arises from real conflicts over land, the lengthy interaction between the British and Native Americans, and the history of its narration, such as "Inkle and Yarico"—a narrative that already emplotted the English economic and territorial betrayal of Amerindians at the level of romance. Similar to *The Fool of Quality* and *The Lady's Drawing Room*, *The Female American* features the marriages of two generations: the marriage of the English landowner Winkfield to the Indian princess Unca and the marriage of their daughter Unca Eliza to her first cousin, also named Winkfield. Christian conversion precedes Unca's marriage to an Englishman, but it does not usher in the Amerindian heroine's life in England. Neither the Amerindian mother nor the mixed-race daughter end up in England permanently. This deviation from other intermarriage narratives reveals, obliquely, some differences in the way constructions of race and marriage operate in regard to a colonized population. Despite this singularity, *The Female American* does not propound a deterministic view of race; this novel, like the others, promotes the notion that however unsettling dark color may be, it is ultimately insignificant.

Narrated by Unca Eliza, the novel initially concerns the story of her Indian grandfather and parents in the colony of Virginia during King James's reign. A revision of the Pocahontas legend, Winkfield is taken by the Indians during a massacre of the colonists, but he is ultimately saved by Unca, the king's daughter, immediately before his beheading because of his physical beauty. Despite the initial emphasis on native American treachery in their massacre of colonists, the narrative depicts them as rational, gentle "savages" otherwise. After rescuing him, Unca clothes Winkfield Indian style and sets him free. Winkfield learns the language and assumes residence there. One of the first ways that Winkfield domesticates himself is by instructing the princess, whose love he now returns, in Christian principles.

Other women often propose marriage to Englishmen. It is a sign of their improper gendering and/or their simple manners, and it is symptomatic of their cultural and religious difference. As in the novels with Muslim women, Unca proposes marriage, which initiates the beginning of a familiar conversion narrative: "As she was a Pagan, though my father sincerely loved her, and wished for that union, he could not help shewing some uneasiness at the proposal" (1:19–20). Winkfield's uneasiness concerns her religion. Just as the prospect of marriage with the Banyan makes Henrietta pause in *The Lady's Drawing Room*, Winkfield views Unca's paganism as prohibitive to marital happiness: "'My God will be angry if I marry you, unless you will worship him as I do'" (1:20). His religious instruction works. Notably, the language describing her conversion closely resembles the parallel scenes in the other intermarriage novels: "In a little time the princess became convinced of her errors, and her good understanding helped to forward her conversion" (20). After her conversion, they marry.

Religious difference, however, is not the only barrier to their felicitous union. At least initially, Unca's dark complexion impedes Winkfield's desire for her, a problem that the tawny-complected narrator finds understandable: "Though a complexion so different, as that of the princess from an European cannot but at first disgust, yet by degrees my father grew insensible to the difference, and in other respects her person was not inferior to that of the greatest European beauty; but what was more, her understanding was uncommonly great" (1:18–19). The narrative mentions Unca's dark color on several occasions; as in the case of the Banyan and the Moroccan emperor, dark complexion is both avowed as an issue impeding attraction and disavowed in its ultimate importance. Native conversion to Christianity validates English cultural superiority and is signified by Unca's donning European dress at her husband's insistence. Unca's rational acceptance of the superiority of Christianity promotes a false view of interracial harmony and native acceptance of British culture. In practice, the English colonists had few successful conversions—either to their way of living or to Christianity. After her marriage, Unca declines to go to England and is eventually murdered by her jealous sister Alluca.

Native Americans are a particularly important group in terms of racial discourse because in Europe there was little consensus about them even by the mid-eighteenth century. Among natural historians, there was possibly the greatest agreement about Indians' physical body in comparison to Europeans: Both Linnaeus and Buffon infuse their taxonomies with cultural and political judgments, in addition to describing generic bodies. Buffon's description emphasizes the limitations of Amerindian government, intellect, and language, and he dismisses them as savages. Linnaeus offers a more mixed categorization: Although copper-colored, quick to anger, and regulated by customs rather than laws, Americans are also a content and free people.[65] Many Britons believed that native Americans were primitive Europeans, untainted by civilization's corruption. Writers who focused on their physical appearance generally claimed an affinity between Amerindians and Europeans. For instance, in *The Natural History of North Carolina* (1737), the author finds Indians darker-complected than northern Europeans but visually pleasing: "The *Indian Women*, as well as the Men, are swarthy, but their features are very agreeable and fine as any People you shall meet with."[66] In contrast to this somewhat favorable view, other writers argued for Native Americans' inferiority based on the perception that they were treacherous, violent, and lacked a civil society. The conflicting views of Indians concurred, however, on the relative difference of Indian beliefs and institutions from Europeans' beliefs, particularly the alarming lack of clear social distinction.[67] Europeans generally considered American Indians less similar to themselves culturally than various Islamic and East Indian societies, a worldview encompassed in the customary reference to them as savages. *The Female American* unites the contradictory interpretations of Americans in the depiction of the gentle Unca and her villainous sister Alluca and therefore does not offer a seamless narrative racializing Indians.

Unca's reluctance to live in England and her tragic demise raise the question: Why isn't she successfully assimilated like her Islamic counterpart in *The Voyages of William Vaughan*, and why is she black? On the face of it, Unca's submission to religious and apparel norms should have been sufficient for British readers to accept her. In Virgina, the setting for *The Female American*, Indians were no longer numerically significant in the mid-eighteenth century and no longer a political threat. The human cost of colonialism—through death, disease, and social change—was evident to contemporaries in their dwindling numbers.[68] Africans, on the other hand, were numerically significant and a political threat at this time in Virginia. In fact, the coloring and death of Unca may be accounted for if she is viewed as a symbolic substitute for a woman of African descent. By placing the narrative during the early seventeenth century, this novel, like *Robinson Crusoe*, finesses the issue of black slavery; the only slaves are Indians.[69] The time and setting of the novel also mean that it is possible to ignore the fact that interracial sex would likely occur between a person of African descent and one of European descent. The most likely Other woman in eighteenth-century Virginia was a black African. When *The Female American* was published, Virginia's population was about 40 percent black and 60 percent white: "No other colony had such large numbers of both blacks and whites as Virginia, nor such a near and long-running balance between the two."[70] Because of the imbalance of white men to all other populations of women, rates of racial mixing were extremely high in Virginia during the seventeenth and eighteenth centuries (37), especially between black and white populations. Furthermore, Virginia was a significant location for contemplating the effects of interracial progeny. The first and greatest racial mixing occurred in the Chesapeake world of Virginia and Maryland.[71]

Another view of Unca's death responds to the liminal status of Native Americans, who were simultaneously a sovereign people and candidates for enslavement. Nevertheless, Indian birth was less of a problem (in legal terms) than African origin, which was evident in rights accorded to the descendants of interracial liaisons. Commensurate with Jamaica's regulations, Virginia's statutory definition of mulattos "extended the taint of Negro ancestry through three generations and of Indian ancestry through only one."[72] Apparently, Unca's origin rendered assimilation dubious, even in fictional terms, and this perception is reinforced by several other novels whose female Indians are depicted as fond wives or suitors of Englishmen who soon die so that the protagonist can return to England unencumbered. The death of an American heroine is especially suspicious in Unca's case, since she is a princess: High rank does not supersede affiliation with Indians. Heroines from noncolonized populations, such as the Ottoman Empire and the East Indies, are not killed in novels and are envisioned as new British subjects. Unlike the absence that characterizes relationships between the British and people of African descent, marriage between Britons and Indians frequently occurs in fiction but rarely lasts. It is up to the mixed-race progeny to bridge the gap.

Unlike the fate of the Indian princess, complete assimilation of Unca and Winkfield's daughter is untroubled despite the narrative's insistence on her hybrid appearance and her delight in masculine pursuits. Unca Eliza's mixed origins reveal themselves in her double name, exotic dress, and her gender ambiguity, which is fostered by an education combining study of classical languages and domestic skills. These factors all indicate that more established ideologies of gender difference and European fashion are responsible for signaling racial mixture than racial ideology itself. In England, Unca Eliza's dress, hair texture, and skin color link her visually to Indians in a way that recalls Linnaeus's snapshot description of Americans, yet her exotic appearance attracts Englishmen's sexual (and financial) desire: "Tawny as I was, with my lank black hair, I yet had my admirers, or such they pretended to be; though perhaps my fortune tempted them more than my person, at least I thought so" (1:47). In as much as her mother's dark color initially disgusts the Englishman in America, Unca Eliza's lighter color makes her attractively exotic in England. No doubt, the rigorous religious instruction that she undergoes from her clergyman uncle helps mitigate the visual impact of her differences. Her knowledge and love of Christianity are key to resolving the plot, which shifts to a Caribbean island.

Unca Eliza's liminal status is given further play when she is abandoned on an uninhabited Caribbean island by an unscrupulous European captain who unsuccessfully demands she marry his son (for her wealth). Instead of "going native," Unca Eliza relies on her Christian and European sensibilities for survival. Fortitude and resourcefulness—colorless national traits—come in handy when she decides to convert the Indians from a neighboring island rather than hide from them. Unca Eliza plans to speak to them through the medium of their pagan idol; in fact, she hopes that her "tawny complexion would be some recommendation" to the process of Christian conversion (1:149). In converting the "real" Indians, which was a man's job, Unca Eliza is eventually regendered and renationalized as a wholly British female.

Unca Eliza's plan to convert the Indians and live with them hinges on her discovery of their towering, androgynous sun idol. The idol represents a thousand years of Indian history, religion, and customs. In a now familiar plot device in intermarriage novels, Unca Eliza dons a disguise. Dressed in the vestments and the rings of their male high priest, Unca Eliza masquerades as the Indians' oracle. Appropriating their religious signs, she instructs the Indians through the body of the enormous idol to accept her as their spiritual leader. Whereas her female gendering made her vulnerable to the greedy captain who abandoned her on the island, it positions her favorably in relation to the Indians once she appears among them as a woman, sent to them by their oracle. Unca Eliza, both English and Indian, appears unthreat-

ening to both populations because she is female and therefore assimilable to
the culture of the men with whom she associates.

The novel's denouement completely replaces pagan signs with Christian ones. The process initiated by Unca Eliza is finished by her English
cousin and another Englishman. Although it becomes possible for Unca
Eliza and her husband/cousin to return to England, Winkfield merely does
so to leave his relations permanently, receive his parents' blessing, and "settle
half of his and [Unca Eliza's] fortune upon his sisters, and leave the rest
for charitable uses" (2:169). After the transferal of wealth to Great Britain,
the final act of the narrative is the destruction of the androgynous idol—the
oracle that symbolizes autonomous Indian history, religion, and customs as
well as Unca Eliza's means of ascendancy. The destruction of the idol is a
symbolic substitution that renarrates British history in America; instead of
natives decimated by disease, pushed away from coastal areas, and uneasily
assimilated, in some cases, by European colonization, this novel destroys a
religious and cultural icon to sever the ties with the Indians' indigenous past
so that they may assume a new Christian identity. The Winkfields and the
other Englishman collect all the gold treasure buried in the idol, and then
they blow it up so that "the Indians might never be tempted to their former
idolatry" (2:169). Ever pragmatic, English expropriation of colonial wealth
appears benign, even generous; it saves the Indians from their past.

What the Winkfields achieve there is what they cannot achieve outside
such a controlled environment: "What with catechising, and his preaching
twice a week, we had greatly the appearance of a christian country. The natural simplicity and purity of the Indian manners greatly accelerated this work"
(2:128). Despite its occasional critique of the effects of colonization, *The
Female American* conveys an optimistic sense of assimilating Caribbean Indians to cherished British ideals primarily because of a theory of human variety
that posited behavior as malleable through changes in climate and education; the novel simply cannot imagine them living in Britain. If a British narrative of a successful Christian nation was unlikely in relation to the American or the Caribbean colonies, happy coexistence with native inhabitants
occurs only away from England and America. Because there are no other
Europeans (except one virtuous man who desires to stay), their Christian
paradise remains a subsistence economy, safely outside circuits of colonial
exchange. As Chapters 4 and 5 contend, consumerism and involvement in
trade are at once forces that can reduce the impact of racial ideology and that
can make an exploited labor force absolutely necessary.

This mixed-race heroine has a happy ending, and there are several reasons for Unca Eliza's success story in comparison with her mother's tragic
ending. First, although the novel emphasizes that she is bilingual and

bicultural, Unca Eliza's Christian upbringing and secular education in England erase the significance of her tawny color. As a result, she is the perfect embodiment of colonial relations, especially in her expansion of a benign Christian and English empire. The intermarriage novels intimate that mixed-race children were more European than Other. Unca Eliza can be the heroine that an African slave, freed woman, or Amerindian could not be because of her high rank inherited from both parents and because of the double standard that distinguished Indians favorably from Negroes.

*   *   *

As the first empire was superseded by the second one in 1763, Great Britain found itself the most powerful European nation. Britain's emergence as a particular kind of Christian nation and empire was marked by debates about population. Many patriots desired increased immigration to bolster the number of its citizens in order to compete more favorably with France.[73] Perhaps the most significant aspect of naturalization was the taking of Anglican sacrament, a requirement that posed particular problems for Catholics for whom the law was mainly devised (41). In all of the narratives that I've examined, the insistence on Christian conversion and religious education not only is a sexual or romantic issue but also responds to a ubiquitous concern about increasing the number of lawful subjects and about building a strong nation based on peaceable subordination. As Eve Tabor Bannet convincingly shows, the Marriage Act of 1753 also addresses the anxiety of ensuring a numerous and industrious citizenry by establishing the legal structure for rearing children within the family that hitherto had been absent.[74]

Intermarriage novels do not simply reflect the material conditions of colonialism, nor are they preoccupied with racial difference; rather, these novels unveil certain culturally tacit views about human variety when they are focused on romance. As many critics have noted, the eighteenth-century novel created a fictional, though authoritative, national history of the present. In its version of Britain, the intermarriage novel revises Englishmen's economic and sexual transactions with Others and thereby make them more palatable than the reality. Repeatedly, intermarriage novels show the British being vindicated in their religion, governance, and national integrity at the same time that they imaginatively construct an England accepting of diversity—within conventional codes of rank and religion. The novels demonstrate that Christianity was still the most important, if idealized, difference from Others.

All of the intermarriage novels erase religious difference and the significance of dark color in the Other partner. In the only example of an un-

happy marriage in *The Lady's Drawing Room*, the Banyan's lack of condescension to his wife, not his race, causes conflict, although by repeatedly
mentioning his tawny color, the novel conveys a general discomfort with
such unions. In midcentury novels, darker complexion and racial traits (e.g.,
treachery) are significant primarily in relation to Indians in the East Indies,
the Americas, and the West Indies—the only groups whose territory the
British occupied in any authoritative way during the eighteenth century.
This discursive phenomenon indicates one of the ways that race and colonialism worked together—to emphasize perceptible differences between the
British and those whom they exploited.

Throughout the rest of the century, as a new ideology of human difference was emerging in natural history and comparative anatomy, cultural
realms that featured the significance of visible distinctions among humans,
novels sustained an increasingly more subversive understanding of human
difference. This paradigm allowed for a selective acceptance of high-rank
individuals despite their dark color or cultural origin because racial ideology
had not yet shifted in all realms to make appearance more important than
behavior. Also, assumptions in novels about skin color and character seem to
rely loosely on a climatic understanding of their origins. The novels simply
dismiss dark color as an obstacle to romantic desire after initially making
it one.

Because none of these narratives contemplates importing other beliefs
or manners into British society, intermarriage with a nonslave population
is neither a negative nor a threatening phenomenon. Midcentury fiction
imagines it as a desirable solution to racial difference. This construction of
intermarriage is a far cry from the social opprobrium interracial sex and its
offspring elicit for much of the nineteenth and twentieth centuries. The absence of black Africans, except as momentary specters, suggests that Sir
George Ellison's ineffable sense of indelicacy in contemplating amalgamation, even in England, may account for the dearth of these characters. Although there were no biological notions that gave voice to political anxieties
associated with racial mixture, the sense that individuals were debased because they were enslaved contributes to this avoidance at the level of representation.

Literary representation of fictional intermarriages also suggests that
their success hinges on the domestic ideology of marriage as much as on
the national origin and high rank of the characters. In England, marriages
in the upper and middle ranks largely concerned the transmission of property, the transference of liquid capital, and the assurance of women's subordinate position in society. As the epigraph from *Pamela* confirms, a woman's

rank was conformable to her husband's class position because of masculine privilege and not vice versa—a phenomenon that reflected the legal definition that there was one body in marriage and that was the man's. The racial identity of these Other women is, to a large extent, inconsequential in marriage because she is a woman. In these novels, we can see the overdetermined meanings attached to Christianity and masculine privilege through the bodies of the heroines. Christian marriage confers acceptable identity on Other women. It is an ideological site safe for depicting an apparently natural racial subordination through the heroine's joyful submission to a loving English husband. Indeed, it is no surprise that many of these narratives feature mixed-race heroines rather than mixed-race heroes. It is through their marriage to Englishmen and their return to England that Other women's success is measured. A mixed-race hero is not, to my knowledge, ideologically likely at this period. Because of his masculine gender, he was not believed to be as assimilable to British authority as his female counterpart, and his allegiances were not believed to be naturally connected to Britain's. The absence of mixed-race sons suggests the difficulty of categorizing them and in imagining their return to Europe as autonomous citizen subjects.[75] Englishwomen are noticeably absent from these interracial romances as they were from novels like Defoe's, which focus on the economic relations of colonialism. At midcentury, a European woman's desire for a dark-skinned, non-European, non-Christian man appears scandalous despite the numerous testimonies, fictional and otherwise, of European men's attraction to Other women.

Intermarriage novels feature a traditional notion of human variety dominant at the time, one that is externally induced by climate and easily changed through education and European accessories. Because of this understanding of human difference, these novels depict British willingness to embrace select Others in the expanding nation. Such a benign vision of the nation, however, is obtained by excluding men and women of African heritage altogether and by erasing other non-European men and Englishwomen. This fictional nation features British men as cultural agents, who, by love, not violence, assimilate the female children of empire and who assume the role increasingly allotted to middle- and upper-class women as agents of civilization.[76] Many of the unarticulated assumptions about race and the connection between physical appearance and state of civilization that show up, sometimes oddly, in midcentury intermarriage novels become more coherently rendered in the theories of human variety and social progress that veritably flood the market in the 1770s.

Chapter 4

Consuming Englishness

On the Margins of Civil Society

To the Lapland dwarf, let the giant of Madagascar succeed. Let the flat-faced African with his black complexion and woolly hair, give place to the European, whose regular features are set off by the whiteness of his complexion and beauty of his head of hair. To the filthiness of a Hottentot, oppose the neatness of a Dutchman. From the cruel Anthropophagite pass swiftly to the humane Frenchman. Place the stupid Huron opposite the profound Englishman. Ascend from the Scotch peasant to the great NEWTON.

—CHARLES BONNET, *The Contemplation of Nature* (1766) [1]

And one may almost venture to say that providence, by throwing Bengal into the arms of Britain, seems to have intended that this, the richest commercial state in Asia, which, through the effeminacy of its inhabitants, should be subjected to Britain, as being the fittest, through similarity of commercial disposition, interest, and modes, to properly govern it; and through her superiority in naval force, the best qualified to defend and protect it.

— *The Present State of the British Interest in India* (1773) [2]

IN publications of the 1770s and later, it was not unusual for Englishmen writing about colonial policy to refer to theories of human variety in making their recommendations, especially in the ongoing discussions about the East Indies. References to their own character and Others' also inflected historical discourse, which is apparent in the many histories of England and the empire published after midcentury. This chapter analyzes two texts with substantial truth claims that typify the range of contemporary racial ideology in the 1770s: Edward Long's *History of Jamaica* (1774) and Samuel Johnson's *Journey to the Western Islands of Scotland* (1775). Long's detailed examination of civil, political, and economic life in Jamaica synthesized a century of colonial research and his own experience of living in Jamaica. Johnson's less systematic record of the Scots resulted from his summer travels with James Boswell in the early 1770s and was influenced by his readings in civil and natural history. Both of these texts participate in a European boom in the human sciences during the final decades of the century, in which the investigation into humans as a "species" and as civil beings gathered momentum.

Johnson's and Long's narratives of British subjects are symptomatic of a paradigm in transition. The older model for comparative analysis of a people derived from the classical tradition. It articulated political relations between the civilized metropole and the barbaric periphery, and it was itself undergoing a certain amount of revision at the hands of the moral philosophers of the Scottish Enlightenment. The newer model of comparative analyses focused on physical typology, and natural histories characterized groups of people in terms of skin color, facial features, and stature. Eighteenth-century racial ideology moves freely between civil and physical characteristics. This fluidity is particularly noticeable in encomiums on Britons' own beautiful white skin color, felicitous government, and polished manners—often all in one sentence. Linnaeus and Buffon, as well as travel writers, demonstrate the simultaneous assessment of bodies and ways of living in their taxonomies of human variety.

Europeanness as a physical and sociopolitical typology was being more aggressively adjudicated than ever before in the proliferation of natural and civil histories, and Englishness was a special concern to writers in the British Isles. Both European and English types were arrived at through a complex amalgam of domestic and foreign contrasts. One example of this process is noticeable in the epigraph. In *The Contemplation of Nature* (1766), the Swiss doctor Charles Bonnet reflects on the astonishing variety of physical and intellectual features around the globe and on their unequal distribution. In his quirky version of what he calls "the universal chain of being," Bonnet illustrates the various hierarchies that Europeans recognized based on stature, complexion, orderliness, civilized behavior, class position, and intellect.

Bonnet was not the only European who suspected that certain Scots ranked among the colonial Others.[3]

In a more sophisticated way than Bonnet but working from a similar set of assumptions, Samuel Johnson and Edward Long each focus on one of the less polished populations to assess more carefully their resemblance to the English. Despite their differing investments in slavery and in the expansion of empire, both writers similarly engage discourses of savagery, consumerism, literacy, and labor to position the various populations of Scotland and Jamaica in relation to each other and to England. Like their contemporaries who were associated with the Scottish Enlightenment, Long and Johnson scrutinize the "savage" past in Africa and the Highlands in order to reflect on the present benefits of English rule. Both writers participate in the assurance that for the Africans and for the Scots, commercial, linguistic, and sexual contact with the English civilizes them. In the process, both racialize Englishness similarly, which helps justify empire building. Similar to Defoe's liberties with fictional depictions of seventeenth-century Africa and the Caribbean, Long and Johnson rewrite African and Scottish history to emphasize the positive effect of contact with the English. Both texts create a hierarchy within the empire based on the realization of English norms of consumer behavior and even physical appearance.

One of the many points that Johnson and Long share is what 1990s motivational speakers call "retail therapy." A comparison of Long's *History* and Johnson's *Journey* shows that many popular beliefs about human difference were inextricable from British experiences of commercial society. Consumption of English goods figures as a primary antidote to savagery and as the key to cultural assimilation in their texts. A shared material culture, they believed, facilitated social solidarity and the cohesion of the empire. It is no small paradox that commercial society held out contradictory possibilities. One potential was for it to retard the force of racial concepts based on assumptions about physical difference through emulation of English behavior, manners, and dress. The other potential was for it to depend on perceived bodily differences economically and culturally. By linking Johnson's text to Long's, I place *Journey* in the thick of contemporary racial ideology and the propensity to racialize British subjects.

* * *

By the time Johnson took his long anticipated journey to the Scottish Highlands and Islands and Edward Long penned his account of Jamaica, Britons had a much greater sense of the physical distinctions among human groups than ever before and showed a lively interest in interpreting them. The two most common paradigms for racializing people were natural history, or the description of the physical body, and four-stages theory. Together they offered a comprehensive sense of the "natural" and civil aspects of human groups. Johnson and Long called on both paradigms to analyze the populations of the Highlands and Jamaica, respectively. Their indebtedness to four-stages theory is evident in their claim that Scotland and Jamaica will be more secure and profitable arms of the empire if the feudal organization of clans and slave-based plantation society is replaced by a commercial model approximating England's own—with less polarization and more socioeconomic gradations. In Johnson's *Journey*, the indebtedness to natural history is most obvious when he contemplates the effects of climate, terrain, and poverty on the stature and beauty of the Hebrideans. In Long's *History*, the nod to natural history is most apparent in his marshaling the explanatory power of skin color to rank the various-colored Jamaican inhabitants in aesthetic and political terms.

Between 1770 and 1780, skin color and physical attributes in general became more central to Britons' understanding of human beings, as is evident in the sheer number of natural histories that they wrote as well as in their references to facial and bodily features in all kinds of documents. A sense of the change is recorded in the difference between the first and second editions of the *Encyclopaedia Britannica*. In the first edition of 1771, complexion and color receive no special treatment. Ten years later in the second edition, "Colour of the Human Species" receives this comment: "Few questions in philosophy have engaged the attention of naturalists more than the diversities among the human species, among which that of colour is the most remarkable. . . . We have shewn [in the entry for "America"] that all arguments which can be brought for specific differences among mankind . . . must necessarily be inconclusive."[4]

Despite the scholarly attentiveness to skin color and race since the 1960s, there has been little analysis of the debate about their meaning in the eighteenth century. The most influential natural historians were committed to the explanation of color resulting from the strong effect of the sun, diet, and other factors on the body's surface. They declared that climate explained all physical human variety and that differences in geography and complexion were the best way to organize various groups of human kind in their taxonomies and essays. If mentioned at all, human understanding was usually assumed to be the same. Occasionally it was said to vary because of the climate; that is, the mind was subject to similar forces that the body was and responded in kind. As a dominant ideology, skin color emerges as the predominant racial category in the mid-1770s within natural history, but its racist implications were initially blunted by widespread disagreement about whether complexion indicated any deeper difference and by a majority of thinkers who subscribed to the belief that all humans partook of the same ability.

Oliver Goldsmith's *History of the Earth and Animated Nature* (1774) is typical, then, of the 1770s when he favors skin color to schematize human differences. Unlike previous speculation that weighed stature, shape of features, and complexion fairly evenly, Goldsmith confidently asserts that "of all animals, the differences between mankind are the smallest.... The chief differences in man are rather taken from the tincture of his skin than the variety of his figure."[5] This usage of color marks a watershed in the human sciences. After this point, skin color is commonly accepted as the best way to organize human variety in taxonomies and essays. Although it could be argued that Linnaeus and Buffon both emphasized color differences in their delineations of humans, Goldsmith is among the first to single it out above all other characteristics by which humans were distinguished. Goldsmith follows Buffon in insisting that climate, nourishment, and custom are sufficient to produce every physical change (1:364). Even though he and others continue to focus on external and changeable factors, he is interested in the possibility of climate influencing mental capability. His brief reference to the correlation between the body and mind departs from Buffon's text, which he usually closely adopts. This connection symptomatically appears only in his discussion of Africans and Europeans. After describing the texture of skin, color, and facial features characteristic of Negroes, Goldsmith considers other physical characteristics. Because of a warm climate and a lack of foundation garments, such as wealthier Europeans then wore, the men's genitals and women's breasts seem "large and languid" to European eyes (372). Goldsmith observes about the connection between the mind and body: "As their persons are thus naturally deformed, at least to our imaginations, their minds are equally incapable of strong exertions. The climate seems to relax their mental powers still more than those of the body" (373). Europeans are the only other population who warrant comment on their intellectual powers. Predictably, Goldsmith observes that "the beauty of their complexions" is matched by "the vigour of their understandings" (374). Despite these conventional associations between climate and humors, Goldsmith maintains that "there is nothing in the shape, nothing in the faculties, that shows their [humans] coming from different originals" (364).

Goldsmith's assumption about the deleterious effects of a hot climate is shared by other writers and doctors. For instance, in his 1775 dissertation,

John Hunter cannot easily dismiss the possible connection between physical attributes and mental qualities either. He believes that mental differences among the world's inhabitants have been exaggerated by previous writers, but he concedes the basic force of their observation: "The mental varieties seem equal to and sometimes greater than the bodily varieties of man."[6] Remarkably, he does not elaborate on the implications of this statement. The increasing attention to the connections between climate, complexion, and mental capacity, however, mirrors the analysis of national character and genius in civil histories.

Despite their dismissive pronouncements about the appearance of entire groups of people, natural historians were still somewhat catholic in their determination of who looked like a European. In two of the most widely read 1770s texts on human variety—by Blumenbach and Goldsmith—they categorized as European most people of the regions bordering on Europe, including much of Asia (west of the Ganges River) and North Africa. In his revised second edition of *On the Natural Variety of Mankind* (1781), Blumenbach expanded the European category to include most of the inhabitants of the northern or arctic regions, such as Laplanders, Greenlanders, and North American Eskimos. Compared with Goldsmith or Blumenbach, Buffon had opted for a more finely calibrated scheme of minute color differences in his 1749 treatment of human diversity, noting variations within France between the darker country peasant and the lighter city dweller.[7] He allowed as European the swarthy and yellow Spanish and the white northern nations. Clearly, the denominations *European* and *white skin* were not synonymous yet. At the same time natural historians were working out the color boundaries for Europeans and others, Scottish Enlightenment writers were figuring out the criteria for the various stages of savagery and civilization. The importance of what people looked like was not quite as fixed as what people did in the determination of difference.

* * *

Some of the most influential civil histories were penned by Scotsmen, and they include several essays and studies by David Hume, Adam Ferguson's *Essay on the History of Civil Society* (1767), James Burnett, Lord Monboddo's *Origin and Progress of Language* (1773), Henry Home, Lord Kames's *Six Sketches on the History of Man* (1774), John Millar's *Origin of the Distinction of Ranks* (1771), and James Dunbar's *Essays on the History of Mankind in Rude and Civilized Ages* (1780). These titles are a small indication of the interest in societal development during the 1770s. Most of the prominent writers of the Scottish Enlightenment analyze the changes wrought by commercial progress in their histories of civil life. Collectively, their speculations solidify portraits of savage, barbarian, and polished societies and map how these societies develop.[8]

What we now call four-stages theory emerged as a significant explanatory system (and validation) of commercial progress such as England exemplified. Through a few general principles, it helped elucidate Europe's Enlightenment in a comprehensive manner. Four-stages theory synthesized commonplaces about England's excellence that had first appeared in the seventeenth century and gained considerable ground after the end of the Civil War. Focused on mode of subsistence to explain the evolution of societies, four-stages theory characterized the most savage societies as those engaged in hunting, fishing, or shepherding activities and the more polished societies as the ones that pursued agriculture and commerce. The theory details the institutions that typify each stage, such as the form of government, the judicial role, state of the arts, technological innovation, and the resulting manners of the people. The chief marks of advancement from one stage to the next are increased protection of private property, refined treatment of women as companions, not servants, and participation in commerce.

Ronald Meek's *Social Science and the Ignoble Savage* (1976), one of the few extensive studies of four-stages theory in eighteenth-century political and historical thought, contends that between 1760 and 1780, four-stages theory became culturally influential, and that between 1780 and 1800, it became more like an orthodoxy.[9] The texts of the Scottish Enlightenment are central to understanding the eighteenth-century investment in civil Britons and the means by which this functioned as a racial ideology. With its emphasis on material culture, four-stages theory provided a conception of human difference that was, on the face of it, antipathetic to the implications of physical typology. By offering an alternative explanatory system, it also forestalled the trend to make notions of race bone deep through the study of comparative anatomy. In this paradigm, like its religious counterpart Christianity, what people do and how they live is important—not what people look like.

Despite agreement about the factors that constituted either a rude or a civil society, the writers who contributed to four-stages theory were uncertain about the causes of the factors that they described. To eighteenth-century British intellectuals, ascertaining origins was the best way to interpret a phenomenon, when possible. Influential seventeenth-century writers, such as Sir Thomas Browne, had limited success in dismissing the sun's heat as a sole cause of color differences on logical grounds. Problems with climatic explanations abated for much of the eighteenth century because no viable alternative explanation was forthcoming. The traditional explanation of the sun accounting for dark skin color was not abandoned but augmented by other climatic factors, such as wind, proximity to water, fertility of soil, and the like. Nevertheless, the explanatory force of climate to account for human variety was tentatively questioned again in the final decades of the eighteenth century.

Although climate remained the most important way to explain why people looked and acted the way that they did and why societies had formed in a certain way, some Europeans wondered if the role of human agency might be much greater than hitherto granted.[10] Scottish Enlightenment thinkers, for example, entertained the possibility of internal conditions driving social progress. From Montesquieu to Millar, however, the exact role of moral causes of human progress was raised but never resolved. Their thinking largely relied on the assumption that climate and terrain bore directly, but in a long-term manner, on the institutions that shaped a society. Many moral philosophers, however, speculated that a goodly amount of innovation and human intervention could improve unsophisticated conditions. Climate occasionally occupied an uncertain role in four-stages theory.

In the predominant assumptions of Scottish Enlightenment thinkers, the fertility of the soil, the food it yielded, the density of the population, the kind of labor the inhabitants performed, their proficiency in arts, and their opportunity to enter into mutual transactions with each other were key to forming national character. According to John Millar, "The variety that frequently occurs in these [soil, terrain, climate, labor], and such other particulars, must have a prodigious influence upon the great body of a people; as, by giving a peculiar direction to their inclinations and pursuits, it must be productive of correspondent habits, dispositions, and ways of thinking."[11] In focusing on external conditions other than the sun's heat, Hume, Millar, and others appeared to question humoral theory. Millar, for instance, claims that weather can't account for profound differences of conduct noted between France and Spain or China and Japan (10–13). The body's response to these factors is unclear to Millar: "We are too little acquainted with the structure of the human body to discover how it is affected by such physical circumstances, or to discern the alterations in the state of the mind, which may possibly proceed from a different conformation of bodily organs" (12). Nonetheless, Millar subscribes to the universal impetus that humans emulate superiority and thereby improve their societies. Speculating that there is "in man a disposition and capacity for improving his condition, by the exertion of which, he is carried on from one degree of advancement to another"

(3), Millar reasons, by extension, that in human society, there is "a natural progress from ignorance to knowledge, and from rude, to civilized manners, the several stages of which are usually accompanied with peculiar laws and customs" (5). Individuals within nations, however, do not display the same uniformity. There is, he observes, often "a great diversity" with respect to individuals, "proceeding from no fixed causes that are capable of being ascertained" (6). As Millar's conundrum suggests, there are several factors to juggle and individual exceptions to synthesize. Generalization is rife with problems.

The considerable uncertainty about their propositions did not stop the many luminaries of the Scottish Enlightenment from putting forth the suspicion that societies were not equally capable of the same achievements, a group that included Hume, Ferguson, and Kames. Even though they gave great credence to the influence of climate and mode of subsistence as ways to account for the different pace at which societies developed, these Scottish Enlightenment writers also gave intellectual sanction to the proposition of unequal advancement and ability. Millar and Hume commented on the startling differences between the Irish, Scots, and English as well as on the gap in achievement between Europeans and all other people. John Millar is helpful in summarizing the concern many writers voiced about the failure of climate alone to elucidate national character in the last two decades of the century:

How is it possible to explain those national peculiarities that have been remarked in the English, the Irish, and the Scotch, from the different temperature of the weather under which they have lived?

The different manners of a people in the same country, at different periods, are no less remarkable, and afford evidence yet more satisfactory, that national character depends very little upon the immediate operation of climate. (13)

Indicating the scope of changes that occurred in the 1770s, John Millar introduced the doubts about climate only in the third edition of *The Origin of the Distinction of Ranks* (1781).

David Hume was one eighteenth-century Briton to question the role of climate. His essays, published in midcentury, probe the distinctly modern British commercial and cultural exceptionality. His ideas about the political, economic, and moral forces operating in civil society influenced an entire generation of Scottish *cognoscenti*. Dunbar, Ferguson, Millar, William Robertson, and Adam Smith all adopted or modified Hume's speculations. Like many of his contemporaries, including Samuel Johnson, Hume had little interest in the inhabitants of most non-European countries.

The change in his treatment of Africans between 1742 and 1777 is symptomatic of wider changes in the perception of human differences, especially as they came to apply more particularly to Negroes than to any other population. In one of his most famous essays, "Of National Characters" (1742), he contends that moral causes, such as type of government, amount of national wealth, and the habits of a people, were more important than physical causes, such as climate, in forming national character. This argument appears to depart from commonplaces of the day, which ascribed national manners and appearance to the workings of temperature, terrain, and diet. Instead, Hume suggests that while nature produced a variety of tempers and understanding in each country, it did not follow that they were produced in the same proportion.[12]

Hume favors an explanation of national character based on the influence of external forces other than climate, such as government, commerce, and geographic situation. His preference is based on his not wanting to concede that the mind responds to outside stimuli similarly to the body in the temperate zone. Despite his consciousness of departing from past rubrics, he maintains the same insights that humoral/climate theory offered. He just doesn't include any of the positive qualities for people outside Europe. All nations beyond the polar circles or between the tropics, he contends, "are inferior to the rest of the species, and are incapable of the higher attainments of the human mind. The poverty and the misery of the northern inhabitants of the globe, and the indolence of the southern, from their few necessities, may, perhaps account for this remarkable difference" without recourse to degrees of heat and cold (207). He concedes that climate may affect the exterior body and organs, but it does not "work upon those finer organs on which the operations of the mind and understanding depend" (214). To refute climate/humoral theory, Hume notes that most conquests originated in the north. Northern nations, he maintains, were spurred on by their poverty, not by any superior courage (211). The characters of nations in the temperate climates "are very promiscuous," by which he means various (208).

Scotland and Jamaica both appear as proof positive of his theory that some nations have not excelled at the same rate as England. As evidence that climate was not as significant as other factors to the formation of national manners, Hume notes that all climatic and physical causes applied equally to Scotland as to England but without the same effect (207): Scots showed little of the industry that Englishmen did. When Hume wishes to underscore the sense that there were original distinctions among the globe's inhabitants not due to climate, he refers to Jamaica and the poems of Francis Williams as proof that no matter where Negroes were or what advantages they had, they did not match Europeans of any rank in learning. The son of free black parents, Williams was educated at Cambridge at the behest of the duke of Montague, who wished to determine " 'whether, by proper cultivation, and a regular course of tuition at school and the university, a Negroe might not be found as capable of literature as a white person.' "[13] His Latin and English poems received much attention from abolitionists, but Hume and Edward Long both dismissed them as merely imitative of English culture, not evidence of African genius *sui generis*. Hume's remarks are especially surprising given that elsewhere in his writings he assumes that the "natural genius of mankind" was the same in all ages "and in almost all countries"; therefore, it was important to identify patterns for imitation, which would lead to a more universal excellence.[14]

To illustrate the hypothesis in his 1758 revision of the essay that both moral and physical causes contribute to national character, Hume includes Africans with all other non-European populations when he writes in a new footnote, "I am apt to suspect the negroes, and in general all the other species of men (for there are four or five different kinds) to be naturally inferior to the whites. There never was a civilized nation of any other complexion than white, nor even any individual eminent either in action or speculation. No ingenious manufactures amongst them, no arts, no sciences."[15] This claim contrasts all the nonwhite populations to the ancient Germans and to the present-day Tartars (Asians). This last group evinces valor and has governing institutions that show the potential for eminence he sees lacking elsewhere. By the 1777 revision of the essay, Hume singles out Negroes as opposite to Whites. The difference of twenty years is subtle but telling when he writes: "I am apt to suspect the negroes to be naturally inferior to the whites. There scarcely ever was a civilized nation of that complexion, nor even any individual eminent either in action or speculation."[16] Regarding this inferiority as a constant difference throughout time, Hume attributes it to "an original distinction" between whites and all nonwhites. Hume's unorthodox religious beliefs made it difficult for some to adopt his opinions at all; others did not share his sense of large differences between Africans and Britons or his conviction that other societies lacked positive attributes. Nevertheless, some Scottish men of letters followed Hume's lead by inquiring into the contribution of moral causes to national excellence and by singling out Africans for special consideration.

In 1767, the Highlander Adam Ferguson also assessed the influence of climate and geography on national advancement. Even though he based his analysis on a cyclical view of history, in which empires became polished and declined and then rose again, Ferguson believed that the regions of Europe *perhaps* belie the natural progress of nations because they were at such a high pitch of achievement compared with other places. This exception gives rise to doubts about external climatic causes of societal development. Like many before him, Ferguson found that the temperate zone was most conducive to human development, and he turned to evidence of cultural and political achievement in Europe for verification: "The arts, which he has on this scene repeatedly invented, the extent of his reason, the fertility of his fancy, and the force of his genius in literature, commerce, policy, and war, sufficiently declare *either* a distinguished advantage of situation, *or* a natural superiority of mind."[17] The first choice fit comfortably with classical thinking; the second choice marked a new way of explaining Europe's history. This new approach to European superiority derived from Hume; Ferguson observed that "the strength of a nation is derived from the character, not from the wealth, nor from the multitude of its people" (61). This departure from standard mercantilist principles to highlight national manners and achievements marked a new emphasis in racializing the English and their imperial prerogative—especially since it dispensed with France's traditional claim to eminence through its large number of subjects (and beliefs about Africa's large population).[18]

To lend credence to his claims about African society, Ferguson referred to their lack of written texts and architectural monuments. This absence suggested to Ferguson that Africa defied natural progress in terms that Edward Long would have recourse to when he used this "fact" to support the benefits of slavery in *The History of Jamaica*. In emphasizing the invisibility of social and political change in Africa, Ferguson unwittingly revealed that it was due, largely, to European inability to interpret African material and oral culture: "Great part of Africa has been always unknown; but the silence of fame, on the subject of its revolutions, is an argument, where no other proof can be found, of weakness in the genius of its people" (110). Ferguson's and Hume's suppositions about Europe's and Africa's singularity were uncertainly dealt with by Henry Home, Lord Kames, who recorded the process by which he arrived at his beliefs. In *Six Sketches on the History of Man* (1774), Kames argued that progress had taken place at vastly different paces in various societies. Ultimately, he too hedged about whether this difference resulted from the stimulus of a people's nature or from the influence of climate (50). He admitted that initially he considered Africans a separate race because of their color, even though he believed that it resulted from the hot climate. Another piece of evidence that Kames offered for thinking that Africans were a separate race was their inferior intellectual discernment compared with Europeans. On second thought, however, he reckoned that their inferior understanding was "occasioned by their condition." If they were subject to the same government and political institutions that Europeans were, and they had to earn wages, then they would show similar intellectual proclivities as Europeans (42). Kames's intellectual meanderings and revisions encapsulated the conjunction of color prejudice and civil anatomy characteristic of the 1760s and 1770s.

The combined force of the speculations of natural and civil historians led to some alarming suppositions, which were backed by a growing body of literature. The sense that bodily, intellectual, and cultural differences might be somehow connected was broached anew in the most influential discussions about human variety during the 1770s and 1780s. In these and other documents, actual economic and political subordination found expression and, occasionally, justification in racial terms; these terms were more likely to include a reflection on the intellectual capacity, and especially the cultural condition, of Europeans and other people than previously in the century. Moreover, this sense of difference was not limited to Africans and Indians whom the British enslaved or to the East Indians, who fell under the rule of the East India Company. It also included Britain's national subjects, particularly the Irish and the Scots. Whether skin color or four-stages theory was the starting point, Europe or England—whichever was called on—emerged preeminent.

*   *   *

Given the way that four-stages theory explained England's special genius and the anatomy of its commercial greatness, it is surprising that it has not been widely treated as a racial ideology. It has been oddly neglected in the current reassessment of race and even in the most complete studies of race, slavery, or imperialism during the eighteenth century. Overall, twentieth-century scholars favor skin color in the analysis of race, possibly because it is the most familiar mode of racialization to us today. Such neglect has resulted in an ahistorical concept of color prejudice in Britain and in attaching undeserved emphasis on minor racial ideologies, such as the chain of being, Ham's curse, and polygenesis, all of which feature variations in skin color from a white norm. Consequently, we have a misleading sense of British beliefs about human difference, one that privileges the physical body over the vaguer and more comprehensive concern with cultural behavior.

Despite his desire to show the political underpinnings of concepts of human difference in Greek and Roman texts in *Race: The History of an Idea in the West* (1996), Ivan Hannaford does not mention the significance of four-stages theory to shaping eighteenth-century notions of race. Like many other scholars, he favors the German and French philosophers over English traditions in the delineation of race. He comes close to recognizing the role of four-stages theory, however, when he notes the influence of Montesquieu's *Spirit of Laws* (1736-43) on British thinking, but he does not examine the group of thinkers whom Montesquieu most influenced—the various writers of the Scottish Enlightenment. This omission has largely characterized the analysis of race for the past thirty years. In two of the most quoted texts on race in the eighteenth century, neither Winthrop Jordan nor Peter Fryer devotes any of his incisive analysis to the role of Scottish moral philosophy in shaping and giving voice to contemporary racial ideology.[19] Two notable exceptions are Marshall and Williams's *Great Map of Mankind* (1982) and Anthony Barker's *African Link* (1978); however, neither of them is cited as frequently as the texts by Jordan, Fryer, or Shyllon, especially among literary critics. In the volume of *Studies in Eighteenth-Century Culture* (1973) devoted to racism, the neglect of four-stages theory results in a narrow focus on the philosophical and medical approaches to race, black skin color, and minor trends in racialization. For years, that volume was a major resource on racism and eighteenth-century Europe. Even in his 1996 article, "From 'Nation' to 'Race': The Origin of Racial Classification in Eighteenth-Century Thought," Nicholas Hudson declines to mention the impact of the terminology and conceptual categories generated by Ferguson, Kames, Millar, and others.

Two anthologies of eighteenth-century writing on race were published in the 1990s, and they will no doubt be influential resources for teaching and scholarly reference. In the critical introduction to *Race and the Enlightenment: A Reader* (1997), Emmanuel Chukwudi Eze ignores four-stages theory entirely and privileges physical typology in his critical apparatus. One of the most historically precise overviews of race in the eighteenth century, Hannah Augstein's introduction to *Race: The Origins of an Idea* (1996), briefly acknowledges climate as the basis of four-stages theory. She notes the interest writers of the Scottish Enlightenment had in the effects of climate on the progress of societies, but she does not explicitly present it as a mode of racialization.[20] In this vein, Linda Colley and Kathleen Wilson, two of the most astute historians of regional divisions within eighteenth-century Britain, frequently use the analytical categories generated by four-stages theory, which implicitly structure their commentary on national and imperial identity, but they do not trace them to the Scottish Enlightenment or treat the way notions of civility and savagery explicitly racialized various groups of Britons.[21]

Essays specifically treating natural history and the early human sciences offer a clearer picture of the Scottish Enlightenment's contribution to racial classification. The collection of essays entitled *Inventing Human Science* (1995) conveys the impression that four-stages theory enabled and shaped the racialization of Britons and Others without, however, explicitly arguing that this was one of its primary accomplishments.[22] Felicity Nussbaum's *Torrid Zones* (1995) provides the most sustained case for connecting climate, four-stages theory, and racialization, particularly as it concerns sexuality. Nussbaum analyzes how writers of the Scottish Enlightenment linked "climate and sexual desire to define a temperate, civilized Europe that possesses the sexual constraint necessary to engage in the work-discipline productive of political liberty and civic virtue, in marked contrast to the libidinous and indolent torrid zones."[23] The general tendency to omit or downplay the contribution of four-stages theory to the history of race and complexion impairs our ability to understand when racial ideology is important and how it operates when skin color is not invoked to arrest our attention.

* * *

Jamaica and Scotland represented very different kinds of colonial spaces, although both were associated with the feudal stage of society. Jamaica stood for excessive indulgence in luxury, which was embodied in the stereotypical plantation owner. To many contemporaries, planters seemed an exotic shell of the civic humanist ideal in which sexual liberty was one manifestation of status conferred by property ownership. Scotland, on the other hand, conjured up a lack of necessities, for which the clan system was believed to be responsible. Nevertheless, the clan chief headed a regulated dynasty in contrast to the slave owner. Neither satellite matched England for its polish, but both contributed to the sense that England was a civil society.[24] In different ways, Jamaica and Scotland raised uncomfortable questions about the extent to which the reality of the empire might be incompatible with English ideals. These concerns often arose in debates on the benefits of luxury and the correlated concern about effeminacy in elite men.

As historians have established, there was an unparalleled flourishing of consumer society during the entire eighteenth century, so much so that foreign commentators envisioned luxury as peculiarly English because it was indulged in by all ranks.[25] Because there was more money to spend and credit to obtain, expenditures of all ranks of people rose dramatically, especially in relation to food and clothing. It is not surprising that these items were important visible, everyday signs of England's civility and commercial greatness.

A proper relationship to luxuries was intimately tied to racializing Britons positively and other people negatively.[26] Consumerism was a patriotic activity that reflected more than cultural chauvinism: Luxury items and consumable goods were the basis of exchange that underwrote civil society and polite sociability. Many of the most popular consumer items, newly affordable to some Britons, came from the crops grown in England's colonies or from the trade networks manned by the East India Company. Sugar, tea, coffee, and tobacco (and their related accouterments), furniture, silk, and printed cotton cloth depended on slave labor and imperial trade. The quantity as well as the quality of these items helped distinguish among ranks of Britons, and they were fundamental items in social rituals like coffeehouses, afternoon teas, and punch bowls at men's clubs. In the colonies, distinctions among masters, servants, and slaves had long been signaled by diet, especially meat and the number of dishes, as well as by the amount and fabric of clothes worn. While the ability to consume luxury items yanked entire groups of people out of the savage realm, it also polarized the consumer and the slave producer. The society that glorified the civilizing benefits of a luxurious nation derived much of that ability from the low cost of slave-generated colonial goods. Slave society in Jamaica contributed significantly not only to the wages and profits accruing to many Britons but also to their own superior sense of civility. Four-stages theory gave the most coherent expression to the benefits of commercial eminence, although its ubiquitousness in British culture may be gauged by commonplaces found in widely read periodicals and essays, such as the following: "Every country must be luxurious before it can make any progress in human knowledge."[27] The correlation between consumption and mental exertion could not be clearer. This was the main idea with which Long assessed Creole society and Johnson viewed the Scots.

Bound up in the increasing conviction about England and Europe's exceptional advancement were the issues raised by widespread luxury. Was more better? Some writers deplored the loss of distinct class subordination and the larger number of effeminate men resulting from increased consumption, not to mention the decline in industry among the elite. On the other hand, the answer was a resounding yes: More luxury was a positive sign. A society that had exceeded basic needs for food, shelter, and clothing was host to a division of labor that resulted in the invention of arts and literature as well as the refinement of them.

The colonies did not simply mirror England's greatness by emulating its style but helped constitute a sense of cultural and physical distinction by providing contrasts. Michael Hechter contends that the English unions with Scotland, Ireland, and Wales functioned as internal colonial efforts from the sixteenth through the twentieth centuries.[28] In his view, the English campaign for Scotland arose from the same forces as overseas colonization in the Americas, including the search for natural resources and security from France's encroachments. The Highlands, in particular, were an internal colony for England. Natural resources and investment schemes based in Scotland and Jamaica contributed significantly to the wages and profits accruing to many English people as well as to Britain's global military strength. Uneven development within a commercial society means that not all regions or ranks of people equally benefit from capitalism. Preserving older modes of subsistence may benefit the English nation and empire as a whole, ensuring the continued dominance of a few regions and the enrichment of already empowered segments of the population. More interesting to me here, however, is that these colonies helped produce a racialized interpretation of Englishness.

*   *   *

During the eighteenth century, Scottish intellectuals most markedly adopted English "as the language of refinement."[29] Moreover, historians have noted the prevalent anti-Scottish reaction of the English populace, especially in the 1760s and 1770s, which was played out in political, cultural, and economic realms.[30] These domestic contexts are crucial to understanding Samuel Johnson's narrative, and so is the larger colonial enterprise. In *Journey*, Johnson constantly refers to commercial activity, refinement of language, and advancement of literature to distinguish the English from the Scots, most particularly from the Highlanders. One of Johnson's main strategies is to compare the clans to various non-European and "savage" populations and to contrast the Highlanders with English counterparts in terms of "the arts, . . . the extent of his reason, the fertility of his fancy, and the force of his genius in literature, commerce, policy, and war."[31] Familiar with the writings of Hume, Kames, and Robertson, Samuel Johnson did not necessarily endorse them in all particulars; nevertheless, the explanatory framework of four-stages theory imbues his analysis.[32] The way in which Johnson conceives his evaluation, rather than only its content, points to the intersection of his writing with contemporary racial ideology. Assessing English character and social conduct as well as the deviations from it was important because of its insight into England's right to govern its empire.

Many critics have analyzed Johnson's *Journey* for its display of English national and cultural authority, but few have mentioned the text as part of the colonial or imperial enterprise, especially his racialization of Britons that

calls on differences both internal to the British Isles and between Europe and
the rest of the world. In fact, one recent critic calls Johnson a "tourist" and
explicitly rejects the connection to imperialism. Doing so treats the text in
isolation from a larger network of meaning. Moreover, to consider Johnson's
text only in terms of English national authority stops short of understanding the broad network of meanings Johnson invokes and the ways that he
racializes the English as well as their Others. The juxtaposition of Johnson's
text to Edward Long's shows that analyzing national character overlapped
considerably with the new mapping of racial character.

Even some of the critics explicitly concerned with colonialism and race
have overlooked or misunderstood the racial ideology operating in Johnson's
work. Simon During's suggestion that the narrative effects of *Journey* illustrate a turning point when modernity intersects with ethnicity is supported
by three important ways to interpret *Journey*: as "a moment in the development of cultural imperialism, or as a moment in the emergence of the tourist
industry, . . . or even as a threshold at which private travelling transmutes into
a rudimentary ethnography."[33] Despite his savvy insights into the historical
significance of Johnson's *Journey*, During misconstrues eighteenth-century
ideas about culture and human differences: "Here [in *Journey*] it is certainly
not a difference between cultures—Johnson and Boswell have no concept
of 'culture,' so they can deplore the Highlanders' 'ignorance' and 'superstition' without relativist qualifications. Nor do they have any notion that the
bodies of those they are visiting have a specific biology—the difference here
is not racial. They do not have any evolutionary schema by which the Highlanders might be called 'primitive' either. . . . Nor, finally, do they have a
strong political or economic sense of the difference: for Johnson and Boswell,
the Hebrides' poverty is merely the result of its inhabitants' 'laziness'" (33).
During's statement is instructive, even if it is incorrect; mid-nineteenth-
century perceptions of race do not transfer to eighteenth-century conditions.
Indeed, in overlooking the eighteenth-century colonial resonances of *culture*,
laziness, and *ignorance*, During misses the terms that connected perceptions
of cultural inferiority to economic conditions. In travel accounts and historical essays, idleness and lack of desire for innovation generally characterize savage societies found in sunny, hot climates among people who have an
underdeveloped appreciation of private property and no institutions to protect it.

The most obvious way that Johnson invokes contemporary racial ideology is through his many references to savages and barbarians. His working
assumption, widely shared among Scots and Europeans, is that northwest
Scotland is in a more savage state of civilization than England. The remote-

ness of the terrain from civil society, the savagery of the inhabitants, and their poverty are Johnson's main focus. Both temporal and spatial, the savagery of the Highlanders and Islanders links northwest Scotland to the most unknown contemporary people. Boswell and Johnson speculate on the similarity of the Highland scenery and the "wilds of America" and on the resemblance between the lower ranks of Highlanders and Native Americans, who were more familiar savages to their readers. The statements comparing Scotland and America conjure up a lesser stage of civilization and inhabitants whose dress, manners, and bodies do not resemble Britons'.[34] Neither the English Johnson nor the Scottish novelist Tobias Smollett expected their English readers to know much about Scotland, particularly the Highlands and Islands. While Smollett selects Japan as a comparably unknown land, Johnson goes further by claiming that even the Lowlanders know little about the region north of them: "To the southern inhabitants of Scotland, the state of the mountains and the islands is equally unknown with that of Borneo or Sumatra. Of both they have only heard a little, and guess the rest. They are strangers to the language and the manners, to the advantages and wants of the people, whose life they would model, and whose evils they would remedy" (96). This passage misleadingly attributes the desire for improving the Highlands and the Hebrides exclusively to the Lowlanders rather than also to members of the conquering English nation. Johnson thereby establishes the Lowlanders as benign, if uninformed, Improvers and the Highlands as a problem in national development that they seek to solve. In this vein, much of *Journey* subtly renarrates Scottish culture, history, and wealth to minimize its contribution to Great Britain.

In *Journey*, savagery defines both the historical and contemporary Highlanders. Johnson's descriptions of Scottish chiefs and their relationship to their clans closely resembles John Millar's comments in *The Origin of the Distinction of Ranks* (1781) about societies in coastal Africa, the East Indies, and feudal Europe (189, 207).[35] Johnson's representation of Scots as savages had a history among Lowlanders as well as English writers. Englishmen had long tended to dismiss the inhabitants at the periphery of the British Isles in ways similar to more distant populations, such as Africans, and for the same reasons: differences of religion and custom. The clans were often Catholic, and they organized family life and labor in a way alien to their southern neighbors. Moreover, they resisted English political and economic incursions. Richard Blome's *Britannia: or, A Geographical Description of the Kingdoms of England, Scotland, and Ireland* (1673) is typical of English responses of the time. The Highlanders, he writes, "are very rude, having much the *nature*, *disposition*, *speech*, and *habit* of the *Tories*, or *wild Irish*"; in the

Western Isles, they "are utterly barbarous."[36] In contrast, Martin Martin, a native of the Western Islands, tends to portray an idealized version of island political and social life in *A Description of the Western Islands of Scotland* (1703). In the 1760s, James Macpherson's—at the time putative—forgeries of Gaelic epics also featured a refined, aristocratic interpretation of clan life. There was more than one way to interpret a previous stage of civilization.

Johnson selects two features of the Highlanders' living conditions to signal the change from the Lowlands to a more primitive existence. The appearance of peat fires—fuel dug from the ground—and the sound of the Gaelic language mark the leaving behind of culture at the verge of the Highlands. In fact, Johnson defines Highland savagery outright in terms of a distinct language, idleness, and "primitive manners" (68) that result from their geographic isolation, lack of commerce, and remnants of Catholicism. The barrenness of their terrain, Johnson remarks, is host to a culture foreign to an Englishman. The barrenness refers both to the small yield of the land in regard to crops or grazing for livestock and to the lack of organized communities with market centers. Compared with England, there were relatively few villages and towns in the Highlands and Islands, which no doubt also contributed to this sense of a more primitive people. Budding urban centers, towns, and villages were signs of civilization deemed important to "converting" the Highlands. Between 1725 and 1769, five planned villages, centered around fishing on the coast and textiles inland, were established; thirty-three appeared between 1770 and 1799.[37]

Other than myriad remarks about noncommercial aspects of Highland and Island life, Johnson betrays a low opinion of Gaelic, which was the sole language of the lower ranks of Highlanders. Johnson's response to Gaelic resembles his contemporaries' contempt for many West African languages; they were sometimes characterized as gibberish and were believed to reflect an undeveloped culture because unwritten and composed of few words. As one contemporary wrote, language "may be considered as the great barometer of the barbarity or civilization of a people. A poverty of dialect is generally accompanied by savageness and ignorance. . . . No authority can, at the same time, so decisively fix the peculiar habits and pursuits of a nation as the sounds by which they articulate their ideas."[38] In one of his many reflections on language, Johnson shifts the responsibility onto his hosts in the Highlands, the native informants, for his paucity of insight into Gaelic: "Of the Earse language, as I understand nothing, I cannot say more than I have been told." Nevertheless, he contends, "It is the rude speech of a barbarous people, who had few thoughts to express, and were content, as they conceived grossly, to be grossly understood" (116).[39]

Johnson frequently refers to the Highland culture as illiterate, thereby willfully ignoring the printed (and recited) Highland poems and lyrics.[40] Johnson attributes this illiteracy to a lack of national genius, which, he argues, results from environmental factors only, including an archaic mode of subsistence and geographic isolation. In this he agrees with Montesquieu and others who examined the characteristics of mountaineers. Johnson equates lack of written history with no history at all and no reverence for the past. The present tense—the failure to preserve the past or plan for the future—is very much a quality associated with savages and slaves. Lamenting that an earlier recorder of life and manners in the islands was not more assiduous in preserving what is now inaccessible, Johnson says of Martin's *Description of the Western Islands of Scotland*: "What he has neglected cannot now be performed. In nations, where there is hardly the use of letters, what is once out of sight is lost for ever. They think but little, and of their few thoughts, none are wasted on the past, in which they are neither interested by fear nor hope. Their only registers are stated observances and practical representations" (79). The problem of no recorded past or preserved edifices is that there are no traces of a recognizable national history: Conjecture supersedes knowledge, and decay overtakes monuments. Even his glimpse of Scottish university life in the Lowlands is rife with visions of decayed buildings and fragments of the past. These sentiments are precisely those that Hume, Ferguson, and Edward Long use to denigrate African culture. Equating oral culture with a paucity of ideas and lack of intellectual complexity, Johnson lays the groundwork for his conviction that the Highlanders' greatest use is as hardy soldiers in protecting the empire.

There is more at stake than Gaelic embodying a less polished culture than England. Gaelic signifies the Catholic, militaristic past of an independent Scotland and is, to Johnson and others, an unfortunate remnant of those barbaric times. Nevertheless, Johnson does not advocate its complete eradication—only its subordination to English. As Fiona Stafford notes about the political conflict enmeshed in language differences within Great Britain, "the survival of the Gaelic language was one of the principal factors dividing the Highlands from the rest of Britain. Not only did it increase the resistance to outside influences, but it also perpetuated the Highlanders' sense of their own special culture and society."[41] Englishmen and some Lowlanders sporadically showed interest in rectifying the Highlanders' separateness from the rest of Britain, and the spread of the English language was long considered a tool to quell Highland political insurgence and minimize their cultural distinction, not to mention a way to rectify their impoverished economic situation.[42]

Formed in 1709, the Scottish Society for the Propagation of Christian Knowledge was charged with establishing schools in the Highlands and Islands in order " 'to teach true religion and loyalty and to strengthen the British Empire.' "[43] The political significance of homogeneous language, culture, and religion when forging a new empire could not be more apparent than in this 1716 observation about Scotland: " 'Nothing can be more effectual for reducing these countries to order, and making them usefull to the Commonwealth than teaching them their duty to God, their King and Countrey [sic] and rooting out their Irish language.' "[44] Johnson's pronouncements about savagery and barbarism reflect this political dimension: Highland savages were not fully British subjects. Boswell reacts to what he fears is Johnson's small-mindedness by comparing his mentor's perception of Scots to the way that ancient Greeks and Romans viewed political outsiders; in this tradition, the civil inhabitants of the *polis*, who govern through the use of reason, are superior to the less civilized inhabitants of the periphery, who speak a different language and belong to a different cultural tradition.[45] Boswell hastens to add, however, that he considers himself, in contrast to Johnson, "a citizen of the world" (166). Boswell means, of course, the European world obtainable through the Grand Tour.

Language and empire go hand-in-hand. When he condemns Earse as an oral rather than a written language (116), Johnson has in mind the power of language in a print culture that produces a sense of similarity among geographically dispersed people within a nation or even an empire. In *Imagined Communities*, Benedict Anderson suggests that language, especially the printed word, figured prominently in the emergence of eighteenth-century European nationalism, since it promoted a feeling of similarity among a certain group of people in a way that theoretically accommodated other differences such as rank, religion, or region: "These fellow-readers, to whom they were connected through print, formed, in their secular, particular, visible invisibility, the embryo of the nationally-imagined community."[46] *Journey* offers an important corrective to Anderson's formulation; it shows the power of the national language and its hegemonic culture to cover up, even erase, regional diversity and to produce norms. Johnson observes about the linguistic assimilation under way, which had accelerated in the eighteenth century: "The conversation of the Scots grows every day less unpleasing to the English; their peculiarities wear fast away. . . . The great, the learned, the ambitious, and the vain, all cultivate the English phrase, and the English pronunciation" (151). Like the wealthy planters and their mulatto children in the West Indies, the Scots elite often educated their sons in English public schools and universities.

That language was so central to assimilation and advancement is evident in comments by Scots and English alike. Traces of a Scottish accent were sufficient to bar professional or political advancement in London.[47] Boswell, for one, repeatedly tried to rid his speech and writing of Scotticisms, and one of the more extreme ways he did so was by avoiding the company of fellow Scots. Anxious himself, Hume advised William Robertson how to eliminate Scottish phrasing from his histories in order to make them more credible to English readers, and evidently the essayist and novelist Tobias Smollett obsessed over his command of written English phrasing.[48] The future seventh earl of Elgin was sent to England to avoid acquiring a Scots accent, despite the number of elocutionists flocking to Edinburgh offering to teach the Scots to speak proper English. High- and low-born Scots and Irish suffered mockery and public humiliation on account of their accents.[49] It is clear from contemporary documents that tone and accent were crucial to policing internal borders of acceptability in the British Isles.

Correct language use was a sign of English political authority; moreover, it marked one as a gentleman.[50] In several installments of the *Rambler*, Johnson features the importance of proper language use and pure pronunciation as an indication of acceptable manliness.[51] To Johnson and his contemporaries, "Language was an index of intelligence and reflected human mentality, knowledge, memory, imagination, sensibility."[52] Thus, Johnson's pronouncements about the Gaelic language and the culture from which it derived must be analyzed in their forceful construction of Highlander inferiority.[53] Despite their relentless occurrence, Johnson's comments on Highlander language and manner favors a changeable notion of national character and human difference. Thus, a longer exposure to English culture may be expected to improve the Scottish character even more by diluting it further.

Precision in spoken and written English became more central to a metropolitan English identity over the eighteenth century. As Nicholas Hudson demonstrates, Johnson was at the forefront of the effort to standardize the written word, which, he believed, was the only way to improve the language.[54] A standard language embodied in print culture signifies civil society because, as Johnson explains about the difference between English and Gaelic, "When a language begins to teem with books, it is tending to refinement. . . . There may possibly be books without a polished language, but there can be no polished language without books" (116). According to Henry Louis Gates, Jr., writing was fast becoming a visible sign of reason during the eighteenth century (when literacy levels were rising in Britain). To some, such as Hume and Edward Long, much of West African society was inferior to Europe because it did not cherish its past in a print culture.

Absence of the arts and sciences such as Europeans practiced raised questions about Africans' command of reason and cultural progress. Absence of literacy, Gates contends, linked racial difference and economic alienation.[55] As Johnson's pronouncements on Highlander language and intellect reveal, it is not only "a culture of color" that gets delimited in reference to Africans, as Gates suggests, but a culture of exclusion affecting the perception and treatment of various colonial populations whose subordination assumed myriad forms.

Inasmuch as Johnson establishes the cultural savagery of the Highlanders through reflections on their language, he also emphasizes the physical embodiment of it by remarking on the oddity of his own corpulent, urban appearance in the Highlands. One of Johnson's first contacts with the lean and fit Highland villagers is permeated by visions of the savage. His depiction of their features dwells on the linguistic, physical, and behavioral peculiarities. He recalls, "The villagers gathered about us in considerable numbers, I believe without any evil intention, but with a very savage wildness of aspect and manner" (62).

In *Journey*, savagery is associated primarily with the lower ranks in the Highlands and Hebrides. Combined with poverty, both characteristics validate the need for change, which Johnson equates with English intervention into the most basic ways of life. Johnson was hardly the first Englishman or Scotsman to accuse the Highlanders of savagery. Nevertheless, some of his contemporaries, including Boswell and Mary Anne Hanway, were embarrassed by his exaggerating the negative and hiding the positive characteristics of life in Scotland.[56] Johnson's largely negative assessment of Scotland prompted some disagreement among reviewers about the merits of *Journey*, although all of the commentators regarded Johnson as a traveling moralist and observer of men and manners.[57] The furor of rebuttals that followed the publication of *Journey* and the nature that praise and criticism took suggest that the merits of Scottish culture (and other pastoral cultures) were at the heart of the debate.[58] Certainly, Johnson's reception in Scotland suggests that the Scots were well aware of his cultural authority, and if they weren't, one suspects Boswell informed them.

The vision of Johnson's enormous bulk weighing down a Highland pony is not the only allusion to urban versus mountaineer bodies. Although Johnson tends to refer to Highlanders most frequently as savages, he also uses other racial concepts to reflect on their lack of regional development. From climatic theories of human variety, he draws the term *mountaineers*, a designation that Montesquieu and Linnaeus use to denote populations made monstrous by the harsh effects of climate on their exposed bodies and by eking out a subsistence existence on barren terrain. Lack of resources and the failure to rectify real wants makes people vulnerable to climate and to the yield of unimproved land. Johnson characterizes Scottish mountaineers as warlike, thievish, and having no reverence for property (i.e., the property of others); all of these epithets were common criticisms of Native Americans, Pacific Islanders, and Africans. Traditionally, the clan owned the land in common and worked it for mutual benefit. This arrangement tended to result in a subsistence existence for all but the chief and tacksman, the latter an intermediate figure between the chief and other clan members, who fulfilled an economic and military function. It was only with the advent of English law and the forcible alteration of the Highlanders' property arrangements, Johnson intimates, that the Highlanders could advance to the margins of civil society.

Inasmuch as many of these mountaineer qualities are more suitable to an earlier stage of civilization, they help provide men stalwart enough to protect the empire against incursions of other Europeans and rebellious indigenous people in North America and the East Indies. In this capacity, the Highlanders' effectivity within a reconfigured Britain relies on their unchanging national character. Part of their character is embodied in their apparel. Johnson analyzes this relationship of distinctive dress to cultural identity: "To allure them into the army, it was thought proper to indulge them in the continuance of their national dress. . . . That dissimilitude of appearance, which was supposed to keep them distinct from the rest of the nation, might disincline them from coalescing with the Pensylvanians [*sic*], or people of Connecticut" (103). The conquering English had banned the traditional tartan dress and arms of the Highlanders to eradicate the most visible distinctions of the vanquished. Allowing their national dress in the colonial army helps preserve the singularity of the Highlanders at a safe distance, keeps them from allying with the Native Americans, and encourages the continuation of fierce militarism now safely rechanneled to secure the British Empire. The kinder, gentler Highland militarism had its limits in the English nation: There was no Scottish militia allowed, and the imperial Highland regiments were not permitted to sail from London.[59]

Johnson favors an explanation of Hebridean character and body based on accidental factors of climate. In one of his observations most resembling other contemporary descriptions of foreign peoples, Johnson's assumption about the different roles of the upper and lower ranks coalesce with aesthetic and intellectual evaluations. The passage below is remarkable for its easy transition from description to evaluation, exactly like contemporary natural histories:

The inhabitants of Sky, and of the other Islands, which I have seen are commonly of the middle stature. . . . The tallest men that I saw are among those of higher rank. In regions of barrenness and scarcity, the human race is hindered in its growth by the same causes as other animals.

The ladies have as much beauty here as in other places, but bloom and softness are not to be expected among the lower classes, whose faces are exposed to the rudeness of the climate, and whose features are sometimes contracted by want, and sometimes hardened by the blasts. Supreme beauty is seldom found in cottages or work-shops, even where no real hardships are suffered. To expand the human face to its full perfection, it seems necessary that the mind should co-operate by placidness of content, or consciousness of superiority.

Their strength is proportionate to their size, but they are accustomed to run upon rough ground, and therefore can with great agility skip over the bog, or clamber the mountain. For a campaign in the wastes of America, soldiers better qualified could not have been found. Having little work to do, they are not willing, nor perhaps able to endure a long continuance of manual labour, and are therefore considered as habitually idle. (92–93)

Johnson assumes that humans and animals, subject to harsh natural forces, suffer the same stunted stature. He does not evince interest in the argument that there might be constant forces impeding improvement, especially moral ones.[60] It is only the upper ranks of people who can be held to a different standard, because their financial resources and education mediate the effects of the natural elements. Overall, this passage demonstrates the way that attention to climate, terrain, stature, and physical abilities can operate as a satisfactory explanation for people's lack of progress or their suitability for protecting the empire. Following the protocol of natural history, Johnson removes people and place from contemporary and historical power relations. Assessment of national character and proclivities masks the impact of power relations with England. Notably, the recent past disappears from Johnson's purview. Disarming the clans, reducing their authority, changing their way of life through economic and political policies—including enclosure of formerly common land—mostly account for men available for military expeditions. The large number of Scots who elected to emigrate to the East Indies, Caribbean, or North America or were forced to join the army did so because they were impoverished by the recent economic policies deemed best for reconstructing Scotland along a commercial model and by the clan chiefs' response to implementing them.

As Johnson and Long both argue, a stalwart body is useful for protecting a civilized nation's colonies; it is in these terms that they envision the Highlanders' and mulattos' place, respectively, in the British Empire. In

contemplating the utility of male Hebridean bodies to expanding and preserving the empire, Johnson calls on the commonplace that physical accomplishments and fit bodies are the basis of distinction in ruder societies. The
aesthetic connected to savagery, elaborated by Buffon, seems ready-made for
thinking about the Scots and English: "Supposing two nations; thus differently circumstanced [a well-governed versus a savage nation], to live under
the same climate, it is reasonable to think, that the savage people would be
more ugly, more tawny, more diminutive, and more wrinkled, than the nation
that enjoyed the advantages of society and civilization. If the former had
any superiority over the latter, it would consist in the strength, or rather in
the hardiness, of their bodies" (3:373). Most European writers agreed that a
hardy body was not necessary in a commercial and polite nation as it was in
a savage one.[61]

In his examination of the Highlanders' mountaineer qualities, Johnson also divorces mental from physical activity and connects them to class
distinctions. One source for the association between ruler and intellect, on
the one hand, and the ruled and physical exertion, on the other hand, was
Aristotle's *Politics* 1:2. According to Hannaford, "Aristotle distinguished between two elements: an element able 'by virtue of its intelligence to exercise
forethought,' and an element 'able by virtue of its bodily power to do what
the other element plans.'"[62] Thus, the savage, despite the common colonial meaning of a pagan, darker-complected non-European, is also a political concept imbued with domestic ideas about class difference, intellectual
inferiority, and beneficial subordination.

Johnson associates savagery with a "limited power of thinking" (201).
Not surprisingly, he sees the necessity of maintaining the clan system in the
Highlands, especially the increasingly endangered intermediate position of
the tacksman, whose role had been primarily a military one, which was now
outdated by increasing commercialism. The tacksman was necessary to combat the inferior acumen for improvement among the lower orders: "As the
mind must govern the hands, so in every society the man of intelligence must
direct the man of labour. If the tacksmen be taken away, the Hebrides must
in their present state be given up to grossness and ignorance; the tenant, for
want of instruction, will be unskilful, and for want of admonition will be
negligent" (95).[63] Discipline prompts industry and both combat the "grossness and ignorance" of more savage populations. After the failure of the 1745
uprising of the clans, they lost considerably more power than in 1715, and
the issue of governance in the Highlands remained in the forefront of English concerns. Contemporary ideologies of class and racial distinctions in
the 1770s feature a concern about governance manifest in discussions about

intelligence versus manual labor and about capacity for feeling versus insensibility. In the logic of Johnson's text is an assessment of the Highlanders' mental and physical fitness for contributing to British commercial success around the globe, both in developing local agriculture and industry and in defending the integrity of trade networks abroad.[64]

*   *   *

Despite appearances to the contrary, cultivating the impression of unadulterated savagery was not the most important thrust of Johnson's many references to it. It would leave an odd impression about the 1707 economic and political Union with England and the influence of the English institutions if Johnson could not show that savagery had abated. The Crowns had been united in a much looser association when James VI of Scotland became James I of England in 1603. Johnson's version of the tour that he and James Boswell took features the continual contrast between the current state of Scotland, especially the Highlands and Hebrides, and its state before the Union. Early in the narrative, Johnson approves of the alacrity with which the Highland distinction was being erased: "There was perhaps never any change of national manners so quick, so great, and so general, as that which has operated in the Highlands, by the last conquest, and the subsequent laws. We came thither too late to see what we expected, a people of peculiar appearance, and a system of antiquated life" (73). Appearing to compliment Scottish industry in this passage, Johnson really congratulates English military and legal intervention. These comments help naturalize English rule and the desirability of England civilizing the Scots, especially since his entire narrative is premised on recording the "peculiar appearance" and "antiquated life" of some Scots, despite his claims to the contrary.

In fact, establishing savagery *and* its abatement in Scotland are the primary ways that Johnson validates the Union of 1707 and the benign rule of the English. As many times as he conjures up savagery, Johnson counters with instances of its partial eradication. The Union has already made inroads into the savagery characteristic of clans from time immemorial, and, to Johnson, Highlanders of the 1770s are not savages as much as they retain traces of savage manners: "The clans retain little now of their original character. . . . Of what they had before the late conquest of their country, there remain only their language and their poverty. . . . That their poverty is gradually abated, cannot be mentioned among the unpleasing consequences of subjection. They are now acquainted with money, and the possibility of gain will by degrees make them industrious. Such is the effect of the late regulations, that a longer journey than to the Highlands must be taken by him whose curiosity pants for savage virtues and barbarous grandeur" (73–74). His sentiment about the possibility of gain from a more commercially oriented Scotland exactly parallels Edward Long's view of the Caribbean Indians' and mulattos' potential as useful British subjects in *The History of Jamaica*. Replacing a subsistence economy with a consumer-driven economy will, they believe, improve the condition and character of Indians, mulattos, and Scots. Samuel Johnson and other contemporaries who write about the Highlands record the transformation in the mode of subsistence that gained momentum in the midcentury; at that time, a pastoral stage, based largely on the sale of black cattle and on the working of limited arable land, was visibly eroding. Slowly displacing this way of life was "a two-class social structure with control over land deriving from rent and accumulated capital and symbolised in and mediated through the English language."[65] Johnson repeatedly conveys the efficiency of the Union in alleviating the poverty induced by the stagnancy of the clan system.[66]

To Johnson, the Protestant religion, like the English language, helps ameliorate savagery in the Highlands. The spread of Protestantism, especially since the 1707 Union, is instrumental not only in abolishing Catholicism but also in eradicating even older pagan superstitions, which, he believes, are endemic to savage societies. Purposely confounding Catholic rites and superstitious practices, Johnson observes: "The various kinds of superstition which prevailed here [Hebrides], as in all other regions of ignorance, are by the diligence of the ministers almost extirpated. . . . They have still among them a great number of charms for the cure of different diseases; they are all invocations, perhaps transmitted to them from the times of popery, which increasing knowledge will bring into disuse" (110).[67] Just as the Union ushered in a new era, so too did the Church of England and Protestantism before it—another significant institution that connected Scotland more firmly to England than to France.

The Union of 1707 between Scotland and England becomes the only important cultural origin for civilization and the impetus to positive change. Boswell admits embarrassment at the credit Johnson repeatedly gives to the Union in public conversations about Scotland (228). In Johnson's reflections on the benefits of the Union to the Scots, he refers to the improvement of private property, the cornerstone of civil society, wrought by the Union: "In Scotland possession [of land] has long been secure, and inheritance regular, yet it may be doubted whether before the Union any man between Edinburgh and England had ever set a tree. . . . Established custom is not easily broken, till some great event shakes the whole system of things, and life seems to recommence upon new principles. That before the union the Scots had little trade and little money, is no valid apology: for plantation is the least expensive of all methods of improvement" (40). Johnson was not the first Englishman to complain about the paucity of trees, although his mentioning it dozens of times possibly singles him out. Edward Burt also remarked on the lack of trees in his *Letters from a Gentleman in the North of Scotland to His Friend in London* (1754), as had Daniel Defoe in *A Tour Through the Whole Island of Great Britain* (1724–26). Johnson refers to the Scots' failure to emulate the English and thereby improve their nation. Calling attention to the lack of trees had multiple resonances—well beyond one critic's neutral interpretation of Johnson's "belief in posterity."[68] Lack of trees conjures up the thriving timber trade that Scotland carried on with Norway before the Union. Johnson characteristically ignores this aspect of Scotland's independent past to feature the seismic nature of the Union. James Dunbar also noted the stripping of the Highland woods, which he attributed to neglect and mismanagement of clans, since cattle often ate the new shoots and the poor used the wood for fuel.[69] Moreover, the treeplanting craze arose largely from recent concerns over imperial expansion, especially having adequate timber for building ships to transport slaves and raw materials as well as finished goods.[70] Putting up with inconveniences and neglecting to improve the land are common criticisms Europeans leveled at Africans and Native Americans.

Johnson presents English culture and commercial enterprise as the necessary segue between the Scottish nation and the British Empire, and the Union substitutes for any other cultural origin. In Scotland, Johnson observes at least two kinds of nations coexisting: one savage because illiterate, unable to innovate, and lacking not only in luxuries but also in conveniences; the other, following the English pattern, is polite because learned, dedicated to improving land and acquiring luxuries. The commercial model, which, he erroneously intimates, was introduced by the Union, is the yardstick by which Scotland as a whole is measured and found wanting. It should be added that Johnson's caustic observations about the lack of improvement and opulence even in the market towns of the Lowlands hardly reflected positively on the parts of Scotland most like England (36). Indeed, several regions in Scotland seem to defy the normal progress charted in four-stages theory—a confusing phenomenon Johnson always remarks on. For instance, he notes that the Scots have produced the liberal arts without developing the manual ones (51). His pronouncements on the lack of progress in Scotland maintain rather than dispel divisions of class and region within Great Britain during the emergent empire through his invocation of racial ideology. For example, part of what defines Englishness and the benefits of the Union in *Journey* is intensive commerce and the circulation of money. Johnson styles himself as a product of a polished nation viewing the most recent imperial acquisition as he diagnoses the source of Scotland's shortcomings in statements such as follows: "The peculiarities which strike the native of a commercial country, proceeded in a great measure from the want of money" (114).[71]

Johnson's propensity for fixing savagery firmly in the pre-Union past does not abate as much as one might expect when he turns his attention to the "lettered hospitality" he receives in the homes of the upper ranks of Scots and the universities. The several crucial attributes of a polished nation are associated solely with England. For Johnson, they are primarily embodied in a preserved historical past with traceable national origins (i.e., through an epic), a language and manners influenced by contact with other nations, and flourishing arts and sciences. In *Journey*, Johnson devotes a considerable amount of space to exploring their weak presence in Scotland. As all of Johnson's comments suggest, the Highland's upper classes have failed to encourage culture or to preserve it, and their carelessness consigns them to imitate the English.

Johnson's comments on the wealthier inhabitants and on the conditions that impede their increased civility become more acerbic when he considers evidence of independent Scottish culture. Acknowledging Scottish culture potentially disrupts the vision of savage Highlanders, but Johnson either ignores or dismisses it as inferior to English culture. Johnson's harshest criticism is reserved for traditional Scottish culture. Clearly, evidence of a significant counterculture would also mean a legitimate challenge to English hegemony. In language, literature, and the preservation of history, Johnson argues that Scotland and its inhabitants must assimilate to the English norm in order to achieve the status of a coequal nation. In a characteristic strategy, Johnson represents the wealthier and more polite Highlanders (and Lowlanders) as more closely approximating the English norm when he desires to praise them. In this construction, they are imitators rather than independent producers of culture, much like Edward Long's condemnation of the poems written by the Cambridge-educated black man Francis Williams. The upper ranks are distinguished from the other Highlanders in the same way that the English differ from the Scots generally—by their command of English, polite manners, ownership of property, and their education. Johnson notes with approval evidence of domestic elegance and intensive cultivation of the land among wealthier Highlanders. In these homes, Johnson finds pockets of heightened civilization owed, he believes, to their imitation of English patterns rather than to longtime association with France or to their own traditions of education and the arts. Johnson consigns the Scots to a recent cultural origin that is legible and hence English.

Journey makes clear that a successful political and economic union requires an ideological union, as the 1745 uprising and its aftermath demonstrated. But English cultural memory could differ from Scottish material reality, and just as Johnson's text ignores the significant products of Scottish culture, it often eliminates English force in its renarration of recent Scottish history. In alluding to the classical empire with which Britons most compared England, Johnson calls on a key historical analogy to justify the cultural and political subjection of the Scots: "What the Romans did to other nations, was in a great degree done by Cromwell to the Scots; he civilized them by conquest, and introduced by useful violence the arts of peace" (51). This paradoxical statement may be elucidated by reference to a more politicized version of Scotland's "improvement" since the Union, especially since 1745. This version would emphasize the violence of conquest and the redistribution of property by noting the "widespread destruction of Highland homes, the execution of many Jacobite supporters, the annexation of forfeited estates to the crown in 1752, and the abolition of hereditary jurisdictions in 1754. For over forty years the forfeited estates were administered by government commissioners, who introduced changes in landholding and agriculture."[72] Johnson did not uniformly support empire building, especially the enslavement of Africans or the forcible subordination of indigenous people, not only because he believed in their right to sovereignty but also because he held the English responsible for failing to improve them. In his political writings, Johnson condemned English annihilation of Amerindians as a despicable part of colonization. Because of its geographic proximity and political importance, subjecting Scotland was far more acceptable than America. As his narrative so frequently testifies, the English had not failed to improve the Scots.

In *Journey*, English military violence, subjection and relocation of some Highlanders, appropriation of their wealth, and weakening of local power bases are all palliated when the end is increased civility and commerce. This worldview is shared by Edward Long, although Long applies it to enslaving Africans. The first part of Johnson's observation below reads as a typical condemnation of culture and manners found in almost any contemporary account of Africa, although it assesses the Scots' change in national character since the Union:

Till the Union made them acquainted with English manners, the culture of their lands was unskilful, and their domestick life unformed; their tables were coarse as the feasts of Eskimeaux, and the houses filthy as the cottages of Hottentots.

Since they have known that their condition was capable of improvement, their progress in useful knowledge has been rapid and uniform. . . . But they must be for ever content to owe to the English that elegance and culture, which, if they had been vigilant and active, perhaps the English might have owed to them. (52)

Edward Burt provides a different view of the Union in regard to the lower classes near Inverness and asks about the conditions conducive to imitation: "What Emulation can there proceed from meer Despair? Cleanliness is too expensive for their small Wages, and what Inducement can they have, in such a Station, to be diligent and obliging to those who use them more like Negroes than Natives of *Britain*." He continues that it is "not any Thing in Nature that renders them more idle and uncleanly than others, as some would inconsiderately suggest."[73] Burt attributes the problem to lack of wealth and opportunity.

Ultimately, Johnson reinterprets Scottish history selectively, minimizing or eliminating entirely their economic achievements and culture prior to Cromwell's invasion and especially the Union of 1707. He also maximizes references to evidence of English manners, organization of property, and government policies that have eradicated or abated the Highlanders' putative savagery. In as much as *Journey* represents a selective rendition of Scotland's inhabitants and their national character, it also provides a crucial insight into the constitution of England's identity in the empire. Polished manners, domestic sophistication, intensive agricultural cultivation, territorial conquest, and commercial activity all define Englishness and justify "useful violence." A polished nation, in fact, relied on state violence to initiate commercial progress. As Ferguson observes, "The employing of force, only for the obtaining of justice, and for the preservation of national rights . . . is, perhaps, the principal characteristic, on which among modern nations, we bestow the epithets of *civilized* or of *polished*." *Polished* originally referred to the state of a nation's laws and government; it also came to indicate a nation's "proficiency in the liberal and mechanical arts, in literature, and in commerce."[74] In all of these areas, Johnson offers a sanguine interpretation of the effects of the Union on Scotland.

Even though he offers conflicting perceptions of Scotland, particularly of the Highlands, Johnson's positive assessment of the overall benefit of English civilizing efforts is largely undisturbed. English national identity and wealth prove themselves compatible with the preservation of more ancient modes of production and ways of life, if not partially constituted by them. Jamaica and the other slave-based colonies represented a more extreme process of incorporating colonial economies into capitalist circuits and national identity. As we will see, the categories of comparison Long uses are almost identical to the ones Johnson employs. Routinely, however, Long's writings have been viewed as racist, and Johnson's have rarely been associated with racial ideology.

*   *   *

Despite the occasional contention that Scotland was the most valuable colony, it was widely recognized by the 1770s that Jamaica was preeminent among Britain's colonies in generating wealth, and Edward Long's three-volume *History of Jamaica* was a testament to that colony's importance. By the 1770s, the overseas colonies had developed different kinds of slave societies, various relations to England, and different histories of the way color and race operated. Long's volumes detailed these aspects of Jamaica's society. Long's authority to write a believable account derived from his experience in both England and Jamaica. Born in England to a Jamaican planter, he lived in Jamaica for twelve years as an adult and married a Beckford heiress, who was from one of the wealthiest land-rich families. Before returning to England, he served the lieutenant-governor, who was his brother-in-law, and was a vice admiralty judge in Jamaica.[75] As lending library records in Bristol show, *The History of Jamaica* was widely read by the middling classes, and the several rebuttals to his work by eminent men of science suggest its contemporary influence.[76]

For the most part, Long's *History*, which describes the topography, government, and trade, as well as the inhabitants, their function, and their potential for strengthening Jamaica, fits comfortably into a tradition of writing about the West Indies. Most other writers also supported slavery and shared his condemnation of the horrific punishments for slaves. They too reported on the various inhabitants' diet, clothes, property, and sexual relations. *The History of Jamaica* is distinguished from its predecessors in its comprehensive treatment of island life, the length of the negative comments about Africa(ns), and the intensive focus on the redemptive potential of consumer desire in regard to several segments of the population. If Long's pronouncements on Africans have garnered the most notoriety, his indictment of the white inhabitants has been strangely neglected by posterity (though not by contemporaries, many of whom used Long's text to argue for abolition).[77]

The section on the inhabitants, which I treat below, has garnered the most attention in the twentieth century, but the main thrust of the text was how to make Jamaica a more secure and lucrative colony for Great Britain. Long hoped for extensive English intervention and planter reform in the island. The problems to which his text responded were the absenteeism among the planter class, the 12:1 ratio of blacks to whites, and the security problems resulting from such an imbalance.[78] By 1780, the 250,000 slaves in Jamaica made it the largest slave society in British America.[79] Long computes Britain's inattention to the colonies in three ways: failing to capitalize on the colonies by intensively cultivating and defending them, disregarding the trade potential with indigenous people, and neglecting the white citizens' needs in Jamaica, particularly their education, an oversight that drains the colony of its leading citizens and disaffects white youth at an early age from the place of their birth.

Edward Long and Samuel Johnson share certain core assumptions about how to analyze societies and people and how to improve them both. In natural histories of the 1770s, the general attention to physical human differences places Long in the mainstream, but his particular interpretation of what skin color signified has earned him a notorious place in twentieth-century histories of race. While his use of facial aesthetics and accusations of African mental inferiority may justly earn him his reputation as the "father of English racism," his beliefs about the efficacious effects of commerce, education, and Christianity in regard to mulatto and Creole black men place him firmly alongside contemporaries such as Hume, Adam Smith, and Samuel Johnson.[80] Long's *History of Jamaica* unravels its racist logic by bringing conflicting views of human differences together; he mixes his contention of a permanent gulf between Africans and Europeans with a belief in the reformist possibilities of consumerism and Christian education.

*   *   *

In the section on inhabitants, Long considers the various subjects in Jamaica in terms of an English standard and finds both Creole, or Jamaican-born, whites and blacks lacking. For nonwhites, the combination of lineage, baptism, ownership of property, and commercial or martial acumen makes the difference between those ordained to be slaves and those who may be usefully included in a new configuration of variously privileged subjects in Jamaica. Even among the planter class, which Long supports in its right to enslave Africans, literacy, modesty, and economic acumen are all found deficient. He attributes these problems to England's inattention and to the multifaceted commerce among whites, blacks, and mulattos, especially between Englishmen and slave women. If Scotland is notable for its paucity of commerce, Jamaica is remarkable for too much of the wrong kind of commerce.

In sync with contemporary natural historians, Long's scheme for classifying the various inhabitants of Jamaica is based primarily on complexion, a scheme he has to explain in detail to British readers because it is foreign to them.[81] Long distinguishes most generally between the white and black inhabitants, and then acknowledges less important differences of nation, religion, and status. The white category is composed of island-born or Creole whites, Scots, Irish, Moravians, who were Scandinavian Protestant missionaries, and Jews. The black category is composed of racially mixed mulattos, freed black slaves, politically insurgent Maroons, island-born or Creole black slaves, and African-born slaves. Twentieth-century historians of the West Indies have noted that the terms of distinction among the inhabitants changed over the eighteenth century: "Whereas in the early part of the century society had been stratified almost entirely according to wealth and status, in the latter part colour in itself became a more and more important element in stratification."[82] Before Long's scheme, British West Indians most frequently spoke of themselves in relation to property and others in relation to the division of labor: inhabitants were customarily divided into masters, servants, and slaves. Long's discussion of the population fuses the kind of observations Johnson made about the Highlanders and Hebrideans to color prejudice.

Perhaps more than any other writer in England at this time, Long looked to African bodies and myths about African life to justify slavery.[83] His focus is typical of other West Indian propagandists. The population that Long identifies as most different from whites is Africans in Africa and those recently imported to Jamaica. Other writers agreed with this sentiment, although they usually resorted to less abrasive ways of expressing themselves. In his *British Empire in America* (1708), John Oldmixon observes that those Africans born in Barbados are more useful than the newly arrived slaves because their language skills and integration into the community were better (124). In his *New History of Jamaica* (1740), Charles Leslie claims that " 'tis observed" that slaves "are simple and very innocent Creatures" when they first arrive.[84] He reasons that they become increasingly corrupt over time because they receive no return on their labor (305). Edward Long intends to defend slavery by any means, and he does this mainly by distancing Africans, or future slaves, from readers by insinuating their putative inferior physical, cultural, and intellectual characteristics.

While Long does not originate a one-to-one correspondence between Africans' origins, color, and inferiority of mind, he centers his argument on this premise more consistently and extensively than previous English writers.[85] Like Hume and Kames, Long believes that white and black people *probably* form two distinct species, of which the white one is visibly superior

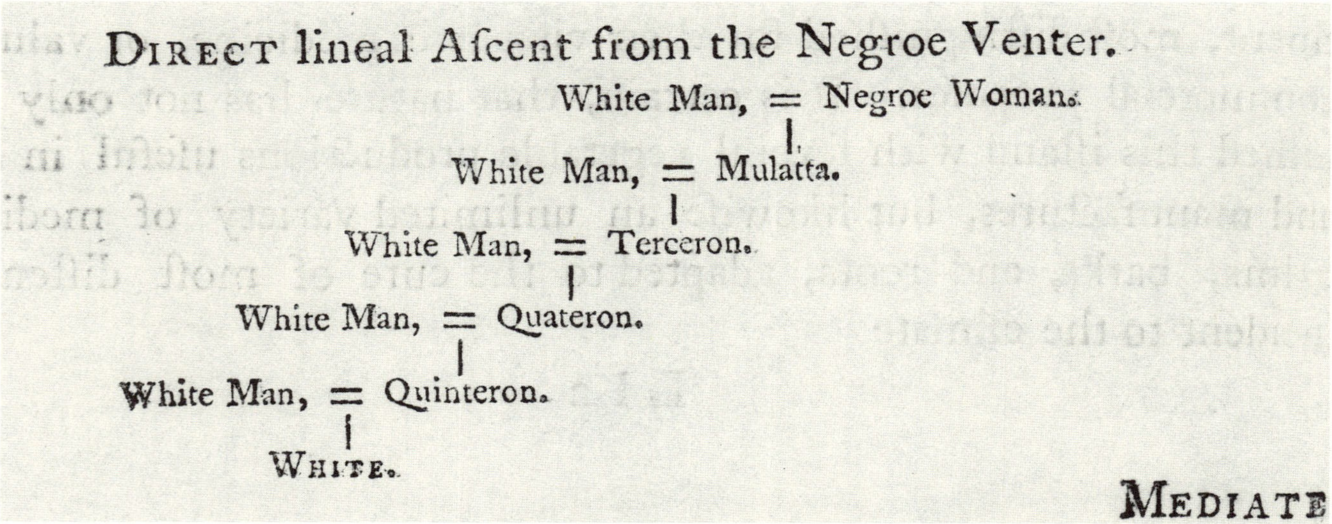

MEDIATE

DIRECT lineal Afcent from the Negroe Venter.

White Man, = Negroe Woman.
|

White Man, = Mulatta.
|

White Man, = Terceron.
|

White Man, = Quateron.
|

White Man, = Quinteron.
|

WHITE.

Figure 12. Chart of Racial Casts. Edward Long, *The History of Jamaica* (London, 1774). Long includes this chart of racial intermixture to distinguish between the Spanish and the British approaches to dealing with interracial sex in the colonies. Long claims that the Spaniards in the New World make the assignment of casts "a kind of science among them." By comparison, the West Indian planters make fewer distinctions; for instance, Long himself tends to use the simpler division signified by the tripartite division white, mulatto, and black to indicate the three main kinds of Jamaican inhabitants in descending order of political and aesthetic currency. The white woman is notably absent as an agent in the chart of racial intermixture. Courtesy of the John Carter Brown Library at Brown University.

MEDIATE or STATIONARY, neither advancing nor receding.

Quateron, = Terceron.

Tente-enel-ayre.

RETROGRADE.

Mulatto, = Terceron. Negroe, = Mulatta. Indian, = Mulatta. Negroe, = Indian.

Saltatras. Sambo de } =Negroe. Meitize. Sambo de } = Sambo de
Mulatta, Indian, Mulatta.

NEGROE. Givero [e].

Figure 12, continued. Chart of Racial Casts with Negro, Indian, and mixed race men featured as sexual agents.

(2:336). The separate origins of humans, or the polygeneticist hypothesis, Long contends, "enables us to account for those diversities of feature, skin, and intellect, observable among mankind; which cannot be accounted for in any other way" (336). Long's resort to polygenesis was a claim that even most other proslavery writers rejected as improbable—or at least too impolitic to print. In Long's scheme, people's visible differences are linked to "invisible" ones, calling on a notion of color and race that is produced by blood in the body rather than by climate or mode of subsistence. When he speaks in black and white terms, his conception of race is not variable.

To emphasize the distinctiveness of African blacks, Long mentions the texture of their hair and their facial features—common enough points of distinction for at least a century or more—and their odor, a newer characteristic he may have gleaned from Buffon.[86] The point of greatest difference, he contends, is skin color. He argues, "The particulars wherein they differ most essentially from the Whites are, first, in respect to their bodies, viz. the dark membrane which communicates that black colour to their skins, which does not alter by transportation into other climates" (351–52). Both the Virginian John Mitchell's "Essay upon the Causes of Different Colours of People in Different Climates" (1744) and Claude Le Cat's *Traité de la Couleur de la Peau Humaine* (1765) amplified the claim that black color was transmitted from an intermediate layer of skin. They favor an anatomical explanation in which skin color is lodged in the mucous membrane, a shift that locates racial distinction in the body and is more akin to biological than climatic explanations. Le Cat also shares Long's suspicion that Africans' numerous differences from Europeans mean that they are not the same species. To Long and Le Cat, color is part of the body and unalterable, which is proof positive of the difference between blacks and whites. Long, then, follows some Continental and colonial investigators in claims about the cause and location of skin color. It was not as common for other Britons to espouse either an anatomical or hereditary concept of skin color during the eighteenth century.

In sync with some of his contemporaries, Long assumes that, aside from the visible bodily differences he details, there is "disparity" in the faculties of the minds of Africans compared with any other people. To offer evidence of their inferior mental acumen, Long does not give a biological explanation or one based on anatomy; instead, he claims that African material and political culture has not progressed for centuries: "Under this head we are to observe, that they remain at this time in the same rude situation in which they were found two thousand years ago" (353). Africa has failed to progress like other nations, and it shows no signs of altering its "rude situation." In this sense, Long's speculation compares with Johnson's, which discovered nothing but the Highlanders' ancientness and moribund sameness until the Union. Long argues that black Africans have failed to absorb important aspects of European culture (that would predispose them to consume) and that they have not progressed because they have failed to emulate the more technologically advanced Europeans: "It is astonishing, that, although they have been acquainted with Europeans, and their manufactures, for so many hundred years, they have, in all this series of time, *manifested so little taste* for arts, or a genius either inventive or imitative" (354–55, emphasis added). Remarkably, this is the same accusation that Johnson levels at the clan culture of the Highlanders. Long's reference to taste reinforces the timeless savagery of the Africans. Colin Campbell analyzes the way that taste functioned in relation to maintaining class distinctions in late eighteenth-century Britain. As Campbell develops his analysis, he indirectly provides a gloss on Long's condemnation of Africans: "Taste as an ethical and aesthetic concept is indispensable to consumer behaviour, both to facilitate choice and to ensure the generation of new wants."[87] Lacking a refined sense of taste prevents Africans from recognizing their static situation and prompts them to indulge in the sensual pleasures of semibarbarians, as Goldsmith puts it.

Repeatedly, Long returns to issues associated with civil society to detail Negroes' inferior understanding. Based on his readings of contemporary philosophy and travel narratives, Long claims that black Africans "seem almost incapable of making any progress in civility or science. . . . They have no moral sensations; no taste but for women; gormondizing, and drinking to excess; no wish but to be idle. . . . Their houses are miserable cabbins. They conceive no pleasure from the most beautiful parts of their country" (353). It is significant that in a later section, Long chooses many of these very ideas to criticize the worst aspects of planters, who frequently exhibit semibarbaric desires. Unlike some of the Scots in Johnson's *Journey*, Long's Africans possess no arts or letters, "no rules of civil polity," no aesthetic appreciation, and no moral rectitude (377–78). In this way, Long rewrites contemporary history in coastal Africa and, like Johnson, offers an exaggerated vision of the present benefits of contact with the English. Long concedes that Africans' "savage manners" abate when they are clothed and inserted into a disciplined life (i.e., enslaved) (503). Thus, his view of their improvement belies his argument about their permanent inferiority. In fact, Long frequently espouses the most common views of national character, which largely arose from humoral/climatic theory—ones that suggest it changes through external stimuli. In his *English Humanity No Paradox* (1778), Long ascribes Africans' cruelty to the hot climate and to their largely vegetable diet. A change of climate and more meat would rectify character defects, in his opinion. In defending the English against charges of cruelty and savagery in the American war, Long claims that the English have eaten more vegetables in the last century and that this dietary change has "wrought a very extraordinary change in our organs, feelings, and propensities," a change that has made the English less fierce.[88] Sticking with beef and pudding, he believes, will eliminate the unmanly meekness that has crept into the English character.

Unlike the nearby Mosquito Indians, whom Long admires for their consumer taste and trading activity, Africans in Africa reveal no complexity or potential. In fact, there is no diversity among the inhabitants at all: "A general uniformity runs through all these various regions of people" (353). This view directly contradicts the commonplace among geographers and natural historians that Africa evinced the most variety of any continent. Take, for example, the illustrations in Goldsmith's *History of the Earth and Animated Nature* (1774), which show men from the major regions of the world: Lapland, America, China, and West Africa. In the 1795 version, a Hottentot from South Africa is added, and Africa is the only continent to warrant two illustrations. Long takes his cue from Hume and Ferguson rather than from natural historians; the former had contended that variety in a society was the felicitous result of mixed and liberal government: The proliferation of professions, ranks, and manners was peculiar to a polished society.[89] The great variety that characterized England meant that it had the least national character of any. In fact, it was usually savage nations that were accused of uniformity in their disposition, customs, and habits.[90]

Like Johnson's Scotland, Long's Africa seems to defy the progression of nations plotted in four-stages theory. The several modes of government observed in Africa seem to have little effect on the inhabitants' attainment of arts or genius, and they possess no recorded history or epics: "They have no mode of forming calculations, or of recording events to posterity, or of communicating thoughts and observations by marks, characters, or delineation; or by that method so common to most other countries in their rude and primitive ages, by little poems or songs" (377). At this time, it was widely agreed that every nation produced poetry in its earliest stages, and this was just one more fictional piece of damning evidence of Africa's exceptional stagnation. Despite the space he gives to enumerating differences of physical features and cultural customs between Africans and Europeans, Long ultimately emphasizes the relative strength of the moral sense and the reasoning faculty to distinguish the two populations (477)—the same categories customarily used to distinguish humans from the animal creation.[91]

The synthesis of various old and new ways of depicting English excellence and African degeneracy finds expression in terms of divine will and the chain of being; most modern critical attention has mentioned Long's racism in this context. The chain provides a visual aide to the various stages of civilization as well as to English power relations in the empire. In Long's vision, degrees of intellect and moral probity coalesce with designations of color, and the mulatto occupies the intermediate position between the slave and European: "The Negroe race (consisting of varieties) will then appear rising progressively in the scale of intellect, the further they mount above the oran-outang and brute creation (371), . . . and ascending from the varieties of this class [Guinea Negroes] to the lighter casts, until we mark its utmost limit of perfection in the pure White. Let us not then doubt, but that every member of the creation is wisely fitted and adapted to the certain uses, and confined within the certain bounds, to which it was ordained by the Divine Fabricator" (375). Long's scheme illustrates the transformation in the use of the chain of being during the Enlightenment. As Arthur Lovejoy shows, for the majority of Britons, the chain was an organizing concept that celebrated the diversity and continuity of the Creation from the lowliest organism to rational human beings. To Long and Charles Bonnet, the chain is a visual metaphor for rigid differences among humans. In Long's analysis, the chain of being joins older ideas about cosmic hierarchy and the benefits of labor subordination to a color binary. His interest is not in celebrating the diversity of Creation but in dramatizing the discrepancies he perceives in humankind. Used this way, the chain of being is a static snapshot of current power relations.

Under Long's pen, the nexus of complexion, intellect, and state of civilization allows one feature to become the signifier for the others. Long's work registers the beginning of a paradigm shift, which was more widely adopted at a later date. *History* lays the groundwork for a deeper and less changeable notion of national and racial differences than was previously fashionable. In *The Order of Things* (1970), Foucault notes an analogous change in the practice of natural history. He suggests that the impulse to systematize according to outward similarities gave way at the end of the eighteenth century to the idea that the surface of the body spoke volumes about invisible traits.

Through a cultural and physical analysis of Africans, Long promotes the benefits of slavery. His version of slavery functions like the Union in Johnson's Scotland: slavery initiates Africans into civil society. Long gives a misleading sense of the institution itself in order to persuade readers about the benefits of forcible African subordination to the British. His version of slavery in Africa combines two related stories (384–401). On the one hand, it demonstrates British compassion in saving the numerous population of

Figure 13. The Chain of Being. Charles Bonnet, *Contemplation de la Nature* in *Oeuvres* (Neuchatel, 1781). A representative Man dominates the rest of the natural world in this typical visualization of the chain of being. A few eighteenth-century writers adapted the general idea of the chain of being to plot hierarchy among humans, usually with black Africans or American Indians closest to the animal creation, and Europeans always at the greatest remove from animals. Nevertheless, it was mostly used as it is here: to demonstrate the gradations of complexity in the natural world. Brown University Library.

Africans from slaughter and torture and, alternatively, the favor the British perform in purging Africa of its criminal element—all justifications found in narratives by slavers in the 1720s and 1730s. Long locates the excesses of slavery and the tyranny of owners in African society rather than in European colonial society, arguing that what distinguishes the white slave owner from his African counterpart is his mild government, polite manners, and just disposition. In other words, he comes from a polished nation, a fact that improves rather than debases the enslaved African (401–3). Moreover, his account of slavery in the West Indies is similarly interested. A picture of leniency under Long's pen, the Jamaican planters give slaves property to manage and provide food, clothing, and shelter for their comfort. Enslavement as an effort to civilize Africans is a concept at odds with an older conviction that slavery debases the enslaved and the enslaver. Nevertheless, even Long concedes that "some few of these poor wretches may have inexorable tyrants for their masters, who may treat them worse perhaps than any person of humanity would treat a brute" (400). Slaves, then, are not animals, despite his occasional insinuations to the contrary.

Long's brief attempt to explain the legal origin of slavery results in unveiling the uncertainty at the heart of the racial ideology he calls on. Long speculates that Jamaican slave regulations transferred Tudor and Elizabethan ideas of class subordination onto a racial hierarchy (495). This explanation, however, creates an ideological tangle about the significance of color and race to enslavement—factors which he privileges elsewhere in his analysis. Suggesting that European custom rather than Negro inferiority laid the groundwork for slave regulation, Long reveals the constructed origins of Africans' inferior racial status: "By what means it happened, that, from the first colonization in the West-Indies, this race of men were so degraded as we find them, is not entirely clear. The English, probably, did no more than follow the steps of the Portugueze [*sic*] and other nations, who had begun, long before, to trade in Negroes as a commodity, and to hold them as mere chattels and moveables." He cautiously adds, "Perhaps the depravity of their nature, much more than their colour, gave rise to a belief of their inferiority of intellect" (497). Long's wavering between nature and color is significant because the two are not yet synonymous despite his consistent juxtaposition of them.

In the origin of slavery discussion and in other parts of *History*, Long adapts sedimented notions of subordination from a society divided according to rank to a society divided according to color. This is nowhere more evident than when Long concludes his encomium on slavery with the thought that slavery is divinely ordained because in all societies God has appointed some to labor (503). Even though slavery is a perversion of "free" wage labor, Long shares this general notion of beneficial subordination with many contemporaries, including Johnson. It was widely agreed that certain bodies were more fit to labor and others to supervise that labor—an assumption governing *Robinson Crusoe, Captain Singleton,* and *Journey to the Western Islands of Scotland.* Britons believed that proper subordination benefited the rich and the poor alike. Liberty was a concept crucial to Britons' self-definition, and it resulted from subordination. As Ferguson explains it, when a citizen has rights of property and station, and when they are protected, then those people are free (239). "Liberty" protects ruling-class men from incursions by the lower orders and slaves.

*   *   *

After his aggressive rewriting of contemporary Africa and Jamaica to dramatize the benefits of slavery to the enslaved, Long counsels rewarding only the most diligent or noteworthy of African descent, thereby securing new classes of subjects by dividing those considered most likely to band together. In Long's proposal for Jamaica's improvement, mulattos, freed blacks, and some island-born black slaves all could achieve various privileges of subjects in order to make Jamaica more secure for whites. Distinctions of color and lineage create niches for them in the commercial network and in the military defense of Jamaica; all of his efforts suggest a desire for a clearly marked social order based on shared interest in Jamaica. The underlying conflicts in Long's proposal in regard to mulattos may be reduced, on the one hand, to a concept of human character as subject to the vagaries of climate and mode of subsistence, and thus changeable by education and supervision, and, on the other hand, to a newer concept of human character as "deeper" and more stable than before.

For Long, lineage and religious conversion rank equally in defining useful and proper subjects, much as it does in Scotland for Johnson. In this way, Christian mulattos may obtain the most privileges in his proposal. For mulattos who inherit independent fortunes and who have a Christian education, he sees little reason to restrict them in any way because they rapidly become worthy citizens lost to Jamaica but gained to England: "For it deserves serious reflection, that most of the superior order (for these reasons) prefer living in England, where they are respected, at least for their fortunes" (322). If fortune and education override dark skin color in Great Britain, Christian conversion only partially compensates a darker complexion in the colonies. Normally, Christian mulattos, or baptized men born of white fathers and

Negro mothers, were not eligible for automatic legal enfranchisement. The Jamaican law, besides requiring three generations' separation from a Negro ancestor, stipulated that the subject be baptized in order to gain the privileges accorded to white men. Surprisingly, Long desires to weaken the severe segregation based on color.

Long's real concern is not upper-class mulattos but the lower ranks who would become the primary military defenders of Jamaica. To make the lower order of mulattos "orderly subjects, and faithful defenders of the country," Long proposes a rigorous plan of religious instruction and education in trade, apprenticeship schemes more formal than the general encouragement recommended for the Indians (333). In Long's thought, education is the only means to equip good subjects adequately, a belief he applies to mulattos as well as to white inhabitants. After religious instruction and apprenticeship, these mulattos would become part of the Jamaican militia to counterbalance the power of the Maroons (334).[92] In these instances, the important goal is to insert mulattos into colonial circuits of defense and trade as independent producers of services and consumers of goods. In *The History of Jamaica*, cultural and material consumption is the most visible way for mulattos to approach English civility, and it is offered as the most rapid way to produce a sense of uniform national manners and common interests among colonial subjects despite differences of language, status, or color. Historians such as David Brion Davis and Winthrop Jordan remark on the singularity of Jamaica's provision for the social ascent of mulattos, but they do not argue as strongly as it seems warranted that the upward mobility responded largely to the overwhelming concern about internal safety.[93] The real interest behind Long's scheme is the protection of white inhabitants and their property against the Maroons and any slave uprisings (344).

Long's plan suggests that mulatto men would effectively become a better distinguished buffer group between ruling whites and slaves. Present-day scholars refer to the ideological and economic place of the Jamaican mulattos and Scottish Lowlanders as buffer groups. The creation of buffer groups contains the heterogeneity of colonial populations according to ideologies of civility and savagery, commercial enterprise and idleness. In fact, buffer groups function similarly to what we call model minorities today: one minority population is embraced as desirable to the detriment of other minority populations. The model minority, however, is privileged because that group is perceived as more faithfully adopting the dominant group's values than other groups.[94] One of the ways that eighteenth-century buffer groups functioned was to mirror back the desirability of English norms of beauty and cultural activity. The contrast between these buffer groups and the more "savage" black slaves or Highlanders was marked by mulatto and Lowlander imitation of English dress, speech, and manners; they aspired to the status that accompanied these visible signs of civility (and were rewarded accordingly).

Long's view of mulattos' and freed blacks' potential service to Jamaica and hence to Britain is reinforced by a racial aesthetic. Each group of inhabitants is distinguished from the group below it on the strength of their resemblance to European features, color, and habits. Mulattos are distinguished from Maroons in beauty of body and complexion as well as in niceness of manners, although they are "equal in hardiness and vigour" of body (335). In turn, the militaristic and free Maroons are visibly superior to native-born African slaves. They speak a more "regular" language than Africans, and they possess well-made bodies and more delicate features than Africans; in fact, Maroons' features are "more of the European turn" (474). Between Jamaican-born slaves and African-born slaves, Long also sees a visible difference: "The Creole Blacks differ much from the Africans, not only in manners, but in beauty of shape, feature, and complexion" (410). His argument for advancing this "better sort" is also based on their potential to enhance the commercial activity of the colony (1:135).

Ultimately, mulattos, free blacks, and a few Creole blacks might be inserted more fully into a network of consumerism, which would hasten their ascent into civility. Eventually their new social and economic position will lead them to "strive for conveniencies [sic], and some even for superfluities. All this must add to the consumption of manufactures, and the cultivation of lands; and the colonies would be strengthened by the addition of so many men, who have an interest of their own to fight for" (503). Thus, consumerism, more readily available to the nonwhite populations, would benefit Jamaica, and it would flourish best when the population aspires to own luxuries, not just necessities, an argument that dangerously suggests the benefits of abolishing slavery altogether. Economically, Long identifies what is called the elasticity of demand, which theorizes that consumers possess an almost infinite desire for commodities, limited chiefly by their income and community customs. The mulattos' desire for luxuries provides the impetus for their continuing industry and its result: a thriving, wealthy society. Long is not just making an economic argument here but is also referring to stages of civilization. Through "free" labor and the ability to purchase British goods, mulattos, freed blacks, and some Creoles will transcend the savagery owed to their African ancestry. In this way, Jamaica would resemble a truly civil society. This dynamic vision of Creole inhabitants contradicts the static conception of race propounded in the chain of being.

Long, even more than Johnson, seems convinced that civilization corresponds to the consumption of British goods. The one-to-one correspondence Long makes between consumerism and civilization is also apparent in his extensive comments about the Indians, the colonial population typically considered most similar to Britons. Like the Lowland Scots, the Indians had already demonstrated the ability to assimilate to British norms by "their annual consumption of British manufactures, by no means inconsiderable; for which they pay us in valuable productions of the Continent" (1:26). Long believes that the Mosquito people will contribute to Jamaica's strength by cultivating the land and expanding trade with proper instruction, but "Preparatory to this, some degree of civilization is necessary; without which, their consumption of British manufactures cannot reach to any great extent. . . . Their wants will undoubtedly increase in proportion as they grow more civilized" (1:318–19). Perceived as fledgling British consumers, Indian conversion to full civility only requires the consumption of more British manufactures. Thus, Long argues that establishing a colony near the Woolvas and Cuckeras Indians would be mutually advantageous because "by fair dealing and a generous communication [the British colony could] wean them from a state of barbarism to civility and industry. It seems, I think, probable, that they might soon become reconciled to much of the English manners in their dress and habitations, and gradually induced to take large imports of cloathing, furniture, implements, and food from us. . . . [O]ur British wares and manufactures might be dispersed to many thousands of people on this continent" (1:324–25). In this way, British commodities become the vehicle of civilization. Increasing the Indians' desire to consume will intensify their emulation of the British, which will, in turn, bring them into the ranks of civility. Long proposes that the Indians' new status would resemble that of foreign Europeans and Jews — a "white" citizenship with all but a few privileges — an increasingly likely scenario, since Indians had been expressly removed from the slave category in Jamaica for thirty years (344). In his treatment of the Indians, Long does not describe them as objects of natural history as much as he positions them as novice consumers.

All of Long's schemes for improved island security meant opening up avenues for the socioeconomic advancement characteristic of capitalist societies. At the moment, however, the extreme legal and economic polarization between most whites and people of mixed and African descent meant that Jamaica bore no resemblance to commercial English society. But there was more than political and economic issues at stake in Long's dwelling on the redemptive possibility of consumer culture. Agriculture was the only culture Jamaica produced, and its failure to propagate arts and letters or technological innovation meant that it was an embarrassing exception to civil society such as the Scottish Enlightenment sketched. As early as 1740, Leslie complained that Jamaica was not a polished society like Britain.[95] Later commentators attributed this lack to the nature of the planters themselves. In *A Descriptive Account of the Island of Jamaica* (1790), William Beckford, Jr. makes this civil failure clear when he describes the planters as indolent and languorous, noting that their society has failed to produce works of genius or the liberal professions.[96] Overseas colonies did not function like the polished nations to which they were attached, not least because their agreed-upon function was to generate personal fortunes for Britons and wealth for England. Given his support for the planter class, it is understandable that Long neglects to mention the culture white Jamaicans have failed to produce. In this way, consumerism is an acceptable substitute to indicate a state of civilization.

Of course, the civilizing benefits of commerce for all Britons explicitly rely on the slave trade. Long, like many before him, enumerates the widespread benefits of the "Negroe trade, which is the ground-work of all" (1:491). Africans are not only the forced labor supply by which astronomical profits are reaped. They are also significant consumers of British goods in their own right, albeit in a different way than the voluntary consumption of the Indians. A captive population, they must be clothed, fed, and given instruments to work with, all of British manufacture. Cannily, Long equates slavery with English patriotism. In fact, his plans for improving Jamaica, and consequently Great Britain, include expanding cultivation and hence increasing the number of slaves. Strategically, Long prefaces his ideas about extending the slave trade with the related benefits that amass to inhabitants in Great Britain: "What a field is here open to display the comforts and blessings of life, which this commerce distributes among so many thousands of industrious subjects in the mother country! what multitudes participate the sustenance and conveniences derived from it, who, without it, would either cease from existence, or not exist to any useful purpose!" (1:508).

Without mentioning actual slaves, Long represents the Jamaican slave system as the bulwark of British industry, commerce, and liberty—concepts synonymous with contemporary notions of civil society. Two earlier observers of Jamaica made similar plugs for the way the enslavement of Africans was equivalent to more British jobs and more widespread enjoyment of delectable commodities.[97] The incitement to consume and the benefit of it were not, therefore, neutral. While the colonies may provide the wealth and trade by which the domestic population of Britain enjoys a higher standard of living and increased civility, the slave system does not foster the like benefits for its laboring populations. It is this anomaly that Long wishes to redress for many segments of Jamaican society, not out of altruism but in the name of whites' safety.

* * *

If Creole black and mulatto men occupy the foreground of Long's concerns about securing civil safety and stimulating commercial activity in the public sphere, black and mulatta women are the focus of the domestic problem. Consistently, Long finds planter degeneracy from a British norm disturbing, and his rhetorical compensations for this troublesome deviation are notable. In order to maintain the civil nature of the planter class, Long counterpoises the savagery of black and mulatta women. Whether Long considers the necessity of education for the island whites or the task of making white women more attractive, the importance of maintaining the purity of the English dialect or of breaking white men of their vicious sexual habits, the source of the problem is black and mulatta women. Thus, to Long, culture, patrimony, marriage, and education are in crisis because of the "superior attractions" of these women, which is his ideological substitute for white men's unrestrained sexuality as a prerogative of masculinity and of forging an empire. Black and mulatta women threaten a view of English masculine identity that is self-controlled and empowered.

When Long analyzes the planters and their white families, he depicts their degeneration in sexual and linguistic terms, attributing their inferiority to the contaminating influence of the social mores of the female slaves who surround them. These degenerations among whites are also gendered. Whereas white men reveal debased morals and a negligent value for their property because of their sexual contact with nonwhite women, white women display their degeneration through their accents and mannerisms, imitated from their slaves. White men's linguistic ability is apparently unimpaired as is white women's virtue.[98]

Long's diatribe against the insidious nature of the slave women dramatizes the problems generated by intensive (sexual, linguistic, and economic) commerce in the empire. Traditionally, the civilizing benefits of commercial exchange were seen to flow in two directions between trading partners trying to accommodate each other. As seen in Chapter 2, however, contact with the English was widely believed to improve other nations, but the unaddressed assumption is that contact with other populations did not necessarily improve the English. For the English, this contact simply made them wealthier. The rise of heterosocial conversation as the process by which Englishmen's

passions would be properly reined in and their manners polished was difficult to duplicate in Jamaica, not least because there were no provisions made
for formal education of white women or men. In fact, as all kinds of colonial documents reveal, there was a frightening proportion of Europeans who
either "went native" or who, like the planters, abandoned the national virtues
most prized by Britons in their pursuit of wealth: commerce could be dangerous. After over a century of writing about the Caribbean colonies, many
observers concluded that Englishness showed alarming evidence of degeneration and vulnerability.

Long emphasizes the many behavioral distinctions between planters
and both Englishmen and white Creole women, including planters' sexual
promiscuity, excessive eating and drinking, and their failure to secure and
improve their patrimony. Most eighteenth-century writers offer a mixed assessment of the white landowners. They describe plantation owners as gay
and hospitable on the positive side, but idle and indolent on the negative
side. These traits were antipathetic to a commercial nation because they im-
paired fortunes and thus injured entire families. Long finds the planters vain,
fickle, haughty, and subject to violent fits of anger; they live too extrava-
gantly, paying too much attention to their dress and equipage, habits that
render them effeminate (265). All of these personal character flaws resemble
contemporary European visions of some African and East Indian men whose
enervated bodies and feminized habits resulted from excessive luxury and
polygamy. Long is alarmed because these traits make for a corrupt ruling
class: White men fail to fulfill the basic obligations of a good citizenry by
not reproducing an unadulterated white race (327). In other words, they are
much more savage and effeminate than their counterparts in Great Britain.

Consumerism assumes a different meaning in relation to Jamaican
planters than to other subjects. To Long, luxury is so rampant among the
planters that it has corrupted them. *The History of Jamaica* initiates a trend
that intensifies in the detailed 1790s depictions of colonial life by Bryan
Edwards, William Beckford, Jr., and John Gabriel Stedman. The composite
picture that emerges from their narratives is of a languid white patriarch
being dressed, coifed, and attended to by slaves in every function of life.
Even the customary meals exceed their wealthiest English counterpart for
number of dishes and amount of alcohol. Never pictured attending to business for very long, they are usually shown as enervated by the climate and
their sexuality. This last component envisions them prey to overseers, slaves,
and colored mistress, all of whom fool the weak planters into giving them
their way.

Long's depiction of the planter class dramatizes the problematic linkage between civilization and consumerism that Britons had been wrestling with throughout the eighteenth century. If some of the nonwhite populations in Jamaica must learn to be more avid consumers, too much consumption saps the drive so essential to generating and preserving wealth among the white inhabitants. In fact, it endangers political rule. Although Great Britain thrives because of the demand for goods created by the planters' extravagant lifestyles, Jamaica itself is weakened and its future endangered. Long's solution to this delicate issue is to introduce new consumers who will be vetted and then regulated by the Jamaican state and to urge the planters to attend to improving their estates rather than simply displaying their wealth. Both strategies co-opt patriotic discourse to buttress the extensive changes they entail.

Inserting planters into acceptable notions of English masculinity proved difficult. Planters fit roughly into the tradition of masculinity and stage of civilization represented by Roman republicanism. Rome was, of course, also a slaveholding society. Other than owning property, the planters were alarmingly free of attributes associated with this ideal. J. G. A. Pocock observes that property and power were, by the 1770s, suspected to be deficient when unalloyed by the control of the passions characteristic of the new economic man of the eighteenth century.[99] *The History of Jamaica* offers an extended picture of the difficulties white Creoles had in ruling themselves and others; the burgeoning mulatto class was simply one visible reminder of insufficiently regulated planters. Most basically, Long hints at the anomaly created by a slave system that included men's uninhibited sexual access to women; the traditional sexual prerogative of ruling-class men was at odds with good governance and island security. In as much as the public sphere in England was conceived ideally as a self-regulating community of equals with satellite subordinates, planter society appeared, even to staunch defenders, unmoored from the philosophical and moral base that anchored ideologies of civic humanism or republicanism.

Long effectively argues that the inhabitants of England and Jamaica neither espouse the same values nor produce the same kind of citizens, not only because of its variously colored inhabitants or the slave system, but also because white male sexuality has run amok in Jamaica and inverted power relations between colors and genders. In contrast to England, Jamaica is "a place where, by custom, so little restraint is laid on the passions, the Europeans, who at home have always been used to greater purity and strictness of manners, are too easily led aside to give a loose to every kind of sensual delight: on this account some black or yellow *quasheba* is sought for, by whom a tawney breed is produced. Many are the men, of every rank, quality, and degree here, who would much rather riot in these goatish embraces, than share the pure and lawful bliss derived from matrimonial, mutual love. Modesty, in this respect, has but very little footing here" (328). These men have transgressed the boundaries sanctioned by British commercial custom by making slavery pleasurable for themselves, not simply useful to economic advancement, a phenomenon Long deplores (333).

The History of Jamaica does not offer a consistent depiction of planter corruption. Countering his vision of their degeneracy, Long's preferred myth of the planters conjures up feudal magnificence. He compares the white planter and his slaves to a Scottish chieftain and his clan with the same nostalgia that Johnson does in wishing to preserve the authority of the patriarchal mode in the Highlands and Hebrides (410). This interpretation favors paternalism over exploitation as the primary mode of interaction, but Long's choice is riddled with inconsistencies. Clans are symptomatic of a barbarous, not a polished, nation, and it is not protection, duty, or affection that binds a planter to his slaves, but violence.

With the advent of the abolition lobby in the 1780s, questions intensify about whether the white Creoles were simply transplanted Britons or a mutant group. The picture of degenerate half-men vied with the vision of feudal grandeur for the dominant representation of the planter ruling class. Both climate and national character were plumbed for explanations. In fact, in his monumental History, Civil and Commercial, of the British Colonies in the West Indies (1793–1801), Bryan Edwards notes that the hot West Indian climate induces planters to "early and habitual licentiousness," which, he believes, hinders their mental improvement. Although it seems to be true, he cannot admit that the Creoles in general "possess less capacity and stability of mind than the natives of Europe."[100]

Despite the litany of landowner deviations from English norms of manliness, there was widespread acceptance of them as misguided Britons, probably because of their rank, ownership of land, and conspicuous consumption. As drama, novels, and poems of the 1770s suggest, there was an active desire to reclaim the West Indian planters and to reconcile their excesses with Britishness. In Elizabeth Bonhote's Rambles of Mr. Frankly (1773), a West Indian makes a cameo appearance. He has recently come to London for the first time. When supplicated for money, the West Indian strikes the beggar, a gesture condemned by the narrator. Commenting that the rich man has forgotten that he has left a land of slaves, the narrator shows a secular conversion scene. The narrator reclaims the West Indian into the national fold when he observes that the colonial son feels remorse. The West Indian, we are told, soon discerns his pity was being importuned, and he gives the beggar five guineas, an act of generosity that shows his true Englishness. The narrator concludes, "The man is a christian and charity will guide him to Heaven."[101]

Richard Cumberland's *The West Indian* (1771) also demonstrates the desire to embrace West Indians by forgiving the foibles of those who return to England and are adjusting to the more strenuous moral climate of London. Emphasizing the newly arrived Belcour's fiery passions (due, the text notes, to the hot climate they were nursed in), the play counters with his generous impulses to relieve the financial distresses of various Britons. The complexity of his unmentioned sexual contact with slave women is played out through his mistaking the young, beautiful, but impoverished Louisa Dudley for a prostitute. The lesson that Belcour must learn is to treat white women of impoverished gentility with dignity. His marriage to Louisa hands over the responsibility to her for regulating him when he errs. As David Solkin shows in his explication of how luxury became consistent with manly virtue over the century, by the 1770s, charity and compassion were essential components of English masculinity at home and abroad.[102] Imperial might was enjoyed most when combined with generosity to the vanquished. Hence the benevolent, if profligate, planter (or his surrogate) appears consistently as hospitable to European strangers in the West Indies and as capable of conversion to English ideals when in Britain. His generosity to fellow Britons excuses other excesses.[103] Colin Campbell's *Romantic Ethic and the Rise of Modern Consumerism* (1987) posits that the Cambridge Platonists initially spearheaded the embrace of secular benevolence; they saw "charity—in the form of a general kindness to all men—as the essence of religion." The goodness displayed through charitable acts evinced "man's capacity for sympathy and feeling" (120).

The History of Jamaica is one of many 1770s texts that contributed to refining an increasingly racialized British identity that prized Englishness because of its superiority to remnants of past unrefined images of savages and present profligate planters. This identity was also about a particular kind of manliness. As Kathleen Wilson demonstrates, one of the achievements of the Seven Years' War was to recover British manliness through imperialism.[104] This new sense of patriotic manliness called into question both the warlike Scottish chief and the effeminate West Indian planter, although it relied on these other identities to differentiate itself. In the 1770s, the cultural ideal urged charity and compassion to fellow countrymen. Complemented by a manly regulation of economic and sexual appetites, this created a model identity for the upper or middling ranks of men.

Because planters deviate from acceptable conventions of manliness by neglecting important duties of citizenship, Long looks to white women for preserving the future of the colony. He sees them as key to reproducing relations of color domination and as linchpins in the transmission of polite culture. In the process of wishing that white women could secure an unadulterated race in Jamaica, Long blames them for not holding the sexual attention of white men (330). He snipes, "One would suppose it no very arduous task to make themselves more companionable, useful, and esteemable, as wives, than the Negresses and Mulattas are as mistresses" (331). According to Long, one of the major impediments to a whiter Jamaica is that European women are less attractive to planters than mulatta and black women. Just as Long envisions the recruitment of mulatto men to supply a new though subordinate citizenry, white women may be improved to add greater security to the island colony by ensuring multiplication of the white race. Education is the most important panacea: It will make white women more desirable than black and mulatta women (although it will not curb white men's inclinations) (279). In addition to rectifying the problem of racial mixture, his plan would also secure more marriages and thereby the integrity of property: "To allure men from these illicit connexions [with nonwhite women], we ought to remove the principal obstacles which deter them from marriage. This will be chiefly effected by rendering women of their own complexion more agreeable companions, more frugal, trusty, and faithful friends, than can be met with among the African ladies" (330). Paradoxically, a feminist demand for improved education secures racist ends.[105]

Long desires the establishment of seminaries in Jamaica to aid white girls in preparing them to be good wives and mothers by weaning them "from the Negroe dialect" and giving them examples of "modest and polite behaviour," presumably from their white instructors (250). The lack of formal education in the colonies had long been a source of concern but only in terms of its effect on young men. In *A New History of Jamaica* (1740), Charles Leslie notes that several large donations had been made to rectify this problem, but no schools were built; he believed that lack of proper education adversely affected men's ability to govern Jamaica disinterestedly. The picture Leslie draws of men raised in Jamaica is one of a gradual dissolution. In his early years, the young boy "diverts himself" with slaves and acquires their "broken way of talking" and their vices (36). Thus, the damage has been done: Schooling is ineffective because the future planter is already willful. Then the young man "rakes with his Equals," which involves more commerce with slaves. Leslie asks, "How can it be supposed one of such a Turn can entertain any generous Notions, distinguish the Beauties of a Virtue, [or] act for the Good of his Country?" (37). Neither Leslie nor Long perceive the planters as able men at some level. Indeed, Long despairs of changing men, but sees hope in white women by asking them to assume the helm of domestic order in Jamaica.

Ideologies of womanhood and of women's education had changed considerably in the midcentury. Commercial society's boast, best elaborated in John Millar's *Origin of the Distinction of Ranks* (1771), was its gentle treatment of women as companions, not its exploitation of them as servants. This belief bolstered the sense of the gulf between Englishwomen and all others. Goldsmith best captures the difference civil society made when he claims, "Her mind is still more prized than her person."[106] Accordingly, women's roles in family life expanded to include the regulation of men's and children's passions, and these new responsibilities entailed more education than formerly, so that women could be pleasing and useful. In Jamaica, this vision of domestic bliss is interrupted by white women's prolonged contact with slaves from an early age, which, some argued, polluted their manners and language: "The constant intercourse from their birth with Negroe domestics, whose drawling, dissonant gibberish they insensibly adopt, and with it no small tincture of their aukward carriage and vulgar manners; all which they do not easily get rid of, even after an English education, unless sent away extremely young" (278).[107] As with the Scots in Johnson's *Journey*, purity of language and dialect is an important sign of sameness with Great Britain, a grave defect in these otherwise "amiable women." From Jonathan Swift to Hannah More, Britons were convinced that "women's conversation was . . . the best way for men to polish theirs." Because women raised sons, it was imperative for women to be educated in grammar and instructed in speaking clearly.[108] The education of young white girls in Jamaica would result in a more stable society. According to Long, "They would, by this means, become objects of love to the deserving youths, whether natives or Europeans, and by the force of their pleasing attractions soon draw them, from a loose attachment to Blacks and Mulattoes, into the more rational and happy commerce of nuptial union" (2:250). Edward Long was not the first to blame Englishwomen for the problems generated by the planters' relationship to slaves. In 1684, Thomas Tryon blamed white women for the poor treatment of female slaves and slave children. It was their responsibility, he reasoned, to prevail more arduously with their husbands to act humanely.[109]

The unsolvable problem seems to be white men's inclinations and the excesses condoned within a slave-based society. Long's afterthought to incite improvement in white women refers to the real source of the problem: "It might be much better for Britain, and Jamaica too, if the white men in that colony would abate of their infatuated attachments to black women"

(327). Regulating elite male sexual behavior and curbing their abuse of power is not commensurate with their privilege and agency.

In Long's narrative of Jamaica, black and mulatta women have a profound effect on the white inhabitants. They are surrogate mothers, companions in youth and puberty, trusted servants, and beloved mistresses. One of Long's narrative strategies emphasizes their savagery by making them agents of contamination. For example, in chastising white mothers for their slack maternal care, he claims that slave women's milk infects the children they nurse and that their speech and manners corrupt young, marriageable white women who spend most of their time in their company (278). Of course, these same charges had been leveled at lower-class women who were wet nurses to families who could afford them in Europe. In this way, black women are blamed for impeding the success of Jamaica and the empire because of their association with white women and children.[110] In this vein, British colonial identity appears weak and malleable as well as constantly endangered.

Long's elaborate plans for improving the various Jamaican subjects noticeably fail to include nonwhite women. Their sexual and domestic contact with whites has apparently failed to uplift them from their putative savagery. Different kinds of education, religious instruction, and apprenticeships are all suggested for white boys and girls, mulattos, and freed black men, but the black and mulatta women seem to have no place except as domestics, field slaves, and sexual partners. In contrast, neither black nor mulatto men appear in the colonial sexual economy at all. Instead, their function is primarily to defend the colony in order to ensure uninterrupted access to liberty and property rights for white men.

Long's revamped Jamaica would increase the contact of all men but would keep women separated and in conflict with each other. Despite the prominence he gives to gradations in complexion, his harping on mental differences, and allusions to the probability of polygenesis, Long subscribes to a theory of human differences similar to Johnson's, not least because of the vast physical and moral "improvements" he finds in the male population of African descent once they are inserted into the colonial economy and have access to education, religious instruction, and consumer goods. In this way, he envisions a cadre of junior Britons who, like Friday in *Robinson Crusoe* and the Black Prince in *Captain Singleton*, would assume a subordinate place in the political and economic life of the empire.

Analyzing the way that assumptions from four-stages theory structure Long's *History* helps uncover the way that Johnson's *Journey* hinges not only on classical observations about the body politic but also on natural history, which was concerned first and foremost with the body. *The History of Jamaica* shows how racialization occurred with and without reference to physical characteristics. Johnson and Long offer similar portraits of the relationship between England and other parts of the empire. Long, like Johnson, perceives the importance of commerce in generating a wealthy and civil society. In *Journey to the Western Islands* and *The History of Jamaica*, cultural and material consumption are the most visible signs of English civility and are offered as the most rapid way to produce a sense of uniform national manners and common interests, despite differences in accent, status, or color.

Consumerism did not erase distinctions of class or color. In fact, it created another kind of hierarchical bond among British subjects based on the emulation of an approved norm. Insufficient consumption of goods or English culture helped delineate differences of station within Britain and the empire. This kind of hierarchy ultimately proved much more negotiable than one based on physical appearance because it could be remedied by changes in government and commerce. Even with the shift to a color hierarchy in natural history, its significance had not yet been fully determined in British culture generally, as the *Encyclopaedia Britannica* (1781) notes. Long's negative use of it suggests that harping on physical differences created a sense of permanent divisions, ones that were not easily bridged.

Chapter 5

The Politicization of Race

The Specter of the Colonies in Britain

What an immense difference exists in Scotland, for instance, between the chiefs and the commonalty of the Highland clans? If they had been separately found in different countries, they would have been ranged by some philosophers under different species.

—*Encyclopaedia Britannica* (1797)[1]

Fleecy locks and black complexion
Cannot forfeit Nature's claim;
Skins may differ, but Affection
Dwells in White and Black the same. . . .
Deem our nation Brutes no longer
'Till some reason ye shall find
Worthier of regard, and stronger
Than the Colour of our Kind.

—WILLIAM COWPER, "The Negro's Complaint" (1788)[2]

THROUGH criticism of the trend, the epigraphs convey the significance Britons placed on the body's exterior, an attention that was especially remarkable in the last two decades of the eighteenth century. The epigraphs also indicate how natural history categories helped in the enumeration of minute differences among groups of people, a phenomenon that made claims about the irrelevance of exterior features difficult to reconcile with the increased propensity to note them. Commonplaces about judging appearance abounded, and even though many scientists tried to distance themselves from the more dubious forms of judgment, such as physiognomy, their own findings, of course, supported such an intimate connection between face and character. Moreover, fashion was as important as deportment and countenance to the task of interpreting appearances, which had regional as well as racial application. The natural historian William Martyn observes about his contemporaries: "We are so accustomed to suffer ourselves to be influenced by external appearances, that if no symptoms of thought and reflection appear in a man's countenance, we too hastily pronounce him to be deficient of ability: we are even weak enough to draw conclusions from the cut of the cloaths, or the curls of the periwig. Men ought therefore to pay some attention to these minute articles; because, in the eyes of strangers, they constitute a part of ourselves, and contribute not a little to the opinion they form of our understanding and manners."[3] Martyn puts his finger on the way a person's appearance provided an automatic commentary on his or her rational capacity. In many late eighteenth-century social and political situations, Britons judged exterior appearance severely, and much seemed to hinge on the accurate interpretation of its meaning. This general climate of belief is one of the many constraints that shapes the former slave Olaudah Equiano's narrative.

Written when the number of slaves Britons transported across the Atlantic was reaching its historic height, Equiano's slave narrative spans his childhood in Africa as the son of a chief man of the kingdom; his kidnapping and subsequent enslavement in England; his labor as a seaman and extensive travels in America, the Mediterranean, Europe, and the Arctic region; his position as a slave overseer; and his cultural and religious education in England.[4] The narrative ends with his marriage to an Englishwoman and his abolitionist work. Reflecting the general shift to a more noticeably color-conscious racial ideology, the narrative shows Equiano's attempts to keep whiteness separate from a notion of Britishness in order for him, a former slave, to claim an authoritative public identity.[5]

Part of positioning himself in relation to his readers involves Equiano's revealing himself to be an avid consumer of British culture and a savvy businessman, which by extension partially accounts for his culminating argument that Africans are poised to become appreciative consumers of British manufactures and civilization once the slave trade is abolished. Throughout the text, Equiano's gender, age, and changing status (enslaved, manumitted, Christian servant, slave driver, abolitionist) position him variously in relation to men and women of different nations, reaffirming that even at the height of the British slave trade, slavery produced contradictions for a man of African descent within dominant racial and gender paradigms and at the level of representation.[6] His text brings to the foreground the way that being a free man overpowers black skin color in Britain and Turkey. In this spirit, Frances Foster Smith's observation deserves attention: "Slaves such as Equiano were more like Defoe's Robinson Crusoe than Defoe's characterization of the ever-faithful and servile black man, Friday."[7] Equiano's narrative also includes instances when dark skin color overrides the privileges of free status and British-coded masculinity in certain contexts, especially in the West Indies and America.

In *The Interesting Narrative of the Life of Olaudah Equiano or Gustavus Vassa, the African* (1789), Equiano calls on prevailing theories of human variety, detailed in the previous chapters, and brings them to bear on his representation of the inhabitants of West Africa, Britain, North America, the West Indies, and, most particularly, his experiences of slavery. In general, Equiano's narrative accords ideologically with other abolitionist writing by emphasizing the shared descent, propensities, and sympathy of Africans and Europeans, which the epigraph from Cowper's "The Negro's Complaint" economically summarizes.[8] *The Interesting Narrative* calls on theories of climate as well as on categories of natural history and four-stages theory to help argue against slavery and, in the process, reveals some of their inconsistencies, including the limits to associating anti-slave trade sentiment with an assumption of human equality. Equiano's efforts, like those of some other abolitionists, demonstrate the difficulty of intervening in ideologies of human variety as they had taken shape by the late 1780s, and of using them to advocate widespread changes in slavery, particularly by trying to argue that Africans were not inferior but only different in some superficial ways.

Equiano's narrative crystallizes some of the most pressing issues connected to racial ideology. On balance, the challenge to proslavery arguments that invoked racial ideology is often limited by the assumptions that pro- and anti–slave trade arguments shared. One of the conceptual obstacles that Equiano must negotiate is the particular shape of racism in the late 1780s. On the one hand, most Britons believed that Africans were inferior to themselves in a number of ways. On the other hand, they did not necessarily believe that they deserved to be enslaved because of that supposed inferiority. This articulation, however, clears a path for broad consensus about race across the political spectrum. Indeed, this space is large enough even for Afro-British writers to inhabit without agreeing that slavery was a necessary evil.

By examining available explanations of human difference in the main arguments for and against slavery, as well as references to slavery and Negroes in representative theories of human difference, this chapter sets up the main context for analyzing Equiano's participation in British narratives of racial difference.[9] His narrative is part of a vast body of eighteenth-century literature that evinces a preoccupation with cultural differences and a sometimes confused concern with the visible appearance of bodies, particularly complexion's meaning. Accounting for the way that slavery shaped these discussions helps us to consider anew the reference to race in slave trade discourse. One remarkable asymmetry is that the anti–slave trade position relied more heavily on appeals to racial similarity than slavery advocates relied on appeals to racial difference.[10] Our historical memory has made the connection between racism and support for slavery seem inevitable and self-evident, but to refuse a closer look at the historical underpinnings of this preconception obscures our understanding of slavery, theories of human variety, and racism.

*   *   *

Henry Louis Gates, Jr., has been instrumental in demonstrating the importance of race to analyses of the Enlightenment, and his scholarship of the 1980s, which continued Richard Popkin's, exposes the racist aesthetics and philosophical systems informing eighteenth-century European thought.[11] Gates examines early slave narratives in terms of racial theories, especially the way that many European literati invoked literacy and reason to distinguish Europeans positively from Africans. Since the seventeenth century, Gates argues, literacy, or the pursuit of arts and letters, was the privileged European sign of civilization that excluded Africans from the human community. If literacy excludes non-Muslim Africans, then it also excludes a great many other people. Samuel Purchas, the compiler of sixteenth- and early seventeenth-century travel narratives, articulated writing as the mark of a polished people in *Hakluytus Posthumus, or Purchas his Pilgrimes* (1625); at the time, it was a new constellation of ideology. Purchas writes, " 'amongst Men, some are accounted Ciuill, and more both Sociable and Religious, by the Vse of letters and Writing, which others wanting are esteemed Brutish, Sauage, barbarous.' "[12] Like their clothing, Europeans' literacy was often a curiosity to peoples in parts of Africa, North America, and the Pacific (41). It is not until the late eighteenth century that Africans were occasionally singled out from other populations. While it is arguable that literacy by itself was the privileged sign of difference—literacy is one of many overdetermined indications of a polished people—it is true that in the seventeenth and eighteenth centuries, writing was considered the queen of the sciences and was believed to make all the learned arts possible. An emblem of civilization, literacy was a sign of Europe's eminence. One of the reasons that literacy was so potent was that traditionally "writing was considered to be among those gifts bestowed on humanity at the creation," and it was certainly key in the exchange between God and Moses in the matter of the Ten Commandments (4). It is no mistake that Crusoe writes a diary on the island where he is stranded, or that Equiano, a former slave, makes much of his acquisition of literacy.

Among all the possible factors to privilege, there is no little irony that literate Britons chose this one. Granted, literacy rates increased during the seventeenth and eighteenth centuries, especially among men, the middling ranks, and city dwellers, but illiteracy was still common.[13] Nicholas Hudson's evidence leads him to conclude that there is "strong evidence that at least half of the British population could both read and write by the middle of the eighteenth century—writing being traditionally a later and more advanced accomplishment than the ability to do simple reading." Literacy intersects with Christianity and commercial society because, as Hudson further notes, "The principal actors promoting literacy were Protestantism, which encouraged individual reading of the Bible, and the rise of the commercial middle classes, a segment of society that prized literacy for its worldly advantages."[14] Thus, literacy and the production of arts, already tools of class and gender distinction, were extended to denigrate many non-European groups.[15]

Black people's writing, especially texts by former slaves, had to be explained. The early slave narratives, Gates contends, "served as a critique of the sign of the Great Chain of Being and the black person's figurative place on the chain."[16] A sampling of documents of the 1780s and 1790s supports Gates's claim that Afro-British writing was, indeed, used to establish Africans' abilities, but slavery discourse in general does not support his other claim that most Britons believed Africans were less than human. His emphasis on the chain of being, while a vivid shorthand, does not capture Britons' dominant view of Africans in the eighteenth century.[17] Featuring the most extreme contemporary observations about human difference, Gates cites texts only by writers who equate black complexion with speculations about Africans' negligible cultural achievement.

Notably, the bulk of his evidence is post-1760, and it is largely culled from philosophic discourse, which posited human differences as more significant and more pronounced than any other realm of discourse.[18] The importance of Gates's argument, as I understand it, is to identify a dominant racial ideology of the late eighteenth century. But, whatever the periodization, the central preoccupation in these documents is slavery and establishing the benchmarks of polished and savage society, not physical features. In as much as Gates demonstrates the constitutive presence of color prejudice and racism in some eighteenth-century writing, he, like others, takes a significant shift in the construction of human variety as the basis for discussing the eighteenth century *tout court*. Nevertheless, Gates's emphasis on literacy is insightful because it emphasizes the prominence of nonphysical differences as a primary constituent of contemporary racial ideology. In more recent material, Gates shifts tactics to argue that Enlightenment ideas about human variety were both racist and antiracist: The Enlightenment's "conceptual grammar of antiracism," their reverse discourses, remain our own today.[19] This insight suggests the urgency of analyzing these dual historical tendencies, especially since most scholarship has focused on the racist conceptions of difference in eighteenth-century thought rather than on the contrary impulse.

Gates's various engagements with race, slavery, and the eighteenth-century intellectual climate remind us that the connection between theories of human variety and slavery has not been easy to elucidate. Despite attempts to distinguish racial thinking from racism, scholars often conflate the two or, in fact, obscure significant changes in racial thinking by failing to differentiate dominant ideology from secondary trends and minority beliefs. Moreover, scholarly assessment of race in the eighteenth century generally occurs in studies of slavery and not in relation to other forces. Beginning at least as early as Eric Williams's 1944 postulation that "racism was the consequence of slavery," historians have debated whether race and racism as we know them today developed as a justification for enslaving Africans, whether slavery resulted from racial prejudice, or whether the two, in effect, developed in conjunction.[20]

Some historians have offered compelling evidence about the primarily political and economic causes of slavery, such as the role of the Dutch in supplying slaves on credit during the English Civil War when the supply of English indentured servants was unreliable and when the rapid conversion to the staple crop of sugar in mid-seventeenth-century Barbados necessitated a larger labor force than before.[21] These analyses indicate that race played little or no role at all in colonists' initial decision to reap profits in the fastest way possible. Economic and political explanations tend to underplay or omit reference to religious and other cultural factors that may have influenced slave owners' decision making or the relative ease with which many colonists tolerated slavery.

The opposite claim that racial prejudice toward African origins dating to the fifteenth and sixteenth centuries helped initiate the slave trade makes Britons' beliefs about Africans seem incorrectly static and monolithic during the early modern era. In this case, some historians and critics identify an often meager trail of evidence dating from the sixteenth to the eighteenth centuries documenting writers who equate Africans with animals or who offer pejorative reflections on their color; it suggests an accretion of similar attitudes that simply increases over time—not shifting attitudes or revisionist ones, as was, in fact, the case.[22] That some Britons subscribed to these ideas is important to know, and it is equally important to know when and if those ideas became ubiquitous and how those beliefs translated into action.

In the wake of Winthrop Jordan's *White over Black* (1968), which concludes that slavery and theories of race mutually reinforced each other over time, even William Green, who favors primarily nonracial explanations for the establishment of slavery, concedes that "[economic] rationality and prejudice are not mutually exclusive."[23] This approach helps explain the continuation of slavery perhaps more than its establishment, since many historians have documented the initial preference for white indentured servants. In a recent attempt to grapple with economic explanations of slavery, David Eltis persuasively contends that "narrowly economic interpretations of history often miss the point" because "capitalists could have made more by selling European convicts for life than African slaves, and more again if the progeny of those convicts, like Africans, had also been bound to a lifetime of service."[24] Eltis's method shows the tacit nonenslavement of Europeans across class and country boundaries in contrast to the relative ease with which certain outsiders were considered appropriate candidates. I find this approach helpful because it includes practices which Britons engaged in and those they declined.

Theories of human variety and defenses of slavery occasionally had significant intersections but were not codependent. Racial ideology and nascent racism in Britain, in one form or another, were available at least from the early seventeenth century, but neither, at this time, provided the governing rationale for the slave system. Racial ideology and racism were both far more indebted to hostility toward foreigners and religious difference than our modern forms, which are more driven by physical appearance. Britons, among others, had multifaceted ways to adjudicate the boundaries of human similarity, and these changed over time. Furthermore, I subscribe to the position that slavery developed in the British colonies before antiblack racism in Britain, which appeared as a rationale much later.[25] The development of racial theories proceeded by fits and starts in Britain and was sometimes informed by color prejudice, which manifests itself sporadically in print culture, from Christian treatises, newspaper articles, and lyric poetry to the reworking of the humor/climate paradigm. Nevertheless, I detect little cultural consensus about the salient components of human variation until the 1770s, when it became a prominent issue in some quarters. The slave trade debates were a catalyst that resulted in the honing of rationales about human difference—or the questioning of them—but, as Chapter 4 demonstrates, the slave trade was not primarily responsible for those theories. The public controversy about slavery helped solidify the parameters of contemporary consensus on racial ideology.

In analyzing how reference to human differences, civil society, and skin color inflected the exchanges between pro- and anti-slave trade factions or, in fact, failed to inform them, one of the most striking findings is that there is no exact correspondence between beliefs about the inferiority of Africans' civilization and their skin color. The scholarship of Gates, Popkins, and others has cued us to expect that defenses of slavery depended on racist claims about black skin, hair texture, and lack of national genius. As will become evident, it was as likely that proslavery positions would present primarily an economic or legal argument as anti-slave trade factions would concede the primitiveness of Africans' society or the significance of their dark skin color. This response held true for Afro-British writers as well.

*　　*　　*

The fifteen years preceding the publication of Equiano's narrative saw an unprecedented flurry of publications concerning complexion, climate, slavery, civil and savage society, and the possible connections among them. To be sure, the early movement to abolish the slave trade spurred many of these debates, as is evident in public response to the Somerset case in 1772 and to Parliament's investigation of the slave trade and the conditions of slavery, which commenced in 1788 and gathered momentum in the 1790s. However, it is also the case that reactions to the American Revolution, the new conquests in the East Indies, and pressures internal to historical and scientific inquiry contributed to this proliferation of texts about human variation. Compared with the first eighty years of the century, the most noticeable change in the way that Britons discussed human differences was their more frequently linking the condition of the body to the development of the mind. This ancient symbiosis assumes a new direction, particularly insofar as Europeans perceived their own ability to divorce the body and mind as great as they believed it unlikely savage people could. Because a very few writers had put forth polygenesis as a possible solution to the question of how human differences originated, several natural historians undertook an explicit refutation of this theory, which also lent a greater uniformity to racial discourse than previously.

All in all, the terrain of racial discourse with which Equiano and other writers engage, though fraught with competing claims, disputes over methodology, and contradictions, displays more detailed consensus about the terms in which the superiority of Europeans was recognizable than at any previous moment, especially claims about the superior beauty of whiteness and the excellence of European civil society. The kind of contradiction that characterizes racial ideology is perceptible in Oliver Goldsmith's comments on East Indians, whom he finds physically pleasing but whose weak national character results in their political dependency. They have a "slender shape, with long strait black hair, and often with Roman noses. Thus they resemble the Europeans in stature and features; but greatly differ in colour and habit of body."[26] Even though Europeans were the standard against which others were measured, physical beauty was, ultimately, less consequential than the negative delineation of national character. Goldsmith follows his statement about the beauty of East Indian women with a general political analysis: "The Indians have long been remarkable for their cowardice and effeminacy; every conqueror that has but attempted the invasion of their country, having succeeded." He attributes this national character to climate: "The warmth of the climate entirely influences their manners: they are slothful, submissive, and luxurious: satisfied with sensual happiness alone, they find no pleasure in thinking, and, contented with slavery, they are ready to obey any master" (1:371). Given this logic, the conclusion of European political and commercial dominion seems inevitable: "The vigour of the Asiatics is, therefore, in general, conformable to their dress and nourishment: fed upon rice, and clothed in effeminate silk vestments, their soldiers are unable to oppose the onset of an European army" (371). Africans were not, then, the only population that was inserted into this logic of race.

Three sets of texts convey the parameters of dominant ideology in the latter part of the eighteenth century in Britain: the first three editions of the *Encyclopaedia Britannica* (1771, 1781, 1797), the successive revisions to Johann Friedrich Blumenbach's *On the Natural Variety of Mankind* (1775, 1781, 1795), and Samuel Stanhope Smith's *Essay on the Causes of the Variety of Complexion and Figure in the Human Species* (1787). These renderings of

Figure 14. The Laplander. Oliver Goldsmith, *An History of the Earth and Animated Nature* (London, 1774). Goldsmith's text is one of the only natural histories in the eighteenth century to have illustrations of varieties of men. The overwhelming majority of plates in natural histories were of animals, insects, and plants. There are no engravings of the European and East Indian, the two varieties Goldsmith represents the most favorably. In the text, skin color is the most important distinction, although this characteristic is less obvious in the ethnographic figures, which are still mainly indebted to a cultural notion of difference. Brown University Library.

Figure 15. The Chinese. The fully clothed Chinese man is flanked by a multistoried pagoda and two other human figures, suggesting modest cultural achievement in architecture and sociability. The Chinese man appears as the most refined of all the varieties depicted. Brown University Library.

Figure 16. The African. The African shares the same body shape and stature with the Chinese, but not with the short Laplander in figure 14. Minimally dressed, he is shown with characteristic housing, distinctive wildlife, and weapons. Brown University Library.

Figure 17. The American. This is the only plate designed by Benjamin West, whom his European contemporaries considered an expert on Native Americans. West's knowledge derived from his residence in Pennsylvania. The American is the only figure shown without any vestige of society. Brown University Library.

Figure 18. Five Varieties of the Human Race. Oliver Goldsmith, *An History of the Earth and Animated Nature* (Philadelphia, 1795). The enterprising printer Mathew Carey pulled the plates from the first London edition, added one, and lined them up for ease of comparison in a new frontispiece to the first American edition. Carey's modern-looking taxonomy did not immediately travel back to England; several early nineteenth-century editions still have the single plates scattered throughout the text. The addition of the Hottentot to suggest variety in Africa does not correspond to Goldsmith's text, which went against the grain of his contemporaries. Most natural historians did not rank Kaffirs, or Hottentots, among Negroes. Goldsmith, on the contrary, argues that "the difference between them, in point of colour and features, is so small, that they may be easily grouped in this general picture." Department of Rare Books, Houghton Library, Harvard University.

human variety are the ones with which Equiano and other abolitionists contend. The changes in these texts over time indicate a slow movement toward a more rigid interpretation of human variety than before and a tendency to view the mind and body as one unit. The assumptions about climate, people, behavior, and appearance are developed at greater length and more coherently in these texts than the condensed references to them in most pro- and anti–slave trade discourse. One of the symptomatic features of these texts is the momentary singling out of Africans and Europeans as exceptional. At the same time that the authors claimed climate, diet, and manners could account for all major variations in the human race, they were also developing the sense that Africans were less like Europeans than any other group. An author's stance against slavery, for instance, was often at odds with the arrangement of material and with the descriptions actually offered.

Largely the brainchild of the Scottish Enlightenment literati, the *Encyclopaedia Britannica* underwent two major revisions in the late eighteenth century. Its first attempt to describe continents is largely limited to neutral geographical descriptions, characterization of the chief forms of government, and the color of the inhabitants; Europe itself is simply defined by geography in the first edition of 1771. *Negroes*, tellingly, is the only entry in which theories of complexion are aired: "The origin of the negroes, and the cause of this remarkable difference from the rest of the human species, has much perplexed the naturalists."[27] The authors further note that eminent thinkers have not yet discovered whether color difference is due to climate or manner of living. Near the end of the entry for *Negroes*, the writers make their stance on slavery clear: "This commerce, which is scarce defensible on the foot either of religion or humanity, is now carried on by all the nations that have settlements in the West Indies" (3:396). The automatic connection between Negroes and slavery—one of the chief legacies of European colonization—haunts descriptions and beliefs about Negroes for at least the next two hundred years. Notably, the writers' preoccupation in the first edition is with European involvement in the slave trade, even though the comment appears under the entry for *Negroes*.

By the second edition of the *Encyclopaedia Britannica* (1781), there is an explosion of information about all continents and their inhabitants that reveals a much more intense general interest in skin color than ten years earlier. *Colour of the Human Species* is a new entry; its inclusion reflects its prominence in the spate of natural histories published during the 1770s and skin color's important ideological status by the 1780s. Indeed, the authors remark, "Few questions in philosophy have engaged the attention of naturalists more than the diversities among the human species, among which that of colour is the most remarkable."[28] The increased interest in color is particularly noticeable in the entry for *America*, the inhabitants of which are described as being anomalous to the rest of the world in respect to their reputedly uniform complexion throughout the continent: "One great peculiarity in the native Americans is their colour, and the identity of it throughout the whole extent of the continent" (1:298). They seemed to defy the implications of climatic theory, which posited that Indians' skin color would vary remarkably from arctic Canada to tropical Florida. The admittedly perplexed authors call for a better comparison between northern and southern natives before they will endorse a statement about their uniform complexion (298). The same entry occurs for *Negroes* as in the first edition; the cross-reference directs readers to *America* and *Colour of the Human Species*, entries that neatly capture the way Native Americans and black Africans were more particularly associated with questions about complexion and other physical differences at this time than other groups. The 1771 protest against the slave trade moves from *Negroes* to *Africa*. In fact, the authors now refer with equal distaste to the savage state of the Africans and to the role of Europeans in the slave trade; they especially condemn those who use the Bible or God's curse to justify slavery (1:110–11).

That bodily and social differences generally seem more important in 1781 is noticeable in the new evaluative statement inserted in the entry for Europe. A typical combination of prejudices about religion, region, government, and complexion, the entry claims that Europe is better peopled and cultivated than other places, and "the inhabitants are all white; and incomparably more handsome than the Africans, and even than most of the Asiatics. The Europeans surpass both in arts and sciences, especially in those called the liberal; in trade, navigation, and in military and civil affairs; being, at the same time, more prudent, more valiant, more generous, more polite, and more sociable than they: and though we are divided into various sects, yet, as Christians, we have infinitely the advantage over the rest of mankind" (4:2860). Statements such as this one that juxtapose European beauty to claims about their superior institutions are common. Nevertheless, whiteness and civility have not yet been equated. White skin color is an attribute of inhabitants and not Europeans' defining feature.

Equiano's narrative falls midway between the second and third editions of the *Encyclopaedia Britannica* (1797). The changes to the entries *Colour of the Human Species* and *Negroes* between 1781 and 1797 suggest that difference was newly pertinent at the level of the body and seems more pronounced than ever before. The singularity of black complexion is represented more negatively than previously; for example, the 1797 entry reads: "In the complexion of negroes we meet with many various shades; but they likewise differ far from other men in all the features of their face."[29] The second part of the sentence considerably outweighs the claims of the first part. The continued stance against the slave trade in the *Encyclopaedia Britannica* coexists with a more negative phenotyping of Negroes and Africans. In the third edition of the *Encyclopaedia Britannica*, Negro women bear the brunt of the negative physical description, which contrasts with the contemporary attention paid by anatomists, among others, to the peculiar beauties of European females. An odd addition to the 1797 edition states: "The negro women have the loins greatly depressed, and very large buttocks, which gives the back the shape of a saddle" (12:794). Gender distinction is more significant in the delineation of human variety than before. In part, this shift heralds a new focus on the ways gender and race differentiate bodies; male and female bodies, and, for some, black and white bodies are increasingly perceived as distinct in myriad ways.[30] *Negroes* is a category that now see-saws erratically between descriptions of Africans in Africa and slaves in the colonies; the distinction between Africans and slaves is one that Equiano and other abolitionists are often mindful to maintain, for reasons sketched in Chapter 2. The description of Africans is now largely interchangeable with some people's beliefs about slaves. Their physical distinction is, the authors allege, matched by their lack of sociability: Negroes are, the authors claim, "strangers to every sentiment of compassion, and are an awful example of the corruption of man when left to himself" (794).[31] The statement about Negroes' putative lack of intellectual, political, and commercial contact with other nations implies that increasing exchange of all kinds would make them more polished and more sympathetic. At this time, in some discursive realms, we see a less elastic sense of human variety than previously, even though there is still an aggressive insistence that these features result from external and natural factors, such as climate, temperature, and diet. The *Encyclopaedia Britannica* is typical in regarding Africans as the group most unlike Britons. The assumption that grounds this claim is that they exemplify the debilitating effects of savagery on appearance and behavior.

Probably the most eminent natural historian of his day, and known today as the "father" of comparative anthropology, Johann Friedrich Blumenbach staked his reputation on the essential similarity of all humans and on their slight variations from one another. Well respected in Britain, and a correspondent of Ignatius Sancho, Equiano, and Joseph Banks, he revised *On the Natural Variety of Mankind* three times in twelve years; most changes occurred between the editions of 1781 and 1795. His findings match many of the trends in the *Encyclopaedia Britannica*. Like many of his contemporaries in the latter part of the century, Blumenbach refines Buffon's ideas, especially his argument that all human variety is detectable to the eye. By considering that differences also reside in anatomical structures, Blumenbach perceives various groups of humans differing by the shape of their skull as well as by their skin color. Nevertheless, he forcefully maintains that the distinctive qualities of skeletons and skin color result from climate, mode of life, and cultural factors.[32]

Blumenbach's 1775 edition of *On the Natural Variety of Mankind* concedes that visible appearances are compelling, if ultimately misleading, especially when writers focus on the three most extremely different groups in isolation from the intermediate groups: "There seems to be so great a difference between the Ethiopian, the white, and the red American, that it is not wonderful, if men even of great reputation have considered them as forming different species of mankind."[33] Similar to most abolitionists, he contends that even though differences seem great, they are, in fact, inconsequential. Skin color, he underscores, "whatever be its cause," internal or external to the body, "is, at all events, an adventitious and easily changeable thing, and can never constitute a diversity of species" (113). The contradictory tendency of Blumenbach's treatise—to avow the general importance of skin color and at the same time to disavow its deeper meaning—is most noticeable when he writes about black skin color.[34]

By the third edition of 1795, Blumenbach introduces the concepts of national varieties of hair, face, color, and skulls, but these more narrowly defined features still apply to broad categories of people, such as Caucasians or Malaysians.[35] These concepts confirm the emphasis on increasingly rigid divisions among human groups. "National features," "national hair types," and "mental capacity" were new categories that rearticulated formerly more broadly conceived features to signal fairly stable generic attributes. The new terminology takes us one step closer to the rigidly defined races of man characteristic of the mid-nineteenth century. This terminology first appears in English, to my knowledge, in John Hunter's *Inaugural Dissertation* (1775), which also referred to a new racial category, namely, "mental capacity." The fact that these concepts do not show up with any regularity until publications of the 1790s indicates to me that it was not a widely employed terminology until that time. This trend appears in the 1797 entries of the *Encyclopaedia Britannica*. The authors' greater effort to systematize the assessment of bodies is facilitated by the emergence of comparative categories like "their constitution and corporal abilities" in reference to Americans and "the effects of climate on hair" in reference to Negroes. This tendency to question the extent of differences—in bodies, minds, as well as states of civilization—is part of the human sciences from the earliest texts of the seventeenth century. The normative impact of these categories is inadvertently furthered by abolitionists, who were compelled to adopt the same terminology to deny significant variations among humans.[36]

Although the German Blumenbach and the American Reverend Samuel Stanhope Smith had never read each other's work in the 1780s, they agreed on most points, although Smith gives more weight to the visible effects of savage life than Blumenbach, possibly because of his Scottish university education. Winthrop Jordan aptly characterizes Smith's inquiry as an "ordinary and unoriginal but thereby highly revealing summation of prevailing thought."[37] Smith displays his indebtedness both to his teachers of four-

stages theory and to his readings of Buffon and Goldsmith. Among his contemporaries, Smith offers the most thorough and aggressive argument on the
extent to which color is externally induced, the many variables accounting for
all shades of complexion, and the vast changes in color to which all bodies are
subject. Smith's *Essay on the Causes of the Variety of Complexion and Figure in
the Human Species* (1787) is the most coherently worked out treatise on the
association of appearance of bodies and the state of civilization and is, therefore, a useful juxtaposition to Equiano and other writers working within the
same logic of human variety. His *Essay on Complexion and Figure* is remarkable for the intimate association of the condition of society and the state
of bodies: "Nakedness, exposure, negligence of appearance, want of cleanliness, bad lodging, and meagre diet, so discolour and injure their form. . . .
These causes will render it impossible that a savage should ever be fair" (47).
Dispensing with the noble savage concept, Smith argues repeatedly that the
human countenance is modified "radically" by the state of society (50).

If Negroes are singled out either to reassure readers of their similarity
to Europeans, despite appearances to the contrary, or to exemplify a particular deformity of feature or character, then Europeans too are seen as exceptional in some way. Despite several different ways of convincing readers how
changeable skin color is according to variations in climate, diet, or terrain,
Smith gets a bit nervous about the implications of this theory for European-
Americans, and it is, I believe, a widely shared colonial anxiety: "The Anglo-
Americans, however, will never resemble the native Indians. Civilization will
prevent so great a degeneracy either in the colour or the features. Even if they
were thrown back again into the savage state the resemblance would not be
complete; because, the one would receive the impressions of the climate on
the ground of features formed in Europe — the others have received them on
the ground of features formed in a very different region of the globe. The
effects of such combinations can never be the same" (23–24). While technically maintaining the spirit of an externally induced theory of human variety,
Smith demonstrates the ease with which it too could serve as a way to intimate near permanent inferiority. In this passage, Smith responds to contemporary debates about the influence of climate but harks back to one of the
long-standing fears of colonists — that leaving England meant leaving their
Englishness.[38]

Smith manages not only to link the uniform effects of climate on the
body and mind more coherently than any other eighteenth-century writer
but also to explain how the body and mind affect each other. His speculations take the theory of climate's influence to its logical conclusion. At first
glance, this theory of the reciprocal effect of the mind and body appears to be

an effort that halts the momentum toward biological notions of race. Nevertheless, it helps establish rigid differences between whites and others that biological racism will supplement and nineteenth-century colonial imperialism will capitalize on: "Mental capacity, which is as various as climate, and as personal appearance, is, equally with the latter [complexion], susceptible of improvement, from similar causes. The body and the mind have such mutual influence, that whatever contributes to change the human constitution in its form or aspect, has an equal influence on its powers of reason and genius. And these have again a reciprocal effect in forming the countenance" (74–75). Encapsulating the dominant position on human variety of his day, Smith's text points to its fraught entanglement with the homology between the body and mind on the one hand, color and capacity on the other hand. This intimate connection will accompany speculations about race from here onward in the political arena.

*   *   *

Given the contours of racial ideology as it was taking shape in natural and civil history, it is surprising to us today that race was not the central component of the slave trade debates. The pamphlets, poems, and essays addressing the slave trade in the 1780s and 1790s often refer to prevailing theories of color, mental capacity, and civility but in unexpected ways. For instance, a writer's belief in monogenesis does not ensure that he considers color or national differences inconsequential, nor is a writer's belief in racial inferiority necessary to defend the enslavement of Africans. Indeed, debates about slavery in the late eighteenth century occur without reference to bodily, cultural, or other kinds of differences. That many writers continued to perceive slavery primarily as an economic and Europeanwide political boon to Great Britain is evident in the reams of pamphlets like *No Abolition* (1789), which does not mention Africans' color, intellectual understanding, or civility, but which cites the potential loss of livelihood that many Britons faced who manufactured goods commonly traded for slaves (like guns in Bristol).[39] John Wesley's *Thoughts on Slavery* (1774) identifies the "grand plea" of proponents of the slave trade in that decade: they were authorized by law.[40] For example, the colonial agent for Barbados, Samuel Estwick, appeals to the legal status of slavery in *Considerations on the Negroe Cause Commonly So Called* (1772), because it is only in the context of law that humans become legitimate trade.[41] Only later in the treatise does he offer an often-repeated argument that the condition of slaves is preferable to the "poorer sort of people" in Great Britain.[42] Operating a plantation in Nevis for eight years, London merchant James Tobin refers more openly than Estwick to the improved condition of Africans under slavery in *Cursory Remarks* (1785), the treatise that Equiano found so objectionable. Because Tobin places this compara-tive argument based on assumptions popularized in four-stages theory near the conclusion, he emphasizes by doing so that he felt the most persuasive arguments were not premised on any essential inferiority of slaves to mas-ters, "except in strength, policy, or good fortune." In fact, Tobin reiterates his position in *A Short Rejoinder* (1787) that slavery is defensible on "politi-cal grounds" only. Even a lampoon of the proslavery position could omit arguments based on color or on societal difference; for instance, Alexander Geddes's *An [Ironical] Apology for Slavery* (1792) drives home the way Chris-tianity, self-interest of individuals, and government interest relied on the system of slavery and the way in which all three were commonly invoked to condone slavery.[43]

The proximity of proslavery and abolitionist positions in many of their recommendations meant that the status quo was maintained. In fact, a large proportion of eighteenth-century Britons concurred that slaves should be treated more humanely and given certain rights but that they should remain enslaved.[44] The ameliorationist position was common ground for the most ardent supporters of West Indian property rights and for those fighting for change. Further, both sides shared a reverence for property and an admira-tion of personal wealth—the same issues that kept European monarchs from demanding their subjects be returned from enslavement in Algiers, Tunis, and Morocco. Tobin's proslavery *Cursory Remarks* shrewdly recounts the as-sumptions that he and his anti–slave trade rival, the Reverend James Ramsay, share, including the nearly ubiquitous belief that some people are naturally subordinate to others, which is central to maintaining social order through consent (8–9). Ramsay begins his influential *An Essay on the Treatment and Conversion of African Slaves* (1784) with the observation that people possess various faculties and abilities and thereby occupy different stations in life, a premise that makes all subordination seem more rather than less accept-able.[45] Beginning with this belief makes it tortuous for Ramsay to prove logi-cally that a master-and-slave relationship is unnatural (3).

Another example of positions shared by contenders for and against the slave trade is detectable in *Narrative of a Five Years Expedition Against the Revolted Negroes of Surinam* (1796). Scottish soldier John Stedman exceeds Equiano or any other abolitionist in terms of enumerating atrocities com-mitted on the bodies of slaves in the colonies, and Stedman offers even more details than former slaves about the depravity of whites—Dutch and British, male and female alike. The proslavery Stedman believes that slaves should have judicial redress, and he even argues that slaves have a well-developed sense of justice and share a common human nature with their masters. For Stedman, their superior stamina and hardy bodies were sufficient reasons to prolong slavery as were the prior property rights of the whites. In his narrative, Equiano appeals to the importance of national prosperity and freedom in Britain (80), as does Edward Long, who in *The History of Jamaica* (1774) cites these same patriotic goals—but in favor of escalating the slave trade. As Christopher Brown comments, "Liberty was an elastic concept in eighteenth-century Britain, serving either progressive or conservative functions."[46]

Since the seventeenth century, when dissenting preacher Richard Baxter admonished his audience that slaves were "reasonable creatures as well as you, and born to as much natural liberty," the shared humanity of Africans and Europeans appeared periodically in references to the condition of slaves.[47] Another typical early reference to slavery and human difference occurs in Robert Robertson's *A Letter to the Right Reverend the Lord Bishop of London* (1730). An inhabitant of one of the Leeward islands, Robertson responds to exhortations from English clergy to Christianize slaves (not to liberate them, of course); notably, references to human difference are not essential to the main thrust of his argument. Indeed, Robertson repeatedly offers variations on the same economic rationale for planters' reluctance to instill Christianity in their slaves: Instruction is equivalent to loss of labor time and, hence, money; thus, conversion is unlikely ever to prove a widespread practice. In conclusion, Robertson notes that slaves are tolerable craftsmen "and consequently that they must be the same Species of Creatures that we are in every respect but Colour."[48] As Chapter 2 contends, defenses of the slave trade were primarily economic in the early eighteenth century, and it was only in the 1780s that a large proportion of British writers felt compelled to confirm or occasionally deny the resemblance of Africans to Europeans. Although pro- and anti–slave trade arguments alike invoked the character of Africans, it was unusual for either position to rely primarily on racial ideology for effect.

If anything, this commonplace about the similarity of Europeans and Africans becomes more specific, frequent, and defensive in the 1780s with the escalation of printed material about the slave trade. In his widely read *Essay on the Slavery and Commerce of the Human Species, Particularly the African* (1786), Anglican clergyman Thomas Clarkson devotes two chapters to dispelling the suspicion that Africans are an inferior link in the chain of nature and thus designed for slavery because of lesser mental abilities, cultural attainments, or dark complexion.[49] Because of his twenty years' residence in the Caribbean islands, clergyman James Ramsay's opinion about the nature of slaves was even more influential than Clarkson's for some people. Appealing to the shared rational capacity of Europeans and slaves, Ramsay contends it is obscured in slaves by their enslaved condition. In *An Essay on the Treatment and Conversion of African Slaves* (1784), he claims about his readers in Britain: "I will not insult the reader's understanding, by an attempt to demonstrate it to be an object of importance, to gain to society, to reason and religion, half a million of our kind, equally with us adapted for advancing themselves in every art and science, that can distinguish man from man, equally with us made capable of looking forward to and enjoying futurity."[50] Despite the suggestion that Britons are greater humanitarians than their West Indian counterparts when it comes to the plight of slaves, Ramsay devotes a good deal of space to addressing the "natural capacity" of slaves and Africans, arguing, along with most natural historians, that education and climate as well as a lack of polished society "naturally produce" any difference of intellect (203).

Writers of African descent responded quite similarly to their European counterparts to issues of power, complexion, religion, and civil society in the context of slavery. This fact is hardly surprising given the workings of ideology and the more local reason that abolitionists were in close contact with each other during the efforts to campaign Parliament and arouse public opinion. For instance, Equiano joined other writers and legal advocates in working against the slave trade. His name often appeared on letters written by the "Sons of Africa" to express thanks for combating what they referred to as " 'the Oran Otang philosophers.' "[51] One of the issues that moves to prominence in discussions of slavery in the 1780s is the trademark of four-stages theory: the way that Africans organized their culture. The unpolished state of African society largely preoccupies most writers for or against the slave trade when they broach noneconomic matters. Indeed, a letter from the Sons of Africa to Granville Sharp confirms the use of the truism in their own correspondence: "It is said that we are the factors of our own slavery, and sell one another at our own market for a price. No doubt but in our uncivilized state we commit much evil."[52] Similarly, elsewhere the former slave Ottobah Cugoano concedes that there is African "ignorance in somethings" and that they are "not so learned, [but] are just as wise as the Europeans."[53] Writing against the slave trade in the mid-1770s, John Wesley identifies the legal status of slavery as the primary defense of the trade. Nonetheless, he symptomatically begins his inquiry into slavery with the nature of Africa's terrain and climate. Wesley demonstrates that it is not "horrid, dreary, and barren" by consulting texts written by men who lived in Africa.[54] He then moves on to the nature of Africans, "of what temper and behaviour" they are in Africa; it is only later that he briefly treats legal matters. Ramsay's *Essay on the Treatment and Conversion of African Slaves* exhaustively attempts to rebut all of the contemporary objections to Africans on physical and mental grounds, and he concludes that these accidental differences derive from the fact that Africans do not live in a polished society.[55] Equiano, too, broaches the issue of African society in his slave narrative; for some people, fathoming its nature bore on the legitimacy of European involvement in the slave trade.

It is no little irony that much intellectual backing for anti-slavery sentiment was provided by the Scottish literati through four-stages theory.[56] As a whole, these works challenge the economic, legal, and moral arguments for slavery and often denounce its practice.[57] Nevertheless, that same body of work elucidates civil society as a key concept defining British eminence, especially the many ways savage nations differ from polished ones. Since antislavery sentiment and racialist thinking shared this way of seeing societies, it makes for a good deal of agreement about the nature of Africans. Numerous contemporary statements about the desirability of increasing the non–slave trade with Africa also articulates this desire through statements about making Africa a more commercial society. For instance, Malachy Postlethwayt, a prolific writer on trade, economically unites perturbation with the unpolished state of Africa to commonly expressed prejudice against dark complexion in his query "Whether the people of this country [Africa], notwithstanding their colour, are not capable of being civilized, as well as great numbers of the Indians in America and Asia have been?"[58] The Quaker Anthony Benezet and Equiano, although both more positive than Postlethwayt in their assessment of African potential, speak out of the same assumption of Africa's unpolished state.

Postlethwayt's conjecture about Africans' black complexion is echoed to a milder degree in much abolitionist writing. Although James Ramsay blames external forces for African cultural inferiority and the European lust for inordinate financial gain for slavery, he stumbles when it comes to the physical appearance of Africans: "It is true, there are marks, that appear now to be established, as if set by the hand of nature to distinguish them from the whites: their noses are flat, their chins prominent, their hair woolly, their skin black."[59] Like natural historians, however, Ramsay claims that despite these superficial attributes, Negroes are not set apart from other humans in a significant way. He develops this line of thinking further: "And, let it be remarked, that the characteristics of negroes shew themselves chiefly about the face, where nature has fixed both the national attributes and the discriminating features of individuals, as if intended to distinguish them from other families, and bind them in the social tie with their brethren" (203–4). While couched in familial discourse, which intimates natural bonds of affection and common parentage, Ramsay manages to convey the sense that because of their visible features, Negroes, like other groups, form a separate "family" from all other people on the earth. Shared features and similar appearance are important, Ramsay intimates, to social cohesion. It may be that Ramsay offers insight into issues such as national preference and prejudice, but his supposition about Negro appearance sits oddly with his efforts to deny that it bears on their enslavement. Despite devoting much energy to the claim that physical differences are inconsequential, and thereby intimating that they are important, Ramsay concludes that slavery is mostly about power, not about race. Poor treatment of slaves and slavery itself, he suggests, are abuses of unnatural power and systemic issues (236).

Skin color has a brief if salient place in most post-1750 writings about slavery. In his *Elements of Moral Science* (1790), James Beattie condemns slavery in no uncertain terms, a discussion that takes place under the heading of "Economics."[60] Within the space of thirty pages, Beattie returns to Africans' physical features, including color, no fewer than six times, either to confirm that some writers cite it as a reason to enslave Africans or to deny that dark color is a legitimate ground for enslavement (81–110). Skin color occupies a similarly symptomatic place in early abolitionist documents by John Woolman and J. Philmore, who begin their works with the assertion that Africans and Europeans are the same kind of men. These documents suggest that dark color and religious difference were prominent rationales espoused by supporters of slavery in the colonies. The superficiality of complexion generally assumes the primary position in a list of reasons not to enslave Africans. Benjamin Rush, for instance, begins his tract with considerations of color before moving on to other issues.[61]

Even though issues of economics and civility dominate exchanges about the slave trade, concerns about skin color have a contradictory place in these texts, not unlike the novels examined in Chapter 3. Afro-British writings, like their white British counterparts, demonstrate repeatedly that dark color raises certain ideological tangles that the discourse on civility does not. Complexion becomes a topic of narration in writings by people of black African descent during the 1770s, a decade after their first known texts appear in the Anglo-American world. In *A Narrative of the Most Remarkable Life* (1772), the young James Albert Ukawsaw Gronniosaw, for instance, wonders if he is despised by God because he is black. The adult Gronniosaw, however, notes that after he is baptized, he wishes to marry an English-woman. He mentions the objections that their friends raise to the intended nuptials, which are based on her poverty rather than on his color or former slave status.[62] Gronniosaw's contemporaries Phillis Wheatley, Francis Williams, Ottobah Cugoano, Equiano, and Ignatius Sancho explicitly mention the standard abolitionist claim of the similarity of blacks and whites despite differences in complexion, but the writers of the 1780s—Sancho, Cugoano, and Equiano—engage more thoroughly with blackness than previous writers and provide evidence that Britons treated blacks in Britain often in the same way that they treated Catholics, Jews, Scots, and the French.

In *Thoughts and Sentiments on the Evil and Wicked Traffic* (1787), Cugoano faces a difficulty many writers did: claiming that color variations are a natural phenomenon (rather than God's curse or an unnatural degeneracy from white skin) and that a variety of skin colors should not signify anything other than the wonder of the Creation. It is, in fact, in the difference between the symbolic cultural significance of blackness and the desire that it be a neutral term of description that the ideological tangle occurs. Citing the proverbial impossible task of washing an Ethiop white, Cugoano asks his British readers: "Can the Ethiopian change his skin, or the leopard his spots? Then, may ye also do good that are accustomed to do evil."[63] In this compilation of permanent (though natural) conditions based loosely on the Christian tradition, the rather strained analogy of complexion to human agency breaks as soon as Cugoano introduces the figurative washing away of sin. Cugoano reasons that none "among the fallen" by themselves can change their nature from "the blackness and guilt of the sable dye of sin and pollution" (45). The Christian exhortation follows that makes the standard association of black with sin and white with redemption; the inherent evil in every man can be removed only through the blood of Jesus and submission to him: "All the stains and blackest dyes of sin and pollution can be washed away for ever, and the darkest sinner be made to shine as the brightest angel" (46). Cugoano argues that extreme differences in colour, embodied in black men, were intended to teach white men that there is a sinful blackness in his own nature, which he cannot change by himself. Nonetheless, Cugoano notes that black skin has nothing to do with God's displeasure, which prompts his comparison of the colors of the rainbow to the variety of human complexion, intimating that both are natural and pleasing. As these comparisons indicate, fluid movement between metaphorical and neutral descriptive registers proves impossible when the black-and-white binary is invoked. The fact that this problem troubles Cugoano is evident because he returns to it several times in the space of a few pages to attack it from different angles. Finally, changing tactics once again in regard to the signification of color, Cugoano contends that the nature and quality of a man is constant, "whether he wears a black or a white coat, whether he puts it on or strips it off, he is still the same man" (47). Rehearsing received stereotypes of blackness and whiteness at the same time that he tries to reject them, Cugoano's narrative exhibits revealing contortions about the many registers of meaning in which complexion signifies.

Complexion carries multiple resonances in Cugoano's *Thoughts and Sentiments*, including positive ones of fellowship. He consistently refers to other Africans or Afro-Britons as men "of my own complexion" (12), as do Equiano and other black Atlantic writers. Indeed, all writers who had lived in the North American colonies and the West Indies tended to accord complexion more conscious importance than their contemporaries who had never been out of Britain—both in their invocation of it as a significant feature of people and as a marker of group belonging. It is also clear from Ramsay's comments in *An Essay on the Treatment and Conversion of African Slaves* that colonists, at least, believed that people with the same skin color had a natural affection for each other.[64] This conviction extends Adam Smith's observations about the natural attachment individuals felt toward their own rank or society in *The Theory of Moral Sentiments* (1759) to the realm of vision.[65] This way of seeing fellowship suggests an important revision to Benedict Anderson's thesis in *Imagined Communities* (1983): Print culture was not the only factor responsible for suturing Britons to a new sense of their identity in the eighteenth century. As the documents I have cited above intimate, visual compatibility among subjects seems to have played a role. It would seem that complexion, widely invoked in the slave trade debates and in natural history writings, helped constitute a conscious sense of group belonging in the colonies quite early on and in Britain by this time as well.

* * *

As the examples from natural history and slave trade discourse have made clear, abolitionists ran into difficulties when they assessed the world in black-and-white terms. The difficulties, of course, were for antiracist thought, not for abolitionist arguments. Equiano encounters similar problems in negotiating racial discourse. For example, when Equiano calls on prevailing discourses of human variety for benign explanatory power, they often fail. This occurs for two reasons. On the one hand, Equiano, like Cugoano and other writers, treats complexion as if there were no cultural baggage attached. Equiano argues that complexion should not connote superiority or inferiority because it is natural and superficial; complexion offers no deeper meaning about a group or individual, and it is not an explanation for behaviors or desires. On the other hand, dark-complected Africans live in a less polite society than Europeans, which makes them less civilized and therefore quite different.[67] Claiming that dark complexion did not matter was easier than arguing that civility did not matter, but the combined force of a black-complected people in an unpolished society was difficult to negotiate. These sometimes contradictory tasks—eliminating negative connotations from blackness and conceding the rude state of African society—prompt a closer scrutiny of these efforts. Indeed, typical abolitionist responses indicate strongly that complexion did, in fact, matter. Through reference to proslavery rationales, we may conclude that visible physical differences likely troubled Britons more than written texts reveal.

One of the main obstacles that Equiano encounters in citing contemporary racial ideology is working within the hierarchy generated through four-stages theory, which generally positioned western Africa among the unpolished societies. Equiano's strategy of comparing the present situation of Africans to agricultural and feudal stages of society has mixed results. In the section on his childhood in Africa, he makes an analogy between Igboes and other contemporary and historical peoples. In this way, he attempts to position Africans similarly to groups who are apparently more acceptable to his audience—the biblical Hebrews, pre-Roman Britons, Native Americans, Greeks, and Scottish Highlanders. As the epigraph from the *Encyclopaedia Britannica* indicates, these comparisons encapsulate the way late eighteenth-century Britons believed that the state of civilization affected bodily and facial features. Complexion and features could vary among classes within a nation or between nations. Thus, the clan chiefs ate a better diet, dressed more thoroughly, and stayed indoors more so that they were able to protect their bodies from the harsh effects of the weather in ways the less prestigious members of the clan could not. Buffon initiates this argument and Samuel Stanhope Smith develops it. To readers today, the comparison of Igboes to Scottish Highlanders most likely seems less problematic than the comparison to the ancient Hebrews or savage Britons, because Scots were, after all, political subjects of Britain and in the process of "moving on up." As Johannes Fabian persuasively demonstrates in *Time and the Other* (1983), temporal separation is a way to deny coequal status.[70]

Nonetheless, to readers steeped in the Bible, Africans' resemblance to the Old Testament Hebrews—separated in time though related by a shared religious heritage—was most likely even more persuasive of similarity than the comparison to contemporary white "savages." In fact, the analogy to biblical Jews was not an uncommon way to argue for savages actually being civilized.[71] The Jews and ancient Britons appear as comparable to Africans in a range of writing, especially in documents urging Britons to expand the non-slave trade in Africa.[72] Claiming Africans as descendants of Abraham, Equiano traces the shared lineage of Africans and Europeans from Adam and Eve and thereby underscores the moral imperative it assumes. Then he calls on categories generated from four-stages theory to compare Igbo and Hebrew laws, customs, and governmental structure, especially the rule of patriarchs and the pastoral state of their societies, such as found in the book of Genesis, "an analogy, which alone would induce me to think that the one people had sprung from the other" (43–44). Ancient Jews were, of course, familiar denizens of various African territories. Equiano's comparison attempts to use Jews as a bridge between Africans and Europeans.[73] Indeed, when Equiano refers to the Bible, he claims he can "see the laws and rules of my own country written almost exactly here" (92). These early homologies set up his later explicit references to the common nature that Europeans and Africans share (232).

If Africans tend to conjure up the Judaic past and a more primitive organization of society, then Equiano's emulation of British manners assures readers about the compatibility between Africa and Great Britain. As many critics have demonstrated, Equiano's narrative emphasizes both his desire and ability to match British national ideals of middle-class masculinity. In the passages when he compares Igboes to people less polished than modern Britons, Equiano tends to leave climate behind as an explanation for the state of African society; he features historical and economic forces instead, though to eighteenth-century Europeans, these two factors were related to climate's long-term effect.

Throughout his narrative, Equiano finds civilization's proximity to Europeanness difficult to undo. Besides his tacit agreement with other Britons that Africans are, in some fashion, less polished than Europeans, Equiano confronts some other problems in comparing Europeans with Africans, especially negotiating the claim that contemporary Africa has not progressed as quickly as Europe. Taking a firm stance that a more primitive society does not excuse enslaving their inhabitants, Equiano intones: "Let the polished and haughty European recollect that *his* ancestors were once, like the Africans, uncivilized, and even barbarous. Did Nature make *them* inferior to their sons? and should *they too* have been made slaves? Every rational mind answers, No" (45). Arguing for any "apparent inferiority" being "ascribed to their situation" of being unfamiliar with the language, religion, and habits of Britons, Equiano tries to set up inferiority as a relative perception and as something that might be rectified ultimately through increased commercial interaction for Africans and education for slaves (45).[74] In this instance,

Equiano appeals to the most neutral version of four-stages theory as elsewhere he relies on the most relativistic version of natural history categories. The unpolished situation of eighteenth-century Africans, due to commercial underdevelopment, is preferable to other options explaining the origin of their color—God's curse or separate creations. As texts like Samuel Stanhope Smith's "proved," however, and as some people observed, the stage of civilization, depth of understanding, and skin color did show remarkable parallels.

In citing prevailing theories of human variety, Equiano faces another major logical problem, which is generated by humoral/climate theory. Climate theory manifested itself in several ways that were not always compatible but that coexisted throughout the century. In one model, Europeans believed that there were polar, temperate, and torrid regions, with inhabitants suited to live in only one of those areas and who would not flourish elsewhere. Based on this assumption, climate accounted for the exterior appearance, disposition, and intellectual capacity of entire groups of people, among whom, however, there would be a range of individual abilities. Seventeenth-century colonization in warm climates puts pressure on this assumption. For example, early English colonists were often at pains to show how well they had adapted to the new world climate or, occasionally, how similar America's climate was to England's. In this way, they emphasized the compatibility between themselves and the land.[68] In a similar vein, some proslavery arguments rested on the claim that Africans were better suited to labor in the West Indian climate than Europeans, a fallacy that many abolitionists tried to refute by reference to the history of labor, which had originally been predominantly European servants.

This traditional view of climate's effect on people coexisted with two other increasingly favored interpretations. Another popular reference to climate/humoral theory was that, while people were possibly best suited to their native climates, they could adapt gradually to a new one with a change in diet, habits, and clothing—what was commonly called "seasoning" in the colonies. Possibly one of the most common beliefs about climate is that it accounted for a person's exterior appearance and influenced one's general disposition, but it did not affect one's rational capability, which is Equiano's most consistently espoused assumption.

As Chapter 4 demonstrates, the majority of Scottish Enlightenment writers questioned climate theory's logical consistency by offering evidence that seemed to belie its comprehensive explanatory efficacy, even as they relied on its assumptions to discuss the way that other external factors, such as division of labor and mode of government, shaped national character.

According to Anthony Barker, toward the end of the century and as a result of the influential speculations of the Scottish Enlightenment thinkers, some Britons found purely climatic theories "ultimately unsatisfactory." Part of the dissatisfaction may have arisen from other Europeans using climate theory against Britons. Undoubtedly, the fact that Britain's cold and damp climate was held accountable for British painters' failure in the arts, compared with the French and Italians, fueled this fire.[69] For some Britons, however, climate's hold over their own bodies and minds was less certain than its effect on non-Europeans. Equiano replicates this tendency to dismiss climate's effects on British character.

The aspect of climate theory almost all British writers could agree on was the fluidity of skin color. Eighteenth-century Britons showed a remarkable desire to believe almost anything about the changeability of skin color based on the effects of the sun, air, and terrain. Almost all natural historians touted the belief that acquiring or losing native color was a slow process, often taking ten to twelve generations in a new climate. Although a few essayists had undertaken to show that the sun's heat was insufficient, in and of itself, to explain human variety, most Britons clung, nonetheless, to climate's explanation for color differences. Another comprehensive explanatory system had not yet appeared as a satisfactory replacement. Equiano's text is particularly interesting because it recovers the contradictory implications of theories based on climate. An analysis of Equiano's narrative crystallizes both the advantages and disadvantages of relying on the heat of the sun and other external factors for explanation of human variations.

Equiano almost always sidesteps one possibility fostered by climate/humoral theory: treating the mind and body as subject to the same forces. Instead, he emphasizes the uniformity of feelings and desires among different colored people. Tactically, this assumption accords well with prevailing sentimental ideology, Christian discipline, and Enlightenment rational ideals. Equiano develops the fraught comparison of ancient Britons with contemporary Africans by introducing the standard abolitionist claim "that understanding is not confined to feature or colour" (45). He also refers to the changeability of skin color in the extended comparison between his village and ancient Hebrews. Ultimately, however, like most of his European contemporaries, he relinquishes the problem of modern color difference as inexplicable: "As to the difference of colour between the Eboan Africans and the modern Jews, I shall not presume to account for it" (44). The claim that color didn't matter, however, largely rested on verifying its origins.

The hybrid appearance of a population that resulted from amalgamation serves as sometimes quirky proof of the natural and superficial changes people undergo in new climates (especially through intermarriage). To argue that all people are subject to alterations in color, Equiano defers to Dr. John Mitchell, a Virginian who wrote an oft-cited explanation of dark skin printed in the *Philosophical Transactions* of the Royal Society of London in 1744. Even though he bases his evidence on anatomical knowledge gained from unnamed experiments on living and dead bodies, Mitchell abides by the influence of climate. Aggressively arguing for the proximity of black and white colors based on scientific examination of skin layers, Mitchell states, "There is not so great, unnatural, and unaccountable a Difference between Negroes and white People, on account of their Colours, as to make it impossible for both ever to have been descended from the same Stock."[75] According to Mitchell, black complexion is not a curse but a blessing, "rendering their Lives, in that intemperate Region [Africa], more tolerable, and less painful" (146). To prove the force of climate's effect on skin color, Mitchell cites the example of the Spaniards in America, which Equiano includes in his narrative. After a prolonged period in the torrid zone, the Spaniards became "dark coloured as our native Indians of Virginia" (Equiano, 44). In a second example, Equiano also uses the physical alteration of Europeans in a hot climate to illustrate how it affects all bodies and manners. In the Portuguese settlement of Sierra Leone, the children of Portuguese and Africans "are now become, in their complexion, and in the woolly quality of their hair, *perfect negroes*, retaining, however, a smattering of the Portuguese language" (45). Indeed, as the examples imply, skin color was believed to shift in the short term at the level of the individual as well as over long periods of time in successive generations of entire populations.

Much of what we might associate with heredity today, Equiano and his contemporaries believed sprang from climate. These examples of the Spaniards and Portuguese who left Europe, Equiano ventures, "while they shew how the complexions of the same persons vary in different climates, it is hoped may tend also to remove the prejudice that some conceive against the natives of Africa on account of their colour." Until this point, Equiano follows Mitchell and Blumenbach closely; both of them refer to these same examples, which were standard ways to signal color's natural mutability. Equiano's additional comment, which follows, tries to challenge the close association between the body's exterior and the mind's capability: "Surely the minds of the Spaniards did not change with their complexions!" (45). Here, Equiano refers to the main stumbling block unwittingly promoted by arguments about the debilitating effects of a hot climate on bodies, minds, and the conduct of societies. The success of these examples of physical mutations in questioning a rationale for slavery is debatable, even though they appeared in the foremost natural histories of the day. Equiano's assurance that over time the Spaniards became Indians in America and the Portuguese became Negroes in Africa was hardly a comfort to Britons, and as we saw with Samuel Stanhope Smith's reasoning, it made some people distinctly uncomfortable.

Although Equiano assumes that complexion changes with an alteration in climate or population, he emphasizes that intellectual probity and refined feelings are common to all humans; he thereby echoes the upshot of William Cowper's widely read "Negro's Complaint" cited in the epigraph to this chapter. When Equiano urges similarities between Africans and Britons, he usually finds occasion to debunk typical proslavery arguments and produce an impression of his own colorless British sensibility. Occasionally, however, the desire to emphasize his similarity to Britons conflicts with the parallels between Britons and other Africans. For example, the most important way that Equiano tries to establish his similarity to Britons is, of course, through his baptism, record of spiritual inquietude, and Christian conversion. When Equiano regards non-Christian slaves and Africans after his conversion, his language reflects the same difficulty posed by the admission that Africa's civilization is inferior to Europe's. After his conversion to Methodism, Equiano divides the world into the converted and unconverted, which is a western European construct that largely supports racial divisions. When Equiano is born again and he sees "with the eye of faith," it means, in part, the eye of a white British man: "Now the Ethiopian was willing to be saved by Jesus Christ. . . . I felt a deep concern for my mother and friends, which occasioned me to pray with fresh ardour; and, in the abyss of thought, I viewed the unconverted people of the world in a very awful state" (190–91). Equiano's new division of the world into converted and unconverted puts Africans on the bottom of a different binary related not solely to skin color but also to enlightenment. Although Equiano's concern focuses on their situation, not their capacities, the non-Christian state of Africans and the widespread ignorance about African religious practices made it difficult to perceive the constant human nature Equiano argued for elsewhere.

Contrary to his usual insistence that the sun affects only skin color, Equiano occasionally invokes climate in a way that suggests its capacity to alter behavior as well, a claim that clashes with the idea that human feelings are identical. Some Britons believed that the heat, air, and climate produced excessive indolence and sexuality, even in European men living in the torrid zones. In theory, a new climate could thus overpower national character. By finding exceptions to the rule, Equiano recounts two incidents in which the causal link between climate, color, and morality shows fissures. By mentioning a British seaman who protects him from bodily harm at the hands of a violent European, Equiano refers to his actions as literally overcoming the infectious climate: "Fortunately a British seaman on board, whose heart had not been debauched by a West-India climate, interposed and prevented him" (108-9). This statement also works on a more figurative level by referring to the corrupt moral climate fostered by slavery. In the space of the same incident, Equiano calls on a standard assumption about the deleterious effects of hot, sunny weather on the moral fiber of the violent man and the exception—a man who has asserted the force of his "true" British character to save him. In another incident, Equiano uses climate as an excuse for his own deviant behavior, which is odd given that elsewhere agency is key to his self-presentation. Following his purchase of a Bible and attempts to live a Christian life, he regrets that he succumbs to the overpowering effect of the hot climate in Montserrat: "All my endeavours to keep up my integrity, and perform my promise to God, began to fail. . . . My resolutions more and more declined, as if the very air of that country or climate seemed fatal to piety" (128). This hyperbole in the last part of the sentence is a barbed reference to the lack of religiosity among the planters, yet Equiano's invocation of the torrid zone to excuse his own slack personal behavior reveals its troublesome explanatory power.

Possibly Equiano's most successful reference to climate is when he simply comments on the shocking effect of the West Indies as a European would: Initially, the sun is "very painful" for him (70). In disclaiming a natural tolerance for the sun's heat, Equiano demonstrates his acclimatization to Europe and that he is not naturally fit to work in a hot climate despite his dark complexion. Equiano declines to use climate to explain white men's lack of feeling in exploiting slaves because he finds (like other contemporaries) exceptions to the rule of harsh slave owners; thus, climate does not work well in regard to analyzing slave owner excesses in the West Indies or to analyzing slavery as a systemic issue. Explanations relying on some versions of climatic/humoral theory tend to undercut human agency, which would undermine the major assumption of abolitionists that planter behavior could change.

The implication of climate affecting both the mind and body is also at odds with the dominant construction of slaves, because, in that case, slaves and masters would partake of a similar degenerate nature. For abolitionist arguments, references to slave society raise the most problems for explanations based in climate or the assumption of uniform intellect among all people. Equiano chooses one small part of the overall climatic package to privilege—the effects of sun on complexion. One of the most challenging negotiations in *The Interesting Narrative* is the representation of himself as a slave and reconciling that image with the dominant ideology of British character. Equiano's general notion of a slave accords with common definitions: passive, especially to be acted upon or immobilized by others, which are the very traits he most assiduously divorces from his self-presentation, even as he enumerates his subjection to physical violence and betrayal by the white men with whom he has contact. A striking example of an abstract reference to slaves that accords with dominant ideology occurs after his manumission when he declares his difference from the enslaved: "I would sooner die like a free man, than suffer myself to be scourged, by the hands of ruffians, and my blood drawn like a slave" (140). Adam Smith's disquisition on the passions in *The Theory of Moral Sentiments* offers a way to interpret this statement anew. Some passions were believed to be necessary parts of human nature. Smith elaborates: "A person becomes contemptible who tamely sits still and submits to insults. . . . [His resentment] enlivens their own [spectators'] indignation against his enemy."[76] Much of Equiano's record of his feelings and actions is indebted to this mode of eliciting sympathy from readers, reaffirming his shared human nature with Britons, and building consensus against West Indian proprietors. David Brion Davis further elucidates the image of active masculinity that Equiano adopts: "Since slavery required physical coercion, its implied antithesis was a perfect freedom of will, instinct, and physical movement, or in other words, a state of self-sovereignty."[77] In Equiano's text, being a slave has as much to do with a state of physical bondage as a state of mind, spiritual health, and politico-commercial power relations. Slavery, then, is an accident of fortune, politics, or trade, and it is not related to the nature of the body, the mind, or the climate.

*   *   *

If the implications of four-stages theory and the several versions of climate theory prove difficult to negotiate, so does working with the religious and aesthetic connotations of blackness and whiteness. Throughout his narrative, Equiano notices color differences within all nations, including Africa ("red," "mahogany," as well as "black" designate various Africans), but instead of developing an analysis about this phenomenon, he initially argues for the operation of a reverse European color aesthetic in Africa. Travelers to Africa often mentioned the way that blackness and other African features were esteemed locally; it was a common enough attempt to argue for a relative aesthetic, rather than a universal one, within a shared humanity (which usually ends up being hierarchical despite claims to the contrary). For in-

stance, in *A New Dictionary of Natural History* (1785), William Martyn repeats the Enlightenment commonplace that every country has its own vision
of beauty, and even the same country defines it differently over time.[78] To
underscore the notion of relative prejudice, Equiano recalls that as a child
in Africa he thought that lighter skin color was inferior: "In regard to complexion, ideas of beauty are wholly relative. I remember while in Africa to
have seen three negro children, who were tawny, and another quite white,
who were universally regarded by myself and the natives in general, as far as
related to their complexions, as deformed" (17).[79] Instead of showing the way
aesthetic assumptions operate culturally, Equiano's example tends to support the acceptability of skin color as a sign of belonging to a nation and the
universality of color prejudice.

Two incidents in his youth show the problem that color prejudice creates for Equiano in Britain. The impasse created by complexion when it
functions as a sign of national identity and communal feeling is dramatized
in an episode that emphasizes Equiano's desire for his black complexion to
be changeable. One of the most poignant scenes of representing his color
difference from Britons occurs when he is a young slave. While on the Isle of
Guernsey, and staying with a ship mate, Equiano's companion is the mate's
young daughter. The British girl is the catalyst for a change in his subjectivity: "When her mother washed her face it looked very rosy; but when she
washed mine it did not look so: I therefore tried oftentimes myself if I could
not by washing make my face of the same colour. . . . I now began to be
mortified at the difference in our complexions" (69). In focusing on the fact
that his complexion does not alter color when scrubbed, Equiano conveys
his heartfelt realization of this indelible difference. The moment when white
skin suffused with red color is common to eighteenth-century encomiums
on the beauty of whiteness. It was widely believed among Europeans that
only they blushed; the rosy tint either displayed "natural beauty" or registered refined sentiments (modesty, embarrassment, resentment). The failure
to change color as much as blackness itself seems of mortifying concern to
Equiano.[80] The scene highlights the glass ceiling of color aesthetics in Britain, and it is prefaced by what Equiano imagined was his sufficient similarity to the British: "As I was now amongst a people who had not their faces
scarred, like some of the African nations where I had been, I was very glad I
did not let them ornament me in that manner" (69). Scarification seems less
important than having white skin for an adequate resemblance to Britons.

Equiano records another incident from his youth of complexion and
features establishing an automatic connection between strangers. His response to the assumption of familiarity based on color is ambivalent: "I was

one day in a field belonging to a gentleman who had a black boy about my own size; this boy having observed me from his master's house, was transported at the sight of one of his own countrymen, and ran to meet me with the utmost haste" (85). This incident on the Isle of Wight appears to confirm that similar complexion gives rise to brotherly feelings, but the events do not initially transpire in this way. Equiano continues: "I, not knowing what he was about, turned a little out of his way at first, but to no purpose: he soon came close to me, and caught me in his arms as if I had been his brother, though we had never seen each other before" (85). After they talked together, they initiated a friendship. This strange interlude supports the uncertainty with which complexion signified for Equiano, at least. To the other boy, Equiano's black complexion was enough to create a bond with a stranger; for Equiano, the identification was not immediate, and in fact, his initial response was avoidance. It is only after a conversation that Equiano accedes to the "natural affection" of countrymen for each other.

In analyzing the difficulties Equiano faced in discussing skin color and its various meanings in eighteenth-century Britain, I have aimed to show the competing implications of discourses about climate, national character, and individual agency—and their quirky collision in the context of slavery. Equiano's typical citation of assumptions from natural history, four-stages theory, and national aesthetic preferences demonstrates the lack of explanatory power the theories possess when juxtaposed. Instead of bolstering each other, they often contradict. Indeed, Equiano's text encapsulates the general lack of coherence in discourses of human difference even in the late eighteenth century.

*   *   *

Another way to interpret the logical inconsistencies and contradictory use of climate theory that I have identified above is that Equiano presents human difference in several ways that disallow any one definition remaining supreme. This is nowhere more evident than in his engagement with skin color. Although black and white complexions both appear in their value-laden meaning in his narrative, he usually invokes them neutrally. Using a two-pronged strategy, Equiano features incidents in which blackness has meaning contrary to prevailing European expectations, on the one hand, and situations in which the superiority of whiteness does not remain unchallenged, on the other hand. These sections prove more successful than using climate or national standards of beauty to explain complexion's meaning.

Equiano combats the reduction of human difference to the intractable shorthand of color, not least by illustrating that race is a composite of signs.

Britons certainly seemed to value their light complexions, but a majority of them did not yet equate whiteness with national character. A brief glance at a recent critic's engagement with race and color in Equiano's narrative shows the tempting conflation of whiteness and Britishness. Susan Marren speculates on the way that whiteness cathected prized aspects of British culture in Equiano's narrative, but her contention misses the way that whiteness was also subject to multiple interpretations because it was not essentialized. Essentialism, or a universal notion based in biology of what it means, in this case, to be a white person, is incongruent with climate theory, as it is with eighteenth-century anatomical theories of skin color. Other than supposing an historical anachronism, Marren elides complexion and national character: "Equiano goes beyond merely measuring himself by white English standards and begins transgressively appropriating whiteness to himself. In eighteenth-century discourse, whiteness is essentialized; it denotes skin color but comes to signify civilization, Christianity, nobility, justice, industry, intellect, truth. While Equiano allows the word *white* to reverberate in the text on every customary semantic level, he ascribes its concomitant virtues to himself and, less consistently, to his fellow slaves, just as he earlier attributes to the white sailors the savagery and irrationality that Western culture associates with dark-skinned peoples."[81] Marren's observation is both insightful and obfuscatory. She demonstrates an appropriately complex notion of race, but she wrongly deems whiteness essentialized and substitutable for national character in the 1780s.

One factor that Marren does not examine is the way that Equiano—and other contemporaries—discovers many of the prized "British" characteristics (justice, industry, intellect) in societies as diverse as his Igbo village, Caribbean Indian culture, and Turkey. In other words, Equiano invests these positive traits in British national character rather than in skin color and attempts to work against one trend of his day that connected them only to descriptions of Europeans.

Equiano argues for a flexibility to the category of whiteness and Europeanness when they are still being adjusted by men of science.[82] By the end of the century, contemporary racial taxonomies generated in Britain or favored by Britons were mainly organized by geographic location, with skin color as the foremost characteristic of inhabitants. The opposite tendency to organize human groups according to color was also present but had tended to appear early in the century with the taxonomies of Richard Bradley, the early versions of Linnaeus's *Homo sapiens*, and the scheme in the *Royal Magazine*, which followed an updated version of the classical custom, dividing men according to white, black, and the intermediate color tawny.

Most recent scholars working with whiteness diagnose it as a powerful, because invisible, category. Its unmarked status allows it to seem not to be racialized at all, just the norm.[83] In *White* (1997), Richard Dyer argues that the "category of whiteness is unclear and unstable, yet this has proved its strength."[84] I would add that whiteness has been more unstable at some times than at others. *White* initially distinguished European-born laborers from African- or Indian-descended servants in the seventeenth-century colonies. Adaptations of geographic or religious affiliation continued to dominate British nomenclature in regard to themselves and others. Throughout the century, *white* was not the privileged British term that designated the ruling classes of Britons or even the Creoles in the various colonies. In the colonies themselves, however, *white* was increasingly used to denominate all classes of people of European descent.[85] Britons did not consider themselves white people, as Marren posits, so much as they believed themselves to be Christians or denizens of a civil society who possessed a white complexion. Many contemporary documents juxtapose the characteristics of a polite society to white skin color, but they are not yet "white" virtues.

Throughout *The Interesting Narrative*, Equiano's reference to whiteness usually function as a neutral description or in conjunction with European descent as a term of identification. Occasionally, whiteness also works as a concept that is itself unstable, ranging from connotations of ugliness, savagery, suspected cannibalism, indiscriminate cruelty to people of all colors, and excessive desires to upright behavior. Whiteness was a site of contestation in the latter eighteenth century, both in terms of what, precisely, it meant and to whom it applied. In fact, Equiano's first physical representation of Europeans reverses commonsense assumptions: They are not white but red-faced and ugly in comparison with Africans. For example, arriving as a slave at the African coast, the young Equiano, manhandled by the crew, believes he has entered "into a world of bad spirits" and that he will be killed: "Their complexions too differing so much from ours, their long hair, and the language they spoke . . . united to confirm me in this belief." He then sees a multitude of "black people . . . chained together," thinking he will "be eaten by those white men with horrible looks, red faces, and long hair" (55). In his African eyes, their visible appearance and linguistic oddity affirm the association with evil intent—a simple reversal of commonplaces from which Equiano usually refrains. Notably, the reference to red faces conjures up the usual positive association of the blush with fair complexions and immediately replaces it with its neutral signification of sunburned, or even a negative connotation, such as red with the exertion of manual labor. Taking an opportunity to drive home how the slave trade brutalizes all concerned in it, Equiano observes, "The white people looked and acted, as I thought, in so savage a manner; for I had never seen among any people such instances of brutal cruelty; and this is not only shewn towards us blacks, but also to some of the whites" (56–57). Slavery, many argued, dehumanized masters as well as their slaves. In these examples, white complexion demarcates a perceived fact; it is not an aesthetic feature as in the youthful face-washing incident.

Other than his first contact with white slavers, Equiano continually finds variations among Europeans based on their behavior; he emphasizes their differences from one another as well as from Africans. For example, on his second sea trip as a slave he is treated better, "quite contrary to what I had seen of any white people before; I therefore began to think that they were not all of the same disposition" (64). After recording his initial negative impression, Equiano consistently refuses to lump white people together, generalize about their nature, or even homogenize traits within one person. For example, as a young boy, his first friend and teacher is a slave owner slightly older than himself, and it is this kind of contradiction Equiano repeatedly faces with kind masters as well as with capricious masters, who are well-intentioned at times or who are deceptive at other moments. In this fashion, Equiano recovers the sense of variety and flux to which all bodies and tempers were believed to be subject. Occasionally, Equiano also refers to whiteness positively, associating it with people who do not sell members of their own country to others and with the "color" of Christianity and enlightenment. For the majority of the time, however, Equiano uses white complexion for description, not evaluation.

One of the most intriguing accounts of the way whiteness and blackness work fluidly in Equiano's text occurs when a sequence of events ends in a color masquerade in which Equiano passes for a white man. This incident reinforces both his repeated point that free black men are among the most vulnerable colonial subjects and that complexion is a superficial difference that can be manipulated. The episode of the color masquerade is occasioned by events that form a condensed slave narrative of John Annis, a "very clever black man," whom Equiano recommends as a cook on his ship. Annis was formerly attached to a man from St. Kitt's, Mr. Kirkpatrick, "from whom he parted by consent" (179). Kirkpatrick tries to regain Annis for sale by deceiving him and then kidnapping him. Eventually, he succeeds and his actions go unchallenged by the captain and crew, who fail to intervene and save their shipmate. Equiano positions himself as Annis's only friend and as a fierce defender of liberty; he finally obtains an injunction against Kirkpatrick, who has set a guard to prevent Equiano's entry into his house. The 1679 Act of Habeas Corpus was central to British liberty. Equiano likely refers to the part that states no Englishman or woman could be sent out of England unless he/she agrees in writing or has been convicted of a felony. Ever resourceful, Equiano explains his ruse to serve the document that would prohibit Kirkpatrick's removing Annis from England: "I whitened my face, that they might not know me; and this had the desired effect." But his effort is ultimately unsuccessful in rescuing Annis from being enslaved again unlawfully (and then tortured to death) because of Kirkpatrick's greater political power (134–35).[86] This episode is largely underexplained in the narrative, but it works on several levels. First, the incident highlights the extreme lengths that some slave owners pursued to keep black men as property and the impunity with which it was regularly done. On a different level, this incident demonstrates that whiteface itself is a powerful disguise for a black man, and here, color is represented simply as a cosmetic difference: Equiano's passing for a white man even fools Kirkpatrick. Third, his artificial whitening is linked syntagmatically to his Christian conversion, which immediately follows—a reversal of the convention discussed in Chapter 3, in which the momentary blackening of Other heroines precedes their baptism and marriage to Englishmen. Finally, Equiano's ruse to free Annis reverses a common eighteenth-century form of protest against the establishment. For instance, bands of disgruntled citizens in Britain blackened their faces before leading riots and American colonists dressed as Indians in redface to raid Boston harbor.

Equiano's own understanding of skin color goes beyond these examples of its changeability or its merely descriptive usefulness: complexion matters because of the way some Europeans treat him *because* of his color. His black color and his racial identity are continually produced for him from Africa to America by instances of disempowerment, threat, bodily harm, denial of rights to his profits from trading, or restriction of his mobility. He exemplifies the very way in which enslavement, not skin color, limits his self-improvement, a delicate negotiation since all three phenomena were often ideologically linked by this time. His text underscores that black complexion is a way of experiencing the world rather than a way of statically being in the world determined by climate, customs, or physical features. Unlike the natural historians—the men of science whose theories Equiano shares—his own concern is not with abstract divisions among humans but with these theories as they affect him or those with whom he has contact. Against these forces, Equiano pits his colorless ingenuity, Christian perseverance, and manly integrity. Equiano's narrative continually spotlights this dilemma of the difference his skin color makes in the colonial world, and yet he maintains the similarity of his mind, feelings, and aspirations to his readers.

*   *   *

Equiano demonstrates repeatedly that the meaning of skin color varies according to place and politics, not least by providing alternative configurations to the negative black and positive white binary. Focusing on geographic changes underscores Equiano's commitment to illustrating complexion's relativity in his comparing Great Britain, Africa, the West Indies, and Turkey. In these various locations, Equiano tries to eliminate the conviction of Africans' singularity and to illustrate his personal achievement of civil behavior in terms recognizable to his readers. Despite the attention he gives skin color on occasion, Equiano characteristically emphasizes manners and customs, heightening similarities and differences among people outside of a color dynamic. These passages are important textual instances of using the language of natural history and the travel narrative to his own benefit. In the section about Africa, for instance, Equiano focuses on language differences and customs, such as circumcision, as the most important distinctions among Africans. In this way, Equiano observes diversity within Africa. Emphasizing the complex social rules that structure African societies, as well as some remarkable differences from Britons, Equiano's reference to laws and customs differentiates Africans positively from Europeans; for example, he notes the extreme cleanliness of Africans, their sobriety, and the absence of swearing, like others before him who wrote about Africa.[87] These behaviors, to some extent, compensate for the lack of commercial and artistic advancement, and they limit the importance of difference between black and white skin.

The main contrast in behavior that Equiano pursues, however, is between slave owners, their lackeys, and himself. By doing so, he detaches national ideals from complexion. Technically a foreign-born alien, Equiano records the process of becoming a virtuous subject of the British nation, despite his color and former slave status.[88] Britishness in its national association is always more positive than its colonial manifestation. Indeed, slave owner behavior in the West Indies shows that these men possess only the name of "Christian" rather than the associated virtues of Christianity or Britishness compared with Equiano himself, Amerindians, or Turks. In this way, Equiano suggests that *Christian* is an outdated nomenclature for describing Europeans abroad, so that the term *white* is actually more applicable. Through his eyewitness account of the routine rape of young slave girls, cruelty to slaves, and the unseemly sexual behavior of planters, Equiano shows, as Edward Long did, the lack of morality and dearth of British social custom characteristic of the colonies.

The white male sexual economy periodically enforces a passive and subordinate masculine identity on the adult Equiano, especially in the West Indies. He tells us that one of his responsibilities as a slave was to care for new cargoes of Negroes. In this role, he was privy to acts of sexual violence and the routine abuse of laborers. He notes that the numerous merchants, plantation clerks, and other white men "commit violent depredations on the chastity of the female slaves; and these I was, though with reluctance, obliged to submit to at all times, being unable to help them. . . . I have known our mates to commit these acts most shamefully. . . . I have even known them [to] gratify their brutal passion with females not ten years old" (104). The argument about his reluctant spectatorship, however, shifts from the issue of violent white male sexuality and his forced complicity to the double racial standard in which Equiano occupies another vulnerable position. As the following passage makes clear, he believes that men of African descent possess the same sexual desires as white men: "And yet in Montserrat I have seen a negro-man staked to the ground, and cut most shockingly, and then his ears cut off bit by bit, because he had been connected with a white woman, who was a common prostitute: as if it were no crime in the whites to rob an innocent African girl of her virtue; but most heinous in a black man only to gratify a passion of nature, where the temptation was offered by one of a different colour, though the most abandoned woman of her species" (104). In this polemical passage, Equiano underscores at once the debased sexuality and corrupt power of white men enmeshed in a slave society and the innocence of black men's sexual desire for white women. It is the black man's passions that are represented as natural, the white prostitute and white men who are monstrous. Virtue and natural desire are conferred alike on the powerless female slaves and free black men, respectively. Here, unlike his younger self, who "relished their [British men's] society and manners," Equiano clearly neither identifies with nor resembles white men in the colonies (77). His job forces him to adopt an impotent position, yet this scene distinguishes him from the debased colonials over whom he has no control.

In *The Interesting Narrative*, the free black man is one of the chief victims of the evils of the slave trade. The West Indies and America offer a narrower distribution of status and tolerance for black color than Africa or Great Britain. As both a slave and a free black, Equiano is constantly threatened by whites. Although the status of mulattos and free blacks nominally challenged the political and racial hierarchies established for the benefit of the whites in the colonies, in several episodes Equiano shows the way that white men attempt to maintain their dominance through legalized violence and thus do not live up to Christian ideals. In this way, Equiano dramatizes slavery's connection to power and profit rather than simply to color difference. Equiano includes several other brief slave narratives within his own, such as the story of a young mulatto who had been free from birth and who married a free woman; he was illegally seized by whites and sold as a slave with impunity (121). These examples show the vulnerability of free blacks and mulattos to white men's greed and that no laws protect their status: "Hitherto I had thought only slavery dreadful; but the state of a free Negro appeared to me now equally so at least, and in some respects even worse; for they live in constant alarm for their liberty, which is but nominal, for they are universally insulted and plundered without the possibility of redress" (122). These aspects of Equiano's narrative tend to support the argument that West Indian slavery, or unnatural power, is responsible for the corruption of Britishness, not climate or other incidental factors.

The West Indies provide an unparalleled opportunity for demonstrating Equiano's British virtues rather than any similarity to the slaves or to the more primitive Indians. In the West Indies, Equiano is an overseer of both enslaved Africans and laboring Indians, whom he styles another "sable people." Equiano identifies with Britons' cultural and commercial superiority in relation to the less civilized indigenous inhabitants. Although *The Interesting Narrative* praises the Indians for their simple way of life, it carefully avoids any personal identification with them. Elsewhere in the narrative, Equiano compares Indians and Africans, but in the abstract rather than in relation to himself (206, 209). Indeed, his way of talking about the Indians is not unlike the narrator's sentiments in Aphra Behn's *Oroonoko* (1688) about the indigenous people of Surinam, Edward Long's views in *The History of Jamaica* (1774), or John Stedman's opinion of them in his *Narrative of a Five Years Expedition Against the Revolted Negroes of Surinam* (1796).[89] In these accounts, the importance of British-Indian trade is emphasized as is Indians' fondness for Europeans. Equiano writes in his travel narrative mode: "The Indians were exceedingly fond of the Doctor. . . . [S]ome Woolwow, or flatheaded Indians, who lived fifty or sixty miles above our river . . . brought us a good deal of silver in exchange for our goods. . . . [O]ur neighboring Indians . . . would not work at any thing for us, except fishing; and a few times they assisted to cut down some trees, in order to build us houses; which they did exactly like the Africans, by the joint labour of men, women, and children" (206). He adds specifically about the Indians' moral character and social custom: "I do not recollect any of them to have had more than two wives," observing about these noble savages, "I never saw the least sign of incontinence amongst them. The women are ornamented with beads, and fond of painting themselves; the men also paint. . . . Upon the whole, I never met with any nation that were so simple in their manners. . . . [T]here was not one white person in our dwelling, nor anywhere else, that I saw in different places I was at on shore, that was better or more pious than those unenlightened Indians" (206). Equiano contends that the Indians are superior to the European slaveholders who are but nominal Christians; however, they are clearly represented as an unpolished people, albeit positively, and quite unlike the Christian overseer Equiano represents himself to be.

His enlightened difference from the sympathetic Indians is most apparent in his attempt to convert one. During his stint as an overseer of slaves, Equiano tries to reconcile the Christian mission with his role as a freedman in the institution of slavery. Noticeably, the issue of enslaving Africans becomes secondary to the religious conversion of an Indian prince that he features. On their way from England to Jamaica, Equiano and his patron encounter four Musquito Indians, one of whom is a prince, a "poor heathen," whom Equiano diligently instructs in doctrines of Christianity (204). But the crew members tease the prince about his Christian pretensions, which prompts him to ask Equiano, "How comes it that all the white men on board, who can read and write, observe the sun, and know all things, yet swear, lie, and get drunk, only excepting yourself?'" (204). While ultimately Equiano is thwarted in his attempts to convert the Indian, he conveys his integrity and Christian commitment as superior to Europeans', which is highlighted when the prince distinguishes Equiano's more circumspect behavior from the rest of the crew. Succeeding better at the business end of the voyage, Equiano helps his patron select slaves and then manages a healthy and productive workforce. While staying within a recognizable paradigm of regarding Indians as virtuous though less polished, Equiano uses these observations to demonstrate his own closer resemblance to Britons in Britain, rather than to the degenerated Creoles in the colonies.

His nickname, "the black Christian," neatly captures the sameness but with a difference in terms of *both* Britons and Africans that his narrative unravels, although the white sailors give him that name (92). As a response to the theory that color is an accident of birth, as well as to the widespread conviction about the passive nature of slaves, Equiano consistently employs one strategy that encourages the perception of him as an active agent: presenting his enthusiastic pursuit of acculturation.[90] Throughout his narrative, Equiano details the process by which he becomes an Englishman, which he never collapses with whiteness but equates with knowledge, behavior, and a worldview. One of the most important ways that Equiano "imbibe[s] their spirit" is through conversion to Christianity, an event that occupies a significant portion of his narrative. The continuing significance of religion to expressing fellow feeling—and to defining British national character—is underscored in the *Monthly Review*'s response to Equiano's record of his conversion: "The sable author of this volume appears to be a very sensible man; and he is, surely, not the less worthy of credit from being a convert to Christianity" (13).

His Christian conversion is bolstered by secular attainments, especially his acquisition of manners through consuming British culture. Signposts of his striving toward a more accomplished servant status (e.g., improving himself in reading and writing, French horn lessons, math instruction, and travel) combine a picaresque narrative form with amassing recognizable signs of British status and upward mobility; they serve to decenter the focus on skin color and focus instead on his class-based desires. These cultural accouterments are an effective way to place himself as recognizably British, but they also recall his lost privileged status in Africa. Characterizing himself as possessing a "roving disposition" and "desirous of seeing as many different parts of the world as I could," Equiano positions himself as an upwardly mobile man, such as the fictional characters Robinson Crusoe, Gulliver, or Roderick Random (171). His desire to travel, including his observations on buildings and customs abroad, also alludes to the narrative style connected to the Grand Tour, the initiation into "human" culture for elite British gentlemen.

One factor underpinning his emphasis on acquiring British culture concerns human similarity and climate. Many Britons believed not only that transplantation into a new climate affected one's appearance but also that a different mode of government, new diet, and foreign manners could influence one's behavior. This result intensified if future generations lived under the same conditions. The assumption that people change if subject to a new institutional arrangement or to a new environment backed the ubiquitous planter claim that Creole slaves were superior to recently imported slaves. It was also the chief component of the argument that Christian religion, British consumerism, and clothing would civilize savages. While Equiano's own example mirrors the mutations of the Spaniards in America and the Portuguese in Africa in cultural terms, his experience is more familiar and more polished than what happened to the Europeans abroad. Hence, Equiano's adoption of English manners shows his resemblance to them and a natural process of adjustment to a new environment, not necessarily the disconcerting assimilation many critics have remarked upon. In this case, color, in theory, might become completely incidental.

If his experiences as a freed man in the West Indies dramatize Equiano's attainment of cherished British ideals of behavior and observation, Equiano's experiences in Turkey also question European superiority. There are several points in his narrative when references to Turkey function as an implicit critique of Britain and as a positive point of comparison to Africa.[91] At the height of his misery in Great Britain, Equiano notes that the Christians he encounters there are "not so honest or so good in their morals as the Turks" (179). In this way, he tries to separate prized British national virtues from Christianity and Britishness just as he did by praising the "pious" if "unenlightened Indians" (206). Drawing distinctions between the West Indies and Turkey also affords Equiano the opportunity to show how black skin color is interpreted in two slave societies. Turkey represents the possibility of extricating himself from the tyranny of color difference in the British Empire. In Turkey, he represents himself as "another" rather than simply Other. Equiano's black skin signifies more positively in Turkey than anywhere outside of Africa because, he implies, his complexion is unimportant in this context.[92] The Turks receive him kindly in Smyrna, and his natural historian's view of them refers to their bodies and most striking characteristics: "The natives are well-looking and strong. . . . In general I believe they are fond of black people" (167). His observation on slavery in Turkey deflects the focus on color as the basis of enslavement: "I was surprised to see how the Greeks are, in some measure, kept under by the Turks, as the Negroes are in the West-Indies by the white people" (167–68). Equiano considers the slavery of the Greeks similar to the enslavement of Africans: as having more to do with power and positionality than with culture or racial features.

Unlike any other place, Turkey represents the possibility of Equiano's being a man rather than a slave. An officer in Smyrna offers him human property (two wives) to establish himself there: "However I refused the temptation, thinking one was as much as some could manage, and more than others would venture on" (169). In wittily dismissing the temptation of polygamy, Equiano defines himself within the public, European norm of sexuality and masculinity (as well as mild misogyny). As Felicity Nussbaum's work on polygamy and the eighteenth-century British Empire suggests, "England's toying with and ultimate rejection of polygamy near the end of the eighteenth century is part of the nation's defining itself both as distinct from and morally superior to the polygamous Other. Monogamy is instituted as part of England's national definition, and whatever practices its explorers might find to tempt them in other worlds, England asserts its public stance that marriage means one man, one wife, at least in law"[93]. This incident allows Equiano to establish his sexuality, moral temperament, and religious conviction against "the polygamous Other" in Turkey and in contradistinction to the slave owners in the West Indies.

*   *   *

Equiano's figurative brush with polygamy in Turkey reminds us that ideologies of sexuality and gender difference are linked to the signification of human variety. Once again, power relations and custom rather than climate seem to account for these constructions in his narrative. As I have shown, Equiano depicts male European sexuality in the colonies as less regulated than either the Indians' or Africans'. Although Britons claimed monogamy, among other domestic virtues, as an attribute of their national character, the perversion of this ideology was especially visible under slavery. The gendering and sexualizing of slaves was not simply an acting out of convictions about the nature of Africans, of course, but sprang from the intricate power relations of slave society. Occasionally, some male slaves and freed blacks seem to have been able to capitalize on the prerogatives associated with masculinity.

Because of an already gendered concept of certain forms of labor, mobility, and behavior in the private and public spheres, male slaves were engendered differently than females from the moment of leaving Africa. The slave trade initiated the new gender distinctions in the types of accommodation and restraint used on most slave ships; for example, separating men and women, men not being given as much freedom to be on deck, but often confined in the holds. The middle passage also made African men's masculinity subordinate to Europeans by forcing them to comply with white men's free sexual access to female slaves on shipboard, in towns, and on the plantations.[94]

Whether male or female slaves were treated similarly or differently was significant in the eighteenth century. The argument about the similarity in the treatment of male and female slaves is meant to shock Britons and indicate the unnaturalness of the slave trade. Anthony Benezet's *A Caution to Great Britain and Her Colonies* (1766) emphasizes the way that the slavers de-sex Africans for the sake of calculating profit and thus the way that they treat humans like livestock.[95] Benezet recounts—in the exact words John Wesley will use a few years later—that British workers strip African women and men alike at the point of sale in Africa: "When the poor slaves, whether brought from far or near, come to the sea-shore, they are stripped naked, and strictly examined by the European Surgeons, both men and women, without the least distinction or modesty" (19). Benezet records the scandal of the slave auction once again on arriving in the colonies: "They are again exposed naked, without any distinction of sexes, to the brutal examination of their purchasers; and this, it may well be judged is to many of them another occasion of deep distress, especially to the females" (22). By commenting on the women's shame, Benezet obliquely refutes the assumption that there was not as great a distinction between men and women in African society as there was in Europe.

If Benezet details the concern African women show about the violation of their modesty, the former slave Cugoano emphasizes a more politicized dimension of the violent gendering African women are subject to in the slave trade, a gendering that exceeds the indecent gaze: "It was common for the dirty filthy sailors to take the African women and lie upon their bodies; but the men were chained and pent up in holes" (15). In these terms, Cugoano insists just as strenuously on the differences in treatment, much as Equiano does. African men and women, despite many similarities in their work assignments and general treatment as slaves, were ranked differently in the colonial labor economy. The kinds of occupations that the men were trained to perform, especially artisan work, permitted greater likelihood of their being able to buy their manumission and support themselves in socially acceptable ways.[96] Nevertheless, the position of male slaves uneasily straddled the production of masculine and feminine gendering because of their status as property.

As Equiano's several references to the routine rape and coercion of slave girls and women suggest, he is careful not to associate female Africans with autonomous sexual power such as Edward Long features in *The History of Jamaica*. The most telling examples of disempowerment in Equiano's narrative include the female slave lodged in the iron muzzle and the slave girls raped by white men. Although represented at this early stage in the rewriting of slavery, the female slave is silent and immobilized, unlike her male counterpart. In fact, the scantily clad, speaking male slave became the symbol of the abolition movement designed by Josiah Wedgwood; he figured the symbolic slave on his knees in chains imploring Britons: "Am I Not a Man and a Brother?"[97]

The critic Chinosole helpfully characterizes Equiano as one who "exists in a state of duality and multiplicity"; the duality she refers to is national, cultural, and religious.[98] The multiplicities, however, exceed even the suggestiveness of Chinosole's essay. As a slave, Equiano must negotiate a different sexual and gendered economy than when he is a freeman, and his narrative represents the uneven process of his interpellation into a masculinity often subordinate to white men's and into a sometimes equivocal Britishness. The vagaries of the way that gender privilege combined with status, especially in terms of self-ownership or ownership of property, meant that Equiano could be the property of others and own it, but not simultaneously.[99]

In legal terms, as a slave, he was the property and chattel of a succession of white men. As Philmore put it rather awkwardly in *Two Dialogues on the Man-Trade* (1760), a slave "may be said to be stolen from himself, being no longer master of himself, or at his own disposal" (22). In those terms, slaves were not owners of property or of their earnings in the way that Britons were. Although custom dictated that some slaves could carry on trade on board ships or at local markets, and keep their profits, Equiano intimates that this custom was subject to the considerable whim of owners and unscrupulous whites. On the other hand, as a freeman, Equiano could and did marry an English wife, who by law was considered his property in the sense that marriage laws recognized one body and that was the man's. This phenomenon suggests that Equiano's male gender and status as a freeman was sufficient at certain times, to "count" more than his color, especially in Britain.

*   *   *

The culmination of Equiano's slave narrative turns to the larger problem of Africa's place in Britain's aspirations for European hegemony. In introducing ideas about enhancing legitimate trade between Africa and Europe, Equiano reaches a similar impasse as when he used skin color or Christianity to think about Europeans and Africans in conjunction. The discourse of civilization resurfaces, a discourse that predicates Africa's inferiority to Europe. In the end, Equiano focuses on the potential of Africans and Europeans as trading partners; the major problem at the time was changing the nature of the current extensive trade.[100] As Chapter 4 demonstrates, the production and consumption of commodities are extremely important factors to understanding how racial ideology informs eighteenth-century colonial power relations. As did several other abolitionists and travelers in the eighteenth century, Equiano attempts to resituate Africa as a future market for British goods. Following Benezet, Cugoano, and Clarkson, Equiano argues in favor of what we would now call imperial colonialism, and his analysis of the African market reads not unlike current government and World Bank publications encouraging multinational Western corporations to establish their businesses in Costa Rica, Malaysia, and Mexico.[101] In Equiano's zeal to make African natural resources and domestic labor power seem a more attractive investment than the slave trade, his text eerily foreshadows Europe's carving up Africa in the nineteenth-century colonial and imperial scramble: "The hidden treasures of centuries will be brought to light and into circulation. Industry, enterprize, and mining, will have their full scope, proportionably as they civilize. In a word, it lays open a field of commerce to the

British manufacturers and merchant adventurers. The manufacturing interest and the general interests are synonimous [*sic*]. The abolition of slavery
would be in reality an universal good" (234). Africa had long been associated
with commodities other than slaves, particularly before the Treaty of Utrecht
(1713), which conferred the Spanish Asiento on England to sell slaves to
their American colonists. Nevertheless, abundant natural resources were not
the same as manufactured goods, art, china, or other ready-made consumer
items. African trade in gum, oil, wood, ivory, and gold did not signal a civil
but a rude society; only European manufactures and division of labor seemed
to qualify as civil trade.

Early in *The Interesting Narrative*, when Equiano is explaining how he
was kidnapped and sold, he focuses on the dissension that European commodities introduce among Africans by creating excessive desires that result
in the selling of slaves. Minimizing the distance between seller and buyer,
Equiano claims, "When a trader wants slaves, he applies to a chief for them,
and tempts him with his wares. It is not extraordinary, if on this occasion
he yields to the temptation with as little firmness, and accepts the price of
his fellow-creature's liberty with as little reluctance, as the enlightened merchant" (39). Such a problem, however, affirms the probable success of more
thoroughly commercializing Africa: The desire for British goods is already
present. The primary obstacle to increasing consumerism in Africa is the
trade in slaves; it is necessary to transform people who were formerly considered commodities into buyers and producers of national wealth for both
Africa and Great Britain.

In eighteenth-century terms, the perception of civilization often rested
on emulation of European standards, a demand for European consumer
goods, enjoyment of luxuries, and ever expanding desires—the arguable
cause and result of a profitable slave trade. As Edward Long and other patriots continually reminded Britons, the slave trade and slavery constituted the
base of Britain's visibly superior claims to civilization. Equiano counters that
claim with the contention that commodities will unite Africa and Europe
in a more mutually beneficial relationship, and Equiano refers to the cor-
relative process of Europeanizing Africa through trade as an added benefit.
In redefining Africa as a market for British manufactures, Equiano's terms
precisely echo Edward Long's plans for civilizing the Caribbean Indians,
discussed in Chapter 4: "The native inhabitants will insensibly adopt the
British fashions, manners, customs, &c. In proportion to the civilization, so
will be the consumption of British manufactures" (175–76). Thomas Clarkson puts the same sentiment even more baldly: "In proportion as we civilize
a people, we increase their wants."[102] Equiano's narrative reveals that part

of the effort to change the slave trade involves positively connecting Africa to the concept of civilization, which was overdetermined by its association with European commercial society and its culture. In discussions advocating increasing trade with Africa, a key silent term is labor. That Africans and Europeans had vastly different notions of labor is evident, and it was a very special kind of labor on which European notions of civilization rested in the eighteenth century: the extraction of surplus value from slave labor. Seen in this light, producers and consumers of civilization occupied nonintersecting positions, a problem that was not visible to contemporary writers.

Like the proposed commercial relations between Africans and Europeans, certain legitimate sexual relations seemed to promise greater harmony and aid in redefining Africans as consumers, not slaves. Equiano responds to James Tobin's proslavery position, which included a stance against amalgamation in Britain. Equiano's response appeared in *The Public Advertiser* in 1788. In his letter, Equiano argues for intermarriage as a measure to halt the rape and ongoing sexual exploitation of female slaves, in particular, but also as a means to create a new tolerance for human differences in general. The similarity of the language of legitimate trade and the language of intermarriage dramatizes the way that both could be marshaled to encourage abolition. The two languages dovetail in Equiano's reasoned response to Tobin's hysterical condemnation: "'The mutual commerce of the sexes of both Blacks and Whites, under the restrictions of moderation and law, would yield more benefit than a prohibition—the mind free—would not have such a strong propensity toward the black females as when under restraint.'"[104] Key to Equiano's proposal is creating a commensurate status between men and women, regardless of color. Although it is clear that Equiano's argument aims to lessen white men's exploitation of black women, it is the sentimental black man, languishing for love and thwarted by social (color) taboos, who again engages our attention and desires legitimating. In Equiano's editorial, the figure of the free black man reappears as the subject of natural sexual desire thwarted by restrictive gendered and racial convention that Tobin advocates. Equiano argues against Tobin's distaste for interracial liaisons, which is based on the assumption of the striking difference between the feelings of whites and blacks (which Equiano contends are shared) and their complexions (which Equiano claims are natural): "If the mind of a black man conceives the passion of love for a fair female, he is to pine, languish, and even die, sooner than an intermarriage be allowed, merely because the complexion of the offspring should be tawney . . . for as no contamination of the virtues of the heart would result from the union, the mixture of colour could be of no consequence" (Equiano, 329).

The issue of complexion appears intractable in its aesthetic manifestation, and Equiano attempts once again to divorce whiteness from merit. Equiano further urges that "a few darker visages" were preferable to the evils arising from clandestine or even open liaisons between black women and white men in the colonies. Because they are extralegal, these connections often result in abortion or murder of infants, practices that endanger women's health (330). His suggestion to establish legal intermarriage in the colonies and even wider social acceptance of it in Britain is based on a moral imperative that regards skin color as inconsequential. He wishes to make way for more "intermarriages at home, and in our Colonies[,] and encourage open, free, and generous love upon Nature's own wide and extensive plan, subservient only to moral rectitude, without distinction of the colour of a skin" (330). Equiano reasons that like legitimate trade, intermarriage would increase virtue in the British state. Comparing his solution to the biblical sanction of intermarriage for Jews as a way to strengthen the nation of Israel, Equiano thereby hints at the positive political effect of such a measure.

Despite the uneven presence of theories of human variety in slave trade discourse, certain ways of seeing Others were crystallized for many reasons. The slave trade debates could have taken place without reference to human differences and simply focused on political and economic issues, but they didn't. There was—both directly and indirectly—an intensification of attention to Africans and Britons. Historians such as Peter Fryer and Anthony Barker have argued that something important changes in the 1770s with regard to racial ideology; they concur that the emergence of modern racism resulted from an acceleration of pro- and anti–slave trade discourse. Fryer, for one, contends that "by the 1770s racism had more than a foothold in Britain."[104] As this chapter has demonstrated, what changed was a greater focus on human differences in many political and cultural realms and a reassessment of the influence of government, climate, and education on the body and mind. Most notably in the 1780s and after, race is politicized in the public domain, along with slavery, which is particularly apparent in the myriad poetic and prose statements about the nature of Britons in the colonies and about slaves.

This book ends on a palpably different note than the one with which it began. In 1789, Equiano offers evidence to prove that he possesses the same reason, feelings, and desires as his readers, despite his skin color and former slave status. In *Robinson Crusoe* (1719), Crusoe believes that the cannibal Friday possesses the same powers, the same reason and feelings as Europeans (212). Working from a rubric in which Europeans, as Christians, received God's light and in which cannibals, as pagans, were denied access to divine revelation, Crusoe settles on the Caribbees as sinners. Equiano's narrative bears traces both of the general importance of Christianity to defining Britishness and of the specific significance of the Protestant "evangelical" revival in Great Britain of the 1770s. To be sure, religious conversion and acculturation into civil society remain vital to acceptability, either fictional or actual. As the other chapters show, Britons maintained an optimistic sense of the efficacy of Christianity, education, and commerce in redressing unpolished manners or erasing the importance of dark skin color, which is evidenced by their embracing select Others as various subordinate, but fellow, subjects of the British Empire: as servants, trading partners, soldiers, and wives in literature and in historical fact. The midcentury, however, marks a new prominence in regard to complexion, though it was often an unsubstantiated and underexplained phenomenon. By the 1770s and 1780s, skin color assumed an importance in several cultural realms and began to appear consistently connected to claims about who Britons were, as well as who Others were.

Equiano's slave narrative helps us see that theories of race and practices of colonialism emerged together in the eighteenth century, though not in a one-to-one correspondence nor at the same pace, and both were overdetermined by international as well as domestic ideological and material pressures. For instance, the abolition of the slave trade in 1807 and the emancipation of slaves in 1832 illustrate the relatively autonomous operation of race and racism in relation to slavery, even in the nineteenth century. Nevertheless, these politico-economic events concerning slaves roughly coincided with other forms of colonial oppression, such as the escalation of political rule in India and the intensification of British cultural dominance there, as well as the colonization of Australia and New Zealand. Racial ideology and British imperial expansion proved highly compatible. Because it was more coherently rendered in scientific discourse, race was often marshaled as a successful political justification of empire formation. This occurred in contemporary newspapers, magazines, and fiction, as well as in economic and legislative policy. Although it is tempting to attribute the development of racial meanings primarily to scientific preoccupation with the classification of human variety or to British colonization, to do so would belie the historical changes that suggest a more complicated relationship among racial ideology, science, colonialism, and the literature that represented them.

Epilogue

Theorizing Race and Racism in the Eighteenth Century

There can be no timeless and absolute standard for what constitutes racism, for social structures change and discourses are subject to rearticulation.

—MICHAEL OMI and HOWARD WINANT
Racial Formation in the United States (1994)

"Race" is, in fact, a rather recent phenomenon; the hierarchical ranking of "peoples" is a much older measuring instrument in the western lexicon of supremacism. . . . It is not the case that an innocent racialness was corrupted by a later ranking of races, but rather that race and racism are fundamentally interwoven.

—RUTH FRANKENBERG, *Displacing Whiteness* (1997)[1]

IN eighteenth-century Britain, the ideology of human variety broadly changed from being articulated primarily through religious difference, which included such things as political governance and civil life, to being articulated primarily through scientific categories derived from natural history that featured external characteristics of the human body—color, facial features, and hair texture. At the end of the century, the contours of racial ideology were more established than a century before, a solidification that accompanied the more important role of race and racism in the intellectual pursuits and structures of everyday life in Britain. The transference from a cultural emphasis to a bodily emphasis was imperfect, of course, and occurred at various paces in different realms that used racial ideology as a reference point.

Cultural and physical ways of racializing people could work separately, but mostly they appeared in conjunction. Early in the century, race was not always visible in ways that we recognize immediately today; it was, however, visible to early modern and eighteenth-century Europeans in the clothing, habitations, and trading behavior of other people. By the end of the century, race was newly important at the level of the body and supported by a respectable scientific and historical artillery, even though there was still disagreement about who was a European or the criteria on which to base racial groupings.

In Britain, references to skin color and its life in racial taxonomy, travel literature, and common parlance often envisioned a world of people with similar capabilities, which were, in many cases, unrealized, but who looked and acted quite differently from Europeans. As Oliver Goldsmith put it, demonstrating ethnocentric optimism at its best, "All those changes which the African, the Asiatic, or the American undergo, are but accidental deformities, which a kinder climate, better nourishment, or more civilized manners, would, in a course of centuries, very probably remove."[2] The terms of race were quite flexible in their oppression or elevation of certain groups: sweepingly general or minutely specific—empirical, aesthetic, or theoretical. Race, though variously articulated through the coordinates of civility and theories of the body, is best understood as a hybrid political, economic, religious, and social construction that, from the 1770s onward, also had a healthy life in the emerging disciplines of moral philosophy, natural history, and comparative anatomy.

Eighteenth-century writers placed great faith in cultural "makeovers" for Others within Britain's borders and beyond. Christian conversion, European clothing, increased trade activity, and desire for ornamental commodities were all components of this process. In representing Britain's Others, all of the authors of the narratives analyzed in this book, despite their considerable differences in rank and politics, typically reveal a desire to remake other people in the image of the English, whether these Others are Catholic and French, Islamic and North African, Native American, or West African. This narrative desire is mainly refracted through non-British characters who freely choose to imitate the British by adopting their manners and dress because of the greater rational appeal of them. Foreigners' recognition of English superiority always garners the intense admiration of Britons, as reports on visitors to Great Britain throughout the century reveal. This narrative desire for peaceful acceptance of English superiority relies on the assumption of a shared human nature and the potential to change. The British ideology of race, however, was motivated by a commitment not to equality but to similarity. In fact, racial ideology relied on ingrained belief in the desirability of subordination, most familiar to Britons through their hierarchy of ranks within the nation as well as their translation to conditions abroad. Racial ideology, like commerce, imagined a world of mutual interdependence and gradual change wrought by foreign emulation of Europeans. One of the best places to discover an anatomy of Britishness was the novel.

Throughout the century, the novel, natural history, and four-stages theory shared the assumption of a changeable but universal human nature. The novel's adherence to a common humanity and a sensible body well into the nineteenth century meant that it maintained older ways of articulating human nature longer than scientific and philosophical discourse, both of which were more driven by the identification of salient differences among people. The novel is one of the many examples of the uneven development of racial ideology within eighteenth-century British society. In fact, the novel was a significant forum for racializing Britons indirectly. By praising commerce, by approving the role of the gentry's younger sons in fashioning an empire, by delineating the benevolent Englishman's rational treatment of women, by encouraging Britons to practice greater self-discipline, and by enjoining them to embrace benign subordination in marriage, the novel offered important domestic focal points for Britons' understanding the innerworkings of a polite and commercial people. This knowledge pertained to the abstract level of society and to the level of individual desire and comportment. The British novel did not delineate whiteness as much as it did the cultural coordinates and desires in which whiteness eventually became a sign of the overdetermined nexus of traits and attitudes connected to civil society.

The novelistic exploration of English domestic virtues, especially polite manners and gendered sensibility, obfuscate, by omission or revision, their colonial corollary—the violence associated with trade and forging an empire. At first glance, gentle manners and sentiment seem antithetical to securing an empire, yet their ideological companion is benevolent governance at home

and abroad and proper subordination between the sexes and "races." To bor-
row Teresa de Lauretis's and Foucault's terminology, the eighteenth-century
novel was a technology of gendered and classed Britishness that worked at
the level of the nation and in the service of a more global racialization. By
demonstrating the importance of rational education and by inculcating exaggerated gender difference, the novel sustained an ideology of identity similar to prevailing racial ideology, but conveyed the impression that these were
peculiarly British traits.

*   *   *

Arguably, race became more racist in the service of an increasingly "objective" view of the world's inhabitants during the nineteenth century. A
brief look at British scientific engagement with racial ideology after 1789
indicates the development of new assumptions about human variety in the
next century. Alterations in one scholar's texts over time show how Britons'
understanding of themselves and others as racial subjects changed. A Christian, physician, and opponent of slavery, James Cowles Prichard's career
spans the first forty years of the century and registers important shifts in the
disciplinary approach to race. Analyzing Prichard's use of the same anecdote
in 1813 and in 1842 marks a significant alteration in views of race from one
of resemblance among human groups to one of essential differences.

   Researches into the Physical History of Man (1813) begins with a fictional situation in which readers are asked to imagine an illiterate Briton,
"bred in some remote corner of England, who had never seen or heard of
any human creatures different from the natives of his own vicinity." This
man is transported to three other continents—to "a horde of the naked and
dusky barbarians who wander on the shores of the Missisippi [*sic*]," then to
a tribe of "yellow and bald-headed Mongoles," and finally to a Negro ham-
let. This Briton, drawing on his background, would "immediately recognise
the beings whom he saw as men, for the expression of rational intellect; the
likeness of the creator which was imprinted on the first of the human kind,
is every where instantly striking and conspicuous."[3] Despite the illiterate
Briton's understandable "emotions of wonder and surprise," he would "not
fail to consider them as fellow creatures." In seeing these other inhabitants
of the earth, Prichard warns, the provincial Briton would observe some differences in the voice, gestures, manners of life, and the unspecified "peculiarities of natural structure" in their bodies (2).

   Thirty years later, Prichard reworks the same anecdote in order to make
an entirely different point about the races of man. The spectator sees fairly

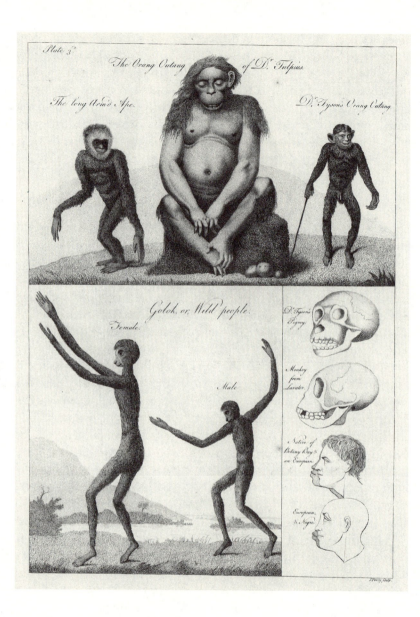

Plate 3.

The Orang Outang of Dr. Tulpius.

The long Arm'd Ape.

Dr. Tysons Orang Outang.

Golok, or, Wild people.

Female.

Male.

Dr Tysons Pigmy.

Monkey from Lavater.

Native of Botany Bay & an European.

European & Negro.

J. Perry Sculp.

similar sights in 1813 and in 1842, but the intervening decades lead his imaginary spectator to opposite conclusions. *The Natural History of Man* (1842) uses many of the plot elements cited above, but the spectator is no longer an illiterate Briton (although he has a European sensibility, of course) but a putatively more objective viewer. Prichard asks his readers to imagine a stranger from another planet who compares the manners of the globe's inhabitants, who now include the Pacific Islanders. This alien first witnesses some "brilliant spectacle in one of the highly civilised countries of Europe," such as the coronation of a monarch; then he views Negroes enjoying themselves with "dancing and barbarous music"; next he is thrust in the midst of "bald and tawny Mongoles" in a desolate landscape. Then the extraterrestrial being is transported to "the solitary den of the Bushman, where the lean and hungry savage crouches in silence like a beast of prey." Finally, the traveler is plunked in the midst of an Australian forest, "where the squalid companions of kangaroos may be seen crawling in procession in imitation of quadrupeds." After painting this human panorama, Prichard then demands, "Can it be supposed that such a person would conclude the various groupes [*sic*] of beings whom he had surveyed to be of one nature, or tribe, or the offspring of the same original stock? It is much more probable that he would arrive at an opposite conclusion."[4] Although Prichard tries to unearth a universal humanity, the way that he goes about it results in our conviction of the great differences among men. Following his stark contrast between civil Europeans and all others, it comes as some surprise that Prichard finds something that all these people share, which reflects their common nature: their rituals of the dead, religious ceremonies, and temples unite civilized and bar-

Figure 19. Humanized Apes and Comparative Racial Profiles. Charles White, *An Account of Regular Gradation in Man* (London, 1799). Because he believes that there are significant and fixed differences among Europeans, Asiatics, Americans, and Africans, White critiques the dominant racial theory of the century. He contends that gradation among several races was a better principle than variety in one race. In his usage, gradation means that there are people with more humanity than others, a minority belief at the time. In the upper half of the plate, the feminine and masculine apes hint at the continuity between humans and animals. The wild people in the lower left portion of the plate are placed in a natural setting, like Africans, Laplanders, and Americans usually were in contemporary iconography. The male and female wild people are indistinguishable, suggesting the significance of exaggerated gender difference to human identity for Europeans. In the lower right portion of the plate is the skull of a pygmy and monkey. Their juxtaposition to comparative profiles of Europeans, native Australians, and Negroes suggests the continuity between animal skulls and non-Europeans. Courtesy of the John Carter Brown Library at Brown University.

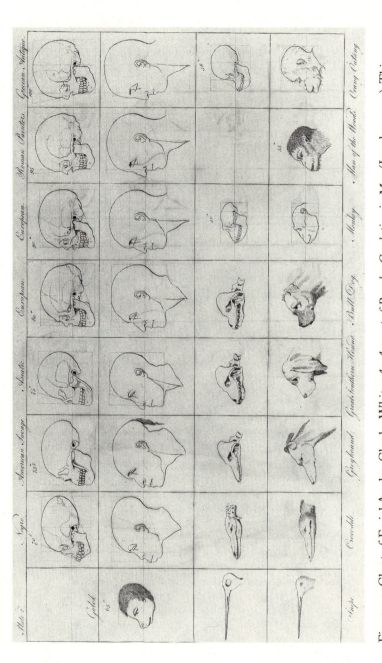

Figure 20. Chart of Facial Angles. Charles White, *An Account of Regular Gradation in Man* (London, 1799). This comparison of facial angles in humans and animals registers over a decade's time lag between Dutch, German, and French comparative anatomists and their British counterparts. White's organizing principle is to show the human groups that most resemble animals in their facial angles: at 58 degrees, the orangutan possesses the facial angle closest to the Negro at 70 degrees. The more perpendicular the forehead, nose, and lips, the closer to the ideal of Greek and Roman statuary. This chart also demonstrates the way that skin color and geography were being superseded by skull shape and facial angle as the best way to organize human groups. Notably, the hierarchy derived from skin color remains unchanged but is now founded on putatively more scientific principles because less easily changed by climate. James Cowles Prichard remarked the general contradiction in 1842 that skulls were the most striking locus of racial difference, yet no two writers could agree on how to arrange them. Courtesy of the John Carter Brown Library at Brown University.

barous nations. It is in this key but very slender circumstance that he contends, against many of his contemporaries, that "all mankind sympathize in deeply impressed feelings and sentiments, which are as mysterious in their nature as in their origin" (492).

Unlike in the 1813 version, Prichard uses the organizing trope of mental endowment in the 1840s text to delineate variation among the world's inhabitants, not physical difference. The commentary on mental capabilities is, notably, articulated through the manners and social organization of various racial types, not through direct claims about their skull size or rational capacity. That is, cultural factors now reflect rational capacity in a fairly stable manner, one which presumes that there is variety in abilities as there is in bodies. Nevertheless, Prichard reasons that if he can establish that humans share a common psychical nature, then, by analogy, he could prove that they are of the same species and origin. He notes that most Europeans would not now assent to the view of a shared origin and common human nature: "For what greater contrasts can be imagined than those which present themselves when we compare in their actual state the different races of mankind?" (487).

What happened to account for such a fundamental change in thirty years? In 1813, Prichard remarks rather derisively that contemporary philosophers had learnt to attribute all discrepancies in the language and manners of the world's inhabitants to accident and education, and to consider the moral diversities of nations as proceeding from external and adventitious circumstances rather than from innate causes (2). Prichard insinuates that the commonplaces arising from blind faith in climate—of the belief in changeability characteristic of the eighteenth century—are outdated and naive in 1813. Furthering the implications of Samuel Stanhope Smith's *Essay on the Causes of the Variety of Complexion and Figure in the Human Species* (1787), which claims that a savage state modifies the human countenance and renders it ugly, Prichard contends that civilization itself is as capable as climate of producing varieties of men (210). He attributes a major role to heredity as a factor that along with climate transmits color—much like Sir Thomas Browne and Sir Robert Boyle in the mid-seventeenth century did. He notes that the variety of color in the races of men "seems to form more general as well as more permanent discrimination than the peculiarities of figure" (17). Skin color, however, had already lost some of its scientific edge to skull shape by 1813. Scientists worried that color was too superficial and changeable—in short, that it wasn't a reliable way to demarcate human differences. Blumenbach, Cuvier, and Camper rapidly convinced other European men of science that anatomy was the best way to establish objective differences among human races (46). The skull, they believed, was supremely suited to signify difference, because the brain and the privileged organs of sense were lodged in it. For instance, the Caucasian's large and shapely skull encouraged many scientists to equate quantity and quality. The myriad forces encouraging the selection of the mind as the privileged organ of sense range from Christian tradition, humanism, Lockean psychology, and the Enlightenment value placed on reason to the belief in moral choices being able to ameliorate the effects of climate.

In 1813, Prichard focuses on physical variations among human groups. In the kind of inversion in climate theory that generally took place during the nineteenth century, Prichard claims that each race's body fits people for their environment. Eighteenth-century racial ideology assumed, in contrast, that the climate and general environment shaped bodies and influenced disposition. In *Researches into the Physical History of Man*, Prichard also argues that the constitutional makeup and physical makeup differ among races: "The Negro is particularly adapted to the wild or natural state of life. His dense and firm fibre renders him much more able to endure fatigue, and the inclemencies of the seasons, than the European with his lax fibre, and delicate constitution. . . . The senses are more perfect in Negroes than in Europeans. . . . This perfection of the ruder faculties of sense is not required in the civilized state, and it therefore gives way to a more capacious form of the skull, affording space for a more ample conformation of the brain, on which an increase of intellectual power is probably dependent" (236). Prichard details the physical structure of the skin, muscle, skull, and their related social functions; his value-laden description reveals not only labor and intellectual capability but also civilizational proclivities. Belief in different kinds of bodies makes it easier to maintain that race is rigidly defined, permanent in its implications, and thus deterministic in nature.

By the 1840s, Prichard is perceived as conservative in race matters. Despite his earlier interest in physical variations among men, he abandons his doubts about climate's effect on bodies and his flirtation with polygenesis. He changes his thinking from equivocating in regard to humans possibly originating separately in 1813 to a firm monogenicist in 1842, despite the large differences that he believes separate human groups. As Nancy Stepan has claimed, "Until Prichard's death in 1848, British racial science was 'Prichardian.' Moreover, it was by the 1840s also 'environmentalist' largely because of Prichard's influential decision to abandon hereditarian notions of racial types and return to climatological ones."[5] Even though Prichard returns to a climate-based racial thinking by the 1840s, racial ideology is bound up in the firm conviction of the essential differences dividing the races; this articulation means that his methodology and assumptions are sometimes at odds.

The Natural History of Man (1842) offers a cautious version of the way that each race has distinct physical characteristics as well as moral and intellectual abilities. Prichard contends that racial groups are best divided according to language groups; the Indo-European, for instance, includes a range of civil and barbaric people.

Offering a sense of dominant racial ideology in midcentury science, Prichard comments on his contemporaries who discerned unbridgeable differences in the races of men, differences that manifested themselves most markedly in the various mental endowments of the races. According to Prichard, his colleagues discovered each race's rational ability in their stature, the size and proportions of their limbs, and the length of their bones (128). In fact, his contemporaries often argued that Negroes, Hottentots, Eskimos, and Australians were organically different and could never be equal to Europeans. Their destiny was either servitude or extinction (6). By this time, most scientists accepted the racial typology evident in the nomenclature promoted by Blumenbach at the very end of the eighteenth century; for example, Ethiopian or Negro, Mongolian, and Caucasian were racial types that show a detachment from geopolitical conceptions of the eighteenth century and a preference for more generic phenotyping.

Prichard's fellow Scot and less illustrious contemporary Alexander Kinmont likely heard the same lectures in moral philosophy at University of Edinburgh that Prichard did, but he drew conclusions from his instruction that departed from Prichard's conviction of a shared human nature and origin. Kinmont spent the last fifteen years of his life teaching in the United States, and he gave a series of lectures on "The Natural History of Man" in Cincinnati. Kinmont's vocabulary links him to the strain of racial ideology that Prichard worked so hard to combat but of which he offered a more benign version. Kinmont's major premise is that each branch of the human family has distinct features, temperaments, genius, and therefore different destinies that connect people to their place of origin. Indeed, he speaks of mental complexions native to each people; these are natural characteristics, by which Kinmont means fixed and designed consistently with each race's nature.[6] The key difference from Prichard is that Kinmont does not believe in the common descent of humans but in multiple creations. For instance, the African's civilization is best suited to him, and it is "a sad error," he contends, to remove Africans from their native regions, because it impedes Africans from attaining their destiny, which, he speculated, would be in the field of theology or some other creative venture (191). Kinmont believes that the human race is one based on a shared human form, but man is composed *ab origine* of several distinct members, some of which show great distinction from each other, like the Caucasians and Negroes, and others which display less distinction from one another. Each race can perfect itself, but only in their own special way: "The Caucasian becomes a noble Caucasian, the Negro a noble Negro, the one the brilliant form of versatile genius, the other the very type itself of affection and of gentleness" (199). In this way, each race can improve, but races need not be considered similar or even as sharing the same qualities in greater or lesser amounts.[7]

Genius and rational thinking, products of a temperate, civilized European environment, become definitively Caucasian traits by the late 1830s. Kinmont, for one, observes that an individual's physical and mental condition results from "all those influences which have acted upon him up to that period." He is not describing what we would call social construction because of the role he ascribes to the European mind. Following contemporary German philosophy and English Romantic ideology, Kinmont sees the environmental influence overpowered in the European man by "the *controlling* power of his will and understanding [which] is always the most important of these influences, and this accordingly modifies and so affects the whole as to give a unity and individuality, certain and indestructible, to that being which he calls himself" (326). The concept of the controlling power of the will is the defining condition of European man, who is the greatest individual because he is the least subject to natural forces. This shift in conceiving of humans, not as products of their environment but as controllers of it, seems to be the "birth" of a distinctly modern notion of stable individuality that many postmodern theorists have mistakenly believed was the *cogito* of René Descartes. It is notable that this model of subjectivity is more explicitly inflected by assumptions of natural and even bone deep racial, class, and gender hierarchies than Descartes'.

Kinmont's ideas show an inversion of eighteenth-century logic: greatness is born in a people and then manifested through their achievements. The major change from eighteenth-century ideology of human variety is that instead of climate, trade, or even government giving rise to progress, societal development now occurs because of racial makeup. For instance, the social institutions in Europe and America, whose object, Kinmont claims, is to secure the greatest good for the greatest number, arises, he contends, from "that hereditary love of freedom and independence, which has distinguished the Anglo-Saxon race,—that *natural* stock of just and manly sentiment, on which the Christian religion has been engrafted, and expanded into a truly rational and moral civilization" (242). He posits, "All improvements in nations, as well as individuals, must spring up naturally, and as it were imperceptibly, from their own peculiar genius and temperament" (264). The manly Caucasians, for example, have a natural instinct to emigrate as much as the Negroes have to stay put (276, 190). In this paradigm, the British

Empire is not motivated by political, economic, or even religious factors, but by racial ones. Thus, national characteristics that had been considered *effects* of climate or of differing stages of civilization during the eighteenth century became *causes* of European superiority and of other races' inferiority by the mid-nineteenth century. For example, commercial acumen, polished manners, or physical beauty, formerly believed to result from the mode of subsistence or geographic chance, could now be independent justifications for European domination of all other people.

The assumptions about human difference and subject formation apparent in much recent race theory frequently call on racial ideology and racism that became dominant only in the nineteenth century, as Prichard's and Kinmont's texts demonstrate. If not adjusted to precise historical conditions and ideology, racial constructions seem monolithic and unchanging. Our contemporary sense of race is heavily filtered through recent assumptions that obfuscate an earlier moment in which biological racism, the white man's moral mission to convert and civilize "heathens," and Europeans' racial destiny as rulers of the world were not inevitable.

Of course, even before there was scientific commentary available, racial factors had been cover stories for territorial expansion, but the assumptions that ground these representations differ from one historical period to the next. For instance, as Theodore Allen, Nicholas Canny, and James Muldoon have shown, fourteenth-century through sixteenth-century legal and ideological renderings of the Irish refer to their savage way of living, their wild appearance, and lack of proper language, religion, and civil institutions as problems English intervention would rectify. English writers' concern about their countrymen in early modern Ireland was more about their remaining civilized than about civilizing the Irish. This same frame of reference, with some adaptations, informed many early English practices and perceptions of Native Americans, Australian Aborigines, and West Africans until the nineteenth century. In fact, the Society for the Propagation of Christian Knowledge in Foreign Parts, a weak entity in the eighteenth century, was overwhelmed by trying to maintain religion and civil society among settlers. Its primary mission was safeguarding Christianity among the maverick Britons in the colonies. The anxiety about English identity signals early modern fears of its instability.

* * *

The transition to an innate and deterministic notion of race accomplished in the nineteenth century raises the question of defining racism. There have been two main trends in regard to theorizing and historicizing racism. On the one hand, some scholars have argued that there was a proto-discourse of race in Britain. Even so, there was no racism in the modern sense, because there was no notion of biology, genetic heredity, or even of fairly rigid interpretations of race. This perspective is persuasive to the extent that it acknowledges historical change, but it defines racism as a purely nineteenth-century phenomenon—as an essentially phenotyping impulse that made race a deterministic construction. Thus, this position considers race more narrowly than is historically appropriate. On the other hand, other historians have argued that there was racism in England from at least the sixteenth century onward. This position incorrectly makes antiblack racism a constant feature of white people's psyche and of the structures of their political and civil institutions. This view also rests on the assumption that race and racism penetrated social, political, and economic thought at the same pace and in the same way. This position is persuasive if race and racism are defined as one and the same and if they are perceived as virtually unchanged in content or context in Britain and the colonies over the past three centuries. This perspective is persuasive only if one ignores the significance of varying assumptions about human nature and the potential for change in different historical periods.

In Britain, Stuart Hall, Catherine Hall, and Paul Gilroy have spearheaded the effort to treat racism as a variable social formation over time; in the United States, Michael Omi and Howard Winant have urged the same position, arguing that "there can be no timeless and absolute standard for what constitutes racism, for social structures change and discourses are subject to rearticulation" (71). Redefining racism is one way to maintain a sense of the eighteenth-century articulation of human variety and to acknowledge that some individual beliefs, intellectual discourses, and societal practices in Britain, the colonies, and commercial networks exceeded the bounds signaled in the concept of ethnocentrism. By treating racism in eighteenth-century terms, it becomes a useful category of analysis. Intellectually and politically, it is imperative to define eighteenth-century race and racism in ways that are not based in biology or determinism. Distinguishing more carefully among historical constellations of race, racism, and ethnocentrism is key to analyzing the past.

This task is made difficult, however, by the fact that xenophobia, patriotism, and national identity blended in with racial ideology in the eighteenth century. A large proportion of English subjects seemed to find most other people, both inside and outside their borders, contemptuous. This suspicion arose mainly from political and religious matters, and it could assume physical or cultural terms. Even those who resembled the English the most closely, such as the French or Irish, were targets of verbal and even physical abuse in the streets of eighteenth-century Britain. Non-English individuals, especially from the upper ranks, might prove themselves exceptions to traditional prejudices of national character, religion, and climate, but Britons' starting point was often fear of the influence of foreigners and distaste for manual labor, scantily clad bodies, and subordinates of all kinds. Although sympathy, for instance, became important in the midcentury as an ideology operative within the domestic borders of Great Britain, particularly its urban areas, it was not always achieved over economic and political interests. Rather, sentiment mediated and palliated these interests, making them more acceptable because overlaid with admirable motives.

The primary form that eighteenth-century racism took was the conviction that people in remote parts of Europe and Asia, most of Africa, all of America, and the Pacific were inferior because they had not become commercial people as quickly or as easily as Europeans. This failure arose from various causes in Britons' minds, namely, the debilitating effects of extremely hot or cold climates, lack of sociability with other nations, and improper regulation of all kinds of desires. These people had not attained the diversity of ranks, pursuits, and monuments to their past that Europeans and a few others had; they certainly had not contributed, in European terms, to a store of knowledge or to improving their general conditions of living. According to convention, it might take centuries for changes to register.

A secondary form that racism took was related to the cultural and political conditions that I have just outlined; it was a physical typology for the various inhabitants of the center, margins, and hinterlands of civil society. Physical typology was not in and of itself necessarily racist, but linking physical variation to mental or moral difference was. Incipient forms of the racial bodies developed over the eighteenth century are, of course, detectable in the Middle Ages and were solidified in sixteenth-century Europe. The typology of most non-Europeans, commonly found in British literature, was largely unflattering and displays a heavily ethnocentric bias that is indistinguishable, in some cases, from racist ideology. Racism was not confined to Britons' beliefs or their actions toward black Africans, but it occasionally assumed a particular constellation in regard to Negroes. For instance, in the period after 1760, white Europeans and black Africans were increasingly polarized for a variety of old and new reasons. In scientific and philosophical discourse, the intensified comparison mostly arose from the fact that the two populations came from radically different climates, a geographic sensibility that had long been informed by humoral theory and classical Greek and Roman treatments of space. It is also the case that scientists and philosophers believed that, through contrast, European and Negro features displayed the most significant differences among humans. Believing that differences were more than skin deep, some Europeans suggested that the societies they had created made contrast inevitable. These explanations were bolstered by the practice of Britons enslaving Negroes and perceiving them as debased because of it. Even though physical typology was coherently rendered and the center of the new science, it, like cultural factors, was believed to arise from climate and other external and changeable forces.

If racism is to be useful to the analysis of eighteenth-century texts and social formations, its myriad forms and difference from the present need to be underscored. For instance, Henry Louis Gates, Jr., contends that the 1980s resembled the eighteenth century in terms of racial discourse.[8] In analyzing eighteenth-century British ideologies of race and racism, however, it is imperative to note that while the categories that we use today to constitute race are similar to those in the eighteenth century—skin color, family and governmental arrangements, the status of women, and the like—the assumptions and the history governing them are, in most respects, different.

Concluding with racism is one way to reflect on the theoretical and historical challenges raised by my study of racial ideology. The seduction of research that reads present political, economic, and racial inequities back on to an earlier period has been difficult to resist, not least because it is generally the most obviously motivated by politically progressive and antiracist commitments; unfortunately, it is also historically misleading. If racial essentialism and its recent history foster a conception of racism that is imperative to combat, it has also spawned resistance—intellectual and activist, known as identity politics. The two tendencies arise from a similar impulse and share certain assumptions about race and racism. It is for this reason, no doubt, that most current scholarship focuses on racist aspects of eighteenth-century literature: It is politically safer and strongly reflects current desires to combat racism through academic study. Challenging racism at this level, however, is not best served by the discovery of an unchanging construction of race. Rather, it is by understanding that race and racism have varied in different times and places that we can more critically assess the present.

Notes

Introduction

1. Robert Boyle, "The Experimental History of Colours Begun," part 2 in *The Works of the Honourable Robert Boyle*, vol. 1 (1664; London: J. and F. Rivington, 1772), 36; Johann Friedrich Blumenbach, *On the Natural Variety of Mankind*, in *The Anthropological Treatises of Johann Friedrich Blumenbach*, trans. and ed. Thomas Bendyshe (1775; London: Longman, 1865), 113. A decade after Boyle's treatise on color, Matthew Hale describes human beauty similarly in *The Primitive Origination of Mankind, Considered and Examined According to the Light of Nature* (London: William Godbid, 1677), but he gives more weight to skin color: It consists equally in figure, symmetry of parts, and color (64). The lighter the color, the more beautiful to Hale: "In the torrid Climates the common colour is black or swarthy, yet the natural colour of the temperate Climates is more transparent and beautiful" (65). Such an understanding of white complexion as beautiful is certainly commonplace but not universal. In delineating key points characteristic of human groups, Hale observes that each nation "hath a certain humour or disposition appropriate to it," which manifests itself in their speech, accent, and pronunciation (164). On the whole, however, he is more diverted by the variations he finds in "improving knowledge and discovery of things," which, he understands, results from sloth, evil custom, barbarousness, or lack of education. These deficiencies in arts and invention are noticeable in parts of Europe, Africa, and Ireland (159). By the eighteenth century, the deficiencies are mainly located in Africa, America, and, to a lesser extent, in Asia.

2. As many other scholars have noted, choice of terminology is a difficult decision. My study of skin color as a component of what we now call race is premised on the fact that race does not reflect an essential condition but is, instead, a historically changing cultural, economic, and political construction in all parts of the globe. Although the use of *race* makes sense to us now as a term that designates fairly rigid distinctions in appearance and even behavior, it did not have the same currency in the eighteenth century. Wherever possible, I've chosen the term *human variety* or *human difference* to underscore eighteenth-century sensibility, which did not always register the sense of difference that the term *race* does today. I have chosen the term *racial* to indicate the main effect of ideology and to distinguish effects that were highly ethnocentric but that weren't necessarily racist. The term *racial* records

the tension between ethnocentric assumptions and racist ones. As I address in the epilogue, racism in the eighteenth century was not based in essentialism.

3. The use of *complexion* in the title to this book incorporates its two main eighteenth-century definitions: "The inclosure or involution of one thing in another," referring to the way that complexion and civility could inhere in each other, and to skin color, or "The colour of the external parts of the body." Samuel Johnson's *Dictionary of the English Language* (London: W. Strahan, 1755) offers three definitions for complexion, the two I cite and a third, which I discuss at length later in the introduction: "The temperature of the body according to the various proportions of the four medical humours." The fact that Johnson includes the adjectival and adverbial forms of "complexion" suggests its common usage.

4. Physicians and philosophers were not sure whether skin color arose from the combined action of the humors and the heat of the sun, whether it was all due to the workings of climate and other external factors, or whether skin color was lodged in a layer of the skin and transmitted by sperm. A few writers believed that black color might originate differently from other colors. Sir Thomas Browne, François Bernier, and Buffon all subscribed to some combination of climate and the intermixture of groups to account for skin color. John Mitchell, Claude Nicolas Le Cat, and Edward Long believed skin color was transmitted by a layer of the skin membrane. Linnaeus, Blumenbach, and Oliver Goldsmith subscribed to climate's formation and transmission of color.

5. Joseph Addison and Richard Steele, *The Spectator*, 5 vols., ed. Donald F. Bond (Oxford: Clarendon Press, 1965), 2:518.

6. Situations such as the one described in Bartholomew Stibbs, *Journal of a Voyage up the Gambia* (1723; London: Edward Cave, 1738) are not isolated incidents. In William Chetwood's *Captain Richard Falconer*, 2 vols. (London: W. Chetwood, 1720), the eponymous hero meets Plymouth, who, he says, identifies himself as an Englishman because he was brought over from Guinea when he was very young (2:18).

7. Georges Louis Leclerc, comte de Buffon, *Natural History: General and Particular*, trans. William Smellie, 35 vols. (1749; London: T. Cadell and W. Davies, 1812), 3:400.

8. Nancy Koehn, *The Power of Commerce: Economy and Governance in the First British Empire* (Ithaca: Cornell University Press), 25.

9. [Oliver Goldsmith?], *The Royal Magazine; or, Gentleman's Monthly Companion* 3 (July–Dec. 1760): 139.

10. See Margo Hendricks and Patricia Parker, eds., *Women, "Race," and Writing* (New York: Routledge, 1994), and Kim Hall, *Things of Darkness: Economies of Race and Gender in Early Modern England* (Ithaca: Cornell University Press, 1995). Dympna Callaghan's "Re-reading *The Tragedie of Mariam, Faire Queene of Jewry*" in *Women, "Race," and Writing* is a particularly important analysis focusing on the ways in which race in the early modern period always encompasses multiple categories of difference in historically specific ways. The essay also distinguishes the specifically different conceptions of race during the English Renaissance from today.

11. A notable recent exception is Felicity A. Nussbaum, *Torrid Zones: Maternity, Sexuality, and Empire in Eighteenth-Century English Narratives* (Baltimore: Johns Hopkins University Press, 1995). Nonliterary studies that treat race as a variable concept and that incorporate non-Africans include Nicholas Hudson, "From Nation to 'Race': The Origin of Racial Classification in Eighteenth-Century Thought," *Eighteenth-Century Studies* 29.3 (1996): 247–64, P. J. Marshall and Glyndwr Williams, *The Great Map of Mankind: Perceptions of New Worlds in the Age of Enlightenment* (Cambridge: Harvard University Press, 1982), Winthrop Jordan, *White over Black: American Attitudes Toward the Negro, 1550–1812* (1968; New York: W. W. Norton, 1977), and Ivan Hannaford, *Race: The History of an Idea in the West* (Baltimore: Johns Hopkins University Press, 1996).

12. The eighteenth century is usually glossed over in other studies of race, which tend to be more interested in the nineteenth and twentieth centuries, as in Stephen Haseler, *The English Tribe: Identity, Nation and Europe* (London: Macmillan Press, 1996), or in the seventeenth and earlier centuries, as in Kim Hall, *Things of Darkness*. Richard Dyer's *White* (London: Routledge, 1997) and David Theo Goldberg's *Racist Culture: Philosophy and the Politics of Meaning* (Oxford: Basil Blackwell, 1993) incorrectly read the nineteenth century back onto the previous century. "Constructing Race," ed. Michael McGiffert, *William and Mary Quarterly* 54.1 (January 1997) focuses on representations of human differences in the sixteenth and seventeenth centuries. My findings differ from all of these texts in arguing for the imprecise articulation of human variety and for the strength of residual racial ideology in the eighteenth century.

13. See Laura Brown, *Ends of Empire: Women and Ideology in Early Eighteenth-Century English Literature* (Ithaca: Cornell University Press, 1993).

14. The exclusive connection between race and black skin has been the topic explored in most eighteenth-century studies. The landmark volume on race is *Racism in the Eighteenth Century*, ed. Harold E. Paglioaro, vol. 3 of *Studies in Eighteenth-Century Culture* (Cleveland: Press of Case Western Reserve University, 1973). The essays prompted discussions we are still pursuing, but the volume does not analyze imaginative literature, and it emphasizes the minor and more overtly racist traditions of preformation, polygenesis, and the chain of being; its source materials for antiblack racism are mostly from non-British European countries. Nevertheless, some signs of change in the disciplinary conception of race are noticeable. Two recent special volumes of *Eighteenth-Century Studies* indicate the potential for a new direction. Felicity A. Nussbaum edited "The Politics of Difference," *Eighteenth-Century Studies* 23.4 (Summer 1990), the express purpose of which was to examine interconnections among gender, race, and class in eighteenth-century culture and narratives (377–78)—an area untouched in the 1973 *Studies in Eighteenth-Century Culture*. Rose Zimbardo's introduction to "African-American Culture in the Eighteenth Century," *Eighteenth-Century Studies* 27.4 (1994) declared the fictionality of race, despite its real effects (527).

15. Studies of what has been called "minor" eighteenth-century literature have featured analyses of savagery, abolitionist fiction, the representation of the American

Indian, and fiction about the East and West Indies, but these have not been central resources for the study of eighteenth-century narrative: Wylie Sypher, *Guinea's Captive Kings: British Anti-Slavery Literature of the Eighteenth Century* (1942; New York: Octagon Books, 1969), Benjamin Bissell, *The American Indian in English Literature of the Eighteenth Century* (New Haven: Yale University Press, 1925), Robert Heilman, *America in English Fiction, 1760–1800: The Influence of the American Revolution* (1937; New York: Octagon Books, 1968), and Maximillian Novak, *Defoe and the Nature of Man* (Oxford: Oxford University Press, 1963). Recent attempts to consider Britain in its imperial and colonial manifestation include Carol Barash, "The Character of Difference: The Creole Woman as Cultural Mediator in Narratives About Jamaica," *Eighteenth-Century Studies*, Special Issue: "The Politics of Difference," ed. Felicity A. Nussbaum, 23.4 (1990): 407–28, Laura Brown, *Ends of Empire*, Elizabeth Bohls, *Women Travel Writers and the Language of Aesthetics, 1716–1818* (Cambridge: Cambridge University Press, 1995), Markman Ellis, *The Politics of Sensibility: Race, Gender, and Commerce in the Sentimental Novel* (Cambridge: Cambridge University Press, 1996), Moira Ferguson, *Subject to Others: British Women Writers and Colonial Slavery, 1670–1834* (New York: Routledge, 1992), and Felicity A. Nussbaum, *Torrid Zones*. Their books constitute a landmark in eighteenth-century literary studies of gender and race. Nussbaum's *Torrid Zones*, in particular, models an analysis of the heterogeneity of colonial and imperial policy, as well as domestic subjectivity while focusing on the global coordinates of oppression, namely, the effects of capitalist expansion, patriarchy, and colonial practices.

16. Critics have analyzed the literature in terms of the emergence of Britain as a national power in Europe, the rise of the middle classes, the intensification of agrarian and market capitalism, and as a technology of gender. I refer to Ian Watt, *The Rise of the Novel* (Berkeley: University of California Press, 1957), Lennard Davis, *Factual Fictions* (New York: Columbia University Press, 1983), Michael McKeon, *The Origins of the English Novel, 1600–1740* (Baltimore: Johns Hopkins University Press, 1987), Nancy Armstrong, *Desire and Domestic Fiction: A Political History of the Novel* (Oxford: Oxford University Press, 1987), and James Thompson, *Models of Value: Eighteenth-Century Political Economy and the Novel* (Durham: Duke University Press, 1996).

17. By contact, I include commercial trading, indentured servitude and slavery, the appropriation of the land belonging to indigenous people, and the taking of natural resources, especially lumber and ore; the contact was most profitable in the East Indies, West Indies, West Africa, and North America. This terminology derives from Mary Louise Pratt, *Imperial Eyes: Travel Writing and Transculturation* (New York: Routledge, 1992), 7.

18. John Brewer, *The Sinews of Power: War, Money, and the English State, 1688–1783* (New York: Alfred A. Knopf, 1988), xvii.

19. Koehn, *The Power of Commerce*, 65.

20. Kathleen Wilson, *The Sense of the People: Politics, Culture, and Imperialism in England, 1715–1785* (Cambridge: Cambridge University Press, 1995), 138.

NOTES TO PAGES 12–19

21. Koehn, *The Power of Commerce*, 75.

22. Addison, *Spectator*, 1: 293–94.

23. Ellis, *The Politics of Sensibility*, 85.

24. Raymond Williams, *The Country and the City* (New York: Oxford University Press, 1973), 97.

25. Gerald Newman, *The Rise of English Nationalism: A Cultural History, 1740–1830* (London: Weidenfeld and Nicolson, 1987), 21.

26. Koehn, *The Power of Commerce*, 58 and chapter 2.

27. Ibid., 41, and Paul Langford, *A Polite and Commercial People: England, 1727–1783* (Oxford: Clarendon Press, 1989), chapter 9.

28. Koehn, *The Power of Commerce*, 49.

29. Ivan Hannaford's *Race: The History of an Idea in the West* (1996) is an excellent guide to the very different conceptions of race and difference in Greek and early modern times. Hannaford is especially useful on the way the term *barbarian* signifies in classical texts.

30. See Denys Hay, *Europe: The Emergence of an Idea*, rev. ed. (1957; Edinburgh: Edinburgh University Press, 1993), 108.

31. There was speculation about the color of Adam and Eve. Not all Europeans believed they were white. Some opted for olive as geographically and climatically appropriate. In the early nineteenth century, there was some suggestion that people were originally black. The conclusion was that white people had progressed farthest from those origins.

32. On the significance of Christianity to British identity, see Michael Adas, *Machines as the Measure of Man: Science, Technology, and Ideologies of Western Dominance* (Ithaca: Cornell University Press, 1989), 22.

33. Hay, *Europe*, 56.

34. Winthrop Jordan, *White over Black*, 55, 21.

35. Linda Colley, *Britons: Forging the Nation, 1707–1837* (New Haven: Yale University Press, 1992), 19, 17; Chris Haydon, *Anti-Catholicism in Eighteenth-Century England* (Manchester: Manchester University Press, 1993), 22–28.

36. Daniel Roche, *The Culture of Clothing: Dress and Fashion in the "Ancien Régime,"* trans. Jean Birrell (1989; Cambridge: Cambridge University Press, 1994), 5, 6, 455, 469, 513; Colin Campbell, *The Romantic Ethic and the Rise of Modern Consumerism* (Oxford: Basil Blackwell, 1987), 159, 160.

37. Marjorie Garber, *Vested Interests: Cross-Dressing and Cultural Anxiety* (New York: HarperPerennial, 1992) 37; Roche, *The Culture of Clothing*, 7, 14, 38.

38. Gordon Sayre, *Les Sauvages Américains: Representations of Native Americans in French and English Colonial Literature* (Chapel Hill: University of North Carolina Press, 1997), 152–3.

39. One of the many colonial aspects to dress was British ready-made wear, which was vital to clothing slaves, servants, and the military. Largely manufactured by British women who were outworkers, ready-made wear also furnished colonists in the Caribbean and America and slave traders in Africa with items of trade

to exchange with indigenous people. See Lemire, *Dress, Culture, and Commerce*, 37, 74.

40. Alan Atkinson, *The Europeans in Australia: A History* (Melbourne: Oxford University Press, 1997), 147–48.

41. George Keate, *An Account of the Pelew Islands . . .* , 3d ed. (London: G. Nicol, 1789), 44.

42. Anna Maria Falconbridge, *Narrative of Two Voyages to the River Sierra Leone During the Years 1791–1793* (1794; London: Frank Cass, 1967), 21.

43. My own conclusions about complexion during the eighteenth century were recently confirmed and furthered by a reading of Mary Floyd-Wilson's dissertation, " 'Clime, Complexion, and Degree': Racialism in Early Modern England," University of North Carolina, 1996. Her analysis of humoral theory, climate theory, and racialism prompted me to reconsider the significance of humors in the eighteenth century and their relation to racial theory. Many of the sources cited and the general discussion of humors that follows is generally indebted to her fine work.

44. Londa Schiebinger, "The Anatomy of Difference: Race and Sex in Eighteenth-Century Science," *Eighteenth-Century Studies* 23.4 (1990): 393.

45. Frederick Sargent II, *Hippocratic Heritage: A History of Ideas About Weather and Human Health* (New York: Pergamon Press, 1982), 70.

46. Nancy Siraisi, *Medieval and Early Renaissance Medicine: An Introduction to Knowledge and Power* (Chicago: University of Chicago Press, 1990), 102.

47. Gail Kern Paster, *The Body Embarrassed: Drama and the Disciplines of Shame in Early Modern England* (Ithaca: Cornell University Press, 1993), 9.

48. Throughout the eighteenth century, there were numerous narratives detailing incidents of wild children reclaimed into domestic and civil life and of non-European men educated in European manners and even in the universities. Foreign celebrities, such as Omai, Prince Lee Boo, William Amo, and numerous native American chiefs who visited Britain, were of intense interest to many. All of these experiments were tests of whether art and a new environment could mitigate the effects of climate or alter the sense impressions received through one's early formative years.

49. Mary Floyd-Wilson, " 'Clime, Complexion, and Degree,' " 135.

50. William Smellie, *The Philosophy of Natural History*, 2 vols. (Edinburgh, 1790), 2: 159, 160.

51. Sir Thomas Browne, "A Digression Concerning Blacknesse," *Pseudodoxia Epidemica; or, Enquiries into Very Many Received Tenents and Commonly Presumed Truths*, ed. Robin Robbins, 2 vols. (1646; Oxford: Clarendon Press, 1981), 1: 526. Mary Floyd-Wilson offers an interpretation of Browne that is somewhat different from my own; see " 'Clime, Comlexion, and Degree,' " 107–14.

52. Boyle, "The Experimental History of Colours Begun," 1:717.

53. Hale, *The Primitive Origination of Mankind*, 201.

54. Immanuel Kant's *Anthropology from a Pragmatic Point of View* (1798) relies on four humoral types but emphasizes that the measure of a man is detectable in his exercise of reason over these temperaments. See Hannaford, *Race*, 220.

55. James Cowles Prichard, *Researches into the Physical History of Man* (London: John and Arthur Arch, 1813), 168–71.

56. *Encyclopaedia Britannica*, 3 vols. (Edinburgh, 1771), 2: 249.

57. John Mitchell, "An Essay upon the Causes of the Different Colours of People in Different Climates," *Philosophical Transactions* 474, vol. 43 (June–Dec. 1744): 114.

58. John Harris, *Lexicon Technicum: or, An Universal English Dictionary of Arts and Sciences* (London: Daniel Brown, 1704) entry for Humours.

59. G. J. Barker-Benfield, *The Culture of Sensibility: Sex and Society in Eighteenth-Century Britain* (Chicago: University of Chicago Press, 1992), 6–9. Barker-Benfield notes that associationist nerve theory became part of the University of Edinburgh's curriculum at an early point and influenced a whole generation of thinkers from Hume to Smith.

60. Jonathan Barry, "Publicity and the Public Good: Presenting Medicine in Eighteenth-Century Bristol," in *Medical Fringe and Medical Orthodoxy 1750–1850*, ed. W. F. Bynum and Roy Porter (London: Croom Helm, 1987), 32.

61. Clarence Glacken, *Traces on the Rhodian Shore: Nature and Culture in Western Thought from Ancient Times to the End of the Eighteenth Century* (Berkeley: University of California Press, 1967), 12.

62. Michel Foucault, *The Order of Things: An Archaeology of the Human Sciences* (New York: Pantheon, 1970), 131–33, 141.

63. Sir William Petty, "The Scale of Creatures," in *The Petty Papers: Some Unpublished Writings of Sir William Petty*, ed. marquis of Lansdowne (1677; London: Constable, 1927), 2: 27, 28.

64. François Bernier initiates this tradition in his widely read essay at the end of the seventeenth century, but it does not become a dominant method until Buffon. Much of the primary information that informed popular and scientific ideas about color and human difference came from male travelers to the East and Levant and from merchants, crews, and physicians connected with the slave trade.

65. See *Philosophical Transactions* 1.3 (1667). Born from a desire "to study Nature rather than Books" in order to create a "Useful Philosophy" (141), the Royal Society of London asked seamen and travelers to keep track of a variety of statistics and phenomena. Among these data are some observations on the inhabitants: "their Stature, Shape, Colour, Features, Strength, Agility, Beauty (or the want of it), Complexions, Hair, Dyet, Inclinations, and Customs that seem not due to Education. As to their Women (besides the other things) may be observed their Fruitfulness or Barrenness; their hard or easy Labor" (188). See *Philosophical Transactions* 1.11 (April 1666).

66. Blumenbach, *On the Natural Variety of Mankind*, 209.

67. The work of Blumenbach reflects the change in terminology, and his ideas about climate closely reflect British practice. Publishing his first treatises on human variety during the 1770s, he was still writing well into the nineteenth century. His third edition of *On the Natural Variety of Mankind* (1795) refers to varieties of mankind; the second edition of *Contributions to Natural History* (1806) uses *races* instead

of *varieties*. In general, that ten-year period seems to be the watershed for ushering in the more rigid conception of race. In 1820, Blumenbach remarks in *A Manual of the Elements of Natural History*: "Races and varieties are deviations from the original specific forms of individual species of organized bodies, resulting from their gradual variation or degeneration." He then distinguishes the specific meaning of *race*: "The word race, however, is in strictness applicable only to a character produced by degeneration, and of such a nature as to become by propagation necessarily and inevitably hereditary" (15). Blumenbach's rationale and terminology are significant because he was eminent in his day and his influence lasted well beyond any of his contemporaries'. He adopted *races* very cautiously to replace *varieties*; quite rightly, he worried that it carried a more fixed connotation. Kant and von Soemmering referred to races in their work from the 1770s onward, but they were not typical of British trends. *Variety* had a range of meanings pertinent to its association with human groups: succession of one thing to another, intermixture of one thing with another, dissimilitude, and deviation, or change from a former state.

68. Samuel Johnson uses the phrase "the race of man" in his dictionary. Johnson's *Dictionary* provides ten definitions of *race*, which are mainly grouped into meanings equivalent to family or breed.

69. Nancy Stepan, *The Idea of Race in Science: Great Britain, 1800–1960* (London: Macmillan Press, 1982), xix.

70. Foucault, *The Order of Things*, 229.

71. John Millar, *The Origin of the Distinction of Ranks*, 3d ed., in *John Millar of Glasgow, 1735–1801: His Life and Thought and His Contributions to Sociological Analysis*, ed. William Lehmann (1781; Cambridge: Cambridge University Press, 1960), 228.

72. Ronald Meek's *Social Science and the Ignoble Savage* (Cambridge: Cambridge University Press, 1976) traces the rise, development, and uses of four-stages theory in the eighteenth century, especially the way that Native Americans were used as exemplary savages in philosophic discourse.

73. Anand C. Chitnis, *The Scottish Enlightenment: A Social History* (London: Croom Helm, 1976), 95.

74. Koehn, *The Power of Commerce*, 183.

75. Stepan, *The Idea of Race in Science*, 3.

76. See ibid., xix. Although some influential men such as Voltaire, David Hume, Edward Long, and Lord Kames suspected that there were separate species of men, most of their English contemporaries found this possibility too distressing to consider seriously. Polygenesis was first broached in the seventeenth century; in the 1770s, it was a topic discussed among European and American men of science, and it evidently had a lot of purchase among planters and more influence on the Continent than in Great Britain. However, polygenesis as an assumption entered British cultural discourse and was particularly popular among plantation owners.

77. David Doig, *Two Letters on the Savage State, Addressed to the Late Lord Kaims* (London: G. G. J. and J. Robinson, 1793), 152.

78. See Londa Schiebinger, "The Anatomy of Difference," 399, and Thomas Laqueur, *Making Sex: Body and Gender from the Greeks to Foucault* (Cambridge: Harvard University Press, 1990), 201, on implications for European women and racial minorities. Notably, both critics use French and German source material.

79. The broadest theoretical impetus informing my interpretation of narratives in the eighteenth century derives from poststructuralist and materialist analyses, which have both focused on issues of heterogeneity in interpretation, though somewhat differently. My sense is that race has been a particularly intractable concept to both poststructuralist and materialist analyses or even methodologies combining the two. For a number of overdetermined factors including our inherited frames of reference in the United States from the legacy of slavery, incomplete civil rights, and still palpable white supremacism, we tend to equate race with blackness — a phenomenon noticeable in the media and politics as well as in the academy. An example of this kind of oversight occurs in Diana Fuss's *Essentially Speaking: Feminism, Nature, and Difference* (New York: Routledge, 1989): In an otherwise insightful work on the complex operations of gender and sexuality, race is equated with blackness.

80. Smellie, *The Philosophy of Natural History*, 2: 159.

81. I am thinking of the biblical passage of the Curse of Ham and its checkered life in Christian teaching, which loses purchase in British documents of the eighteenth century after the first two decades. I have found it mentioned less than a handful of times, though it was more popular in the seventeenth century and in the colonies. The chain of being is another example. While it was a heuristic readily available to Europeans, and it was invoked, it was less frequently used to establish a hierarchy of races. Edward Long in the 1770s and Charles White in the 1790s are exceptions. In fact, Nancy Stepan notes in *The Idea of Race* that the use of the chain for racist purposes was not typical even in the early nineteenth century (9). She ascribes this neglect to Blumenbach's explicit rejection of it. Most Britons did not subscribe to this idea, since it was sacrilegious. Finally, although there are negative comments about black skin color in the eighteenth century, it is often treated as a descriptive characteristic. This tendency changes most noticeably during the abolitionist debates of the 1780s and beyond.

82. Hazel Carby's *Reconstructing Womanhood: The Emergence of the Afro-American Woman Novelist* (New York: Oxford University Press, 1987), Toni Morrison's work, especially *Playing in the Dark: Whiteness and the Literary Imagination* (Cambridge: Harvard University. Press, 1992), bell hooks's *Black Looks: Race and Representation* (Boston: South End Press, 1992), and Michele Wallace's *Invisibility Blues: From Theory to Pop* (London: Verso, 1990) all attend to the white part of the dominant color binary and examine the intricate historical relations among classes, genders, and races in relation to slavery and cultural production in the United States — a project also undertaken by white feminists such as Minnie Bruce Pratt, Peggy McIntosh, and Ruth Frankenberg.

83. In the past thirty years, social movements and academic theorizing have alerted us to certain characteristics of these binary pairs and directed our attention to

them in specific ways. First, the civil rights movement, black power, and feminism made power dynamics more visible; there was a new consciousness of the unequal structuring of social relations, including marriage, employment, and education. Second, the new social and economic visibility of women of all colors and black men particularly attracted attention to the subordinate constituency of common binary pairs. In the 1990s, there has been renewed attention to the dominant terms, especially whiteness and masculinity. Through this process of revision, the monolithic character of both binary terms has been successfully questioned, if not partially dismantled in academic work, including a greater interest in looking at the differences within ethnicities.

84. In Homi Bhabha's "Signs Taken for Wonders: Questions of Ambivalence and Authority Under a Tree Outside Delhi, May 1817," in *"Race," Writing, and Difference*, ed. Henry Louis Gates, Jr. (Chicago: University of Chicago Press, 1986), for example, hybridity is a concept that gathers psychosexual energy unconfined by the dichotomy colonizer and colonized. Hybridity is one way to theorize the imprecision of colonialism: "The paranoid threat from the hybrid is finally uncontainable because it breaks down the symmetry of self/Other, inside/outside. In the productivity of power, the boundaries of authority—its reality effects—are always besieged by 'the other scene' of fixations and phantoms" (177). See Bhabha's "Interrogating Identity: The Postcolonial Prerogative," in *Anatomy of Racism*, ed. David Theo Goldberg (Minneapolis: University of Minnesota Press, 1990), for the explanation of hybridity as the vacillating psychic, cultural, territorial, and linguistic boundaries produced by colonialism and the difficulty of drawing the line between where one begins and ends (202). Frantz Fanon's and Albert Memmi's meditations on the unstable production of subjectivity and mixed cultures in colonial situations are significant precursors that have informed this more recent research.

In fact, there has been a trend in recent postcolonial scholarship to account for the ambiguous aspects of racial identities under "high" colonialism in the late nineteenth and twentieth centuries and to scrutinize the practices that belie dominant ideology. See Aijaz Ahmed, *In Theory: Classes, Nations, Literatures* (London: Verso, 1992), Nicholas Thomas, *Colonialism's Culture: Anthropology, Travel, and Government* (Oxford: Polity Press, 1994), and Robert Young, *Colonial Desire: Hybridity in Theory, Culture, and Race* (London: Routledge, 1995). Their methods have influenced my own approach to reading race in the eighteenth century and are thoughtful guides to negotiating some of the major terms that appear in this book, especially *nation, culture*, and *colonialism*.

85. Trinh Minh-ha, *Woman, Native, Other: Writing Postcoloniality and Feminism* (Bloomington: Indiana University Press, 1989). Isaac Julien and Kobena Mercer claim that Bhabha's theory of the colonial situation is transhistorical, which is accurate in one sense but fails to detect its nineteenth-century assumptions of colonialism. See their "De Margin and De Centre," in *Stuart Hall: Critical Dialogues in Cultural Studies*, ed. David Morley and Kuan-Hsing Chen (London: Routledge, 1996).

86. Nicholas Thomas, *Colonialism's Culture: Anthropology, Travel, and Govern-*

ment (Oxford: Polity Press, 1994); Ann Laura Stoler, "Rethinking Colonial Categories: European Communities and the Boundaries of Rule," *Society for Comparative Study of Society and History* 31 (1989).

87. Marxist economic notions of competition, struggle, and domination—the workings of capitalism—bear a remarkable similarity to Darwinian concepts of racial types and their confrontation. To some race scientists of the 1830s and beyond, the racial struggle, for example, explains the eventual rise of some types of man from barbarism to civilization. That is, embedded in Marxist theory is an unrecognized assumption about race that is incompatible with eighteenth-century ideology. A few salient differences from the historical, economic, and intellectual conditions of the eighteenth century that are at odds with their assumptions include the following: Neither the state, the repressive state apparatuses, nor formal education had the same effects on large segments of the populace that inform, differently, Gramsci's and Althusser's theory. Indeed, the eighteenth-century concept of civil society, its constitution and role, was an incipient form, at best, of Gramsci's and Althusser's notions of civil institutions and their function.

88. As Terry Eagleton in *Ideology: An Introduction* (London: Verso, 1991) and Stuart Hall have forcefully contended, some ideologies reveal ties to a particular class interest and others do not. According to this view, ideology functions dynamically, such as Volosinov envisioned, but not with his assumption of class struggle as the only or primary struggle in cultural domains. I do not, however, subscribe to Eagleton's statement that racism and sexism are nonclass ideologies (148). A more nuanced statement is that racism and sexism have occasionally shown a disappointingly stubborn life that traverses different classes but are not primarily about class concerns. I think it is ill advised to imagine racisms and sexisms don't help constitute class ideologies in certain historical circumstances.

89. Stuart Hall, "Gramsci's Relevance for the Study of Race and Ethnicity," in *Stuart Hall: Critical Dialogues in Cultural Studies*, ed. David Morley and Kuan-Hsing Chen (London: Routledge, 1996), 421.

90. Stuart Hall, "On Postmodernism and Articulation: An Interview with Stuart Hall," ed. Lawrence Grossberg, in ibid., 147.

91. Ann Laura Stoler's analysis of Foucault's engagement with race bears out this sentiment. See her *Race and the Education of Desire: Foucault's "The History of Sexuality and the Colonial Order of Things"* (Durham: Duke University Press, 1995).

92. Hall, "On Postmodernism and Articulation," 158.

93. Louis Althusser, "Ideology and Ideological State Apparatuses (Notes Toward an Investigation)," in *Lenin and Philosophy, and Other Essays*, trans. Ben Brewster (New York: Monthly Review Press, 1971), 170.

94. Most work in postcolonial feminist theory also privileges nineteenth- and twentieth-century conditions, although there is a significant body of feminist work on race and early colonialism in Renaissance studies. See *Women, "Race," and Writing in the Early Modern Period*.

95. Indeed, while many scholars have critiqued Edward Said's *Orientalism* for

its omissions of gendered considerations or for its monolithic construction of the Orient and the West, most have not noted the way that nineteenth-century European imperial rule overdetermines Said's categories of inquiry.

96. Technically, the eighteenth-century West Indies and some American colonies were slave societies rather than colonial societies; nevertheless, because of the many populations that coexisted temporarily and permanently in these regions, I retain the term *colonial* to describe the eighteenth-century Atlantic, especially since colonial societies encompass various forms of exploitative labor arrangements.

Chapter 1. Christians, Savages, and Slaves

1. William Fleetwood, Lord Bishop of St. Asaph's annual sermon for the Society for the Propagation of the Gospel in Foreign Parts encapsulates a transition from thinking of colonists as Christians to regarding them as the more narrowly defined Englishmen. The sermon is typical of the yearly reassurance that the Church of England offered to slaveowners about the compatibility of Christianity and slavery.

2. For many social critics, including Toni Morrison, Robinson Crusoe and Friday are paradigmatic of power relations between whites and nonwhites. Bernard McGrane's *Beyond Anthropology: Society and the Other* (New York: Columbia University Press, 1989) and Patrick Brantlinger's *Crusoe's Footprints: Cultural Studies in Britain and America* (New York: Routledge, 1990) are exemplary cultural analyses of Robinson Crusoe and Friday as a paradigm of colonial relations. McGrane examines the shifting history of European conceptions of difference from the sixteenth through the nineteenth centuries. *Robinson Crusoe* was McGrane's choice as a representative text of the Enlightenment's concept of the Other. That is, the representation of Friday tells us not about Caribs but about the British.

3. Toni Morrison, ed., *Race-ing Justice, En-gendering Power: Essays on Anita Hill, Clarence Thomas, and the Construction of Social Reality* (New York: Pantheon Books, 1992), x.

4. Some critics speculate that Selkirk and Defoe actually met, including Angus Ross, editor of *The Life and Adventures of Robinson Crusoe* (1719; London: Penguin Books, 1965), who notes that since the eighteenth century, *Robinson Crusoe* has been believed to be "based on the central incident in the life of an undisciplined Scot, Alexander Selkirk" (301). Selkirk's adventures are a disputed source for Defoe's novel.

5. The scientific racism of the mid-nineteenth century featured everything from skull measurements to nationalized notions of blood types; this is the idea of race that informs Morrison's observations. See Nancy Stepan, *The Idea of Race in Science: Great Britain, 1800–1960* (London: Macmillan Press, 1982), for a general discussion of the historical development of race in the nineteenth century. In comparison with scientific racism, the most basic difference of Defoe's time is that human variety was generally thought to result from external factors, such as the sun, or chance historical conditions.

6. There are other national confusions in Morrison's account of the novel. She recalls a scene of Spanish mutineers, some of whom Crusoe saves, she speculates, because worthy, and some of whom are singled out as villains for slaughter. Morrison observes in *Race-ing Justice*: "This discrimination [recognition of difference within a group] is never applied to Friday's people" (xxvii). In fact, in the novel the mutineers are English. The effect of replacing the English with the Spanish confounds whom Crusoe valued and whom he didn't and thus (falsely) solidifies her case for the insignificance of the native. Morrison neglects to mention that Friday and his father are represented as different from the rest of the cannibals in significant ways. In another example, Morrison mistakenly points out that Friday's father does not return from his island but that the Spaniard does: "Once his services [Friday's father] are no longer needed, there is no mention of him again" (xxvii). But both the Spaniard and Friday's father remain outside the text after they go to retrieve the other Spanish and Portuguese men. In fact, neither resurfaces until volume 2, *The Farther Adventures of Robinson Crusoe* (1719).

7. While one could contend that Morrison's complaint of contamination is true of all discourse, I agree with her argument that a bicultural or minority person entering hegemonic discourse and assuming a relatively empowered position frequently entails such damage. Thus, hegemonic discursive power relations are particularly complex for a bicultural or minority person and should be discussed accordingly. Not everyone enters them equally, contaminated though they "always already" are or negotiates them similarly.

8. Sumi Cho, "Korean Americans vs. African Americans: Conflict and Construction," in *Reading Rodney King: Reading Urban Uprising*, ed. Robert Gooding-Williams (New York: Routledge, 1993): 196–214, identifies the production of a model minority as "an embrace of 'racist love'" because the basis of that love is "to provide a public rationale for the ongoing subordination of non-Asian people of color. Because the embrace or love is not genuine, one cannot reasonably expect the architects truly to care about the health or well-being of the model minority" (203).

9. Eric Williams, *Capitalism and Slavery* (1944; reprint, Chapel Hill: University of North Carolina Press, 1994), 23. Williams reports that the losers in this numbers game in terms of their status were small white farmers and African slaves. The white flight to other islands was enormous: In 1645, there were about 11,000 small white farmers and about 5,500 Negro slaves in Barbados; in 1667, there were 745 large plantation owners and about 82,000 slaves (23).

10. In volume 2, *The Farther Adventures of Robinson Crusoe*, ed. George Aitken (1719; London: J. M. Dent, 1899), Crusoe acknowledges that Friday is not, in fact, Carib: "The savages who came to my island were not properly those which we call Caribbees, but islanders, and other barbarians of the same kind, who inhabited something nearer to our side than the rest" (52). I have retained the term *Carib* because the novel uses it to signify savagery, especially cannibalism; such a specific reference, even if later repudiated, indicates its ideological power as a term of opposition to *European*. Peter Hulme's *Colonial Encounters: Europe and the Native Caribbean, 1492–1797* (1986; London: Routledge, 1992) provides a thorough examination of the asso-

ciation between Carib and cannibal and the etymology of other Caribbean islander naming, especially in the introduction and chapter 1. Cannibalism usually referred to eating those outside one's community; see Philip Boucher, *Cannibal Encounters: Europeans and Island Caribs, 1492–1763* (Baltimore: Johns Hopkins University Press, 1992), 15.

11. Several studies of *Robinson Crusoe* have connected the plot's impetus to colonialism, desire, and fear; see John Richetti, *Defoe's Narratives: Situations and Structures* (Oxford: Clarendon Press, 1975), chap. 2; Maximillian Novak, *Defoe and the Nature of Man* (Oxford: Oxford University Press, 1963), 25–26, 34, and 37; Maximillian Novak, *Economics and the Fiction of Daniel Defoe* (New York: Russell and Russell, 1976), esp. chap. 2; Ian Watt, "*Robinson Crusoe* as a Myth" in *Robinson Crusoe: An Authoritative Text, Backgrounds and Sources, Criticism*, ed. Michael Shinagel (New York: W. W. Norton, 1975): 311–31.

12. In *Robinson Crusoe*, the word *Africans* refers to black Africans south of Morocco on the west coast (near present-day Senegal, opposite the Cape Verde Islands where the Portuguese ship finds Crusoe and Xury). In this chapter, I frequently refer to black Africans as West Africans; either generic term, however, is a "trap" because they both homogenize the diverse histories and physical features of coastal Africans and make Africa appear as a unified continent or nation.

13. Daniel Defoe, *The Life and Adventures of Robinson Crusoe*, ed. Angus Ross (1719; London: Penguin Books, 1965), 38–39.

14. In *Robinson Crusoe*, the term *Moors* signifies Muslim inhabitants of northwest Africa, particularly Morocco. Moors were part of the governing structure of the Ottoman Empire in North Africa. The *OED* indicates that people from Algeria and Mauritania, who were of mixed Berber and Arab ancestry, were also called Moors. While Europeans popularly considered Moors very swarthy or, indeed, black until well into the seventeenth century (*OED*), there were other factors that acknowledge this European "myth" and that Moor was an unstable category. For instance, there was a common distinction between tawny Moors and white Moors which recognized that not all Moors were black. There was, however, the simultaneous usage of Moor as a popular synonym for Negro. In British literature through the eighteenth century there was a tradition of the Moorish quality ennobling black Africans. See Wylie Sypher, *Guinea's Captive Kings: British Anti-Slavery Literature of the Eighteenth Century* (1942; New York: Octagon Books, 1969), 234, 237. Anthony Barthelemy's *Black Face, Maligned Race: The Presentation of Blacks in English Drama from Shakespeare to Southerne* (Baton Rouge: Louisiana State University Press, 1987) features an excellent history of the evolution and complexities of the term *Moor*, especially in chap. 1. He makes several crucial arguments: *Moor* (similar to *Turk* and *Indian*) is difficult to define but shares with these other terms the connotation of alien or foreigner (6). In Spain, the earliest form of *Moor* distinguished Christian from non-Christian (10). *Moor* could refer to people of different colors and religions; the only certainty is that a Moor is not a European Christian (7).

15. François Bernier, "A New Division of the Earth, According to the Differ-

ent Species or Races of Men Who Inhabit It," *Journal des Sçavans*, in *Memoirs Read Before the Anthropological Society of London*, ed. Thomas Bendyshe (1684; London: Longman, 1865), 360–64.

16. In reference to English slaves held by the Moors, see John Wolf, *The Barbary Coast: Algiers Under the Turks, 1500–1800* (New York: W. W. Norton, 1979). He shows that although "Cromwell was the first to use naval power effectively for both the protection of commerce and the ransom of prisoners," "Slaves not yet sold could be freed, but slaves purchased by individuals had become 'private property,' and both the English and the French kings respected 'private property' even though it happened to be an Englishman or a Frenchman" (159). Thus, as the novel confirms, all bodies can be property. For some it is an accident of fate; for others it is their fate. Historically, the publication of the novel coincides with a well-known release of English slaves. In 1720, Commodore Stewart, on orders from George I, ransomed 296 British subjects from North Africa, a fraction of the captive British population. See Stephen Clissold, *The Barbary Slaves* (Totowa, N.J.: Rowman and Littlefield, 1977), chaps. 8 and 9.

17. David Eltis, "Europeans and the Rise and Fall of African Slavery in the Americas: An Interpretation," *American Historical Review* 98.5 (December 1993): 1420.

18. Winthrop Jordan, *White over Black: American Attitudes toward the Negro, 1550–1812* (1968; New York: W. W. Norton, 1977), 55–56.

19. Morgan Godwyn, *The Negro's and Indians Advocate, Suing for their Admission into the Church* (London: J.D., 1680), 28.

20. Appearing in several editions of the popular Hakluyt's *Principal Navigations* (1589), the success of the 1554–55 voyage was "recruiting" kidnapped Africans whom the Englishmen wanted for training guides and interpreters for future expeditions; English merchants were more interested in ivory, metals, and spices than in slaves at this point. These guides, evidently very useful, were referred to as "our Negros." See Alden Vaughan and Mary Vaughan, "Before *Othello*: Elizabethan Representations of Sub-Saharan Africans," *William and Mary Quarterly*, 3d series, 54.1 (January 1997): 26.

21. A comprehensive historical analysis of the Moriscos' changing position relative to Europeans and to the peoples of the Islamic East, based on the Moriscos' own Aljamiado literature, is found in Anwar Chejne, *Islam and the West: The Moriscos. A Cultural and Social History* (Albany: State University of New York Press, 1983). For a skeleton history of the Moriscos' outsider status, especially in relation to Spain and in Spanish literature, see Israel Burshatin, "The Moor in the Text: Metaphor, Emblem, and Silence," in *"Race," Writing, and Difference*, ed. Henry Louis Gates, Jr. (Chicago: University of Chicago Press, 1986), 117–18, 132.

22. Chejne, *Islam and the West*, 7.

23. The critical treatment of Xury, while not as extensive as the interest in Friday, elicits similar confusion about Xury's color and national origins. See Stephen Hymer, "Robinson Crusoe and the Secret of Primitive Accumulation," *Monthly Re-*

view 23.4 (September 1971): 11–36; Lennard Davis, "The Fact of Events and the Event of Facts: New World Explorers and the Early Novel," *Eighteenth Century* 32.3 (1991): 240–55. In contrast to Hymer's identification of Xury as an African, Davis claims that Xury is not easy to classify in terms of national origins: "Xury, whose exact racial origin is unclear, although he is clearly 'Other,' is the prototype of the friendly native" (242). In the following sentence, however, Davis does try to distinguish Xury from West Africans: Xury "is somewhat moorish and in this case the natives are 'Negroes' " (243).

24. Maximillian Novak reprints "Robinson Crusoe & His Boy Xury on the Coast of Guinny Shooting a Lyon" in *Realism, Myth, and History in Defoe's Fiction* (Lincoln: University of Nebraska Press, 1983), 38. This illustration was one of six plates added to the sixth edition of 1722. It must be noted that there are several sets of illustrations connected with various eighteenth-century editions of the novel, and at different times, Xury is European in features and black African.

25. Daniel Defoe, *Robinson Crusoe* (abridged; Dublin, 1774), 20. Daniel Defoe, *Robinson Crusoe*, (abridged; Birmingham: J. Skechley, 1765) also has Xury speak in pidgin but leaves out the reference to his "broken tone." This pidgin—the liberal use of *de* and *dat* for *the* and *that*—characterizes the representation of Indians in the West Indies in William Chetwood's *Voyages, Dangerous Adventures, and Imminent Escapes of Captain Richard Falconer* (London: W. Chetwood, 1720). There is no apparent correlation between alterations in Xury's speech and his representation as a Negro.

26. Hilary Beckles, *White Servitude and Black Slavery in Barbados, 1627–1715* (Knoxville: University of Tennessee Press, 1989), 22. Stuart Schwartz, "The Formation of a Colonial Identity in Brazil," *Colonial Identity in the Atlantic World, 1500–1800*, ed. Nicholas Canny and Anthony Pagden (Princeton: Princeton University Press, 1987); 15–50, calls attention to the historical transformations of status display in colonial Brazil (in which *Robinson Crusoe* seems to participate): "Lacking these external proofs of gentility [titles and other marks of European nobility], the colonists sought to demonstrate their nobility by a seigneurial lifestyle, including a landed estate, numerous slaves and retainers, liberality, patriarchal attitudes, and personal justice" (29). This observation describes the style of Crusoe's governance on the island and his own understanding of his desires.

27. William Chetwood, *Captain Richard Falconer*, is typical of this tendency in the description of St. Kitt's: "The island is inhabited by both English and French, who even in Time of War live very friendly together" (22).

28. Savagery is a traditional discourse of absolute difference traceable to Herodotus. See Hulme, *Colonial Encounters*, for excellent historical and analytical work on savagery in the Caribbean, especially the introduction and chap. 1.

29. Philip Boucher, *Cannibal Encounters: Europeans and Island Caribs, 1492–1763* (Baltimore: Johns Hopkins University Press, 1992), 10.

30. *Wild Majesty: Encounters with Caribs from Columbus to the Present Day*, ed. Peter Hulme and Neil Whitehead (Oxford: Clarendon Press, 1992), 4.

31. Frank Lestringant, *Cannibals: The Discovery and Representation of the Cannibal from Columbus to Jules Verne* (Berkeley: University of California Press, 1997), 141.

32. W. Arens, *The Man-Eating Myth: Anthropology and Anthropophagy* (New York: Oxford University Press, 1979), 170–71.

33. In *The Problem of Slavery in Western Culture* (New York: Oxford University Press, 1966), David Brion Davis sketches the shifts in European policies and attitudes toward Amerindians as slaves (167–70). From time to time in North and South America, enslavement of the Amerindians was forbidden; in the earliest Spanish colonies, there was an ongoing conflict between the pope and the demands of colonists, who were often backed by the Crown. The need for a law forbidding the enslavement of Amerindians tends to indicate that in practice they were regarded as "legitimate" slaves at this time, even if ideologically there were reasons not to regard them as natural slaves. Also see Jordan, *White over Black*, 89–95, for a discussion of why "Indian slavery never became an important institution in the [North American] colonies" (89). Richard Popkin, "The Philosophical Basis of Eighteenth-Century Racism," *Studies in Eighteenth-Century Culture*, vol. 3, *Racism in the Eighteenth Century*, ed. Harold E. Paglioaro (Cleveland: Press of Case Western Reserve University, 1973), 245–62, is also helpful concerning the hybrid position of Amerindians.

34. See the introduction to *Cannibalism and the Colonial World*, ed. Francis Barker et al. (Cambridge: Cambridge University Press, 1998), for a summary of the scholarship.

35. Boucher, *Cannibal Encounters*, 7.

36. Arens, *Man-Eating Myth*, 48–49. Arens explicates this in terms of Spanish ideology; he contends that by the sixteenth century, "Resistance and cannibalism became synonymous and also legitimized the barbaric Spanish reaction."

37. Boucher, *Cannibal Encounters*, 10, 117, is particularly helpful in showing lines of influence from French authors to English writers. In the last quarter of the seventeenth century and the early eighteenth century, several popular books made somewhat more positive views of Caribs available (108–10).

38. Hulme and Whitehead, *Wild Majesty*, 130.

39. Richard Bradley, *A Philosophical Account of the Works of Nature* (London: W. Mears, 1721), 169. For the contrast between beardless Indians and Europeans, see Londa Schiebinger, "The Anatomy of Difference: Race and Sex in Eighteenth-Century Science," *Eighteenth-Century Studies* 23.4 (1990): 387–405. Observing that the beard was historically considered a sign of virility, Schiebinger notes that "the absence of a beard in native American males led to great debate. Many natural historians took this to be a sign that they belonged to a lower class of humans; some even argue that this absence of hair follicles on the chin proved that they belonged to a separate species" (391). Many Britons regarded this argument as spurious and refuted it. For instance, the 1771 *Encyclopaedia Britannica* included accusations that Americans did not have beards, but subsequent editions included the commentary that ridiculed this point of view. This criterion is particularly curious given that

it was customary even by the late seventeenth century for Englishmen to be clean shaven, a custom which was almost universal in the eighteenth century.

40. Boucher, *Cannibal Encounters*, chap. 5, argues that British representations of Caribs were more negative than their French counterparts. The frontispiece to William Chetwood's *Captain Richard Falconer* is typical of this tendency to represent Indians as similar to Europeans in facial features and skin color, even though scantily clad. The Indian warriors burning the English hero at the stake are the same hue as he is—despite the fact that he refers to his Indian wife as his "Tawny Rib." By the sixth edition of 1769, however, the Indians are dark in color and have short curly hair.

41. Hayden White, *Tropics of Discourse: Essays in Cultural Criticism* (Baltimore: Johns Hopkins University Press, 1978), 186.

42. Richard Blackmore, "The Nature of Man," in *A Collection of Poems* (1711; London: W. Wilkins, 1718), 250. On the effects of the sun's heat, see 180.

43. Daniel Defoe, *Serious Reflections During the Life and Surprising Adventures of Robinson Crusoe . . .* , vol. 3, *The Works of Daniel Defoe*, ed. G. H. Maynadier (1720; London J. M. Dent, 1899), 240–41.

44. Gordon Sayre, *Les Sauvages Américans: Representations of Native Americans in French and English Colonial Literature* (Chapel Hill: University of North Carolina Press, 1997), 152–53.

45. In one of the several taxonomies that Crusoe creates, he states: "I have not clothes to cover me," but on the positive side, he counters: "But I am in a hot climate, where if I had clothes I could hardly wear them" (83). As we find out later, he is clothed as thoroughly as if he were in a sub-Alpine climate. This initial naturalization and justification of his own near-nakedness gives way to an emphasis on the symbolic value of clothing as a sign of difference from savages.

46. *Tawny* represented not one but several possibilities in the late seventeenth and early eighteenth centuries, and here it is clearly meant to convey pure color and hence attractiveness. Often it was the intermediate shades that elicited derision.

47. Theodore Allen, *The Invention of the White Race*, vol. 2, *The Origin of Racial Oppression in Anglo-America* (London: Verso, 1997), 351.

48. Beckles, *White Servitude*, cites a 1675 description of Barbados's population that emphasizes the significance of *free* to distinguishing among people in the Caribbean: the four categories were freeholders (landowners), freemen (former indentured servants), Christian servants, and Negroes (141). As these categories suggest, ownership of property, station, religion, and color all apply variously to the different populations.

49. Jordan, *White over Black*, 95.

50. Ibid., 81–82; Michael Goldfield, "The Color of Politics in the United States: White Supremacy as the Main Explanation for the Peculiarities of American Politics from Colonial Times to the Present," *The Bounds of Race: Perspectives on Hegemony and Resistance*, ed. Dominick La Capra (Ithaca: Cornell University Press, 1991), 116; and Davis, *Problem of Slavery*, 132, convincingly argue that slavery in all

of the British colonies shifts to a more permanent, hereditary state between 1660 and 1710.

51. Stephen Haseler, *The English Tribe: Identity, Nation, and Europe* (London: Macmillan Press, 1996), 10.

52. Allen, *The Invention of the White Race*, 2:351 n. 39.

53. *Colonising Expeditions to the West Indies and Guiana, 1623–67*, ed. Vincent Harlow, Hakluyt Society, 2d series, vol. 56 (London: Bedford Press, 1925), xix–xxi.

54. This Other may be gendered female and/or racialized. In general, I contend that Friday is not feminized but that he is accorded a subordinate masculinity. The trend delineating Other men as feminized is one of the less historically precise conventions of psychoanalytic theory. See Robyn Wiegman, "Economies of the Body: Gendered Sites in *Robinson Crusoe* and *Roxana*," *Criticism* 31.1 (1989): 33–51. In a parallel between Thomas and Friday that she doesn't draw, Toni Morrison notes about the treatment of Judge Thomas in the media and the Senate that "the black man's body is voluptuously dwelled upon in biographies about them, journalism on them, remarks about them. . . . What would have been extraordinary would have been to ignore Thomas's body, for in ignoring it, the articles would have had to discuss in some detail that aspect of him more difficult to appraise—his mind" (*Race-ing Justice*, xiv).

55. Daniel Defoe, *Robinson Crusoe*, (abridged; Birmingham: J. Skechley, 1765) adds the following comment after Crusoe's lengthy description of Friday: "Such handsome features, and exact symmetry in every part, made me consider, that I had saved the life of an Indian prince," whom he compares to Oroonoko (133).

56. Although the physical description may be flattering in ethnocentric terms, it is an unflattering picture in behavioral terms. It was unheard of for Caribbean islanders to flee their captors (as was Friday's captor's inability to swim). Also, Carib islanders were very familiar with firearms and sails (Boucher, 126–27).

57. A. J. Dulaure, *Pognologia; or, A Philosophical and Historical Essay on Beards* (London: R. Thorn, 1784), 76.

58. Edward Ward, *Trip to Jamaica in Five Travel Scripts Commonly Attributed to Edward Ward* (1698; reprint, New York: Columbia University Press, 1933) is one example of the connection between tawny and mulatto. He describes a story of an English woman whose husband had also married a mixed-race Jamaican woman, whom she refers to as "a *Gipsy*, a Tawny Fac'd *Moletto* Strumpet, a Pumpkin colour'd Whore" (9).

59. Boucher, *Cannibal Encounters*, 8.

60. That this illustration appears in volume 3 when Crusoe is nowhere near the Caribbean and Friday is dead has been explained by the argument that the engraver did not have the first volume of the novel at hand when he produced the frontispiece of black savages for the third volume; see David Blewett, *The Illustration of Robinson Crusoe, 1719–1920* (Gerrards Cross, Buckinghamshire: Colin Smythe, 1995), 28. While this may be so, it doesn't account for the failure to alter the illustrations once the mistake was discovered or the way readers and illustrators alike remember Friday

as an African. Another logical explanation for the appearance of the black Caribees in the frontispiece to volume 3 is the sensational ability of the illustration to sell this final, less riveting volume of adventures.

61. Eltis, "Europeans and the Rise and Fall of African Slavery in the Americas," 1402.

62. Nancie Gonzales, "From Cannibals to Mercenaries: Carib Militarism, 1600–1840," *Journal of Anthropology Research* 46 (spring 1990): 25. The distinction Crusoe makes between Friday's color ("very tawny") and the other cannibals' ("ugly yellow nauseous tawny") inverts a common distinction Europeans made between the gentler Yellow Caribs, a.k.a. Island Caribs, and the more aggressive Black Caribs.

63. That Europeans often confounded Black Caribs and African slaves is borne out by a remark made by Louis XIV about the maroon communities of Black Caribs: "It would be much in the interest of the islands if all these negroes could be destroyed so that those who have the desire to run away would no longer have an assumed haven'" (Boucher, *Cannibal Encounters*, 103).

64. Hulme and Whitehead, *Wild Majesty*, 150; Boucher, *Cannibal Encounters*, 95.

65. The narrative time roughly corresponds to Cromwell's Commonwealth and the Restoration, a time when both Portugal and Spain were more powerful nations than in 1719, by which time English merchants largely controlled Portuguese trade. Defoe wrote the novel after the gaining of the Asiento from Spain in 1713, a monopoly on the slave trade in the Atlantic; after the formation of the Royal African and South Sea Companies, two of the most powerful and lucrative organizations responsible for trade in slaves, gold, and other raw materials between Europe and parts of the Atlantic empire; and after the establishment of the Bank of England, a reliable institutional and financial partner of the slave trade. The mid-seventeenth century was also the height of Corsair activity, and Brazil was the leading exporter of sugar, not the West Indies; these conditions changed by the early eighteenth century. Although the narrative time predates these events, it is crucial to account for the differences these events make to the emphasis on and nature of the slave trade and representations of Africa and the Caribbean in *Robinson Crusoe*.

66. David Galenson, *Traders, Planters, and Slaves: Market Behaviour in Early English America* (Cambridge: Cambridge University Press, 1986), 2.

67. Davis, *Problem of Slavery in Western Culture*, 132; Boucher, *Cannibal Encounters*, 93.

68. Goldfield, "The Color of Politics in the United States," 116.

69. Williams, *Capitalism and Slavery*, 9.

70. Beckles, *White Servitude*, 13–14.

71. I wish to emphasize that in practice, planters were not as selective in terms of choosing a more desirable labor force until later in the seventeenth century.

72. Eltis, "Europeans and the Rise and Fall of African Slavery," for one, has argued that nonslave ships tended to carry fewer servants per ton (1405); evidence seems to support this, but abuses of this general rule were also rife.

73. Hulme, *Colonial Encounters*, 205.

74. David Blewett, *Illustration of Robinson Crusoe*, 15.

75. Jordan, *White over Black*, 52–53.

76. Frank Pitman, *The Development of the British West Indies* (New Haven: Yale University Press, 1917), 35. It is remarkable that this slippage does not occur once they reach Europe; the novel represents Friday's position unambiguously as a servant (see 284). Also, at the end of the novel, in Europe, Crusoe's status among other Europeans is cast in terms of the labor power he commands. Because Friday is "too much a stranger to be capable of supplying the place of a servant on the road" (284), Crusoe hires an English sailor as an additional servant. The other European men assign Crusoe the position of command based on his superior age and number of attendants.

77. Daniel Defoe, *The Great Law of Subordination Consider'd* (London: S. Harding, 1724), 140.

78. Charles Gildon, *The Life and Strange Surprizing Adventures of Mr. D——DeF——, of London*, 2d ed. (London: J. Roberts, 1719), ix. The exchange among Crusoe, Friday, and Defoe culminates in a characteristic early eighteenth-century moment, however, when Crusoe commands Friday to force-feed Defoe the volumes of *Robinson Crusoe* and they toss the author in the air until he defecates—and then Defoe wakes from a dream, so he thinks, until he smells himself.

Chapter 2. Racializing Civility

1. Francis Moore, *Travels into the Inland Parts of Africa*, (London: Edward Cave, 1738), xi–xii.

2. The second edition of 1988 includes the European norm that governs the entire definition: "[A Negro is] an individual (especially a male) belonging to the African race of mankind, which is distinguished by a black skin, black tightly-curled hair, and a nose flatter and lips thicker and more protruding than is common amongst white Europeans."

3. *Africa* and *African* were not transparent or monolithic terms in the eighteenth century; our present-day notions have no parallel in the seventeenth and eighteenth centuries. *Africa* and *African* have no less heterogeneity today, but ideologically and geographically many Westerners have created a more unified picture of Africa than its various histories, customs, religions, and languages demand. Novels such as *Captain Singleton* are part of this homogenizing tradition. I use the term *African* most frequently as a substitute for *black* or for the eighteenth-century terms *Negroe* and *Native*, although this practice also has a homogenizing tendency. Nevertheless, as a term of reference, it reflects the eighteenth-century tendency to think of people in relation to the continents where they or their ancestors were born. For analysis of the European invention of Africa versus heterogeneous definitions of Africa, see Kwame Anthony Appiah, *In My Father's House: Africa in the Philosophy*

of Culture (New York: Oxford University Press, 1992), 25, and V. Y. Mudimbe, *The Invention of Africa: Gnosis, Philosophy, and the Order of Knowledge* (Bloomington: Indiana University Press, 1988), 69.

As opposed to *African*, current since the ninth century, *European* was a relatively new term; the *OED* lists the first citation in the early seventeenth century. Its first meaning reveals the way its usage emerged in response to colonialism: "In India, *European* (not 'English' or 'British') was the official designation, applied to the troops sent from the United Kingdom as distinguished from the native soldiers." *European* also signified a "person of European extraction who lives outside Europe; hence, a white person, especially in a country with a predominantly non-white population." The first entry appeared in 1696.

4. Jennifer Morgan's " 'Some Could Suckle over Their Shoulder': Male Travelers, Female Bodies, and the Gendering of Racial Ideology, 1500–1770," *William and Mary Quarterly*, 3d series, 54.1 (January 1997): 167–92, analyzes the symptomatic interest Englishmen showed in Other women's breasts and physical appearance, especially African and native American women. The long time span of her study tends to ignore the writings that do not reflect an equation between British profits and slave women's bodies. For a more nuanced analysis, see Felicity A. Nussbaum, *Torrid Zones: Maternity, Sexuality, and Empire in Eighteenth-Century English Narratives* (Baltimore: Johns Hopkins University Press, 1995).

5. Alta Jablow, "The Development of the Image of Africa in British Popular Literature, 1530–1910," Ph.D. diss., Columbia University, 1963, 2 ff., also considers the issue of racialized categories applicable to Africans and Europeans. See P. J. Marshall and Glyndwr Williams, *The Great Map of Mankind: Perceptions of New Worlds in the Age of Enlightenment* (Cambridge: Harvard University Press, 1982), chap. 8, for an extremely helpful summary of trends in eighteenth-century narratives to Africa. See also Anthony Barker, *The African Link: British Attitudes to the Negro in the Era of the Slave Trade, 1550–1807* (London: Frank Cass, 1978). Marshall and Williams question Barker's thesis that the depiction of Africans is not uniformly negative in the eighteenth century. Barker argues that even though many of these writers were participants in the slave trade, "their attitudes, both to slavery and to Negro culture, were not monolithic" (18). Marshall and Williams agree with Barker that these earlier accounts do not depict Africans as subhuman, but they do not accept his related contention that "the Negro image was little different from that of the rest of the uncivilized world" (Barker, 120). Marshall and Williams suggest that in comparison to contemporaneous narratives of other non-Europeans, accounts of Africa possess a "sharper, more denigratory tone of language" because the writers' preoccupation was the slave trade (229). My own position is that although there was no uniform depiction of Africans, only contradictory stories, there was a negative view of African society especially that even detractors of the slave trade were aware of and worked against, such as Atkins and Moore.

6. For example, *The National and Private Advantages of the African Trade Considered* (London: John and Paul Knapton, 1746) and *The African Trade, the Great*

Pillar and Support of the British Plantation Trade in America (London: J. Robinson, 1745) appeal to the national advantage of continuing trade, the cheapness of Negro labor, and the importance of African trade to English hegemony in Europe. At most there are appeals to the ways that Africans are constitutionally more fit to sustain the toil of planting in hot climates (*The African Trade*, 14).

William Dodd, no supporter of the slave trade, suggests in *The Royal African; or, Memoirs of the Young Prince of Annamaboe* (London, 1749) that some Britons believed that Africans were slaves because of their color (iii) and their ignorance: "For whatever some Men may think, human nature is the same in all Countries, and under all Complexions; and to fancy that superior Power or superior Knowledge gives one Race of People a title to use another Race who are weaker or more ignorant with Hautiness or Contempt, is to abuse Power and Science" (vii–viii).

7. *The National and Private Advantages of the African Trade Considered*, 4.

8. Margo Hendricks and Patricia Parker, eds., *Women, "Race," and Writing in the Early Modern Period*, (New York: Routledge, 1994), 1–2, and Kim Hall, *Things of Darkness: Economies of Race and Gender in Early Modern England* (Ithaca: Cornell University Press, 1995).

9. Alden Vaughan and Virginia Vaughan, "Before *Othello*: Elizabethan Representations of Sub-Saharan Africans," *William and Mary Quarterly*, 3d series, 54.1 (January 1997), 44. This essay is a recent examination of these traits in early modern travel literature. The Vaughans' essay contends that English representation of Africans became more negative in the second half of the sixteenth century. This trend, they believe, persisted into the eighteenth century. With few exceptions, they argue, black skin color was believed to be unattractive and was occasionally seen as a stigma of divine punishment. Their religion was unworthy of being called such and their governments were dismissed as petty; their communities primitive, and their character uncivil. Many other scholars agree with this general summary. On the contrary, I find not a progressive trend but conflicting stories in the representation of Africans. The idea that blackness resulted from a curse had some purchase in popular belief, particularly in the fifteenth and sixteenth centuries, but no credibility in philosophical or scientific writings. See essays on the curse of Ham by Benjamin Braude, "The Sons of Noah and the Construction of Ethnic and Geographical Identities in the Medieval and Early Modern Periods," and Robin Blackburn, "The Old World Background to European Colonial Slavery," both in *William and Mary Quarterly*, 3d series, 54.1 (January 1997): 65–102, 103–142.

10. Peggy McIntosh, "On the Invisibility of Privilege," *Peacework*, Working Paper 189 (Wellesley, Mass.: Wellesley College Center for Research on Women, 1991).

11. Emily Bartels, "*Othello* and Africa: Postcolonialism Reconsidered," *William and Mary Quarterly*, 3d series, 54.1 (January 1997): 46.

12. Robin Hallet, *The Penetration of Africa: European Exploration in North and West Africa to 1815* (London: Frederick A. Praeger, 1965), 39.

13. *The Compleat Geographer: or, The Chorography and Topography of All the*

Known Parts of the Earth, 4th ed. (London: J. Knapton et al., 1723), 137 and entry for *Europe*. The same entries appeared in the 1709 first edition.

14. Moore, *Travels*, 120.

15. François Bernier, "A New Division of the Earth, According to the Different Species or Races of Men Who Inhabit it," *Journal des Sçavans*, in *Memoirs Read Before the Anthropological Society of London, 1863–4*, ed. T. Bendyshe (1684; London: Longman, 1865), 361–62.

16. Richard Bradley, *A Philosophical Account of the Works of Nature* (London: W. Mears, 1721), 169.

17. Mungo Park, *Travels into the Interior of Africa* (1799; reprint, London: Eland Books, 1983), 102.

18. *A New General Collection of Voyages and Travels*, 4 vols. (London: Thomas Astley, 1745–47), 2:255.

19. John Ogilby, *Africa* (London: Thomas Johnson, 1670), 318.

20. For example, in Defoe, at least, constructions such as "black *Negroe-man*" appear (43). According to the *OED*, the first entry for the noun *black* referring to a person with black skin occurs in Samuel Purchas, *Purchas His Pilgrimes* (1625). The equation of *black* with *Negro* was never as stable in Britain as in the colonies. The *OED* suggests *black* "appears to be a translation of *Negro*, which was in earlier use." *Negro* carries a broader menu of features than *black*, as the epigraphs indicate.

21. See John Atkins, *A Voyage to Guinea, Brasil, and the West-Indies* (London: Caesar Ward and Richard Chandler, 1735), 180, for a typical statement about the way Negroes acquire their facial features from human manipulation.

22. Moore, *Travels*, 131.

23. Sir Thomas Browne, *Pseudodoxia Epidemica; or, Enquiries into very many Received Tenents and Commonly Presumed Truths*, ed. Robin Robbins, 2 vols. (1646; Oxford: Clarendon Press, 1981), 1:516.

24. Robert Mayo, *The English Novel in the Magazines, 1740–1815* (Evanston: Northwestern University Press, 1962), 18.

25. *The Athenian Oracle*, 2d ed., 3 vols. (London: Andrew Bell, 1704), 1:29–30.

26. Michael Adas, *Machines as the Measure of Man: Science, Technology, and Ideologies of Western Dominance* (Ithaca: Cornell University Press, 1989), 65–66.

27. Religion, use of reason, and orderly government were characteristics used by later writers to segregate Africans, Lapps, and other populations from Europeans as opposed to distinguishing all humans from animals. At either end of the seventeenth century are two substantial inquiries into apes and the features that separate men from animals: Edward Topsell's *History of Four-Footed Beasts and Serpents* (London, 1607) and Edward Tyson's *Orang-Outang . . . or, the Anatomy of a Pygmie Compared with that of a Monkey, an Ape, and a Man* (London: Thomas Bennet, 1699). Both focus on inward anatomical resemblance and exterior similarities between apes and humans. Tyson finds many anatomical parallels between humans and orangutans: women's breasts, in particular, link humans to apes and pygmies more than do men's penises or testicles. Topsell's earlier text suggests that the etymology

of simia comes from the Greek *simos* "signifying the flatness of the Nostrils" (2). Flatness of the nose also signified a tendency to venery: "Men that have low and flat Nostrills are Libidinous as Apes that attempt women" (3). Attempts to make the body legible are noticeable; these efforts were originally linked to court culture but were increasingly useful for an urban culture in which meeting strangers and making decisions about them could increase profit accordingly.

28. Kenneth Davies, *The Royal African Company* (London: Longmans, Green, 1957), chap. 6. Francis Moore, a factor for the Royal African Company during the 1730s, details the delicate balance of power of Europeans living on the African coast, the daily politics of being foreigners, and the vulnerability of the English living in Africa. Historically, only a very small number of Englishmen had contact with Africans; see Philip Morgan, "British Encounters with Africans and African-Americans, circa 1600–1780," in *Strangers Within the Realm: Cultural Margins of the First British Empire* (Chapel Hill: University of North Carolina Press, 1991): "About 350,000 Britons had some measure of direct contact with blacks on the African littoral from 1600 to 1780" (160). See John Thornton, *Africa and Africans in the Making of the Atlantic World, 1400–1680* (New York: Cambridge University Press, 1992), chap. 2, for an excellent account of the early modern give-and-take between Africans and Europeans in regard to items of trade and its general organization.

29. Morgan, "British Encounters with Africans and African-Americans," 182–84.

30. William Smith, *A New Voyage to Guinea* (1744; London: Frank Cass, 1967), 138, and James Houstoun, *Some New and Accurate Observations Geographical, Natural and Historical . . . of the Coast of Guinea* (London: J. Peele, 1725), 24–25.

31. Barker, *The African Link*, 14.

32. Thornton, *Africa and Africans in the Making of the Atlantic World*, 317.

33. Felicity Heal, *Hospitality in Early Modern England* (Oxford: Clarendon Press, 1990), 103–20.

34. See the definitions for *civility* offered in Samuel Johnson, *A Dictionary of the English Language* (London: W. Strahan), 1755.

35. Scenes like this are typical of the early eighteenth-century narratives. European clothing, for instance, occasionally elicits mixed feelings. In *A Voyage to Guinea, Brasil, and the West-Indies*, John Atkins deplores European behavior and slavery; he also characterizes the people he meets as naked, idle, ignorant, and lacking a government (61), and he claims to find African women contemptible (50). Yet the report of his meeting with King Pedro of Sesthos suggests a different dynamic at work. In detailing the palaver rooms where business is transacted, Atkins comments on the very government he accuses the Africans of lacking elsewhere. Before European ships can obtain wood and water, the king expects a *dashee*. The king makes the Englishmen wait an hour before he enters attended by 100 *"naked Nobles"* (64). Atkins reports that the king's dress—a dirty bays gown—looks "antick" because it is a patchwork of various colors and has a train. He sports a full bottomed wig, an old hat too small for the wig, coarse shoes and stockings, and a heavy brass chain around

his neck (65). While he may look comical to the Englishmen, he finds their *dashee* insufficient and asks for items of their clothing to supplement it (65). In another situation, European dress does not elicit contempt as much as approbation, perhaps because it is combined with the profession of sincere Christianity. Receiving the Englishmen in European dress, Seignior Joseph of Sierra Leone had traveled to England and Portugal and been baptized a Catholic. Atkins approves of his effort to propagate Christianity among his subjects. Another laudable act Atkins reports is that this Christian Negro had "by the Advantage of Trade" "removed the Wants of his own Family (his Towns)" (55).

36. Daniel Defoe, *The Life and Adventures of Robinson Crusoe*, ed. Angus Ross (1719; London: Penguin Books, 1965), 141.

37. Fernand Braudel, *The Structures of Everyday Life: The Limits of the Possible*, vol. 1, *Civilization and Capitalism: Fifteenth–Eighteenth Century*, trans. Siân Reynolds (1979; Berkeley: University of California Press, 1992), 205.

38. On Atkins's second trip to see King Pedro, he finds him in a more casual setting, smoking with two of his wives: "His Dress and Figure, with the novelty of ours, created mutual Smiles which held a few Minutes" (67). In this situation, the reciprocal oddity apparently strikes both parties, and the shared moment works similarly to the one in Snelgrave's text.

39. Gary Scrimgeour, "The Problem of Realism in Defoe's *Captain Singleton*," *Huntington Library Quarterly* 27 (1963–64): 23.

40. On the travel narrative quality of the novel, see Francis Watson, *Daniel Defoe* (1952; New York: Kennikat Press, 1969), 193. As the editor of the Penguin edition notes, until the 1780s *Captain Singleton* was not advertised as a fictional work by Defoe (vii); it thus circulated as a "true," if sensational, memoir. The title page accentuates the travel book quality and builds interest especially around Africa: "The Life, Adventures, and Pyracies, of the Famous Captain Singleton: Containing an Account of his being set on Shore in the Island of *Madagascar*, his Settlement there, with a Description of the Place and Inhabitants: Of his Passage from thence, in a Paraguay, to the main Land of *Africa*, with an Account of the customs and Manners of the People: His great Deliverances from the barbarous Natives and wild Beasts: Of his meeting with an *Englishman*, a Citizen of *London*, among the *Indians*, the great Riches he acquired, and his Voyage Home to *England*."

41. Arthur Secord, *Studies in the Narrative Method of Defoe* (1924; New York: Russell and Russell, 1963), 129–30, looks at travel narratives with which Defoe was familiar and which were in his personal library. At the time of the novel's publication or, indeed, one hundred years later, few Britons could have questioned the accuracy of Defoe's depiction.

42. Scrimgeour, "The Problem of Realism," 21.

43. Madagascar especially elicited European speculation about establishing plantations during the seventeenth and early eighteenth centuries—not in any coherent way but in several offhand statements in travel accounts and geographies. It was strategically located for the East India Company's base of operations. R. K.

Kent, "Madagascar and the Islands of the Indian Ocean," in *General History of Africa*, ed. B. A. Ogot, vol. 5, *Africa from the Sixteenth to the Eighteenth Century* (Berkeley: University of California Press, 1992) refers to two attempts at English colonization, one of them a group of Puritans that was sent to Madagascar in 1644–45 to establish a colony (863). Richard Boothby, *A Brief Discovery or Description of the Most Famous Island of Madagascar* (1646) in *A Collection of Voyages and Travels*, 2 vols. (London: Thomas Osborne 1745), 625-63, calls Madagascar "the paradise of the world" (2:633). Boothby believed that the fertile island could be wealthy, "especially if once inhabited with Christians or civil people, skillful in agriculture and manufactures, and all sorts of mechanic arts and labours" (633). Similarly, Robert Morden, *Geography Rectified; or, A Description of the World* (London: Robert Morden and Thomas Cockerill, 1693) repeats such sentiments and makes the same equation between civility, the Christian religion, and more beneficial trade—all characteristic English notions of their identity: "Pity it is, that so noble an Island, and so populous, should continue so long uncivilized, and corrupted with Mahumetism [*sic*] and Heathenism, and estranged from God and Virtue, and seated so advantageously for Traffick with all the World" (538). Morden's text was familiar to Defoe and used in *Captain Singleton*; see Secord, *Studies in the Narrative Method of Defoe*, 138.

Given Defoe's familiarity with the attractions of Madagascar and that it was a well-known depot for pirates, it is little surprise that Singleton believes Madagascar the best place in the world to settle (36). To the British, Madagascar represents potential for settlement as well as expanded trade in Africa. Singleton's sense that violent intervention was the only way to settle successfully (i.e., profitably) reflects a desire not so much to settle Africa with Europeans as to control the flow of goods to Europe. Madagascar was an important source of slaves during the late seventeenth century. West Indian planters felt undersupplied by the Royal African Company and turned to Madagascar. According to Kenneth Davies, *The Royal African Company* (London: Longman, 1957): "Between 1675 and 1690 numbers of Malagasy slaves were brought to the English colonies, and the company was powerless to stop the trade. Madagascar lay within the limits of the charter of the East India Company, but that body had no interests there and turned a deaf ear to appeals for help in restraining interlopers" (100).

44. Willem Bosman, *A New and Accurate Description of the Coast of Guinea* (in Dutch) (London: J. Knapton, 1705), 86.

45. Barker, *The African Link*, 4.

46. Vaughan and Vaughan, "Before *Othello*," 26.

47. Laura Brown, *Ends of Empire: Women and Ideology in Early Eighteenth-Century English Literature* (Ithaca: Cornell University Press, 1993), 162.

48. Walter Rodney, *A History of the Upper Guinea Coast, 1545-1800* (Oxford: Clarendon Press, 1970), 154.

49. David Galenson, *Traders, Planters, and Slaves: Market Behavior in Early English America* (Cambridge: Cambridge University Press, 1986), 13.

50. Davies, *The Royal African Company*, 41.

51. Adas, *Machines as the Measure of Man*, 112.

52. Atkins, *A Voyage to Guinea*, 86, 99, 106, makes the same contradictory statements about trade and civility that Defoe does.

53. Rodney, *A History of the Upper Guinea Coast*, 171, observes that, although not as attractive as some other items of trade, European coins were imported by Africans for ornamentation. In the novel, however, the value-added labor is European, not African. Eighteenth-century travelers note ornamentation in general was popular among Africans: Some painted their bodies and faces, others scarified them. Atkins, *A Voyage to Guinea*, 61, records that on the Grain and Malaguetta coasts, the men wore jewelry on their wrists, ankles, fingers, and toes.

54. Rodney, *A History of the Upper Guinea Coast*, 184.

55. Atkins, *A Voyage to Guinea*, 76.

56. Thornton, *Africa and Africans*, 44–45, contends that preindustrial Europe offered Africa little it did not already produce. African interest in ornamentation was not a sign of their savagery; it was, he argues, a testament to the strength of local markets and reflected conspicuous consumption of novel items.

57. See Bosman, *A New and Accurate Description of the Coast of Guinea*, 52, 82, 334, and Snelgrave, *A New Account of Guinea*, 2.

58. Rodney, *A History of the Upper Guinea Coast*, 172.

59. The Portuguese foresaw the possible erosion of their local power with the dissemination of European technology and officially refused to trade in weapons (ibid., 175). "Between 1703 and 1719, the [Royal African] Company requisitioned a large variety of firearms for the African trade" (175), although arms did not penetrate inland as easily (176–77); guns and other European weapons were not as significant in the early part of the eighteenth century as they were later as a major British export to Africa.

60. Daniel Defoe, *A Review of the State of the British Nation* 5:140, (1709; New York: Columbia University Press, 1938), 560.

61. Scrimgeour, "The Problem of Realism," 26. A. W. Secord, *Studies in the Narrative Method of Defoe* (1924; New York: Russell and Russell, 1963) was one of the first to observe this phenomenon: "Singleton's remarks concerning the people and the country are cautiously general" (128).

62. Typical of contemporary accounts of Africa, "white men" is the most common reference to Europeans in the novel (179, 160–61, 134, 68). According to the *OED*, the adjective form of *white* first appeared to distinguish Europeans from other people in the early seventeenth century. The noun *white* did not appear in the *OED* until 1671.

63. Snelgrave, *A New Account of Guinea*, 25.

64. Smith, *A New Voyage to Guinea*, 182.

65. The possibility of Africans being cannibals is dismissed early in the novel (13). Although there were isolated allusions to interior peoples being cannibals in some travel accounts, John Atkins, *A Voyage to Guinea*, agrees with Defoe: Africa and cannibalism were not related (xxiii). Other narratives that include reference to Afri-

can cannibalism generally copy from previous sources, although many eighteenth-century travel accounts dismiss the possibility of cannibalism. Geographies, however, generally include cannibalism as part of the African disposition.

66. Scrimgeour, "The Problem of Realism," 29.

67. Tzvetan Todorov, *The Conquest of America: The Question of the Other*, trans. Richard Howard (1984; New York: HarperPerennial, 1992), 34, 36.

68. Thornton, *Africa and Africans*, 50.

69. Other critics have mentioned that nakedness forms a crucial sign of non-Europeanness. See Timothy Blackburn, "The Coherence of Defoe's *Captain Singleton*," *Huntington Library Quarterly* 61.2 (1978): 125, and James Sutherland, *Daniel Defoe: A Critical Study* (Cambridge: Harvard University Press, 1971), 145.

70. Another possibility is that African nakedness, which almost always involves some covering, if scanty by European standards, offends the commercial desires underwriting much of the narrative. Africans do not consume enough! As Davies, *The Royal African Company*, shows, reexports were increasingly important to the British and global economies. Cloth, especially East India cottons, calicoes, and prints, "commanded a ready sale in Africa" (170). English cloth played a significant role as well in the later seventeenth century; domestic manufacture completely replaced cloth bought from Amsterdam for sale in Africa at this time (175). English woolens were the most important domestic manufacture shipped to Africa (176–77).

71. Adas, *Machines as the Measure of Man*, 28.

72. One of the continuing fascinations of eighteenth-century travel narratives was with European men who lived among the natives not as company factors but as captives or renegades. *Captain Singleton* features three such inset narratives of Europeans that reveal quite a bit about important racial boundaries. The other two narratives of hybrid Europeans take place in Ceylon. In both of these narratives, the interest focuses on what, if any, admixture has occurred in Europeans' behavior by prolonged distance from civil society.

73. According to Susan Jeffords, "Compromising Narratives: The Ideological Structure of Epistolaries, Conduct Books, and the Eighteenth-Century English Novel," *Quarterly Journal of Ideology* 10.3 (1986): 24, Defoe's conduct books, especially *The Compleat English Gentleman* (1729), argue that "a gentleman should be distinguished, not by his *blood*, but by his *behavior*."

74. Two exceptions are in *Captain Singleton*, 54, 73. Contemporaries noted that the number of prisoners of war had burgeoned because the Europeans inflamed historical tribal differences within Africa and created new ones to increase the flow of slaves. For information about procurement of slaves for sale to Europeans, see David Brion Davis, *The Problem of Slavery in Western Culture* (New York: Oxford University Press, 1966): "As late as 1721 the Royal African Company asked its agents to investigate the modes of enslavement in the interior and to discover whether there was any source besides 'that of being taken Prisoners in war time'" (183).

75. For example, in *An Essay upon the Trade to Africa* (London, 1711), Defoe refers repeatedly to the continuation of the slave trade under the Company's direc-

tion as benefiting the nation (15); usually, he criticizes the free traders and praises the Company. In defending the necessity and viability of the Royal African Company, Defoe expressed a minority position; see Davies, *The Royal African Company*, 130, 150. See Defoe's *Review* 1:44 (1713) and *Review* 5:140, 557 for Defoe's assigning mutual blame to the Company, government, and free traders. Defoe not only wrote about but invested in the Royal African Company and the South Sea Company; see John Moore, *Daniel Defoe: Citizen of the Modern World* (Chicago: University of Chicago Press, 1958), 86. He invested £800 for two shares "which fell so in price that he got less than £100 for them. By June, 1710, he had no investment in the [Royal African] company" (289).

76. Barker, *The African Link*, 9.

77. Brown, *Ends of Empire*, 162.

78. Morgan, "British Encounters with Africans and African-Americans," 201.

79. Singleton ends his journey at Cape Coast Castle, which was the major English garrison at the time of the novel's publication, with about 100 Europeans, or about half of the British population on the Gold Coast; see Morgan, "British Encounters with Africans and African-Americans," 182.

80. Snelgrave, *A New Account of Guinea*, justifies slavery in ways that continued to be popular over the eighteenth century. He begins by asserting that slavery has been an African custom "time out of Mind," and that before Europeans bought slaves, Africans "were often obliged to kill great Multitudes" (158) because polygamy had overpopulated the continent (160). He erases the European role in the increase in the number of slaves and the different conditions of African slavery. On the other hand, Atkins, *A Voyage to Guinea*, emphasizes that slaves result from wars carried on among Africans and that many Europeans lured Africans onto their ships for trade. He critiques the notion that slavery improves the lot of Africans because slavery removes people from their families, friends, and homeland, which "must be highly offending against the Laws of natural Justice and Humanity" (178).

81. Snelgrave, *A New Account of Guinea*, 4.

82. See Felicity A. Nussbaum, "The Other Woman: Polygamy, *Pamela*, and the Prerogative of Empire," *Women, "Race," and Writing in the Early Modern Period*, ed. Margo Hendricks and Patricia Parker (New York: Routledge, 1994), 145.

83. Two exceptions are John Richetti, *Popular Fiction Before Richardson: Narrative Patterns, 1700–1739* (Oxford, Clarendon Press, 1969), and Virginia Birdsall, *Defoe's Perpetual Seekers: A Study of the Major Fiction* (Lewisburg, Pa.: Bucknell University Press, 1985). They both interpret interracial sex between the Portuguese pirates and native women similarly—as a reflection on Singleton. Richetti mentions only the one incident in Ceylon as evidence that Singleton is superior to the Portuguese with whom he travels (87–88), and Birdsall characterizes these scenes of (sexual) violence simply as evidence of Singleton's "failure to control the appetites of his men" (63). The other significance Birdsall draws focuses on the irony of the lack of control displayed by "ostensibly civilized human beings in their relationship with 'uncivilized' ones" (64).

84. Also used in the similar encounter in Ceylon with the native women, *homely* means rough or rude, according to the *OED*. In this passage, it takes on its dominant usage, which conveys an excuse: "Often apologetic, depreciative, or even as a euphemism for 'wanting refinement, polish, or grace.'"

85. B. R. Burg, *Sodomy and the Perception of Evil: English Sea Rovers in the Seventeenth-Century Caribbean* (New York: New York University Press, 1983), and Hans Turley, "Piracy, Identity, and Desire in *Captain Singleton*," *Eighteenth-Century Studies* 31 (winter 1997–98): 199–214.

86. Luce Irigaray, *This Sex Which Is Not One*, trans. Catherine Porter (Ithaca: Cornell University Press, 1985), 157–58.

87. Defoe's *Review* 1:44, 89. In a similar vein, James Houstoun, *Some New and Accurate Observations of the Coast of Guinea* in *The Works of James Houstoun, M.D.* (London: S. Bladon, 1753), writes about the importance of trade to Africa: "What a glorious and advantageous Trade this is . . . it is the Hinge on which all the Trade of this Globe moves; for put a Stop to the peopling the *European* Plantations Abroad . . . without depopulating *Europe*; I say, put a stop to the *Slave-trade*, and all others cease of course. Pray who digs the rich Mines of *Peru*, *Brazil*, &c? Nay, who sweetens the Ladies Tea, and the generous Bowl? And who reaps the Profit of all?" (147–48). During the first three decades of the eighteenth century, there was a consensus that the trade to Africa was of the greatest importance to Britain's wealth. What was more in dispute was the value of the Royal African Company versus separate traders (i.e., monopoly vs. free trade).

88. Hazel Carby, "White Woman Listen! Black Feminism and the Boundaries of Sisterhood," *The Empire Strikes Back: Race and Racism in 70s Britain* (London: Hutchinson, 1982), 221–22. Carby's wording misleadingly conveys the impression that all women in Britain were white in the eighteenth century, but her point about general benefits to the national population, including women, is timely.

Chapter 3. Romanticizing Racial Difference

1. Samuel Richardson, *Pamela: or, Virtue Rewarded*, ed. Peter Sabor (Harmondsworth: Penguin Books, 1980), 441; Benjamin Rush ("By a Pennsylvanian"), *A Vindication of the Address to the Inhabitants of the British Settlements, on the Slavery of the Negroes in America* (Philadelphia: John Dunlap, 1773), 4. The nineteenth-century term *miscegenation* often describes interracial sex, marriage, and the children—and usually refers to white and black relations only. I have retained the eighteenth-century terms *amalgamation* and *intermarriage*. The negative connotation of *miscegenation* is striking for its assumptions about race compared with *amalgamation*.

2. Daniel Defoe, *The Life and Adventures of Robinson Crusoe*, ed. Angus Ross (1719; London: Penguin Books, 1965), 299.

3. Although in novels such as *The Farther Adventures of Robinson Crusoe* (1719) and William Chetwood's *Captain Richard Falconer* (1720) Englishmen marry Caribbean women, they do not bring these wives back to England.

4. Robert Heilman, *America in English Fiction, 1760–1800: The Influence of the American Revolution* (1937; New York: Octagon Books, 1968), 84. He calculates that "two editions indicate considerable attention, three positive popularity" (84). Heilman suggests another way to judge the readership and reception that the intermarriage novels enjoyed in the eighteenth century: between 1760 and 1800, two thousand novels were published; 75 percent were never reprinted.

5. Jerry Beasley, *Novels of the 1740s* (Athens: University of Georgia Press, 1982), 59.

6. Jennifer Goodman, "Marriage and Conversion in Late Medieval Romance," in *Varieties of Religious Conversion in the Middle Ages*, ed. James Muldoon (Gainesville: University Press of Florida, 1997), 115, 124.

7. Edward Long, *Candid Reflections Upon the Judgement . . . On What is Commonly Called the Negroe-Cause* (1772), quoted in Peter Fryer, *Staying Power: The History of Black People in Britain* (London: Pluto Press, 1984), 157.

8. In the 1772 Somerset case, it was ruled that a master could not force his slave to go out of England; this was an updated version of an older law that applied to masters and servants (ibid., 126). This ruling did not, of course, ban slavery in England.

9. Winthrop Jordan, *White over Black: American Attitudes Toward the Negro, 1550–1812* (1968; New York: W. W. Norton, 1977), 137, 171.

10. A characteristic public discussion of planter-slave sexual relations is found in letters written by Barbadian men in *Carribbeana. Containing Letters and Dissertations, Together with Poetical Essays, On Various Subjects and Occasions: Chiefly Wrote by Several Hands in the West-Indies, And Some of Them Gentlemen Residing There*, 2 vols. (London: T. Osborne, 1741); at this point, interracial sexual relations are eroticized, being widely considered the most convenient way for Englishmen to gratify their passions.

11. Abena Busia, "Miscegenation as Metonymy: Sexuality and Power in the Colonial Novel," *Ethnic and Racial Studies* 9.3 (1986): 367.

12. Jordan, *White over Black*, 162–63.

13. Fryer, *Staying Power*, 161.

14. Brief statements against amalgamation occur in F. Freeman, *The London Chronicle* (1765); Anonymous, *The London Chronicle* (1773); Samuel Estwick, *Consideration on the Negroe Cause* (1772); Edward Long, *The History of Jamaica* (1774); Charles Johnstone, *The Pilgrim* (1775); and Philip Thicknesse, *A Year's Journey Through France and Part of Spain*, 2d ed. (1778). See Fryer, *Staying Power*, 155–65, for details. Folarin Shyllon, *Black People in Britain, 1555–1833* (London: Oxford University Press, 1977), 110–12, cites seven public statements associated with the West India lobby against black/white intermarriage, which, like above, are short remarks in treatises addressing other issues. Five of them follow the Somerset case; the other two appear in the mid- and late 1780s. Gretchen Gerzina, *Black London: Life Before Emancipation* (New Brunswick, N.J.: Rutgers University Press, 1995), offers another explanation for intermarriages in England: "Mixed-race marriages tended not to be

seen as problematic to the English because they primarily occurred among the lower working classes" (21).

Although they clearly marshal incipient racism, both Long and Thicknesse regarded the French, as well as blacks, as agents of contamination for the English population. See Paul Langford, *A Polite and Commercial People: England, 1727–83* (Oxford: Clarendon Press, 1989), 506, on Thicknesse against the French, and consult Edward Long, *English Humanity No Paradox: or, An Attempt to Prove, that the English Are Not a Nation of Savages* (London, 1778). In attempting to vindicate the English in their conduct of the American war, Long often juxtaposes black Africans and the French in a negative way.

15. The various West Indian assemblies dealt with interracial sex somewhat differently. Jordan, *White over Black*, 140, suggests that even though North American colonies had more legal bans against intermarriage, interracial liaisons were more evenly distributed among white men and women than in the West Indies, which had fewer legal strictures, but on many islands, it was unthinkable for white women of any class to be connected with a black man. Montserrat, where there was a large free black population, was the only island to ban intermarriage.

16. George Fredrickson, *The Arrogance of Race: Race, Class, and Consciousness* (Middletown, Conn.: Wesleyan University Press, 1988), 196.

17. Henry Gally, *Some Considerations upon Clandestine Marriages*, in *The Marriage Act of 1753: Four Tracts* (1750; New York: Garland, 1984), 36, 1.

18. Thomas Perry, *Public Opinion, Propaganda, and Politics in Eighteenth-Century England: A Study of the Jew Bill of 1753* (Cambridge: Harvard University Press, 1962), 13–14, notes that in the Marriage Act of 1753, Jews were allowed exemptions because most acts were aimed at Catholics.

19. Jordan, *White over Black*, 95.

20. Morgan Godwyn, *The Negro's and Indians Advocate, Suing for their Admission into the Church* (London: J. D., 1680), 61.

21. Fryer, *Staying Power*, 146.

22. Sarah Scott, *The History of Sir George Ellison*, 2 vols. (1766; London: F. Noble and J. Noble, 1770), 1:27.

23. Ibid., 2:48.

24. Kathleen Wilson, *The Sense of the People: Politics, Culture, and Imperialism in England, 1715–1785* (Cambridge: Cambridge University Press, 1995), 138.

25. In characterizing a new phase of the British Empire in the 1760s, T. O. Lloyd, *The British Empire, 1558–1983* (New York: Oxford University Press, 1984), argues that the most significant difference from the seventeenth and early eighteenth centuries was the acquisition of new subjects: "The changes of 1757–63 mark the point at which the British moved on an appreciable scale into the imperial activity of gaining new subjects in the process of expansion" (84).

26. W. R. Chetwood, *The Voyages, Travels, and Adventures of William Owen Gwin Vaughan*, 2 vols. (London: J. Watts, 1736). The novel also appeared in 1740 and in a second London edition in 1760, as well as in a Dublin edition of 1754. Chet-

wood was already known for stories of adventure and interracial sex from his previous popular novels.

27. In narratives about the Ottoman Empire, male European travelers and fictional characters repeatedly encounter circumstances wherein they represent themselves as the object of Muslim men's desire; however, this bisexual or homosexual desire is rehearsed as a specifically Muslim propensity.

28. Chetwood, *Voyages of William Vaughan*, 2:144, 132.

29. Attributed to Charles Brachy, there is a Dublin edition of 1760. Before it was printed on its own, the novel appeared in the very popular collection of Madame de Gomez's *Cent Nouvelles Nouvelles* (1744) in both the original French and in the English translation.

30. Carl von Linné, *A General System of Nature, Through the Three Grand Kingdoms of Animals, Vegetables, and Minerals* (1735 [rev. 1758]; London: Allen Lackington, 1802), 7.

31. Georges Louis Leclerc, comte de Buffon, *Natural History: General and Particular*, trans. William Smellie, 35 vols. (1749; London: T. Cadell and W. Davies, 1812), 3:351, 431.

32. Laugier de Tassy, *A Compleat History of the Piratical States of Barbary* (London: R. Griffiths, 1750), v.

33. Thomas Shaw, *Travels, or Observations Relating to Several Parts of Barbary and the Levant* (Oxford: Printed at the Theatre, 1738), 304.

34. De Tassy, *Piratical States of Barbary*, iv, 287.

35. Janet Todd, *The Sign of Angelica: Women, Writing, and Fiction, 1660–1800* (New York: Columbia University Press, 1989), 103.

36. Linda Colley, *Britons: Forging the Nation, 1707–1837* (New Haven: Yale University Press, 1992), 103.

37. The most widely reviewed of any of these intermarriage novels, *The Fool of Quality* received encomiums from the *Monthly Review* (vols. 35 and 42), the *Critical Review* (vol. 22), and the *Gentleman's Magazine* (vol. 36). It appeared abridged in the *Universal Magazine* shortly after its initial publication; see Mayo, *The English Novel in the Magazines*, 181. Leigh Hunt included the novel, heavily excerpted, in *Classic Tales* (1806–7), a collection "intended to contain the best short fiction of the previous age" (Mayo, 255). In 1780, John Wesley edited the novel and recommended it for religious instruction.

38. Gerald Newman, *The Rise of English Nationalism: A Cultural History, 1740–1830* (London: Weidenfeld and Nicolson, 1987), 127.

39. Linda Colley, *Britons*, 102, observes that Catholicism and Islam were considered antithetical to the British version of Christianity because of the way that authority figured in them: "Asia, like Catholicism, was for many Britons synonymous with arbitrary power." Similarly, P. J. Marshall and Glyndwr Williams, *The Great Map of Mankind: Perceptions of New Worlds in the Age of Enlightenment* (Cambridge: Harvard University Press, 1982), 150, argue, "Oppressive despotisms and obscurantist religions, the normal 'moral' elements in Asian immobility, were but the 'Popery' and 'slavery' of authoritarian Catholic Europe writ large. Britain was presumed to

be a country governed under known laws with the consent of at least some sections of its population; British Protestantism rested on reason and placed no obstacles in the way of scientific inquiry and the pursuit of individual advantage."

40. Homoerotic attraction is not reserved solely for cross-dressing heroines. In fact, "sympathy"—a platonic though complex form of attraction and bond—provides the intuitive connection. The way that the elder Harry Clinton's attachment to Louisa is signaled is through another same-gender encounter. At the opera, Harry meets "one of the loveliest young fellows I ever beheld" (5:135). The stranger explains his attraction to Harry in terms of immediate "sympathy" (136). The object of this immediate sympathy turns out to be Louisa's brother.

41. Louisa's mother explains that she cannot convince her husband to let the two marry because "he inquired your character among the English; and, notwithstanding the report of the nobility of your birth, and your yet nobler qualities, hearing also that you had acquired part of your fortune in trade, he conceived an utter contempt for you, and took an utter aversion to you" (5:145-46).

42. There was a historical basis for this perception: "By the early 1700s, most comparable institutions [to Parliament] had ceased to meet, as the estates general had in France, or had been emasculated, like the diets in most German states": Colley, *Britons*, 50.

43. *Royal Magazine; or Gentleman's Monthly Companion* 2 (January-June 1760): 286.

44. De Tassy, *Piratical States of Barbary*, 363.

45. The younger Harry's first introduction to the Moroccan strangers is accidental. At the docks, he sees the "savage populace," who are "insulting, beating, and dragging a number of unhappy foreigners, without any apparent provocation, save that their garb, complexion, and language, were different from their own; the very reason that should have induced them to have treated these abused strangers with courtesy and kindness" (5:199). Savagery is associated with the lower orders of English society rather than with the Moroccan strangers. Despite such a hostile reaction to the "London barbarians" (5:200), their response physically enacts Harry's initial negative ideas about the black Moor and his attendants.

46. John Barrell, *The Political Theory of Painting from Reynolds to Hazlitt: "The Body of the Public"* (New Haven: Yale University Press, 1986), 31-40.

47. *The Lady's Drawing Room* (London: M. Cooper and A. Dodd, 1744; reprint, New York: Garland, 1974), 101. The novel was published in London in a second edition of 1748 and in Dublin in 1746. Henrietta's inset narrative was popular in its own right; it was published in 1750, 1800, and 1820. Zoa's history also appeared separately in 1808 and 1815; it typically mentioned her mother's narrative as a selling point for her own.

48. François Bernier, "A New Division of the Earth, According to the Different Species or Races of Men Who Inhabit It," *Journal des Sçavans*, in *Memoirs Read Before the Anthropological Society of London, 1863-4*, ed. T. Bendyshe (1684; London: Longman, 1865), 361.

49. See, for example, John Henry Grose's *Voyage to the East-Indies*, 2d ed.

(London, 1767). He notes that the English controlled Bombay: "The houses of the black merchants, as they are called; though some are far from deserving the appellation of black; are for the most part extremely ill distributed" (53). In a section devoted to the climate, Grose observes, "The natural color of the inhabitants is black: but the Bramins, and generally the Morattoes, are yellowish, little differing from a tawnish Portuguese" (340).

50. Robert Sencourt, *India in English Literature* (1923; Port Washington, N.Y.: Kennikat Press, 1970), remarks that *heathens* was the most typical reference to East Indians in the seventeenth century, especially since there was very little precise or firsthand knowledge about the inhabitants. Samuel Johnson was one of the more eminent English writers who considered "the native inhabitants barbarians" in the late eighteenth century (203). Warren Hastings, "'Letter to Nathaniel Smith,' from *The Bhagvat-Geeta*," in *The British Discovery of Hinduism in the Eighteenth Century*, ed. P. J. Marshall (Cambridge: Cambridge University Press, 1970), 189, comments in a 1784 letter, "It is not very long since the inhabitants of India were considered by many, as creatures scarce elevated above the degree of savage life; nor, I fear, is that prejudice yet wholly eradicated, though surely abated."

51. David Solkin, *Painting for Money: The Visual Arts and the Public Sphere in Eighteenth-Century England* (New Haven: Yale University Press, 1993), 26.

52. William Alexander, *The History of Women from the Earliest Antiquity to the Present Time*, 2 vols. (London: Dilly, 1772), 1:103.

53. Rev. William Smith of Philadelphia made an almost identical statement as the characters in *The Lady's Drawing Room* in relation to intermarriage with Amerindians. He alludes to forgetting civilization, not to sexual scandal. About the women who had married Indian men, Smith writes: "'For the honour of humanity, we would suppose those persons to have been of the lowest rank. . . . For, easy and unconstrained as the savage life is, certainly it could never be put in competition with the blessings of improved life and the light of religion, by any persons who have had the happiness of enjoying, and the capacity of discerning, them.'" See James Axtell, "The White Indians of Colonial America," *William and Mary Quarterly*, 3d series, 32.1 (1975): 65.

54. My analysis is much indebted to Marjorie Garber, *Vested Interests: Cross-Dressing and Cultural Anxiety* (New York: HarperPerennial, 1992) and work on blackface by Eric Lott, "'The Seeming Counterfeit': Racial Politics and Early Blackface Minstrelsy," *American Quarterly* 43.2 (June 1991): 223–54, and Michael Rogin, "Blackface, White Noise: The Jewish Jazz Singer Finds His Voice," *Critical Inquiry* 18.3 (spring 1992): 417–53. I have liberally adapted their incisive theoretical insights to a different historical/ideological moment.

55. Garber, *Vested Interests*, 37, and Lott, "'The Seeming Counterfeit,'" 238.

56. Eric Lott, *Love and Theft: Blackface Minstrelsy and the American Working Class* (New York: Oxford University Press, 1993), 28, 57.

57. Rogin, "Blackface, White Noise," 420, 434.

58. Robert Orme, *Historical Fragments of the Mogul Empire, of the Morattoes,*

and of the English Concerns in Indostan From the Year M.DC.LIX, ed. J. P. Guha (1782; New Delhi: Associated Publishing House, 1974), 301.

59. Michael Edwardes, *The Sahibs and the Lotus: The British in India* (London: Constable, 1988), 33.

60. Nancy Armstrong, *Desire and Domestic Fiction* (Oxford: Oxford University Press, 1987), 30.

61. Kenneth Ballhatchet, *Race, Sex, and Class under the Raj: Imperial Attitudes and Policies and Their Critics, 1793–1905* (New York: St. Martin's Press, 1980), 96–97.

62. Gerald Bryant, "Officers of the East India Company's Army in the Days of Clive and Hastings," *Journal of Imperial and Commonwealth History* 6.3 (1978): 203–27, 209.

63. Ballhatchet, *Race*, 97, 98.

64. *The Female American; or, The Adventures of Unca Eliza Winkfield*, 2 vols. (London: Francis Noble and John Noble, 1767). It was reprinted in 1790, 1797, 1800 and 1814. A similar plot appears in James Annesley's purportedly factual *Memoirs of an Unfortunate Young Nobleman* (1743), which also contains tragic elements.

65. Buffon, *Natural History*, 3:412–13, and Linnaeus, *The System of Nature* (1735), 7.

66. John Brickell, *The Natural History of North Carolina. With an Account of the Trade, Manners, and Customs of the Christian and Indian Inhabitants* (Dublin: James Carson, 1737), 287.

67. For these different yet historically simultaneous interpretations, see David Brion Davis, *The Problem of Slavery in Western Culture* (New York: Oxford University Press, 1966), 167, and Marshall and Williams, *Great Map of Mankind*, 26–33, 187–226.

68. James Merrell, " 'The Customes of Our Countrey': Indians and Colonists in Early America," in *Strangers Within the Realm: Cultural Margins of the First British Empire*, ed. Bernard Bailyn and Philip Morgan (Chapel Hill: University of North Carolina Press, 1991), 140 ff.

69. Davis, *The Problem of Slavery*, 181, reckons, "Although Indians and Negroes were both cruelly exploited and often reduced to the same status as chattel slaves, it is undeniable that the European conscience was more troubled by the plight of the native American."

70. Joel Williamson, *New People: Miscegenation and Mulattoes in the United States* (New York: Free Press, 1980), 35.

71. Some historians have gone so far as to claim that "the entire interracial sexual complex did not pertain to the Indian" because colonists advocated intermarriage with Indians in some cases; see James Kinney, *Amalgamation! Race, Sex, and Rhetoric in the Nineteenth-Century Novel* (Westport, Conn.: Greenwood Press, 1985), 163. William Byrd was one such advocate, and Patrick Henry twice pushed a bill through two readings in the Virginia House of Burgesses that offered monetary rewards for Indian-European marriages (163). In general, the advocacy of intermarriage with Indians was a minority position.

72. Jordan, *White over Black*, 163.

73. Perry, *Public Opinion*, 40–41.

74. Eve Tabor Bannet, "The Marriage Act of 1753: 'A Most Cruel Law for the Fair Sex,'" *Eighteenth-Century Studies* 30.3 (spring 1997): 233–54.

75. Henry Home, Lord Kames, *Six Sketches on the History of Man* (1774; Philadelphia: Bell and Aitken, 1776), offers one explanation of why so few foreign men and mixed-race sons arrive in England: "The master of a family is immediately connected with his country: his wife, his children, his servants, are immediately connected with him, and with their country, through him only. Women, accordingly, have less patriotism than men" (196).

76. For a development of this argument, see Sylvana Tomaselli, "The Enlightenment Debate on Women," *History Workshop* 20 (autumn 1985): 101–24.

Chapter 4. Consuming Englishness

1. Charles Bonnet, *The Contemplation of Nature*, 2 vols. (London: T. Longman, 1766), 1:68–69.

2. *The Present State of the British Interest in India: with a Plan for Establishing a Regular System of Government in that Country* (London: J. Alman, 1773). Although I have featured the discursive framing of Scotland and Jamaica in terms of racialized discourse, during the 1770s much was written about the East Indies and the role of the British. Most frequently, writers concerned with the future of the empire in India focused on the conjunction of national character and right to govern. Most writers did not argue for original distinctions between Britons and the various populations of the East Indies; although many of them had recourse to the long-term effects of a hot climate and the Mogul government to argue for the improved position of the inhabitants under British rule. As scores of books attest, in comparison to the Negro in Africa, there was more debate about the Indian character, far less assurance of its inferiority, and intense interest in the languages, history, and religions of this region.

3. Charles Bonnet, *The Contemplation of Nature* 2 vols. (London: T. Longman, 1766), 1:68–69. Bonnet's eminent contemporary and the foremost natural historian of his generation, Johann Friedrich Blumenbach, remarks on a dubious link that other Continental scientists had noticed between Highlanders and Negroes. Observing for the first time in the third edition of *On the Natural Variety of Mankind* (1795) that "it is generally said that the penis in the Negro is very large," Blumenbach notes that the same was said of the Highlanders. He is not yet sure if this claim is universally true of Negro anatomy, but he asserts that it is not a correct generalization about the northern Scots; see *The Anthropological Treatises of Johann Friedrich Blumenbach*, trans. and ed. Thomas Bendyshe (London: Longman, 1865), 249. Some French and Scots claimed that the penis of Native Americans was smaller than the European average in the 1770s. See Winthrop Jordan, *White over Black: American*

Attitudes Toward the Negro, 1550–1812 (New York: W. W. Norton, 1977), 163. Nonetheless, the Highlanders are consistently the only Europeans who are associated with the most "savage" European Others.

4. *Encyclopaedia Britannica*, 2d ed., 10 vols. (Edinburgh: J. Balfour, 1781), 3:2083.

5. Oliver Goldsmith, *History of the Earth and Animated Nature in Four Volumes* (1774; Philadelphia: Carey, 1795), 1:364.

6. John Hunter, *An Inaugural Dissertation*, in *The Anthropological Treatises of Blumenbach*, 389.

7. Blumenbach, *On the Natural Variety of Mankind* (1781), 100; Georges Louis Leclerc, comte de Buffon, *Natural History: General and Particular*, trans. William Smellie, 35 vols. (London: T. Cadell and W. Davies, 1812), 3:445.

8. Although these Scottish Enlightenment thinkers shared a general approach to theorizing civil society, John Brewer, among others, has correctly argued for the salient differences among them; consult his "Adam Ferguson and the Theme of Exploitation," in *British Journal of Sociology* 37.4 (1986): 470, 473. The nuances of their different approaches to history, progress, and four-stages theory are treated in various essays; see Alan Swingewood, *A Short History of Sociological Thought*, 2d ed. (New York: St. Martin's Press, 1991), 16–20.

9. Ronald Meek, *Social Science and the Ignoble Savage* (Cambridge: Cambridge University Press, 1976), 176.

10. The additions to John Millar's introduction between the first edition of *The Origin of the Distinction of Ranks* (1771) and the third edition of 1781 are telling. The unreliability of climate as a determining factor in national character appears in the time lapse (12–14). See John Millar, *The Origin of the Distinction of Ranks* (London: J. Murray, 1781), 3d ed.

11. Ibid., 2–3.

12. David Hume, "Of National Characters," in *Essays: Moral, Political and Literary* (1742; Oxford: Oxford University Press, 1963), 202.

13. Peter Fryer, *Staying Power: The History of Black People in Britain* (London: Pluto Press, 1984), 421.

14. Hume, *Essays*, 134.

15. Hume, *Essays Moral, Political, and Literary*, ed. T. H. Green, 2 vols. (London: Longmans, 1875), 1:252.

16. Hume, *Essays Moral, Political, and Literary* (London: Grant Richards, 1904) 213.

17. Adam Ferguson, *An Essay on the History of Civil Society*, ed. Duncan Forbes (1767; Edinburgh: University of Edinburgh Press, 1966), 108–09, emphasis added.

18. John Oldmixon, *The British Empire in America* (London, 1708), repeats the commonplace: "'Tis said, people are the Wealth of a Nation" (xix). Eve Tabor Bannet examines this truism in "The Marriage Act of 1753: 'A Most Cruel Law for the Fair Sex'" in *Eighteenth-Century Studies* 30.3 (spring 1997): 233–54.

19. Winthrop Jordan, *White over Black*, 287, gives credence to the impact of

"environmentalism" in the second half of the century, but he offers no particular discussion of the Scottish Enlightenment. Fryer, *Staying Power*, gives most weight to
political factors in the developing discourse of race, not to climatic or institutional
theories. The influence of the planter lobby and merchants involved in the slave trade
are most important for his argument.

20. Hannah Augstein, *Race: The Origins of an Idea, 1760–1850* (Bristol:
Thoemmes Press, 1996), xiii.

21. See Kathleen Wilson, *The Sense of the People: Politics, Culture, and Imperialism in England, 1715–1785* (Cambridge: Cambridge University Press, 1995), 170. The
chapter headings Colley chooses suggest her indebtedness to four-stages theory as
much as the research itself: see Linda Colley, *Britons: Forging the Nation, 1707–1837*
(New Haven: Yale University Press, 1992).

22. For the shared assumptions of civil and natural historians, see Emma
Spary, "Political, Natural, and Bodily Economies," and Paul Wood, "The Science of
Man," both in *Cultures of Natural History*, ed. N. Jardine et al. (Cambridge: Cambridge University Press, 1996). Robert Wolker, "Anthropology and Conjectural History in the Enlightenment," Philip Sloane, "The Gaze of Natural History," and
David Carrithers, "The Enlightenment Science of Society," in *Inventing Human
Science: Eighteenth-Century Domains*, ed. Christopher Fox et al. (Berkeley: University of California Press, 1995), highlight the intellectual context and points about
savage and civil people from four-stages theory but do not explicitly argue that this
was a dominant racial ideology.

23. Felicity A. Nussbaum, *Torrid Zones: Maternity, Sexuality, and Empire in
Eighteenth-Century English Narratives* (Baltimore: Johns Hopkins University Press,
1995), 10.

24. Jack P. Greene, "America and the Creation of the Revolutionary Intellectual World of the Enlightenment," in *Imperatives, Behaviors, and Identities: Essays in
Early American Cultural History* (Charlottesville: University of Virginia Press, 1992),
esp. 357–63, is an excellent analysis of the role of the American colonies in helping
define European notions of civility.

25. Neil McKendrick, "The Commercialization of Fashion," in *The Birth of
a Consumer Society: The Commercialization of Eighteenth-Century England*, ed. Neil
McKendrick et al. (Bloomington: Indiana University Press, 1982), 9–10.

26. Oliver Goldsmith, *History of the Earth*, 1:284.

27. *Royal Magazine; or, Gentleman's Monthly Companion* 2 (June 1760): 341.
This anonymous author, believed to be Goldsmith, provides an "intellectual map" of
the world. Because of the extreme temperatures at either end of the globe, the people
"are incapable of being reduced into society, or any degree of politeness" (341). The
severe climate precludes leisure for advancement and the conditions to produce luxuries. In contrast, the English crown Europe; their excellence derives from their mode
of government: "They are distinguished from the rest of Europe by their superior
accuracy in reasoning . . . [which] is only the consequence of their freedom." On
England, see *Royal Magazine* 2 (September 1760): 140.

28. Michael Hechter, *Internal Colonialism: The Celtic Fringe in British National Development, 1536–1966* (Berkeley: University of California Press, 1975), 31–34.

29. Charles W. J. Withers, *Gaelic Scotland: The Transformation of a Culture Region* (London: Routledge, 1988), 59.

30. Paul Langford, *A Polite and Commercial People, 1727–83* (Oxford: Clarendon Press, 1989), 327.

31. Ferguson, *An Essay on the History of Civil Society*, 108–9.

32. Consult Karen O'Brien, "Johnson's View of the Scottish Enlightenment in *A Journey to the Western Islands of Scotland*," in *The Age of Johnson* (New York: AMS Press, 1991), 4:60–61, for Johnson's reading of Scottish Enlightenment thinkers. Pat Rogers's book, *Johnson and Boswell: The Transit of Caledonia* (Oxford: Clarendon Press, 1995), offers the most complete cultural context for Johnson's *Journey* yet attempted; he looks at travel narratives, at the discoveries in the South Pacific, and at the ideas of "primitive" and "savage" from the Scottish Enlightenment as the primary cultural interests that inform Johnson's *Journey*. Although our interests overlap, our conclusions and methodology differ. My study is ultimately quite different from Rogers's because I am interested specifically in racial discourse as it inflects *Journey*, in the political implications of narrativising race, and in reading the text as symptomatic rather than simply reflective of British culture in the 1770s.

33. Simon During, "Waiting for the Post: Some Relations between Modernity, Colonization, and Writing," *Ariel* 20.4 (1989): 33.

34. R. K. Kaul, "*A Journey to the Western Isles* Reconsidered," *EIC* 13.4 (1963): 341–50, analyzes Johnson's attitude toward contemporary and feudal Scotland by referring to Johnson's dictionary for definitions of savagery. "1. Wild; uncultivated. 2. Untamed; cruel. 3. Uncivilized; barbarous; untaught; wild; brutal" (341). James Boswell *The Journal of a Tour to the Hebrides* (1786; Harmondsworth, Middlesex: Penguin Books, 1984), defines a Highland servant as "a fellow quite like a savage" (288). In this definition, *savage* means idle, dirty, and inadequately clothed. Although I agree with many critics that Johnson sympathized with the Indian's position, documented in his political writings, most of Boswell and Johnson's references to Indians are not sympathetic but derogatory in terms of their savagery and unadvanced state of civilization.

35. Millar, *The Origin of the Distinction of Ranks*, 189, 207.

36. Richard Blome, *Britannia; or, A Geographical Description of the Kingdoms of England, Scotland, and Ireland* (London: Thomas Roycroft, 1673), 292. Martin Martin, *A Description of the Western Islands of Scotland* (London, 1703).

37. Withers, *Gaelic Scotland*, 92.

38. John Richardson, *A Dissertation on the Languages, Literature, and Manners of Eastern Nations* (Oxford: Clarendon Press, 1777), 1–2.

39. Many Highlanders held English in similar contempt. See Fiona Stafford, *The Sublime Savage: A Study of James Macpherson and the Poems of Ossian* (Edinburgh: Edinburgh University Press, 1988), 16.

40. Withers, *Gaelic Scotland*, 345.

41. Stafford, *The Sublime Savage*, 16.

42. Withers, *Gaelic Scotland*, 15.

43. *The Rev. Dr. John Walker's Report on the Hebrides of 1764 and 1771*, ed. Margaret McKay (Edinburgh: John Donald, 1980), 20.

44. Stafford, *The Sublime Savage*, 16.

45. Ivan Hannaford, *Race: The History of an Idea in the West* (Washington, D.C.: Woodrow Wilson Center Press, 1996), 21, 77–79.

46. Benedict Anderson, *Imagined Communities: Reflections on the Origin and Spread of Nationalism*, rev. ed. (London: Verso, 1995), 44.

47. J. G. A. Pocock, *Virtue, Commerce, and History: Essays on Political Thought and History, Chiefly in the Eighteenth Century* (Cambridge: Cambridge University Press, 1985), 128.

48. J. G. Basker, "Scotticisms and the Problem of Cultural Identity in Eighteenth-Century Britain," in *Sociability and Society in Eighteenth-Century Scotland*, ed. John Dwyer and Richard Sher (Edinburgh: Mercat Press, 1993), 84–87.

49. Langford, *A Polite and Commercial People*, 326.

50. Withers, *Gaelic Scotland*, 60; see the *Rambler*, nos. 98, 194, 195.

51. Michèle Cohen, *Fashioning Masculinity: National Identity and Language in the Eighteenth Century* (London: Routledge, 1996), 53.

52. Anand Chitnis, *The Scottish Enlightenment: A Social History* (London: Croom Helm, 1976), 111.

53. Ian Haywood, *The Making of History: A Study of the Literary Forgeries of James Macpherson and Thomas Chatterton in Relation to Eighteenth-Century Ideas of History and Fiction* (Rutherford: Fairleigh Dickinson University Press, 1986), has shown the way that the epic form signified a legitimate national identity in the eighteenth century. David Radcliffe, "Ossian and the Genres of Culture," *SiR* 31.2 (1992): 21, develops this idea by focusing on the way that Ossian's poems validated an alternative to the commercial ideals of a polished nation: "Rather than presenting culture as a gradual refinement of manners through commercial exchange and material progress, Macpherson describes how a society regulated by 'the natural affection of the members of a family' was supplanted first by feudalism and then by the establishment of laws and regular government; 'As the first [stage] is formed on nature, so, of course, it is the most disinterested and noble.'" This argument over the past—whether it was barbaric or noble—has a great deal to do with the force of racialization in the present.

54. Nicholas Hudson, *Writing and European Thought, 1600–1830* (Cambridge: Cambridge University Press, 1994), 102.

55. Henry Louis Gates, Jr., "Introduction: Writing 'Race' and the Difference It Makes," in *"Race," Writing, and Difference* (Chicago: University of Chicago Press, 1985), 8.

56. Mary Anne Hanway, *A Journal to the Highlands of Scotland. With Occasional Remarks on Dr. Johnson's Tour* (London: Fields and Walker, 1775), 67.

57. See Malcolm Andrews, *The Search for the Picturesque: Landscape Aesthetics*

and Tourism in Britain (Stanford: Stanford University Press, 1989), 198, and Ralph Jenkins, "'And I Travelled after Him:' Johnson and Pennant in Scotland," *Texas Studies in Literature and Language* 14.3 (1972): 461–62.

58. J. D. Fleeman, ed., introduction to *A Journey to the Western Islands*, by Samuel Johnson (Oxford: Clarendon Press, 1985).

59. Howard Weinbrot, *Britannia's Issue: The Rise of British Literature from Dryden to Ossian* (Cambridge: Cambridge University Press, 1993), 512.

60. John Radner, "The Significance of Johnson's Changing Views of the Hebrides," in *The Unknown Samuel Johnson*, ed. John Burke Jr. and Donald Kay (Madison: University of Wisconsin Press, 1983), 136, 145, emphasizes Johnson's preference for explanations of difference based on climatic determinism.

61. Georges Louis Leclerc, comte de Buffon, *Natural History: General and Particular*, trans. William Smellie, 35 vols. (1749; London: T. Cadell and W. Davies, 1812), 3:201. To Buffon, a strong body "which would be highly valuable in the savage state, is of little use among polished nations, where more depends on mental than corporeal powers, and where manual labor is conferred to the inferior orders of men" (3:201). Adam Smith, *The Theory of Moral Sentiments*, ed. D. D. Raphael and A. L. Macfie (Oxford: Clarendon Press, 1976), 185, observes that sensibility is the characteristic most suitable to a civilized country and hardiness to barbarians.

62. Hannaford, *Race*, 53.

63. Previously, Johnson described the hierarchy of the clan system: "Next in dignity to the Laird is the tacksman; a large taker or lease-holder of land. . . . The Tacksman is necessarily a man capable of securing to the Laird the whole rent, and is commonly a collateral relation. . . . He held a middle station, by which the highest and the lowest orders were connected. He paid rent and reverence to the Laird, and received them from the tenants. This tenure still subsists, with its original operation, but not with the primitive stability" (94–95).

64. Mercantile theory envisioned such an enhancement of Britain that tends to illustrate Hechter's thesis about internal colonialism and its relation to overseas expansion. The center of the empire, England, was compared to the hub of a wheel, its colonies to the spokes. Trading around the rim was strictly forbidden, because it meant that the colonies might benefit independently and that England might lose control of natural resources and money. Illegal trade flourished, of course, which is one of the main reasons pirates were so reviled by the government (usually not by the populace who bought the desirable goods).

65. Withers, *Gaelic Scotland*, 42. The efforts to disarm Highlanders and forbid Highland dress, punish wealthy chiefs from the 1745 Rebellion, and annex their estates "are seen to have been successful in accelerating the transition of a Highland society from one stage to the next—from a military-feudal type of social organization to the commercialization of agriculture under a more capitalist system of landownership." See Karen O'Brien, "Johnson's View," 66.

66. Not all commentators viewed the clan system as the responsible party for widespread impoverishment or the Union as an effective antidote. James Dunbar,

Caledonia: A Poem (London: T. Cadell, 1788), offers several instructive footnotes about the desperate situation in the Highlands that departs somewhat from Johnson's account. Although they both comment on the lack of employment, the problem of massive emigration, and the little money in circulation, Dunbar outlines the difficulty of gainful employment in the Highlands and makes concrete suggestions for alleviating the poverty that accompanied the destruction of subsistence clan living. He suggests giving wool and flax to the Highlanders to spin into yarn for stockings to sell to the army, which would augment the income for men and women who primarily tend flocks. In the coastal regions, he suggests encouragement of the fishing industry. More labor will result in more money in circulation, "which is much wanted" (57). If they had a sure market for their goods, then they would be more industrious and not think of emigrating to America. Views of the benefits of the Union did not simply divide along national lines.

67. Johnson observes about the uniformity Catholicism encouraged: "We therefore who came to hear old traditions, and see antiquated manners, should probably have found them amongst the Papists" (125). Edward Long reaches a similar conclusion about introducing slaves to religion: Catholicism would surely appeal more than Protestantism because of its resemblance to superstitious rites (2:429–30).

68. Edward Tomarken, "Travels into the Unknown: 'Rasselas' and 'A Journey to the Western Islands of Scotland,'" in *The Unknown Samuel Johnson*, 150–70.

69. Dunbar, *Caledonia*, 57.

70. Richard Grove, "The Island and the History of Environmentalism: The Case of St. Vincent," in *Nature and Society in Historical Context*, ed. Mikuláš Teich et al. (Cambridge: Cambridge University Press, 1997), 155.

71. In her informative essay on Johnson's *Dictionary* and *Journey*, Deidre Lynch, "'Beating the Track of the Alphabet': Samuel Johnson, Tourism, and the ABCs of Modern Authority," *ELH* 57.2 (1990): 357–405, provides two interpretations of Johnson's efforts: Johnson "on an ethnographic safari" and "Johnson as *conquering* hero: not so much on a tour as on a victor's triumph, putting power on display, and wielding his English learning in a manner designed to overawe an underdeveloped North Britain" (360).

72. Margaret McDonnell, *The Emigrant Experience: Songs of Highland Emigrants in North America* (Toronto: University of Toronto Press, 1982), 7.

73. Edward Burt, *Letters from a Gentleman in the North of Scotland to his Friend in London . . . began in the Year 1726*, 2 vols. (London: S. Birt, 1754), 1:108–9.

74. Ferguson, *An Essay on the History of Civil Society*, 200, 205.

75. Anthony Barker, *The African Link: British Attitudes to the Negro in the Era of the Atlantic Slave Trade, 1550–1807* (London: Frank Cass, 1978), 41, and Fryer, *Staying Power*, 157.

76. Marshall and Williams, *The Great Map of Mankind*, 57.

77. Philip Morgan, "British Encounters with Africans and African-Americans, circa 1600–1780," in *Strangers Within the Realm: Cultural Margins of the First*

British Empire (Chapel Hill: University of North Carolina Press, 1991): 157–219, is one of the few to analyze Long's treatment of whites.

78. Once sugar production edged out smaller landowners, the larger profit margin encouraged those who could afford to leave to go to England. Absenteeism produced several related problems. In the owners' absence, it was believed that overseers more flagrantly abused slaves, which often prompted slave rebellions. An absent owner also paid less attention to improving the plantation. Overall, the flight of inhabitants weakened the security and attractiveness of the colony.

79. Philip Morgan, "British Encounters with Africans and African Americans," 174.

80. Folarin Shyllon, *Black People in Britain, 1555–1833* (London: Oxford University Press, 1977), 98, calls Long the father of English racism.

81. Edward Long, *The History of Jamaica*, 3 vols. (London: T. Lowndes 1774), 2:260. All references are to volume 2 unless otherwise indicated. It is this section of his text about the various inhabitants of Jamaica that critics and historians commonly cite as evidence that Long is one of the most virulent racists of the eighteenth century. Most of Long's twentieth-century readers have failed to observe that Long made significant distinctions between Africans in Africa and all others in the British colonies; it is only Africans in Africa who are consigned to unchangeable realms of inferiority. See Barker, *The African Link*, 42, and Gates, *"Race," Writing and Difference*, 11. Anthony Barker is one of the few to suggest the complexity of Long's text, including his criticism of the excesses of slavery (42, 70). Thus, no modern consensus about Long's contribution has been reached. While the tendency has been to note the importance of his pseudo-scientific racism, such as Fryer, *Staying Power*, 159, and to attribute his ideas as representative of certain vocal, though minority, elements in Great Britain, Barker has questioned Long's representativeness, describing him as a marginal influence on ideas about race but agreeing with others that his ideas about slavery were increasingly influential. My argument supports the view that on the whole, he is within a range of the mainstream of writers who employ racial ideology.

82. J. H. Parry et al., *A Short History of the West Indies*, 4th ed. (New York: St. Martin's Press, 1987), 134.

83. Barker, *The African Link*, 41, notes that the period of the early 1770s is key in the history of attitudes about the Negro (and, I would add, as opposed to all other populations at this time) because "for the first time men began to argue to the derogatory extreme about the Negro's place in nature."

84. Charles Leslie, *The New History of Jamaica* (London: J. Hodges, 1740), 306.

85. Important earlier considerations of color's relation to enslavement include Morgan Godwyn's *Negro's and Indians Advocate* (London: J.D., 1680), which dismisses it, and *The Importance of Jamaica to Great Britain, Consider'd in a Letter to a Gentleman* (London: A. Dodd, n.d. [post 1722]), which considers color among a range of possibilities for enslaving Africans.

86. Buffon, *Natural History*, 3:383.

87. Colin Campbell, *The Romantic Ethic and the Rise of Modern Consumerism* (Oxford: Basil Blackwell, 1987), 157.

88. Edward Long, *English Humanity No Paradox . . .* (London, 1778), 28.

89. Ferguson, *An Essay on the History of Civil Society*, 290.

90. Goldsmith, *History of the Earth*, 1:373–74.

91. Long mentions the moral sense, a notion associated with Shaftesbury's *Characteristics of Man, Manners, Opinions, Times* (1711); it was an "understanding of what is good and right, as well as a natural desire to carry it out." See Campbell, *The Romantic Ethic*, 150.

92. Since Jamaica had been taken from the Spanish in the late seventeenth century, a group of Spanish-owned black and mulatto slaves fled to the interior mountains and harassed the British planters on and off for decades in guerrilla warfare ending in 1739. Ultimately, they prevented cultivation "to the great prejudice and diminution of his majesty's revenue, as well as of trade, navigation, and consumption, of British manufactures", which is why peace was sought. See Long, *History*, 2:342.

93. Jordan, *White over Black*, 177.

94. Sumi Cho, "Korean Americans vs. African Americans: Conflict and Construction," in *Reading Rodney King: Reading Urban Uprising*, ed. Robert Gooding-Williams (New York: Routledge, 1993), 45–54.

95. Leslie, *New History*, 35–37.

96. William Beckford, Jr., *A Descriptive Account of the Island of Jamaica* (London: T. and J. Egerton, 1790), 376.

97. Leslie, *New History*, 336; *A Letter to a Member of Parliament, Concerning the Importance of Our Sugar-Colonies to Great Britain, by a Gentleman, who resided many years in the Island of Jamaica* (London: J. Taylor, 1745), 26.

98. My argument differs from Carol Barash's. As opposed to many of the earlier texts that linked debased white female sexuality with linguistic hybridity (largely because then most white women were servants in the colonies), this phenomenon had changed by the 1770s when indentured white servitude had all but ceased and the overwhelming majority of white women were wives or daughters of resident planters and merchants. See Barash, "The Character of Difference: The Creole Woman as Cultural Mediator in Narratives About Jamaica," *Eighteenth-Century Studies* 23.4 (summer 1990): 407–28.

99. Pocock, *Virtue*, 106.

100. Bryan Edwards, *The History, Civil and Commercial, of the British Colonies in the West Indies*, 3 vols. (London: J. Stockdale, 1793–1801), 1:15.

101. Elizabeth Bonhote, *The Rambles of Mr. Frankly*, 2 vols. (Dublin: Sleater, 1773), 2:34.

102. David Solkin, *Painting for Money: The Visual Arts and the Public Sphere in Eighteenth-Century England* (New Haven: Yale University Press, 1993), 193–200.

103. The extent of the recovery effort that viewed planters and other colonial

beneficiaries as prodigal sons may be gauged by the earlier literature about the West Indies. Initially, Jamaica had been incorporated into the English cultural imagination by its association with deviant sexuality, especially lower-class white women's, as is evidenced by salacious anonymous narratives like *Jamaica Lady* (1720) and *The Fortunate Transport* (1742). Conventionally, the Caribbean and American colonies were regarded as a repository for Britain's least desirable citizens. Colonial narratives about Jamaica and Virginia in the late seventeenth and early eighteenth centuries are replete with references to perversely sexualized Britons, most of whom are criminalized in the fiction and travel accounts. Such a representation had altered somewhat by the time that Long wrote about Jamaica because of the rapid decline of white indentured servitude after the initial sugar boom in the late seventeenth century and because those who returned to Britain were the absentee plantation owners and their children, who were significantly wealthier and more privileged than the British serving classes in the colonies.

104. Wilson, *The Sense of the People*, 195.

105. Moira Ferguson, *Subject to Others: British Women Writers and Colonial Slavery, 1670–1834* (New York: Routledge, 1992) investigates this phenomenon in a larger context than simply education.

106. Goldsmith, *History of the Earth*, 1:285.

107. Long's allegations are hardly new. An earlier defender of Jamaica suggested that because children are breastfed by slaves, it "causes those that have not an opportunity of a better education, in their Pronunciation, to speak in a drawling broken *English* like the Negroes." See *The Importance of Jamaica to Great Britain*, 7–8.

108. Cohen, *Fashioning Masculinity*, 30–31.

109. Thomas Tryon, *Friendly Advice to the Gentlemen-Planters of the East and West Indies* (London: Andrew Sowle, 1684), 106.

110. Elsewhere Long observes that white men's sexuality had been naturalized to new domestic configurations that transgressed property inheritance as well as shocked conventional morality: "On first arriving here, a civilized European may be apt to think it impudent and shameful, that even bachelors should publickly avow their keeping Negroe or Mulatto mistresses; but they are still more shocked at seeing a group of white legitimate, and Mulatto illegitimate, children, all claimed by the same married father, and all bred up together under the same roof" (2:330). This scenario restores the agency to white men denied when focusing on black and mulatta women.

Chapter 5. The Politicization of Race

1. This observation on Highlanders did not appear in the previous 1781 edition, and it is symptomatically part of an entry on *Negroes* (12:795). Even though the entry states that Scotland is a polished nation, it underscores the many shades

of complexion found in any population, and it slyly refers to the vogue for taxonomic liberties, especially the way that superficial differences seemed to weigh more heavily than ever before. That this comment applies specifically to the severe effects of diet and way of living on the human countenance is evident because it is taken from Samuel Stanhope Smith's *Essay on the Causes of the Variety of Complexion and Figure in the Human Species* (Philadelphia: Robert Aitken, 1787), 53.

2. William Cowper, "The Negro's Complaint," *The Poems of William Cowper*, vol. 3, ed. John D. Baird and Charles Ryskamp (Oxford: Clarendon Press, 1995), 13–14.

3. William Frederic Martyn, *A New Dictionary of Natural History*, vol. 2 (London: Harrison, 1785), s.v. "Man."

4. Vincent Carretta has presented new evidence that Equiano may have been born in South Carolina. See his "Three West Indian Writers of the 1780s Revisited and Revised," in *Research in African Literatures* 29.4 (Winter 1998): 85.

5. Richard Kain, "The Problem of Civilization in English Abolition Literature, 1772–1808," *Philological Quarterly* 15.2 (1936): 103–25, offers a wide range of materials and an incisive analysis of abolition literature in poetry, essays, and tracts. He deals well with the way that primitivism was used strategically and the way that the issue of civilization informed the abolitionist argument. His section on how this literature tried to separate color and abilities is especially pertinent to my argument (112–16).

6. Philip Morgan argues this point cogently in relation to historical forces in Britain and the colonies in "British Encounters with Africans and African-Americans," in *Stranger Within the Realm: Cultural Margins of the First British Empire* (Chapel Hill: University of North Carolina Press, 1991): "Race relations not only varied between and within societies but also according to the status of individuals and groups interacting across racial lines" (193). In my analysis of difference and multiplicity in Equiano's narrative, I draw on implications in work by Chinosole, "Tryin' to Get Over: Narrative Posture in Equiano's Autobiography," in *The Art of the Slave Narrative: Original Essays in Criticism and Theory*, ed. John Sekora and Darwin Turner (Macomb: West Illinois University Press, 1982): 45–54, and William Andrews, *To Tell a Free Story: The First Century of Afro-American Autobiography, 1760–1865* (Urbana: University of Illinois Press, 1989). Both authors offer compelling analyses of the complexity of Equiano's text and historical position. Their interest is primarily issues of slavery and narration, not race.

7. Frances Foster Smith, *Witnessing Slavery: The Development of Ante-bellum Slave Narratives* (Westport, Conn.: Greenwood Press, 1979), 48.

8. Despite similar goals, Equiano's tone is consistently less patronizing toward Africans in Africa than most abolitionists; even the most ardent of monogeneticists had difficulties with ideas such as cultural relativity. Compare a typical example, such as Anthony Benezet's *Some Historical Account of Guinea* (1771; London: J. Phillips, 1788): "Hence it appears they [Africans] might have lived happy, if not disturbed by the Europeans; more especially, if these last had used such endeav-

ours as their christian profession requires, to communicate to the ignorant Africans that superior knowledge which providence had favoured them with" (2).

9. Previous critical work on Equiano has been interested in establishing Equiano's importance to abolition, introducing him as a crucial eighteenth-century Anglo-African, communicating the gist of his experiences from the slave narrative and other documents, or providing a theoretically informed reading of the structure and major tropes of his slave narrative. Critics of Equiano's work have tried to account for the more troublesome aspects of his narrative, such as when he is ambiguous about slavery or praises Europeans. Some critics have remarked on the impossible narrative dilemma of his position as a former slave, writing in a language and conceptual universe in which he is not positioned as if he were a powerful subject. The lack of language available to talk about slavery from the position of the enslaved is a central problem, especially for the earlier Anglo-African writers, since abolitionist discourse was just emerging in a very conservative political climate, and in Great Britain it focused primarily on abolishing the slave trade not slavery. Also, abolitionist discourse often positioned slaves and other Africans in subordinate terms, making abolitionist discourse not a solution for Anglo-Africans but another discursive challenge.

10. Christopher Brown, "Foundations of British Abolitionism: Beginnings to 1789," Ph.D. diss., Oxford University, 1994, finds that two-thirds of the 123 tracts written between 1760 and 1788 were antislavery; over half appeared in 1788, the year before Equiano's slave narrative was published (222).

11. See Henry Louis Gates, Jr., *Figures in Black: Words, Signs, and the "Racial" Self* (Oxford: Oxford University Press, 1985), esp. chap. 2, and "Introduction: Writing 'Race' and the Difference It Makes," in *"Race," Writing, and Difference* (Chicago: University of Chicago Press, 1986); Richard Popkin, "The Philosophical Basis of Eighteenth-Century Racism," in *Studies in Eighteenth-Century Culture*, vol. 3, *Racism in the Eighteenth Century*, ed. Harold E. Paglioaro (Cleveland: Press of Case Western Reserve University, 1973), 245–62. Other significant studies of racial thinking in eighteenth-century science and philosophy include Philip Curtin, *The Image of Africa: British Ideas and Action, 1780–1850* (Madison: University of Wisconsin Press, 1964), and Anthony Barker, *The African Link: British Attitudes to the Negro in the Era of the Atlantic Slave Trade, 1550–1807* (London: Frank Cass, 1978). Gates has contextualized the earlier slave narratives as the initiators of an African-American tradition. Placing most of his discussions in the context of the Enlightenment discourses of the great chain of being and theories of blackness, Gates's interest focuses on the way that blackness came to signify an absence in European discourse; see his *Figures in Black*, 14. The operative assumption that many Europeans worked from is that reason was legislated on a case-by-case basis rather than indicating a general characteristic of Africans.

12. Nicholas Hudson, *Writing and European Thought, 1600–1830* (Cambridge: Cambridge University Press, 1994), 40.

13. Ibid., 4–5, and R. A. Houston, *Scottish Literacy and the Scottish Identity:*

Illiteracy and Society in Scotland and Northern England, 1600–1800 (Cambridge: Cambridge University Press, 1985), chap. 2.

14. Hudson, *Writing and European Thought*, 5.

15. In *Elements of Moral Science* (Edinburgh: T. Cadell, 1790), the eminent Scottish academic James Beattie explicated a nuance that underlies literacy's cultural significance to Enlightenment thinkers. Because there were no written documents, a savage nation was not able to contribute to the exploration of human intellect in an active way: "By means of writing, human thoughts may be made more durable than any other work of man; may be circulated in all nations; and may be so corrected, compared, and compounded, as to exhibit . . . the accumulated wisdom of many ages" (1:25–26).

16. Henry Louis Gates, Jr., *The Signifying Monkey: A Theory of Afro-American Literary Criticism* (New York: Oxford University Press, 1988), 167.

17. See Johann Friedrich Blumenbach, *On the Natural Variety of Mankind*, in *The Anthropological Treatises of Johann Friedrich Blumenbach*, trans. and ed. Thomas Bendyshe (London: Longman et al., 1865). In 1795, Blumenbach wrote to Sir Joseph Banks: "I am indeed very much opposed to the opinions of those, who, especially of late, have amused their ingenuity so much with what they call the continuity or gradation of nature" (150–51). This reference to the recent European resurgence of interest in gradation and the scale of nature appears only in his 1795 revision of *On the Natural Variety of Mankind*, specifically in its application to ranking human variety. In the first edition of 1775, Blumenbach had observed that the principal question of his dissertation was "*Are men, and have the men of all times and of every race been of one and the same, or clearly of more than one species?*" He remarks that this "question [is] much discussed in these days, but so far as I know, seldom expressly treated of" (97–98). His footnotes refer to five writers who express an opinion in favor of separate creations. Barker's *African Link* provides evidence for Blumenbach's conclusion that polygenesis was bandied about rather than examined in Britain; see 45, 47, and chap. 9 for the little printed attention given to racialist arguments based on the chain of being or gradation.

18. See the proslavery position of James Tobin, *Cursory Remarks upon the Reverend Mr. Ramsay's Essay on the Treatment and Conversion of the African Slaves in the Sugar Colonies* (London: G. and T. Wilkie, 1785). Tobin fingers the philosophers as particularly responsible for negative views of Africans in 1785: "Mr. Ramsay's fifth chapter [which is entitled "Objections to African Capacity, drawn from Philosophy, Considered"] is entirely employed in endeavouring to restore the negroes to that equality with the whites, from which many very ingenious philosophers have lately attempted to degrade them. . . . I cannot indeed consider the merits of this famous controversy of much consequence, even to the open and advowed advocates for slavery (if any such there are) as it has never been pretended, that the slaves either of the Jews, Greeks, or Romans of old, or the European and Asiatic slaves of modern times, were, or are, any way *inferior* to their masters, except in strength, policy, or good fortune" (140–41). Another proslavery advocate makes a similar reference; see

Gordon Turnball, *An Apology for Negro Slavery*... (London: J. Strachan, 1786), 34. It is possible, of course, that criticizing the philosophers was a smoke screen to distract from their own similar beliefs. James Beattie, *Elements of Moral Science*, nicely sums up the particular importance of philosophy: It was believed to be the most complex form of thinking because both reason and the knowledge of nature were necessary. Its significance as a realm of discourse to twentieth-century critics might best be explained by Beattie's elaboration on philosophy and its truth claims: "Philosophy is founded in the knowledge of nature, that is, of the things that really exist" (1:8).

19. Henry Louis Gates, Jr., "Critical Remarks," in *Anatomy of Racism*, ed. David Theo Goldberg (Minneapolis: University of Minnesota Press, 1990), 323.

20. Eric Williams, *Capitalism and Slavery* (1944; Chapel Hill: University of North Carolina Press, 1994), 3. The introduction of Theodore Allen's *Invention of the White Race*, vol. 1, *Racial Oppression and Social Control* (London: Verso, 1994), provides a helpful overview of the different approaches to the relationship between slavery and racial prejudice. Eric Williams is credited with launching this debate in 1944. He contends that the origin of Negro slavery was economic, not racial: "It had to do not with the color of the laborer, but the cheapness of the labor" (19). Whether slavery was primarily an economic or racial phenomenon, according to historians, is thoroughly reexamined in William Green, "Race and Slavery: Considerations on the Williams Thesis," in *British Capitalism and Caribbean Slavery: The Legacy of Eric Williams*, ed. Barbara Solow and Stanley Engerman (Cambridge: Cambridge University Press, 1987). The article critiques the lineage of historiography contributing to this international debate and suggests that most 1980s scholarship broadly agrees with Williams about racism resulting from power relations. See William McKee Evans's suggestive article "From the Land of Canaan to the Land of Guinea," which mounts a persuasive case for fairly constant stereotypes about slaves in all slave societies (23–25). Although they adapt to new socioeconomic forces over time, stereotypes about slaves remain remarkably similar whether the slave population is African or Circassian. My general approach is indebted to Winthrop Jordan, *White over Black*, and Anthony Barker, *The African Link*, both of which offer a rich historical sense of color, religion, and savagery as divisions pertinent to slavery.

21. Green, "Race and Slavery," 44–48.

22. Winthrop Jordan, *White over Black*, and Peter Fryer, *Staying Power*, are two of the most influential historians to do this on occasion; Anthony Barker's *African Link* attempts to revise this tendency. For a similar view of the teleological trap of forcing early modern conditions into a framework dictated by our contemporary race relations, see Green, "Race and Slavery," 34.

23. Green, "Race and Slavery," 48.

24. David Eltis, "Europeans and the Rise and Fall of African Slavery in the Americas: An Interpretation," *American Historical Review* 98.5 (December 1993): 1423.

25. Arguably, Britons insisted on Africans' humanity more routinely after 1780.

26. Oliver Goldsmith, *History of the Earth and Animated Nature in Four Volumes* (1774; Philadelphia: Carey, 1795), 1: 370.

27. *Encyclopaedia Britannica*, 3 vols. (Edinburgh: A. Bell and C. Macfarquhar, 1771), 3:395.

28. *Encyclopaedia Britannica*, 2d ed., 10 vols. (Edinburgh: J. Balfour, 1781), 3:2083.

29. *Encyclopaedia Britannica*, 3d ed., 18 vols. (Edinburgh: A. Bell and C. Macfarquhar, 1797), 12:794.

30. Thomas Laqueur, *Making Sex: Body and Gender from the Greeks to Foucault* (Cambridge: Harvard University Press, 1990), 155.

31. Slave owner William Beckford, Jr. made the same claim that appears in the *Encyclopaedia Britannica* (1797) in *Remarks on the Situation of Negroes in Jamaica* (1788), 84. Beckford observes, "A slave has no feeling beyond the present hour, no anticipation of what may come, no dejection at what may ensue: these privileges of feeling are reserved for the enlightened." Beckford's statement reveals its peculiarly late eighteenth-century inflection in his contrast between slaves and the enlightened. Claiming slaves' or Africans' equal capacity for sensibility and sympathy was one way that Britons affirmed their common humanity. As the Cowper epigraph illustrates, abolitionists emphasized the similarity of feelings and the common nature of Africans and Europeans as a way to refute proslavery claims. In a typical statement, Anthony Benezet demonstrates through contemporary travel accounts "that the Negroes are equally intituled [*sic*] to the common Privileges of Mankind with the Whites; that they have the same rational Powers, the same natural Affections, and are as susceptible of Pain and Grief as they": *Short Account of that Part of Africa, Inhabited by the Negroes* (1762; London: J. Phillips, 1788), 78. Hannah More felt compelled to heavily footnote her "Slavery, A Poem" (New York: J. and A. M'Lean, 1788); in the text the narrative addresses those who impugn slave character: "Plead not, in reason's palpable abuse, / Their sense of feeling callous and obtuse / . . . tho' few can reason, all mankind can feel" (11). The footnote reads, "Nothing is more frequent than this cruel and stupid argument, that they do not *feel* the miseries inflicted on them as Europeans would do" (11).

32. For an extended analysis of Blumenbach and trends in racialization, see Londa Schiebinger, "The Anatomy of Difference: Race and Sex in Eighteenth-Century Science," *Eighteenth-Century Studies* 23.4 (1990): 387–405.

33. Blumenbach, *On the Natural Variety of Mankind*, 105.

34. This trend of homogenizing all black-complected Africans into "Negroes" and singling them out from all other groups is also discernible in Blumenbach's *Contribution to Natural History* in *The Anthropological Treatises of Johann Friedrich Blumenbach*, trans. and ed. Thomas Bendyshe (1790 and 1806; London: Longman, 1865). Blumenbach's own beliefs are less abrasive than the authors of the *Encyclopaedia Britannica* (1797), and his ends are different. Blumenbach's chapter entitled "On the Negro in Particular" reflects the more embattled position of people who defended variety in one human species near the century's end. Blumenbach perceived

the danger of singling out Negroes negatively in the manner that the *Encyclopedia Britannica* does, because he devotes the chapter to emphasizing that variety among Negroes is as striking as among Europeans.

35. Blumenbach, *On the Natural Variety of Mankind*, 209, 227, 234.

36. David Turley, *The Culture of English Antislavery, 1780–1860* (New York: Routledge, 1991), rightly notes that antislavery agitation was not at many levels about race: "Antislavery was part of a religious, philanthropic and reform complex which embraced missionary activity, temperance, peace, free trade and limited political reform" (6). He identifies a crucial point about the leaders of abolition that explains the contradictions frequently noticeable in their statements: Most of them displayed "ambivalence or opposition" to "agitations which not only drew heavily on popular support but challenged middle-class notions of appropriate relations of power in society and implicitly questioned the adequacy of reformist procedures" (6).

37. Samuel Stanhope Smith, *An Essay on the Causes of the Variety of Complexion and Figure in the Human Species*, ed. Winthrop Jordan (Cambridge: Belknap Press of Harvard University Press, 1965), viii–ix.

38. This phenomenon is ably discussed by Karen Ordahl Kupperman, "Fear of Hot Climates in the Anglo-American Colonial Experience," *William and Mary Quarterly*, 3d series, 41.2 (April 1984): 215. I am generally indebted to James Egan's discussion of American colonists' representation of their bodies in relation to the New World climate in *Authorizing Experience: Refigurations of the Body Politic in Seventeenth-Century New England Writing* (Princeton: Princeton University Press, 1999), chap. 1. Egan shows that many seventeenth-century New England promoters commented that colonization confirmed the apparent paradox that "English bodies adapted better to alien environments than did any other body type."

39. *No Abolition; or, An Attempt to Prove to the Conviction of Every Rational British Subject, that the Abolition of the British Trade with Africa, Would Be a Measure as Unjust as Impolitic* (London: J. Debrett, 1789).

40. John Wesley, *Thoughts on Slavery*, in *The Works of the Rev. John Wesley*, vol. 16 (London: Thomas Cordeux, 1813), 454.

41. Samuel Estwick, *Considerations on the Negroe Cause Commonly So Called . . .* (London: J. Dodsley, 1772), 11–13, 34–35.

42. Ibid., 30. See Anthony Barker, *The African Link*, 47–48, for an important change between the first and second edition of the same year, which degrades the Negro to a different species.

43. Tobin, *Cursory Remarks*, 141; James Tobin, *A Short Rejoinder to The Reverend Mr. Ramsay's Reply . . .* (London: G. and T. Wilkie, 1787), 24; Alexander Geddes, *An [Ironical] Apology for Slavery; or, Six Cogent Arguments Against the Immediate Abolition of the Slave-Trade* (London: J. Johnson, 1792).

44. I am indebted to Christopher Brown for the point that the private attitudes of many abolitionist authors were more progressive than their public statements. Black and white abolitionists worked in a political context in which emancipation

was dangerous to espouse and believed impossible to achieve. Their language and public statements reflect this constraint.

45. James Ramsay, *An Essay on the Treatment and Conversion of African Slaves in the British Sugar Colonies* (London: James Phillips, 1784), 1.

46. Brown, "Foundations of British Abolitionism," 21.

47. Richard Baxter, *Abstract from Richard Baxter's Christian Directory* (1673), 4.

48. Robert Robertson, *A Letter to the Right Reverend the Lord Bishop of London, from an Inhabitant of His Majesty's Leeward-Caribee-Islands* (London: J. Wilford, 1730), 33.

49. One of the more agonized aspects of Thomas Clarkson, *An Essay on the Impolicy of the African Slave Trade* (Philadelphia: Bailey, 1788), is his concern over the color original to humans (many of his contemporaries argued it was white). Finally, he decides that it must be a dark olive, "a just medium between white and black" (120).

50. Ramsay, *Treatment and Conversion*, iv.

51. "For the Diary; or, Woodfall's Register, 25 April 1789," in Olaudah Equiano, *The Interesting Narrative and Other Writings*, ed. Vincent Carretta (New York: Penguin Books, 1995), 344. Equiano's and Cugoano's names were usually included with several other Afro-Britons'; this reference appeared in a letter the Sons of Africa wrote to William Dickson in response to the publication of his *Letters on Slavery* (1789).

52. Folarin Shyllon, *Black People in Britain, 1555–1833* (London: Oxford University Press, 1977), 267.

53. Ottobah Cugoano, *Thoughts and Sentiments on the Evil and Wicked Traffic of the Slavery and Commerce of the Human Species*, in *Unchained Voices: An Anthology of Black Authors in the English-Speaking World of the Eighteenth Century*, ed. Vincent Carretta (Lexington: University Press of Kentucky, 1996), 153, 156.

54. Wesley, *Thoughts on Slavery*, 443.

55. Ramsay, *Treatment and Conversion*, 225–29.

56. See David Brion Davis, *The Problem of Slavery in Western Culture* (New York: Oxford University Press, 1966), chaps. 13 and 14.

57. Brown, "Foundations of British Abolitionism," 220.

58. Malachy Postlethwayt, *The Universal Dictionary of Trade and Commerce*, 4th ed. (London: W. Strahan 1763), 1:vii.

59. Ramsay, *Treatment and Conversion*, 203.

60. James Beattie, *Elements of Moral Science*, 1:81.

61. J. Philmore, *Two Dialogues on the Man-Trade* (London, 1760), 37–38; John Woolman, *Some Considerations on the Keeping of Negroes* (Philadelphia: James Chattin, 1754), 2; Benjamin Rush (a Pennsylvanian), *An Address to the Inhabitants of the British Settlements on the Slavery of Negroes in America* (Philadelphia: John Dunlap, 1773), 1.

62. James Albert Ukawsaw Gronniosaw, *A Narrative of the Most Remarkable Particulars in the Life . . .* (1772) in *Unchained Voices*, ed. Carretta, 38, 49.

63. Ottobah Cugoano, *Thoughts and Sentiments on the Evil and Wicked Traffic of the Slavery and Commerce of the Human Species* (1787; London: Dawsons of Pall Mall, 1969), 45.

64. Ramsay, *Treatment and Conversion*, 208 and 235.

65. Adam Smith, *The Theory of Moral Sentiments*, ed. D. D. Raphael and A. L. Macfie (Oxford: Clarendon Press, 1976), 376.

66. In "Critical Remarks," in *Anatomy of Racism*, ed. David Theo Goldberg (Minneapolis: University of Minnesota Press, 1985), Gates explains the distinction between nominal and essential essences that arises from John Locke's *Essay Concerning Human Understanding* (321).

67. For example, Equiano adopts the natural historian's stance in this passage: "We are almost a nation of dancers, musicians, and poets. . . . As our manners are simple, our luxuries are few" (14). "Our cleanliness on all occasions is extreme" (15).

68. Egan, *Authorizing Experience*, chap. 1.

69. Anthony Barker, *The African Link*, 63–64, 99; Kay Dian Kriz, *The Idea of the English Landscape Painter: Genius as Alibi in the Nineteenth Century* (New Haven: Yale University Press, 1997), 102. As Kriz demonstrates, in late eighteenth-century art circles, Germans and Frenchmen observed "that the cold, damp English climate prevented native artists from producing a successful school of history painting," which roused considerable indignation (102). These accusations also elicited denials that climate and national culture were related. During the eighteenth century, other Europeans often chose to associate England with a northern climate, while most Englishmen preferred to think of their country as part of the temperate zone.

70. Johannes Fabian, *Time and the Other: How Anthropology Makes Its Object* (New York: Columbia University Press, 1983).

71. The most extensive contemporary example of this rhetorical move is James Adair's monumental *History of American Indians* (1789) in which he demonstrates the myriad similarities of social structure, customs, and rites between the Jews and Amerindians in an effort to reflect positively on the Amerindian culture. His comparisons extend even to similarities of language.

72. See Barker, *The African Link*, 118, for a more detailed argument. Chapter 6 treats British responses to African culture and is a useful resource because Barker shows what Britons chose to ignore about African manufactures, especially textiles.

73. In seeking to delineate similarities between Africans and Christians, Equiano selects the more ancient European Other, the Jew. Even though the Jews were integrated into the commercial networks of most European nations, they were socially ghettoized and did not enjoy the full rights of citizens.

74. Ronald Richardson, *Moral Imperium: Afro-Caribbeans and the Transformation of British Rule, 1776–1838* (Westport, Conn.: Greenwood Press, 1987), cogently analyzes abolitionist goals and discursive strategies. According to Richardson, Thomas Clarkson "believed that Africans were backward, indeed, but not because they happened to be black. Their backwardness reflected their lower stage on the ladder of social evolution. All abolitionists could agree with this notion. No one

thought of advancing the thesis of social or cultural equality between Africa and Europe" (150).

75. John Mitchell, "An Essay upon the Causes of the Different Colours of People in Different Climates," in *Philosophical Transactions* of The Royal Society of London, no. 474, vol. 43 (June–December 1744): 131. Mitchell suggests that it is only the unscientific who are apt to believe in polygenesis or any significant differences between whites and blacks (131).

76. Smith, *Theory of Moral Sentiments*, 88.

77. David Brion Davis, *The Problem of Slavery in the Age of Revolution, 1770–1823* (Ithaca: Cornell University Press, 1975), 372.

78. Martyn, *A New Dictionary of Natural History*, vol. 2, s.v. "Man."

79. Like other European travelers, Equiano marvels at albinism and the wonders of changeable complexions. He recounts "a remarkable circumstance relative to African complexion" in London: "A white negro woman . . . had married a white man, by whom she had three boys, and they were every one mullattoes, and yet they had fine light hair" (167). Albinism in Africans was most interesting to eighteenth-century inquirers because it encompassed the most extreme change; Blumenbach treats this condition in *On the Natural Variety of Mankind* (1775) 130, 137 and (1797) 259–60.

80. About the time that this passage was written, elsewhere in his writing Equiano depicted his adult color differently in a response published in *The Public Advertiser* to James Tobin's proslavery arguments about the condition of slaves in the West Indies. Equiano writes about his visible umbrage: " 'I confess my cheek changes colour with resentment against your unrelenting barbarity' " (328). Oliver Goldsmith, *History of the Earth*, interprets the changeability of whiteness that typifies the aesthetics of skin color in the eighteenth century: "Of all the colours by which mankind is diversified, it is easy to perceive that ours is not only the most beautiful to the eye, but the most advantageous. The fair complexion seems, if I may so express it, as a transparent covering to the soul; all the variations of the passions, every expression of joy or sorrow, flows to the cheek, and, without language, marks the mind. . . . [T]he African black, and the Asiatic olive complexions, admit their alterations also; but these are neither so distinct nor so visible as with us" (1:375).

81. Susan Marren, "Between Slavery and Freedom: The Transgressive Self in Olaudah Equiano's Autobiography," *PMLA* 108.1 (1993): 100.

82. As an indication of the competing notions of how to divide humans, Blumenbach in *On the Natural Variety of Mankind* recounts the known ways of dividing human groups in 1795: two races (Meiners, Metzger), three primitive nations of mankind (Pownall), four races (Bernier, Linnaeus, Kant, Klugel), six races (Buffon), seven varieties (Hunter). Some use geography to divide humans; some use color. The most extreme is Christoph Meiners in *Grundriss der Geschichte der Menschheit*, 2d ed. (1793), who "refers all nations to two stocks: (1) handsome, (2) ugly; the first white, the latter dark" (268).

83. David Roediger, *Towards the Abolition of Whiteness: Essays on Race, Politics,*

and Working-Class History (London: Verso, 1994), 12; George Lipsitz, *The Possessive Investment in Whiteness: How White People Profit from Identity Politics* (Philadelphia: Temple University Press, 1998), 1; Ruth Frankenberg, "Introduction: Local Whitenesses, Localizing Whiteness," in *Displacing Whiteness: Essays in Social and Cultural Criticism* (Durham: Duke University Press, 1997), 3, 6; Richard Dyer, *White* (London: Routledge, 1997), 44.

84. Dyer, *White*, 20.

85. Henry Mackenzie, *Julia de Roubigné* (London: W. Strahan and T. Cadell, 1777), 4.

86. Olaudah Equiano, *The Interesting Narrative of the Life*, ed. Robert Allison (Boston: Bedford Books of St. Martin's Press, 1995), 6. In his introduction, Allison mentions that Annis was eventually murdered at Kirkpatrick's instigation.

87. For a sense of Equiano's borrowing from British writing about Africa, see *The Interesting Narrative*, ed. Carretta, 241, notes 42–43.

88. Seymour Drescher, *Capitalism and Antislavery: British Mobilization in Comparative Perspective* (Oxford: Oxford University Press, 1986), 41.

89. Barry Weller, "The Royal Slave and the Prestige of Origins," *Kenyon Review* 14.1 (1992): 65–78, offers a thoughtful analysis of connections between *Oroonoko* and Equiano's narrative, especially the issue of exalted lineage in representing enslaved black men.

90. Many other critics have remarked upon his process of acculturation. See Geraldine Murphy, "Olaudah Equiano, Accidental Tourist," *Eighteenth-Century Studies* 27.4 (1994): 551–68. Murphy offers a strong analysis of the function of the gaze and discourses of travel in Equiano's narrative; she contends that both help establish his "bourgeois subjecthood" (567).

91. Ian Duffield and Paul Edwards, "Equiano's Turks and Christians: An Eighteenth-Century African View of Islam," *Journal of African Studies* 2.4 (1976): 437. In regard to Equiano's narrative, Duffield and Edwards contrast Islam to Christianity and link the representation of the Igbo people to Islamic practices. I consider the comparison as less symmetrical than their analysis suggests: The Turks are civilized but non-Christian, which links them to the Europeans in some ways and to the Indians and Africans in other ways.

92. Equiano's perception that the Turks were fond of black people did not mean that they did not also enslave them. Blackness and slavery carried different meaning in Turkey. Muslim slavery, though not race- or color-based in the same way as European slavery, possessed certain characteristics in which color signified. For instance, black eunuchs guarded the female slaves of all colors; white eunuchs surrounded the body of the sultan. In addition, the sexual ideology of slavery differed from the West by publicly acknowledging sexual rights to enslaved women. By law, Muslim slave owners were entitled to the sexual use of slave women. Free Muslim women might own male slaves, but they had no equivalent sexual privileges. See Bernard Lewis, *Race and Slavery in the Middle East: An Historical Inquiry* (New York: Oxford University Press, 1990), 14.

93. Felicity A. Nussbaum, "The Other Woman: Polygamy, Pamela, and the Prerogative of Empire," in *Women, "Race," and Writing in the Early Modern Period* (New York: Routledge, 1994): 149.

94. See Hortense Spillers, "Mama's Baby, Papa's Maybe: An American Grammar Book," *Diacritics* 17.2 (1987): 65-81, for a different argument than mine about gendering and the middle passage (esp. 67, 69, 72).

95. Anthony Benezet, *A Caution and Warning to Great Britain and Her Colonies, in a Short Representation of the Calamitous State of the Enslaved Negroes in the British Dominions* (Philadelphia: Henry Miller, 1766), 9.

96. On a typical Jamaican plantation, "The female/male ratio, which was low in the 1760s, turned to a female majority by 1810. . . . His [Dunn's] data show that 95 percent of female adult slaves became prime field hands, compared with only 65 percent of males. Females were excluded from jobs as craftsmen and drivers and from miscellaneous other skilled occupations." See Solow and Engerman, eds., *British Capitalism and Caribbean Slavery*, 17.

97. "Am I Not a Woman and a Sister" did not appear until 1828. See Clare Midgley, *Women Against Slavery: The British Campaigns, 1780-1870* (New York: Routledge, 1992), 97-99. The quintessential slave in discourse and illustrations was male.

98. Chinosole, "Tryin' to Get Over," 51.

99. Gates's reading points to the way that property figures in the production of slave subjectivity and the shifting in the narrative between Equiano as property and an object of discourse to Equiano as owner of property and the subject of discourse. See his *Signifying Monkey*, 155.

100. For example, Benezet ends *Some Historical Account of Guinea* with a similar proposition: "A farther considerable advantage might accrue to the British nation in general, if the slave trade was laid aside, by the cultivation of a fair friendly, and humane commerce with the Africans" (120). He believes that this change will help civilize Africans: it will "introduce the arts and sciences amongst them, and engage their attention to instruction in the principles of the Christian religion, which is the only sure foundation of every social virtue" (121). Ottobah Cugoano's proposal is much more detailed than Equiano's in its plan for the abolition of slavery and in urging instruction in "Christian religion and laws of civilization" for Africans (131). He argues similarly to Equiano that "as the Africans become refined and established in light and knowledge, they would imitate their noble British friends" (133).

101. Ralph Austen and Woodruff Smith, "Images of Africa and British Slave Trade Abolition: The Transition to an Imperialist Ideology," *African Historical Studies* 2.1 (1969): 69-83, point to the historical irony of abolishing the slave trade; they argue that "reform-oriented English penetration into Africa became a part of the whole notion of ending the slave trade. It is not surprising that the abolition of the slave trade marked the beginning of serious missionary work by the British, supported by the government" (80)—and the beginning of colonizing Africa.

102. Clarkson, *Impolicy of the Slave Trade*, 115.

103. Equiano, *The Interesting Narrative*, ed. Carretta, 329.

104. Fryer, *Staying Power*, 161.

Epilogue

1. Michael Omi and Howard Winant, *Racial Formation in the United States: From the 1960s to the 1990s*, 2d ed. (London: Routledge, 1994), 71; Ruth Frankenburg, "Introduction: Local Whitenesses, Localizing Whiteness," in *Displacing Whiteness: Essays in Social and Cultural Criticism* (Durham: Duke University Press, 1997), 9.

2. Oliver Goldsmith, *History of the Earth and Animated Nature in Four Volumes* (1774; Philadelphia: Carey, 1795), 2:380.

3. James Cowles Prichard, *Researches into the Physical History of Man* (London: John and Arthur Arch, 1813), 1–2.

4. James Cowles Prichard, *The Natural History of Man*, 3d ed. (London: Hippolyte Bailliere, 1848), 887–88.

5. Nancy Stepan, *The Idea of Race in Science: Great Britain, 1800–1960* (London: Macmillan Press, 1982), 43.

6. Alexander Kinmont, *Twelve Lectures on the Natural History of Man and the Rise of Philosophy* (Cincinnati: U. P. James, 1839), 332, 236.

7. This same metamorphosis had already occurred for European men and women, who were increasingly considered as two different entities that complemented each other. The older model, which did not disappear entirely, posited that women were inferior men. I believe a similar logic operates in regard to racial ideology and changes between the eighteenth and nineteenth centuries. For discussion of this phenomenon, see Thomas Laqueur, *Making Sex: Body and Gender from the Greeks to Foucault* (Cambridge: Harvard University Press, 1990), and Londa Schiebinger, "The Anatomy of Difference: Race and Sex in Eighteenth-Century Science," *Eighteenth-Century Studies* 23.4 (1990): 387–405.

8. Henry Louis Gates, Jr., "Critical Remarks," in *Anatomy of Racism*, ed. David Theo Goldberg (Minneapolis: University of Minnesota Press, 1990), 322–23.

Index

Abolition, 153, 228, 236-37, 241, 248-49, 251, 253-60, 287, 350 n. 8, 351 n. 9, 355 n. 36, 357 n. 74, 360 n. 101

Adas, Michael, 100, 119

Africa, 23, 35, 66, 94-95, 101-2, 106-8, 136, 209-11, 256, 323 n. 3; change in nomenclature for inhabitants, 98; change in treatment of inhabitants, 92, 185-88, 247, 249-50, 301-2; inhabitants of, 3-4, 10, 15, 21, 37-38, 46-48, 55, 58-60, 90, 95, 102-36, 175, 347 n. 81; and illustrations of, 10, 18, 24, 34, 36, 118, 245, 247, 290, 292; absent in intermarriage novels, 141-44, 170, 173-75; female slaves in Caribbean, 225-32, 275, 281-82; male slaves in Caribbean, 57, 220-23; in natural histories and taxonomies, 5, 19, 23-27, 29, 36, 40, 96-98, 176, 180, 214-19, 245, 247-51, 291-99; representation as people versus slaves, 128, 250, 279. See also Moors

Albinism, 4, 269, 358 n. 79

Alexander, William, 162

Allen, Theodore, 74, 299

Althusser, Louis, 41

Amalgamation, 131-34, 83, 137-75, 163, 185-86, 212-13, 225-32, 264, 333 n. 1, 334 n. 10, 334 n. 14, 338 n. 53, 339 n. 71, 349 n. 110

America, 14, 16, 83; inhabitants of, 10, 19, 35, 37, 67, 78, 167-73, 290; and illustrations of, 18, 34, 36, 165, 246-47; and skin color, 4, 248-49; and tragedy, 167-68, 170, 172-73; exceptional treatment of, 248; in natural histories and taxonomies, 19, 30-31, 36, 96-97, 169, 176, 246-48, 252-53, 291, 293-94, 340 n. 3

Anatomy, 2, 26-27, 31, 33, 38, 150-51, 174, 182, 214, 250-51, 265, 292-99, 326-27 n. 27, 340 n. 3

Anderson, Benedict, 192, 260

Annesley, James, 139

Arctic zone, 22-24, 30, 38, 71, 100. See also Climate theory; Humoral theory

Arens, W., 68

Armstrong, Nancy, 140, 166

Asia, 34-37, 76, 336 n. 39; inhabitants of, 151-52; and illustrations of, 18, 34, 36, 120, 244, 246; in natural histories and taxonomies, 160, 242, 291-94; and women, 166, 242

Athenian Oracle, The, 99-100

Atkins, John, 101-2, 106, 109, 113, 129, 327-28 n. 35

Augstein, Hannah, 189

Barker, Antony, 101, 186, 189, 264, 324 n. 5, 352 n. 17

Barrell, John, 158

Barry, Jonathan, 27-28

Bartels, Emily, 94

Beards, 19, 69, 73, 79, 80, 96, 119, 121-22, 319 n. 39

Beattie, James, 258

Beauty, 1, 7, 10, 23, 25, 38-39, 68-69, 93, 95-99, 142, 164, 177, 180, 221-22, 242, 249, 268-69, 271, 286

Beckford, William, Jr., 224, 226

Beckles, Hilary, 85-86

Behn, Aphra, Oroonoko, 47, 126-27, 277

Benezet, Anthony, 257, 281-82, 350 n. 8

Bernier, François, 96, 160, 304 n. 4

Bhabha, Homi, 41, 312 n. 84-85

Binary pairs, 2, 30-31, 38-45, 50, 53, 95-96, 98, 116, 123, 143, 148, 156, 214, 217

Black Caribs, 83, 322 n. 62

Black skin color, 1-4, 10, 24-26, 31, 39, 51-52, 58, 78, 83, 91-93, 97, 147, 249, 251,

Black skin color (*continued*)
    257–61, 268–69, 274, 323 n. 3, 326 n. 20;
    and Caribbean Islanders, 69, 277; and
    East Indians, 160–61; and humors, 3;
    origins and causes of, 98–100; values
    attached to, 97–99. *See also* Skin color
Blackmore, Richard, 71
Blome, Richard, 194–95
Blumenbach, Johann Friedrich, 1, 25, 28,
    30–31, 181, 250–51, 295, 297, 309–10 n. 67,
    352 n. 17
Body, 2, 5, 7, 15, 19, 20, 26–27, 32, 39, 78–80,
    95–96, 100–101, 119, 129, 139, 174, 177–79,
    182, 185, 199–201, 211, 220, 222, 232–37,
    242, 249–53, 257, 264, 280, 283, 289, 296,
    301, 325 n. 6, 345 n. 61, 355 n. 38
Bonhote, Elizabeth, 228
Bonnet, Charles, 176–78, 217–18
Boucher, Philip, 68, 78
Boyle, Robert, 1, 25–26, 99, 295
Bradley, Richard, 69, 96, 100, 271
Braudel, Fernand, 105
Brewer, John, 11
Britain, and gender, 38, 139, 175, 229–30;
    and whiteness, 235, 266, 271–72, 286;
    singled out, 155, 173
Brooke, Henry, 139, 154–58, 160–61
Brown, Christopher, 255, 351 n. 10, 355 n. 44
Brown, Laura, 11, 110, 115, 126
Browne, Sir Thomas, 24–25, 99, 182, 295,
    304 n. 4
Buffon, Georges Louis Leclerc, comte de,
    4–5, 10, 28, 30, 152, 160, 169, 177, 180–81,
    202, 214, 250, 252, 261, 304 n. 4
Burt, Edward, 205, 208
Busia, Abena, 143

Callaghan, Dympna, 304 n. 10
Campbell, Colin, 215, 229
Cannibalism, 54, 58–59, 67–69, 72–73, 76,
    78, 80, 272, 330–31 n. 65
Canny, Nicholas, 299
Capitalism, 12–13, 39–40, 55, 66–67, 102,
    122, 172, 192, 203
Carby, Hazel, 135
Caribbean, 9, 19, 46, 54–56, 66, 77, 81, 88–
    89, 101, 110, 171; Creoles, 210–33, 276–77,
    279; inhabitants of, 12, 50, 54–55, 65–

73, 76–84, 88, 117, 172, 223, 277; Jamaica,
    177–79, 185–86, 190, 209–33, 284
Carretta, Vincent, 350 n. 4
Categories of difference, 1–50, 54, 65–66,
    71–80, 88–89, 92, 95, 97, 100, 102, 115–
    24, 138–41, 146, 158, 168–73, 210–11,
    249–51, 253, 261, 270, 287, 289–91, 314
    n. 1, 340 n. 2. *See also* Racial ideology
    and individual categories: Cannibalism;
    Catholicism; Christianity; Civil society;
    Clothing; Freedom; Language; Literacy;
    Manual labor; Muslims; Rank; Savagery;
    Skin color; Slavery; Technology
Catholicism, 16–17, 61, 76, 144–45, 154, 173,
    194–96, 204, 259, 290, 336 n. 39, 346 n. 67
Chain of Being, 188, 217–18, 222, 238, 255,
    311 n. 81
Chambre, Marin Cureau de la, 9
Chetwood, William Rufus, 75, 139, 304 n. 6,
    318 n. 27, 320 n. 40
Chinosole, 282
Christianity, 7, 9, 15–17, 19, 22, 31, 43, 46,
    47, 49, 54, 56–57, 60–61, 65, 69–72, 74,
    75, 100, 103–4, 121, 138–39, 144–51, 153,
    161, 164, 171–73, 210, 220–21, 266, 278–79;
    and clothing, 20–21; and Protestantism,
    16, 204, 238, 287; and single Creation, 15,
    102, 262; and skin color, 2, 4, 221, 259–60,
    266, 273–74, and superiority, 249
Civil society, 7, 14, 34–36, 161–62, 177, 190,
    222, 224, 241, 252, 257, 290; and Africa,
    104, 109, 250, 256, 261; and America, 252;
    and clothing, 118, 122, 244; and skin color,
    3–4, 22, 252, 253; denotes rational capa-
    bility, 214–15; measured by the condition
    of women, 162, 231
Civility, 7, 15, 91, 102–7, 110–17, 123–24, 136,
    150, 158, 178, 207, 222, 224–25, 249–50,
    261–62, 289–90
Clarkson, Thomas, 255–56, 284
Classical tradition, 6, 14–15, 22–24, 28, 30,
    35–36, 177, 197, 202, 227, 301
Climate theory, 1, 2, 5, 15, 21–28, 32, 47, 71,
    81, 95, 98–100, 155, 160, 174, 179–81, 183–
    88, 201, 215, 241, 247–48, 250–53, 262–67,
    270–79, 299, 301, 342 n. 27, 355 n. 38, 357
    n. 69
Clothing, 14, 17–21, 39, 58, 60, 72–73, 78–

80, 97, 117–18, 163–64, 235, 327 n. 35, 331
n. 70; and gender distinction, 19, 117–18,
122, 242. *See also* Gender disguise
Colley, Linda, 16–17, 153, 189
Colonialism, 12, 39, 45, 54–55, 59, 65–66, 74,
81, 83, 88–89, 98–99, 102–3, 110, 135, 141,
167–68, 173, 252, 276, 345 n. 64; and race,
10–11, 177, 287
Commerce, 5, 11–14, 102–3, 106, 108, 109–
17, 128, 134–36, 147, 150, 155, 158, 176, 204,
210, 225–26, 228, 232–33, 238, 242, 257,
262, 283–87, 290, 301; and knowledge, 191
Complexion, 2–5, 9, 30, 36, 46, 65, 75, 91,
98, 304 n. 3; concept incorporating skin
color but not limited to it, 2, 22–28
Consumerism, 11, 43, 47, 136, 178, 190–91,
210, 222–27, 233, 235–36, 283–84
Cowper, William, 234, 236, 266
Cugoano, Ottobah, 256, 259–60, 282
Curse of Ham, 99–100, 188, 259, 263, 311
n. 81
Cumberland, Richard, 229

Davis, David Brion, 221, 268, 319 n. 33
Defoe, Daniel, 12, 75, 158, 175; *Captain
Singleton*, 20, 46, 91, 101–36, 138, 232;
Farther Adventures of Robinson Crusoe, 68,
71, 76; *Great Law of Subordination Con-
sider'd*, 88; *Robinson Crusoe*, 46–89, 131,
138, 148, 232, 236, 286; *Serious Reflections
of Robinson Crusoe*, 76, 81; *Tour through
the Whole Island of Great Britain*, 205
Degeneration, 15, 100, 122, 143, 216, 225, 259
Descartes, René, 298
Desire, 139–41, 148–49, 157–58, 162, 168, 175,
290; and narrative, 139, 174, 290; based on
similar appearance, 160
Doig, David, 37
Dunbar, James, 181, 184, 205
During, Simon, 193
Dyer, Richard, 272

Eagleton, Terry, 313 n. 88
East Indies, 14, 153, 158–59, 166–67, 176–77,
241, 287; inhabitants of, 10, 100, 165–67;
in natural histories and taxonomies, 30,
71, 160, 242

Education, 162, 220, 225–26, 230–32, 262,
287
Edwards, Bryan, 226, 228
Ellis, Markman, 11–12
Eltis, David, 240
Encyclopaedia Britannica: first edition, 26,
177, 248, 319 n. 39; second edition, 177,
233, 248–49, 319 n. 39; third edition, 234,
249, 251, 261, 319 n. 39
Enlightenment, 7, 9, 21, 28, 99, 182, 239,
264, 273, 296
Equiano, Olaudah, 47–48, 235–37, 260–87,
256–57
Estwick, Samuel, 253
Europe, illustrations of, 8, 10, 18, 34, 36,
63–64, 82, 165, 292; in natural histories
and taxonomies, 36, 95–97, 176, 180–
81, 289–99, 302; singled out, 95. *See also*
Britain
Eze, Emmanuel Chukwudi, 189

Fabian, Johannes, 261
Falconbridge, Anna Maria, 21
Female American, The, 167–73
Feminist theory, 39–41, 311 n. 82, 311–12,
n. 83
Ferguson, Adam, 33, 181, 184, 186–89, 196,
208, 220, 216
Ferguson, Moira, 11
Floyd-Wilson, Mary, 23, 308 n. 43
Foucault, Michel, 28–29, 32, 38, 43–44, 217,
291
Four-stages theory, 7, 14, 21, 33–38, 179, 181–
91, 204–6, 216, 224, 232, 251–52, 256–57,
261–63, 290, 299, 344 n. 53
Fredrickson, George, 144
Freedom, 74–75, 220, 236, 268, 273–74,
276–77
Fryer, Peter, 91, 143–44, 189, 286

Gally, Henry, 144–45
Garber, Marjorie, 17, 163
Gates, Henry Louis, Jr., 198–99, 237–39,
241, 302, 351 n. 11
Geddes, Alexander, 254
Gender disguise, 148–49, 151, 154–58, 163,
171
Gildon, Charles, 89

Gilroy, Paul, 300
Glacken, Clarence, 6, 28
Godwyn, Morgan, 57, 62, 146
Goldsmith, Oliver, 30, 40, 180–81, 215–16, 242–47, 252, 289, 358 n. 80
Goodman, Jennifer, 140
Government, 5, 15, 17, 74, 95, 140, 152, 155, 176–77, 216, 227, 242, 290–91
Gramsci, Antonio, 24, 41
Green, William, 240
Gronniosaw, James Albert, 258–59

Hale, Matthew, 25, 99, 303 n. 1
Hall, Catherine, 300
Hall, Kim, 93
Hall, Stuart, 41–43, 300, 313 n. 88
Hannaford, Ivan, 189, 202
Harris, John, 27
Harvey, William, 27, 32
Hay, Denys, 16
Hechter, Michael, 192
Hudson, Nicholas, 189, 198, 238
Hulme, Peter, 54, 86
Human variety. See Racial ideology
Hume, David, 181, 183–87, 192, 196, 198–99, 210–11, 216
Humoral theory, 2–3, 22–28, 71, 100, 174, 215, 263–67, 301; in the work of Hume, 185; Linnaeus, 152; Long, 215–16; Wesley, 257
Hunter, John, 181, 251

Ideology, 42–45, 54, 174–75, 231, 256, 281, 287. See also Racial ideology
India. See East Indies
Intermarriage, 46, 143–44, 166–67, 170, 285–86
Interracial sex. See Amalgamation
Irigaray, Luce, 133

Johnson, Samuel: Dictionary, 3, 38, 304 n. 3, 310 n. 68; Journey to the Western Islands, 47, 177–78, 192–210, 214–15, 220; Rambler, 198
Jordan, Winthrop, 16, 57, 87, 91, 100, 142–43, 189, 221, 240, 251

Kames, Henry Home, Lord, 37, 181, 184, 187–88, 192, 211, 340 n. 75
Kinmont, Alexander, 297–99
Koehn, Nancy, 12
Kriz, Kay Dian, 351 n. 69

Labor. See Manual labor
Lady's Drawing Room, The, 139, 158–67, 174
Language, 15, 52, 62, 95, 136, 192, 195–99, 204–6, 225, 231–32, 348 n. 98; and assimilation, 198, 222
Laplanders, 24, 29, 38, 96, 176, 181, 243, 247
Lauretis, Teresa de, 291
Lavater, Johann Caspar, 10
Le Cat, Claude, 214, 304 n. 4
Leslie, Charles, 211, 230
Lestringant, Frank, 67, 73
Linnaeus, 25, 28, 30, 96, 98, 151, 160, 169, 177, 180, 199, 271
Literacy, 15, 196, 237–39, 210, 216, 352 n. 15
Locke, John, 27, 296
Long, Edward, 37, 47, 141, 143, 147, 162, 177–79, 187, 191, 193, 196, 199, 201, 204, 206–8, 209–33, 255, 275, 277, 282, 284, 304 n. 4
Lott, Eric, 163

Madagascar, 112, 116, 328–29 n. 43
Manual labor, 55, 65, 74, 76, 81, 113, 121–22, 126, 128, 142, 211, 217, 220, 222, 272, 281, 285, 330 n. 53, 360 n. 96
Marren, Susan, 271
Marriage Act, 144–45, 173
Marshall, P. J., 189, 324 n. 5
Martin, Martin, 195–96
Martyn, William, 235, 269
Marxist theory, 41–42, 94, 313 n. 87
Masculinity, 91, 119, 122, 127–29, 138, 157–58, 175, 198, 225, 229, 262, 268, 274, 276, 280–81; and racial ideology, 298, 321 n. 54
McIntosh, Peggy, 40, 93
Meek, Ronald, 182
Memoirs of the Remarkable Life of Mr. Charles Brachy, 139, 150–51
Millar, John, 33, 35, 181, 183–84, 194, 231
Minh-ha, Trinh, 41

Mitchell, John, 26–27, 214, 265, 304 n. 4, 358 n. 75

Monboddo, James Burnett, Lord, 181

Montagu, Mary Wortley, Lady, 20–21

Montesquieu, Baron de, 33, 183, 189, 196, 199

Moore, Francis, 95, 101–2, 109

Moors, 19, 56–58, 145, 148, 151, 153–54

Morgan, Jennifer, 324 n. 4

Morgan, Philip, 327 n. 28, 350 n. 6

Moriscos, 50, 54–65, 141

Morrison, Toni, 50–54, 69, 88

Mosquito Indians, 51, 216, 223, 278

Muldoon, James, 299

Multiplicity, 38–45, 50, 54–57, 59, 66, 78, 88–89. *See also* Categories of difference

Muslims, 16, 20, 48, 57–58, 60–62, 87, 97, 140, 145, 148–53, 154, 156, 290, 316 n. 14

Nakedness, 58, 63, 66, 72–73, 115, 117, 119, 123, 252

Natural history, 1, 5, 9, 14, 21, 24–33, 37, 77, 95–98, 174, 177, 179, 201, 232–35, 248, 257, 274–75, 280, 289–99; illustrated, 243–47

Negroization of non-Negroes, 62–64, 78, 81–84. *See also* Racial masquerade

Neville, Henry, 138

Noble savages, 69, 81–82, 169, 277

Novels, 7, 9, 19, 43, 45, 89, 108–9, 138–41, 166, 290–91

Nussbaum, Felicity A., 11, 190, 280, 305 n. 11, 305 n. 14, 306 n. 15, 324 n. 4

Ogilby, John, 98

Oldmixon, John, 211

Omi, Michael, 288, 300

Orme, Robert, 166

Park, Mungo, 20, 97, 108–9, 130

Patriarchy, 39, 78, 106, 162, 228

Petty, William, Sir, 29–30, 96

Philmore, J., 258, 283

Physiognomy, 9–10, 235

Pocock, J. G. A., 227

Polygenesis, 37, 102, 188, 214, 232, 242, 263, 296–99, 310 n. 76, 352 n. 17, 358 n. 75

Popkins, Richard, 241

Postlethwayt, Malachy, 35, 257

Prichard, James Cowles, 26, 32, 291, 293–97

Prisoners of war, 87, 71, 125, 139

Purchas, Samuel, 33, 237

Racial ideology, 2, 4–7, 9–12, 14–16, 21, 30–32, 37–48, 50, 53, 56, 89, 91–92, 98, 100–101, 128–29, 138–39, 142, 147, 156, 159–60, 167, 175, 177, 179–80, 182–83, 188, 193, 202, 220, 232–33, 235–36, 239–42, 247, 252–53, 256, 260–61, 270, 286–302, 303 n. 2, 311 n. 79, 358 n. 82; and assimilation, 173–74, 178; and gender, 147–48, 162–63, 170–71, 173–75, 225, 249–50, 286–87; and rational capability, 96, 101, 179–81, 186, 191, 200–202, 211, 214–16, 219, 232, 235, 242, 250–56, 263–67, 274, 286–87, 289, 291–98, 325 n. 6, 352 n. 18. *See also* Categories of difference

Racial masquerade, 139, 148, 151, 155–58, 163–64, 273–74; and assimilation, 164

Racism, 11, 14, 43, 45–46, 51, 57, 91, 143, 210, 217, 236, 239–40, 253, 286–88, 291–302, 313 n. 87, 314 n. 5, 353 n. 20.

Ramsay, James, 254–58, 260

Rank, 7, 39, 46, 55, 58, 75, 103, 117, 126, 128, 134, 137, 139, 141, 143, 145, 155, 164, 173–75, 199–200, 202, 205–6, 219–20, 290, 301, 337 n. 45

Robertson, Robert, 255

Robertson, William, 184, 192, 198

Roche, Daniel, 17

Rogers, Pat, 343 n. 32

Rogin, Michael, 163–64

Royal Magazine, The, 155, 271, 342 n. 27

Rush, Benjamin, 137, 258

Savagery, 7, 34–36, 46, 51–52, 54, 58–59, 67–70, 76, 80, 107, 111, 115–17, 121, 191, 193–96, 199, 202–6, 215, 226, 249, 251–52, 257, 261–62, 273, 343 n. 34

Sayre, Gordon, 72

Scotland, 18–19, 23, 35, 47, 177, 185–90, 192, 194–209; inhabitants of, 144, 181–82, 191, 194, 228, 234, 259, 261, 340 n. 3; illustration of, 18

Scott, Sarah, 140, 146–48

Scrimgeour, Gary, 115
Secord, Arthur, 328 n. 41
Sensibility, 154–57, 229, 258, 260, 268, 270, 285–87, 290, 354 n. 31
Servitude, 52, 54, 60–61, 75, 80, 84–88, 125, 147, 287, 297, 322 n. 71–72
Sexuality, 132, 225, 227, 275–77, 280, 281–82, 285, 348 n. 98, 349 n. 103, 349 n. 110
Sharp, Granville, 256
Shaw, Thomas, 152
Shyllon, Folarin, 143, 189
Siraisi, Nancy, 22
Skin color, 1–11, 14, 25–27, 30–31, 33, 36, 46, 50–54, 58, 60, 69, 73–75, 78–80, 91–93, 97, 99, 100, 130, 139, 153, 156–57, 159–60, 166–69, 179–80, 210–11, 214, 219, 241, 248, 251, 260, 264–65, 268–70, 275, 286–87, 289, 338 n. 49; and Adam and Eve, 15, 307 n. 31, 356 n. 49. *See also* Black skin color; Complexion; Tawny skin color; White skin color
Slave trade, 14, 39, 46, 54–56, 83, 89, 92, 101, 106, 110, 125–26, 133, 135, 224, 235, 248, 272, 284
Slavery, 16, 43, 46, 51, 54–61, 65, 74, 83–89, 91–92, 100, 107, 125, 128, 136, 210, 219, 228, 268, 277–80; and Europeans, 56–58, 148, 280; and gender, 236, 281–82; and race, 10–11, 128, 147, 239–41, 253, 255, 267–68, 287; and religion, 146; and skin color, 46, 102, 236; mainly economic justifications of, 107, 128–29, 253–58
Smellie, William, 24, 38
Smith, Adam, 33, 154, 184, 210, 260, 268
Smith, Samuel Stanhope, 251–53, 261, 263, 266, 295
Smith, William, 130
Snelgrave, William, 101–6, 109, 116, 130
Solkin, David, 102, 161, 229
Spaniards, 19, 68, 74–77, 80, 102, 265–66, 279
Spectator, The, 3, 12, 33, 158, 161
Spencer, Jane, 140
Sprat, Thomas, 29
Stafford, Fiona, 196

Stedman, John Gabriel, 226, 254–55, 277
Stepan, Nancy, 32–33, 296, 311 n. 81
Stoler, Ann Laura, 41
Sugar plantation, 62, 65–66, 84–85, 135, 239; owners of, 209–13, 219–32, 267, 275, 280
Swift, Jonathan, 134, 231

Tassy, Laugier de, 152
Tawny skin color, 73, 79–80, 156, 159, 161, 164, 171, 173, 174, 227, 269, 271, 320 n. 46, 320 n. 58, 322 n. 62
Technology, 72, 79, 114, 117, 119, 127–28, 136, 223–24, 330 n. 59
Temperate zone, 22–23, 30, 100. *See also* Climate theory; humoral theory
Thomas, Nicholas, 41
Thompson, James, 140
Tobin, James, 254, 285, 352 n. 18
Todd, Janet, 140, 152
Todorov, Tzvetan, 117
Torrid zone, 22–24, 30, 71, 100, 122, 266–67
Tryon, Thomas, 231

Vaughan, Alden, 93, 325 n. 9
Vaughan, Mary, 93, 325 n. 9
Voyages of William Owen Gwin Vaughan, The, 148–50

Wedgwood, Josiah, 282
Wesley, John, 253, 256–57, 281
White, Charles, 292–94
White, Hayden, 70–71
White skin color, 2, 10, 26, 31, 39–40, 74, 80, 93–94, 97–100, 242, 249, 269–74, 330 n. 62, 358 n. 80; and Christianity, 4; and Englishness, 47, 123; origins of, 100. *See also* Britons
Williams, Eric, 86, 239, 315 n. 9, 353 n. 20
Williams, Glyndwr, 189, 324 n. 5
Williams, Raymond, 13, 41–42
Wilson, Kathleen, 12, 147, 189, 229
Winant, Howard, 288, 300
Women, "Race," and Writing, 93
Woolman, John, 258

Acknowledgments

THIS book bears the traces of the teachers, mentors, and friends whose ways of thinking profoundly influenced my own. Without the theoretically informed and politically motivated feminists at Syracuse University in the late 1980s and early 1990s, I would never have conceptualized this project. Their seminars, essays and books, conversation, and the reading groups they participated in meant that I had the experience of learning from them at the same time I worked through significant intellectual problems with them. Linda Alcoff, Beverly Allen, Dympna Callaghan, Steve Cohan, Jim Duncan, Felicity Nussbaum, Linda Shires, Robyn Wiegman, and Tom Yingling were all central to my intellectual growth. The generally encouraging climate for my work has been sustained by many people, but no one more singly important than Felicity Nussbaum. Her perceptive scholarship, including her dedication to historical precision and theoretical sophistication, is a model that has long inspired me. No one could hope for a mentor more generous with her time or insightful in her comments than Felicity. Her impact on my work and life is profound.

If one of the most rewarding aspects of writing this book has been the continuing support tendered by long-time mentors like Felicity Nussbaum and Dympna Callaghan, one of the most delightful experiences has been meeting new friends, who are now valued colleagues. Spring 1997 at the Huntington brought together a fabulous constellation of people, many of whom dedicated a great deal of time to reading my work. Chris Brown, Dian Kriz, Terri Snyder, Blakey Vermeule, and Natalie Zacek all provided incisive critique at the most crucial point in my project. In various ways, they all led me to think more carefully about my claims and the structure of the individual chapters that they read. Long past the time we left California, Chris Brown, Dian Kriz, and Margaret Newell continue to pose challenging questions about the issues we tackle in our different disciplines. Personally and professionally, I have gained so much from the past two years spent talking to Dian about race in the eighteenth century. Having a close friend steeped in eighteenth-century colonial culture who is also a part of daily life reminded me of the best that the academy has to offer—an intellectual companion.

The Huntington fellowship was also indirectly responsible for introducing me to my editor at University of Pennsylvania Press, Jerry Singerman. His initial interest in this project and patience with its completion has been a reliable source of strength over the past few years. Vin Carretta and Kris Straub, the readers of the manuscript, offered thoughtful feedback that spurred the last round of revisions. Their continued input has given me the best of all worlds: esteemed mentors, excellent colleagues, and friends. Ursula Appelt, Carson Bergstrom, Susan Comfort, Jim Egan, Michelle Jensen, and Ashley Montague all gave reassurance and smart critique in the last months of revision. Craig Smith and Allen Larson have always been there for "intellectual therapy."

In the several stages of writing this book, I have been helped considerably by the generosity of institutions and individuals who supported graduate student and junior faculty development. A Syracuse University Graduate Research Grant first opened the British Library to me, and a Pennsylvania State System of Higher Education Faculty Professional Development Grant permitted me to return some years later. I was also fortunate to have access to the fine resources at the William Andrews Clark Memorial Library through a short-term fellowship, an experience that inspired me to try to return to the West Coast. A Security Pacific and Andrew W. Mellon Foundation Fellowship at the Huntington Library allowed me to revise the manuscript, and if any one event could be said to be a happy turning point in a career, this was it. I was also helped by an Indiana University of Pennsylvania Senate Research Committee Award, for which Ginger Brown, then Associate Dean for Research, encouraged me to apply. She also generously supported my leave with a much-needed laptop computer and other material resources. In the final year of writing and researching this book, I was given the most important gift of all—time to think—as well as money and a place full of wonderful resources with which to work, by the National Endowment for the Humanities, which made possible one of the most productive and fulfilling years of my professional life at the John Carter Brown Library. The President of Indiana University of Pennsylvania, Lawrence Pettit, and the Provost, Mark Staszkiewicz, offered vital supplementary financial assistance for which I am truly grateful.

Earlier versions of Chapters 1, 2, and 3 appeared, respectively, as " 'My Savage,' 'My Man': Racial Multiplicity in *Robinson Crusoe*," *English Literary History* 62 (1995): 821–61, © 1995 The Johns Hopkins University Press; "Limited Visions of Africa: Geographies of Savagery and Civility in Early Eighteenth-Century Narratives," in *Writes of Passage: British Colonial and Post-Colonial Travel Writing*, ed. James Duncan and Derek Gregory (London: Routledge, 1999); and "The Complexion of Desire: Racial Ideology and Mid-Eighteenth-Century British Novels," *Eighteenth-Century Studies* 32.3 (Spring 1999): 309–332, © 1999. American Society for Eighteenth-Century Studies, reprinted by permission of the Johns Hopkins University Press.

Punctuation and capitalization of quotations follow seventeenth- and eighteenth-century convention, except that I have silently changed the long "ſ" to the modern "s."

This book is dedicated to Larry and Joan Wheeler, who have lovingly supported me and my work without question.